I0722137

Future Imaginaries

Indigenous
Art
Fashion
Technology

Autry Museum of the American West, Los Angeles
in association with
University of Washington Press, Seattle

Foreword

In introducing *Future Imaginaries: Indigenous Art, Fashion, Technology* and its focus and exploration of Indigenous futures, my objective is to connect that subject to the deep and abiding context from which Native artistic expression springs. I do so against the following background.

I have served as the director of two museums that hold substantial and significant collections of Native art objects and other cultural materials. In that capacity I have overseen (1) the development of art exhibitions that are inspired by and reflect changes during the past generation in Native art history and (2) the curation and interpretation by museums and the academy of the work of contemporary Native artists.

In addition, my views concerning Native arts, in an important sense, are lived and genetic. My father, Walter Richard West Sr., was an artist and active participant in the Native fine arts movement that blossomed in the last half of the twentieth century in Oklahoma. I had a quite personal engagement with the thinking that went through the mind of this Native artist as his creativity went from brush to canvas and chisel to wood.

I grew up not far from Tulsa, where the Philbrook Art Center (now the Philbrook Museum of Art) and the Gilcrease Museum are located. Both hold substantial collections of Native art and other cultural materials. Since my father's work and career took him to both institutions with some frequency, he would sometimes take me with him. On one of those visits when I was a child, probably under ten years of age he and I took a tour through the Philbrook galleries. We came upon a Northwest Coast object, a Tlingit ceremonial dish, as I recall. Dad told me initially about the object's remarkable aesthetic beauty, including its material, the artist's technical skill, the use of color, and the splendid lines of the piece. Then, with a slight chuckle, he added, "The only problem is—that's not what it really means. For the maker and his community, it had deep ceremonial meaning and cultural importance and value. It guided their lives."

And there sits an axiom that fundamentally differentiates Native artistic expression and its creation from Western art history and its guiding canons that descend from the Enlightenment and have shaped the curation and interpretation of American art collections and exhibitions for more than a century. Significantly, many contemporary Native fine artists view the matter similarly. Rick Hill, an artist, academician, and former director of the Institute of American Indian Arts Museum of Contemporary Native Arts in Santa Fe, puts the matter this way:

The main difference between Indian and non-Indian
artists is that we are still community-driven. . . . Art is the
cement that binds the Indian people together, uniting
us with our ancestors and with generations yet to be
born. Through art we can take a look at why language is
important, why ritual is important, why land is important.[1]

With his characteristic frankness and edge, contemporary
Apache sculptor Bob Haozous, the renowned son of the
renowned Allan Houser and a brilliant artist in his own right,
makes the same point regarding the essential nature of
Indian art:

I want to see people participating in my work. That's totally
contrary to what we're taught in America—the artist as an
individual, the genius. I don't want to see that in my work at
all. I'd rather see, at the most, a cultural reflection of being an
Apache. I've been fighting those concepts of individualism,
uniqueness, and universalism, concepts that are totally contrary
to tribalism. Individualism denies a future or a past awareness.
You claim it, you own it, but you're not a part of it.[2]

This perspective regarding Native arts is incompatible with the
creation and organization of Western knowledge systems that
have come to us from the Middle Ages and the Enlightenment.
Knowledge is not a neat row of vertical disciplinary silos—art
and history over here, and culture and anthropology over there.
To the contrary, to invoke the words of the academy itself, it
is, instead, a knowledge system that is interdisciplinary and far
more integrated and holistic in impact and outcomes. For Native
peoples and communities, boundaries or divisions between
knowledge areas are mutually permeable, always, in the name
of the whole. Native artistic expression should be viewed
through this rather different lens.

A former colleague of mine at the National Museum of the
American Indian and now a distinguished professor of history
spoke directly to this point when she wrote:

[T]he Native artist . . . [values] the creation [of art] . . .
over the final product. Process speaks *to historical
or cultural significance* because it is testimony *to
cultural continuity and change*. It is the evidence of lost
traditions, innovations, preserved cultural knowledge,
historic perspective and *vision of the future*. . . . It takes
into account a sort of "spiritual evidence" that is integral
to the creative process. The integrity of the creative
process is foremost. The object is *meaningless without
it*.[3] [emphasis mine]

The work of the Native artists in *Future Imaginaries* remains consistent with the deep and long-standing traditions that have shaped the content and forms of Native artistic expression from the beginning. The most fundamental of those traditions is the capacity for change and adaptation. The current focus may be grounded, even diminished, by that which has been. But it lives in the present, with its focus ever on the prospective and the future of Native communities.

No aspect of knowledge can escape the Native artists' gaze, and all are relevant and at play, including science and technology. As Dr. Amy Scott states in her essay in this volume:

> For [Native artists], making art about the future offers healing by challenging the inevitability of colonial notions of "progress," and reclaiming one's destiny from the politicians, technocrats, and industrial developers vying to conquer "the final frontier." This is true not only for those peoples who have suffered colonization, but for all of us.

W. Richard West Jr. (Cheyenne)
Founding Director and Director Emeritus
National Museum of the American Indian, Smithsonian Institution

President and CEO Emeritus
Ambassador, Native Communities
Autry Museum of the American West

1 Rick Hill, personal communication, ca. 1990–92.
2 Bob Haozous, personal communication, ca. 1990–92.
3 Anonymous, personal communication, ca. 1990–92.

Director's Statement

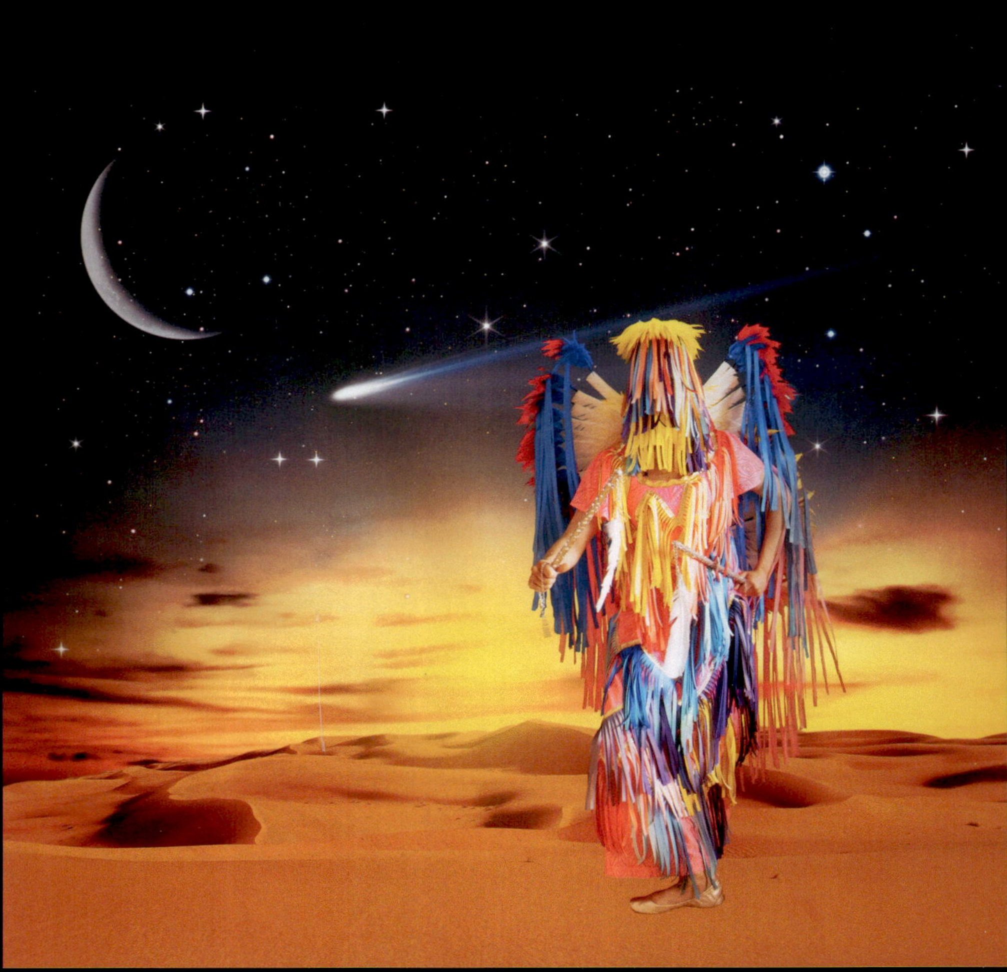

Fig. 1. Wendy Red Star (Apsáalooke), *Stirs Up the Dust* from the *Thunder Up Above* series, 2011. Pigment print on FineArt Pearl, 27 × 30 in. Courtesy of the Autry Museum of the American West

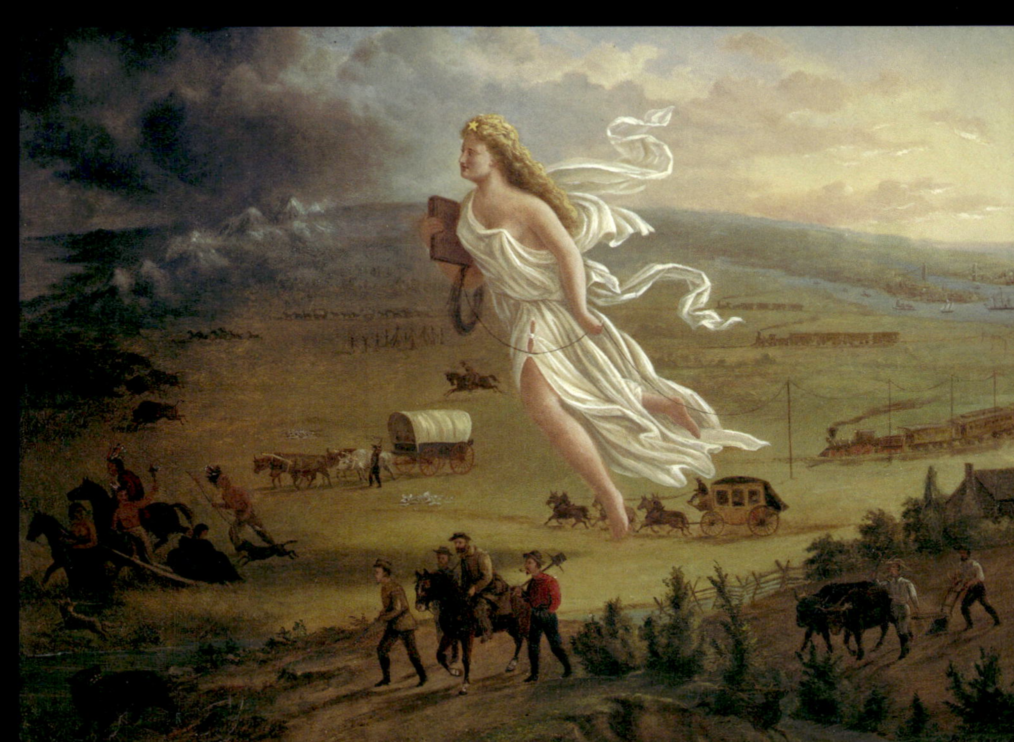

Fig. 2. John Gast, *American Progress*, 1872. Oil on canvas, 11½ × 15¾ in. Courtesy of the Autry Museum of the American West

This companion volume to the exhibition *Future Imaginaries: Indigenous Art, Fashion, Technology* at the Autry Museum of the American West explores the fertile and forward-facing artistic creations that have come to be grouped under the construct of "Indigenous Futurism." But while readers of the book and visitors to the exhibition may hope for a single definition and clear set of boundaries, they will discover Indigenous *Futurisms* that elude easy categorization. Rather than coalescence, this project complicates (and pluralizes) our understanding of Indigenous Futurisms. Indeed, like Indigenous artists and cultures more broadly, Indigenous futurists reach back to their traditions while looking forward in many directions. Still, amid the diversity of voices and visions within these pages and the accompanying exhibition, commonalities emerge that draw on worlds past and imagine worlds to come to upend colonial expectations, trumpet cultural survival, and spotlight environmental sustainability (fig. 1).

Of particular significance to the Autry Museum, with its principal focus on the history of the American West, is how Indigenous Futurisms challenge long-standing rhetorical and artistic tropes about "the vanishing Indian." Not surprisingly, the Autry's ongoing *Art of the West* exhibition includes numerous works that exemplify the once widespread conviction among white Americans that Indians were destined for extinction. Among these, consider as "exhibit A" John Gast's 1872 painting *American Progress* (fig. 2). Thanks to its endless reproduction in the late nineteenth century and its continuing appearance inside (and sometimes on the cover) of countless U.S. history textbooks over the last 150 years, this artwork has become one of the most familiar visual representations of Manifest Destiny, which it is sometimes mistitled. In Gast's panorama, the link between American expansion and Indian expulsion is made clear: on the far left, Indians and bison retreat into the shadows and off the canvas. Their fate is sealed by the course of American progress, and for them there is no future.

The Autry does not leave Gast's and similar visions of doomed Indians unchallenged. Alongside depictions by white artists of vanishing Indians are historical works by Native creators that present very different views about Indian peoples and their ways. The museum's galleries also feature more recent works by Native artists that contradict the myth of Native American extinction and affirm Indigenous cultures' survivance and vitality. *Future Imaginaries* takes the challenge further by firmly planting an Indigenous flag in the world ahead. The Indigenous lens offers fresh perspectives on fashion, science fiction, and technology. And like the best imaginings about the future, the works in the exhibition and the essays in this publication allow us to reckon with the past and better understand the present.

Stephen Aron, PhD
Calvin B. and Marilyn B. Gross Director and President and CEO
Autry Museum of the American West

Acknowledgments

Every exhibition project has a backstory. For *Future Imaginaries: Indigenous Art, Fashion, Technology*, that story begins in 2019 when the Getty Foundation announced the theme of *Art & Science Collide* for the next iteration of PST ART, the recurrent exhibition series that sprawls across Southern California every few years. As the theme implies, as fields of inquiry, these concepts are not so easily separable. Likewise, the Autry's collections of material culture, historical artifacts, and art by diverse peoples from across the American West have long blurred the boundaries between traditional museological categories, such as media or nationality. In considering the Autry's interdisciplinary approach to art alongside the museum's mission to connect past to present to inform our shared future, the opportunity presented by PST ART: *Art & Science Collide* to create an exhibition that showcases the entwined nature of technology and artistry that pervades so much of contemporary Indigenous art became clear. Yet the future can be an elusive concept, as many of the artists and authors in this volume suggest. By foregrounding the technological knowledge embedded in Indigenous art, *Future Imaginaries: Indigenous Art, Fashion, Technology* has the potential to disrupt the colonial biases that circulate still within American society while creating a space for Indigenous voices to mediate their version of what lies ahead.

I am immensely grateful to all the colleagues, curators, artists, and institutions that have supported these efforts and whose many contributions have deeply and profoundly shaped this project. Chief among them is W. Richard West Jr., director of the Autry Museum when the PST ART: *Art & Science Collide* initiative was first announced, who supported my ambitions to realize not one but two projects within this framework. He and his successor, Stephen Aron, share a love of the American West and an understanding of the essential ways contemporary art operates within a history museum, partly by challenging our preconceived ideas about the past and opening space in the present to renegotiate their meaning.

Foundation support for this project has been instrumental in its success. I would like to thank Dr. Joan Weinstein and Dr. Heather MacDonald at the Getty Foundation for their critical contributions in the form of major research and implementation grants, which both launched the project and helped see it through to completion. Dr. Teresa Carbone and the Henry Luce Foundation also honored the Autry with a significant grant. I am likewise grateful to the board of the Carl & Marilynn Thoma Foundation of Santa Fe; Feelie Lee, James Trotta-Bono, and the board of the Ethnic Arts Council in Los Angeles; Caryll and

William Mingst at the Mildred E. and Harvey S. Mudd Foundation;
and the Pasadena Art Alliance. These foundation gifts were
essential in realizing this project, and your generous support
humbles us.

For the thematic structure of the exhibition, the original scholarship
included in these pages, and the collegial, collaborative spirit
that pervaded our many meetings, I am forever grateful to our
curatorial team of scholars, Amber-Dawn Bear Robe (Siksika),
Kristen Dorsey (Chickasaw), and Dr. Suzanne Newman Fricke.
These formidable women contributed a unique combination of
specialized knowledge, curatorial experience, and artistic insight,
advancing many of the incredible works of art and important ideas
within these pages. Project advisor Dr. Nancy Marie Mithlo (Fort
Sill Chiricahua Apache) of the University of California, Los Angeles,
was instrumental in offering commentary and feedback throughout.
Your collective insights have transformed the exhibition and book,
and I am honored by the generosity and freedom with which you
shared your knowledge and experience. I am equally appreciative
of the additional scholars and artists who agreed to write for this
publication; in your words, we can see the complexity of this topic
and glimpse its many dimensions. In addition to the aforementioned
curators and advisors, my thanks go to Amanda Wixon (Chickasaw),
Autry Museum associate curator of Native history and culture;
scholar and curator Dr. Matthew Ryan Smith; Concordia University
professor Jason Edward Lewis (Kanaka Maoli/Samoan), Dr. Manuela
Well-Off-Man of the IAIA Museum of Contemporary Native Arts in
Santa Fe, New Mexico; and the artists Weshoyot Alvitre (Tongva/
Scottish), Sonny Assu (Ligwiłda'xw of the Kwakwaka'wakw Nations),
Mercedes Dorame (Tongva), Cannupa Hanska Luger (Mandan/
Hidatsa/Arikara/Lakota), and Virgil Ortiz (Cochiti Pueblo). I would
also like to extend a very special thanks to Gerald Vizenor (White
Earth Nation), whose groundbreaking work in Indigenous science
fiction has served as a beacon for many. It is an honor to publish
your work; thank you for being a part of this project.

One of the primary goals of the curatorial team was to deploy
an artist-driven methodology, which meant inviting artists
into conversations about the show's development early on,
creating opportunities for dialogue around content as it evolved
in real time. To the many artists we spoke with, I am forever
grateful for the knowledge, insights, and artworks you shared
with the Autry team, as well as the gift of being able to show
your art at the Autry Museum. For your generosity in all these
things, I am grateful to Barry Ace (Odawa), KC Adams (Cree/
Ojibway), Neal Ambrose-Smith (Flathead Salish/Sho-Ban/
Métis/Cree), Sonny Assu (Ligwiłda'xw of the Kwakwaka'wakw
Nations), Nanibaa Beck (Diné), Catherine Blackburn (Dene/

European), Mona Cliff (Aaniiih/Nakota/Eastern European),
Wally Dion (Salteaux), Mercedes Dorame (Tongva), Orlando
Dugi (Diné), Chase Kahwinhut Earles (Caddo), Andy Everson
(K'ómoks/Kwakwaka'wakw), Nicholas Galanin (Tlingit/Unangax̂),
Jeffrey Gibson (Mississippi Band of Choctaw Indians/Cherokee
descent), Luzene Hill (Eastern Band of Cherokee Indians), Shawn
Hunt (Heiltsuk), Margaret Jacobs (Akwesasne Mohawk), Brian
Jungen (Dane-zaa), Jontay Kahm (Plains Cree), Rykelle "Ahlazua"
Kemp (Mvskoke Creek Nation), Kite (Oglala Lakota), Cannupa
Hanska Luger (Mandan/Hidatsa/Arikara/Lakota), Meryl
McMaster (nêhiyaw/Métis), Caroline Monnet (Anishinaabe/
French), Jamie Okuma (Luiseño/Shoshone/Bannock), Virgil Ortiz
(Cochiti Pueblo), Celeste Pedri-Spade (Anishinabekwe/Ojibwe),
Pat Pruitt (Pueblo of Laguna), Wendy Red Star (Apsáalooke),
Cara Romero (Chemehuevi), Diego Romero (Cochiti Pueblo),
Devin Ronneberg (Hawaiian/Okinawan), Nep Sidhu (Punjabi
Sikh), Rose B. Simpson (Santa Clara Pueblo), Ryan Singer
(Diné), Skawennati (Kanien'kehà:ka [Mohawk]), Matagi Sorensen
(Yavapai-Apache), Adrian Stimson (Siksika), Tammy Tallchief
(Cayuga), Jeffrey Veregge (Port Gamble S'Klallam), Marie Watt
(Seneca), Will Wilson (Diné), Lucille Wright Payotapaihpiyakii
(Dancing the opposite direction woman) (Siksika), and X
(Koasati/CHamoru). It is an honor to share the gallery and these
pages with such incredible creativity. Through the power and
vibrance of your work, we can all see a brighter future.

This exhibition has benefited enormously from the expertise
and artworks shared by institutional lenders, art galleries, and
private foundations. These include the Albuquerque Museum,
the Casey Kaplan Gallery in New York, the Dallas Museum of
Art, the Denver Art Museum, the Eiteljorg Museum of American
Indians and Western Art, Equinox Gallery in Vancouver, Garth
Greenan Gallery in New York, as well as Gallery Hózhó in
Albuquerque; the Trotta-Bono Collection in Santa Fe, Patel Brown
in Toronto, and the Vancouver Art Gallery. Thanks also go to
Holly Harrison at the Thoma Foundation and Laura Findlay Smith
at the Tia Collection, both in Santa Fe. We are likewise grateful to
individual lenders John O'Connell at Davis Rea Ltd. and George
and Martha Richards.

Ultimately, *Future Imaginaries* was realized through the talent
and dedication of the Autry Museum staff. Jennifer A. Doyle,
who edited both the museum's PST ART books, facilitated
our many conversations with artists, and coordinated several
project variables, deserves a special mention; her keen eye and
thoughtful attention to detail have been critical at every step.
LaLena Lewark, vice president of exhibitions, collections, and
conservation; Sarah Signorovitch, senior registrar for loans and

exhibitions; and conservator Lily Doan ensured safe transit and display for all works of art. Eugene Wyrick, associate director of exhibition design, created a stunning, vibrant, and dynamic installation, while senior media producer Anton Lieberman oversaw multimedia and video installations. Project coordinator Sarah Mitchell kept the trains running on time, and Virginia Scharff, chair of Western history, had us covered at the end. Lastly, this book went from an idea to a reality in no small part thanks to Donna Wingate and Kestrel Rundle of Marquand Books, and publication designer Sébastien Aubin (Opaskwayak Cree); I would also like to thank Nicole Mitchell, director of the University of Washington Press. I am grateful for your belief in this book and your guidance in shepherding it throughout the publication process.

And to Harris, who will be nine years old when this project is realized, the future is always bright with you.

Amy Scott, PhD
Executive Vice President, Research and Interpretation
Marilyn B. and Calvin B. Gross Curator of Visual Arts
Autry Museum of the American West

In Memoriam

Jeffrey Veregge
Port Gamble S'Klallam
1970-2024

A marvel to us all.

Future Imaginaries:
A Curatorial Conversation

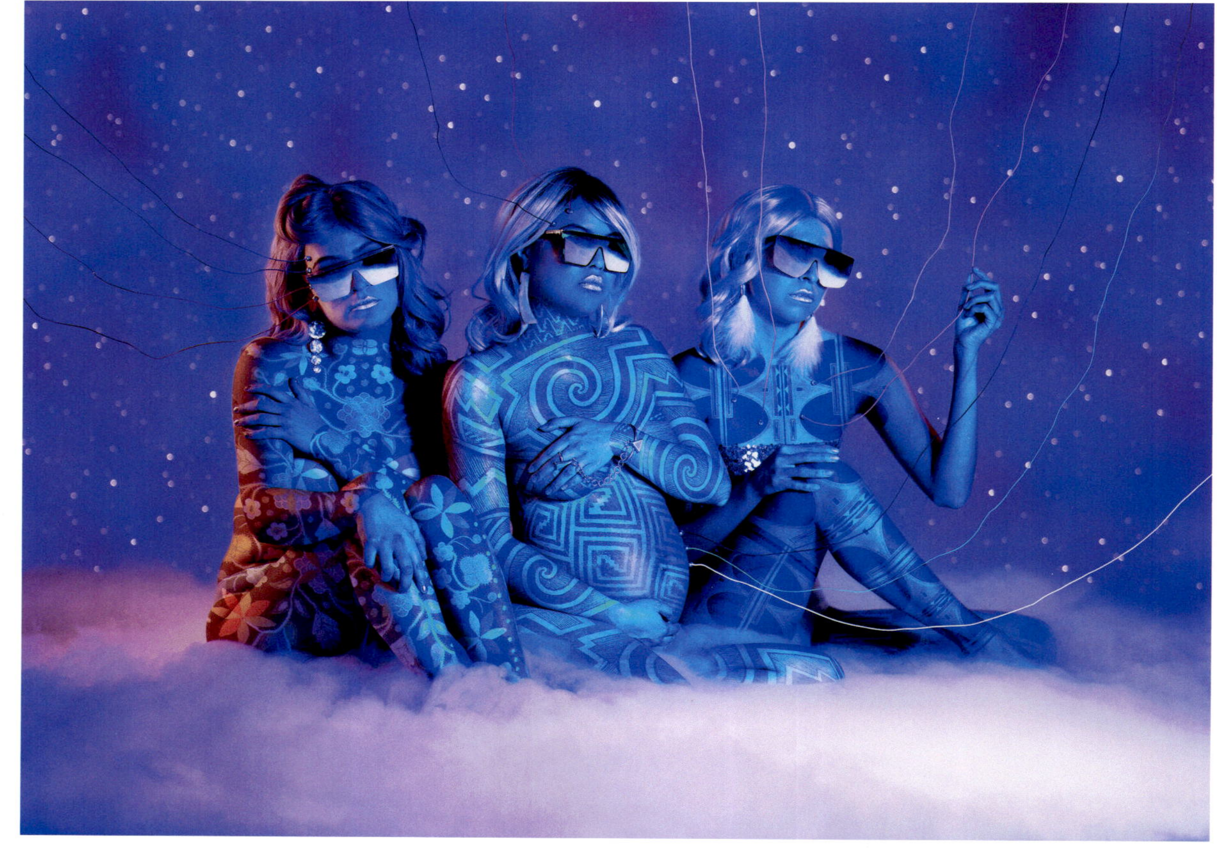

Cara Romero (Chemehuevi), *Three Sisters*, 2022.
Limited edition archival photograph, 40 × 55 in.
Courtesy of the artist

Amber-Dawn Bear Robe, Kristen Dorsey, Suzanne Newman Fricke, and Amy Scott

The term "Indigenous Futurisms" was first published by scholar Grace Dillon in 2012 in reference to a growing movement in Indigenous literature, visual art, and other media that sought to express Indigenous perspectives on the future and their relationship to both our colonial past and present reality.[1] In the years since Dillon coined the term, many scholars, artists, and authors have also contributed their research, artwork, and perspectives to the field, expanding and diversifying the meanings of Indigenous Futurisms and the possibilities it holds for artists and audiences alike. This includes scholar (and contributor to this volume) Jason Edward Lewis, who developed the concept of the "Future Imaginary" to encompass "how a culture thinks collectively about its future," a way of structuring meaning that shapes ideas about the past and behaviors in the present, giving rise to shared ideas about the future. Drawing upon Lewis's concept for its title, this publication represents yet another contribution to this dynamic and evolving conversation.

On September 12, 2023, the four curators of *Future Imaginaries: Indigenous Art, Fashion, Technology* gathered to discuss the exhibition and its companion volume. In these excerpts, Amber-Dawn Bear Robe, Kristen Dorsey, Suzanne Newman Fricke, and Amy Scott speak to their wide-ranging visions for the exhibition and thoughts on Indigenous Futurisms, its varied meanings, and importance as an artistic genre. Virginia Scharff, Autry Museum chair of Western history, served as moderator.

Virginia
To understand the exhibition, can you describe how you envision *Future Imaginaries* and Indigenous Futurisms? Kristen, what would you say is your approach to Indigenous Futurisms?

Kristen
Indigenous Futurisms encompass world building by drawing upon Indigenous knowledge systems for future generations. Futurism is not a new concept for Indigenous societies. We are always innovating and strategizing for the next generation. A good entry point to understanding the artwork in this show is that it reflects the writings of curator and professor of visual arts at the University of Regina David Garneau (Métis), that Indigenous art is an active, not static, process, and that artists work as researchers. Artists conduct research and expand their knowledge through their tribal communities and nations, returning to ancestral knowledge and incorporating that into their vision of what is happening now and what will happen in the future. I see each artist in this exhibit doing that, experimenting with new technologies and images. Part of that research is

posing questions, seeking answers, and critiquing and analyzing systems, all for the sake of our future kin, both human and nonhuman.

Amber-Dawn
Future Imaginaries represents and reclaims the narrative, structuring our Indigenous presence now and moving forward. Indigenous peoples are widely thought of as "Edward Curtis Indians," a romanticized image stuck in the past, preventing or making it more difficult to have useful discussions within larger American society about present-day Indigenous realities. When the general population thinks of Indigenous fashion, they imagine beads and leather. We need to excavate the Edward Curtis Indian to reframe current narratives, putting ourselves in the future and reframing it from our perspective.

Star Wars, *Star Trek*, and other popular sci-fi narratives are part of the larger public discourse relating to what people think of as Indigenous Futurisms. I understand the place for incorporating popular sci-fi; my approach to Indigenous Futurisms is different.

Virginia
Suzanne, you have published on the topic and curated *Indigenous Futurisms: Transcending Past/Present/Future* in 2020 at the IAIA Museum of Contemporary Native Arts in Santa Fe, New Mexico, as well as other exhibitions about Indigenous Futurisms. Would you please discuss your view of this field? How is *Future Imaginaries* distinctive?

Suzanne
Amber-Dawn and I differ in our views on Indigenous Futurisms, but the field is broad enough to encompass different perspectives. Indigenous Futurisms envision the future based on the aesthetics, history, and ideas of the past. In doing so, it reaches to the past and the future, converging in a new vision for the present. Artists like Diné painter Ryan Singer, Port Gamble S'Klallam printmaker Jeffrey Veregge, and K'ómoks/Kwakwaka'wakw printmaker Andy Everson directly incorporate the characters and scenes from popular sci-fi. They are not appropriating something outside their experience but expressing something from deep in their imagination. It is evident that these worlds live within their consciousness, and their work articulates this part of their imagination. Sci-fi is the ultimate playground, open to everyone, as seen in the work of Kanien'kehà:ka (Mohawk) digital artist Skawennati, who created an online forum in *Second Life* that offers a wider range of skin tones, body types, and hairstyles for avatars to express their identities as part of AbTeC (Aboriginal Territories in Cyberspace), an organization she co-founded.

As a museum show, *Futures Imaginaries* suggests how the field of Indigenous Futurisms has expanded. Other Indigenous Futurisms shows are focused on *Star Wars*, *Star Trek*, and the Marvel Universe. This show reflects that influence but expands the definition of Indigenous Futurisms by embracing many different artists with unique viewpoints. As Amber-Dawn said, this show counters the view of the Edward Curtis Indian since the artwork looks forward while embracing Indigenous culture and history.

Amy
Professor Kristina Baudemann suggests that Indigenous Futurisms bridge the perspectives Amber-Dawn and Suzanne outlined, embracing the field's heterogeneous nature. Regardless of their work or background, these artists are carving out space in an allegedly all-encompassing meta-narrative to express their own ideas about what lies ahead. This is an artistic act—it's not resistance, it's not rebellion, it's more of a rewriting of these narratives that draw attention to processes of colonial erasure. And in doing so, they also highlight the erasure of Native culture by emphasizing the idea of an Indigenous future.

Virginia
What you're suggesting is that Indigenous Futurisms expand how Indigenous peoples are viewed. How does that change our understanding of futurism and futures more broadly?

Amber-Dawn
It's hard to define all of this, though that's what art history often tries to do-put everything in neat packages. I am approaching the exhibition from the perspective of Indigenous fashion. At this point, there is very little scholarship in Indigenous fashion and theory. There's anthropological work, but there's no research and theory in the larger academic field of fashion history. Contemporary Native art history is also new to the discourse of art history when looking at the canon. Fashion history grew out of art history, which means that we're still trying to use a language that originated from a predominantly white, male, and Western viewpoint to define Indigenous fashion. From my perspective, this discussion is, by nature, changing and ongoing. I don't think we should have a conclusion for the show. This show must generate more productive dialogue.

Amy
That's a good point. This show is not about establishing a definitive narrative or art historical canon. The 2020 exhibition *Indigenous Futurisms: Transcending Past/Present/Future* at the IAIA Museum of Contemporary Native Arts in Santa Fe was

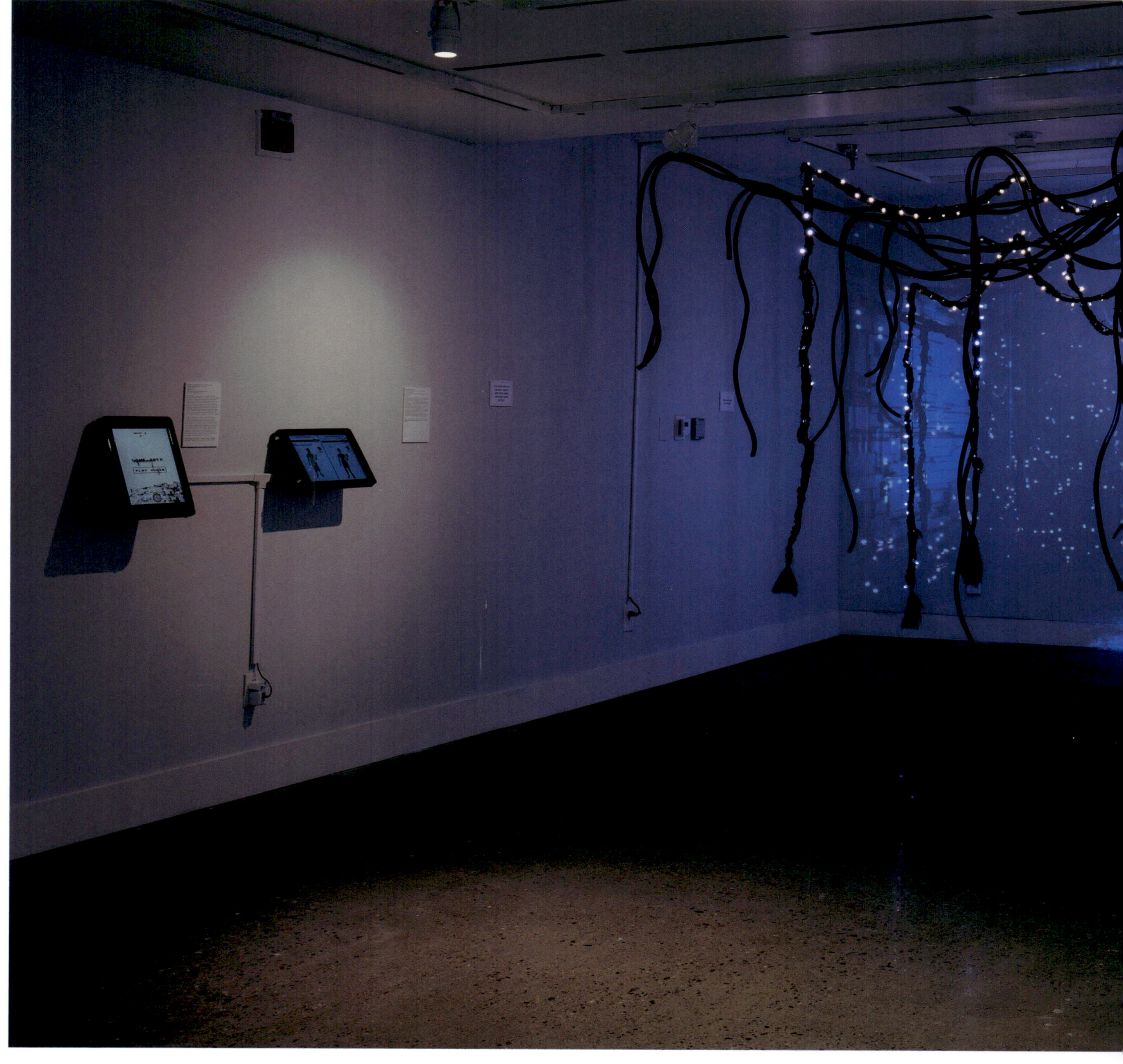

an important effort and helped establish what Indigenous Futurisms was in that moment along with its major players. Yet the field, and the phrase "Indigenous Futurisms" along with it, has continued to expand at such a rate that it is already inherently changed; this show lays the groundwork for further artistic and curatorial conversation by showcasing, among other things, the energy, diversity of views, and momentum that characterize the field today and points toward what it might be tomorrow.

Virginia
How does Indigenous Futurisms describe an Indigenous point of view on Indigenous creative work?

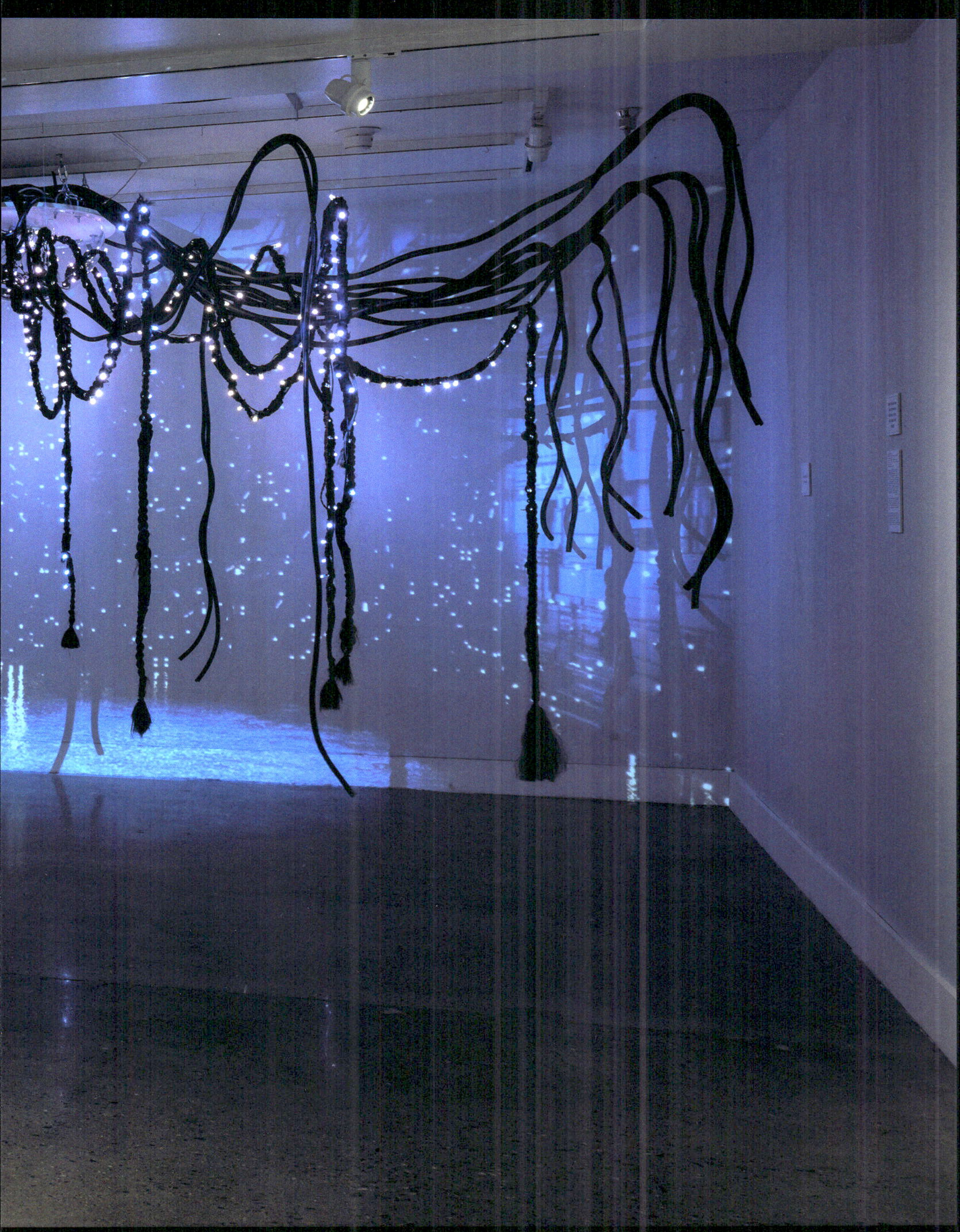

Fig. 1. Installation view of *Inyan Iyé (Telling Rock)*, 2019, by Kite (Oglala Lakota) and Devin Ronneberg (Hawaiian/Okinawan), from the exhibition *Indigenous Futurisms: Transcending Past/Present/Future*, IAIA Museum of Contemporary Native Arts, February 13, 2020–January 3, 2021. Courtesy of the IAIA Museum of Contemporary Native Arts, Santa Fe, NM. Photography by Jason S. Ordaz

Kristen
While it is impossible to generalize Indigenous creative practices because each one is unique to their personal lived experience, artistic training, and community, Futurism encapsulates Indigenous creative expression because these expressions translate knowledge from ancestors for future generations. Indigenous ways of being and doing, such as practices of relationality, can be communicated through the visual arts. For example, I see relationality embedded in Indigenous fashion because you're actually clothed in the knowledge of your ancestors, clothing that's made for you now. It's reaching through time, upending the idea that time is linear. It's generational knowledge transfer.

Indigenous Futurisms describe the now. It's dynamic and expansive while also grounded in our Indigenous societies. It also differs from what the dominant settler society thinks of as futurisms. Stereotypical Western futuristic imaginings can be bound up with discovery and claiming, concepts which fuel imperialism. Many of the works in the exhibition push back on these settler colonial concepts of individualism. It's generational knowledge transfer.

Virginia
How are these ideas expressed in the exhibition?

Suzanne
The show is divided into three parts. "Suiting Up: Armor, Regalia, Haute Couture" includes fashion and regalia. Clothing, whether a business suit, space suit, or ceremonial regalia, articulates who you are and what you are doing. It serves as a protective layer. It serves a function, but it's highly aesthetic. "Suiting Up" introduces the show to the viewer. When you walk into that section, everything relates to the human form.

Of the three sections, "Indigenizing Sci-Fi" aligns most closely with what often comes to mind when considering Indigenous Futurisms, with artists incorporating the characters, locales, technologies, and narratives from popular sci-fi but expressed from an Indigenous perspective. For example, Jeffrey Veregge's work depicts the *Millennium Falcon* from *Star Wars*, but it's illustrated using the formline designs common to Northwest Coast tribes. Formline designs are built from basic building blocks, such as an ovoid, a U-shape, circles, and crescent shapes. In works like *She's Got It Where It Counts*, Veregge demonstrates the affinity between sci-fi designs and formline shapes (pl. 26). Not only are the designs compatible, but this visual language allows the artist to suggest new meanings, such as the conflation of the *Millennium Falcon* and the figure of Raven, an important character in Northwest Coast oral histories.

The final section, "Critical Mass: Indigenous Technologies, Ecologies, and the Future," explores the primary importance of ecological issues and Indigenous technologies and knowledge systems when looking to the future. Cara Romero's (Chemehuevi) *The Zenith* depicts another artist, George Alexander (Muskogee Creek), as an astronaut in a space helmet with ears of corn floating around him (pl. 36). The image suggests the importance of corn and other heirloom crops in developing agriculture in space. This image challenges the history of corn, which has become industrialized and overproduced, reliant on genetically modified seeds and chemical fertilizer. *The Zenith* suggests how crops that have long formed the cornerstone of Indigenous lifeways can provide solutions to growing food in the future.

Amy
We started with the works of fashion—all of it wearable art—
because they offer a great way to introduce visitors to the show.
In terms of their scale, they lend a human point of reference
but are also fierce and avant-garde. The fashion section of the
exhibit features all the symbolism and status associated with
haute couture in Western society. These bespoke, beautiful, hand-
tailored ensembles give the wearer certain powers status, and
authority, reframing them in an Indigenous, future-forward context.

And, of course, when worn by Indigenous people and of Indigenous
design, these clothes also speak to the ongoing significance
and resilience of certain aesthetic traditions, depending upon the
designer's culture and personal history. These are clothes for a
new society, suitable not just for the runways of New York or Paris
but beyond, into outer space, or wherever else the future takes us.
There's a fabulousness to it all that also poses serious challenges
to Western high fashion, especially who gets to make it, who gets to
wear it, and in what settings.

The force of these clothes is compounded by a regalia component,
seen in the show where the artists deliberately insert elements of
traditional cultural wear in designs made for these future worlds.
They emphasize the importance of continuity in Indigenous design,
timeless and contemporary at the same time.

Kristen
For me, the Anishnaabe/French artist Caroline Monnet bridges
the "Suiting Up" and the "Critical Mass" sections. For *Future
Imaginaries*, Monnet shared aspects of her *Echoes from a
Near Future* series, which features clothing she made from
construction materials, including a photograph with outfits worn
by powerful women and *Aïcha's Regalia*, a cape made from the
under material for laminate flooring (pls. 11 and 12). These pieces
reimagine construction waste as wearable sculpture. I'm excited
about how Monnet's work calls attention to overconsumption
within the fashion and construction industries. Overconsumption
and waste are symptoms of capitalism, settler society, and the
environmental crisis. Indigenous artists are engaging with these
urgent issues and offering insights into life outside of capitalism.

Amber-Dawn
Fashion is a form of wearable art. Everybody wears clothes, so
there's an immediate connection for the viewer. This section is
relatable for people who may feel alienated when visiting an art
museum. Fashion is a powerful visual tool and global language,
along with body tattooing, scarification, and jewelry. Of course,
this depends on how one defines fashion. People's understanding
of Indigenous future fashion, particularly in Los Angeles, does not

necessarily bring palm trees and sand to mind. In other words, designs in this show will expand notions of Indigenous creations and their diversity. There are no obvious items people might look for, such as feathers, headdresses, or fringe. The nature of the collection of works in the exhibition will push people beyond what they're comfortable seeing concerning Native North American art. Some may think this isn't Native art or "authentic" Native art, which is an anthropological standard. We're encouraging the audience to think beyond what they may know or not know of contemporary Native art, fashion, and science.

Virginia
Let's talk about technology, not just within the framework of the *Star Wars* universe, but rather more generally, because that's a way to get to the significance of *Future Imaginaries* for interpreting contemporary Native art in Los Angeles. What is the stance you're taking toward technology?

Suzanne
Years ago, in a conversation with Amanda Wixon and other contributors, we wanted to redefine the word "technology." Technology is not a computer. Technology is not your phone. It is not a circuit board. Technology is any process that has been refined. I had a conversation yesterday with Virgil Ortiz about how ceramics are a technology. Artists need to understand how materials work and how they come together. It's a highly technical skill. So we're trying to reimagine the word "technology"; we need to respect that these are technologies. Technology is related to food sovereignty, especially in the exhibition's "Critical Mass" section, because why are we introducing heirloom seeds, radishes, corn, and bees? We need these technologies to move into the future.

These works also suggest a different relationship to technology. *Ínyan Iyé (Telling Rock)* by Kite (Oglala Lakota) and Devin Ronneberg (Hawaiian/Okinawan) describes technology not as something nonhuman but something that has a soul (fig. 1 and pl. 44). The lights and sounds of this interactive installation change as people move through it, suggesting an alternative intelligence. Kite notes that in Lakota cosmology, inanimate objects can have souls, so her computer-generated braids and lights should be treated respectfully.

Kristen
In the "Critical Mass" section, I'm especially excited about Margaret Jacobs's (Akwesasne Mohawk) *Old Growth Series* (pl. 45). She works with traditional medicinal plants from her community, forging them in steel and creating a contemporary tool kit anyone can use. Plants are also framed as critical tools

in Tammy Tallchief's (Cayuga) *Space Farmer with Radishes* (pl. 37). I had the honor of interviewing Tammy for an essay in this book, which I co-wrote with my PhD advisor Dr. Nancy Marie Mithlo (Fort Sill Chiricahua Apache). Tallchief researched how radishes were grown on the International Space Station and how they're the perfect food because they are so nutritious. She said, "If we can do it with radishes, then we can do it with our corn, beans, and squash." Tallchief's work argues that we can bring our plant medicines, foods, and heirloom seeds with us into space. Seed keeping is critical to Indigenous food sovereignty projects and many tribes have seed banks. Heirloom seeds are Indigenous technologies and are being used to re-create Indigenous food systems because the current Western capitalist food system is broken.

Amy

One of the things that differentiates Indigenous technologies and knowledge systems from classic Western science is the definition and relative understanding of technology and how it is made and wielded. Too often, we're thinking about a piece of hardware, a computer or a phone, the static, inanimate things that do wonderful and amazing things for us all the time. But they're just products. The Indigenous view of technologies and knowledge systems suggests a greater awareness of entire systems, including intimate knowledge of specific ecologies passed down through generations. It is generational and ancestral and shows awareness of and attunement to the world around us, organic and otherwise.

Virginia

Let's talk about the significance of this exhibition to the local audience in Southern California. How will this exhibition change how people think about art in Los Angeles?

Suzanne

To outsiders, Los Angeles is the place of dreams. That is where you go to create your dream, whether it's a movie or a TV show. The mythology it creates is highly problematized. Nevertheless, LA is the locale for dreams in the nation's consciousness.

Amy

LA is the mythmaker and the contemporary storyteller for American culture writ large. Of course, LA is where *Star Trek* and many science fiction shows come from; LA as the generator of these fictions and of science fiction—Western science fiction in particular—deserves a mention. And so this exhibition draws upon that history while also helping rewrite it.

Kristen
LA is also the home of cutting-edge conceptual artworks and installations. This exhibit will dialogue well with the contemporary art scene of Los Angeles.

Amber-Dawn
Hollywood is the world's stage for creating narratives, whether true or not; the movie industry here informs American identity on the global stage. That includes the Wild West, which made the "Hollywood Indian." The Hollywood Indian is as ingrained as American apple pie—a stuck image leaving little room for reality.

Kristen
The Autry Museum is situated on Tongva land. I hope our audience leaves the exhibition with the understanding that Tongva creative practices like Mercedes Dorame's offer vibrant visions for Tongva lands, serving as important voices in the Los Angeles art world. Mercedes's work is about rebuilding relationships with the land for herself and her community. I think of her practice, which pictures the Tongva presence and worldview through the land, as based in portraiture rather than landscape (see Dorame essay in this volume and pl. 39).

Amber-Dawn
This show is a form of visual communication, and fashion is communication. Hopefully, it will also bring attention to the fact that this is Native land—palm trees, sand, and all. We hope the show will expand people's ideas of diversity because, for many, diversity and inclusion stop at slavery. Diversity in the larger public discourse does not see Indigenous people; we are considered the "other" demographic even in voting charts. The very fabric of North America is the Native North Americans who experienced genocide, a fact and history of the violent making of America.

This exhibition represents important narratives that have always been there but are unknown. Indigenous technology, fashion, and science have always been there, but now, due to a societal change in awareness, people are finally paying attention.

Amy
Visibility for contemporary Indigenous art in Los Angeles is beginning to change and grow, thanks in part to some of the artists in this show; Mercedes Dorame recently created an enormous installation for the Getty Museum, and Cannupa Hanska Luger (Mandan/Hidatsa/Arikara/Lakota) designed and produced the 2020 opera *Sweetland*, which was performed on the banks of the Los Angeles River, on Native land. But showings of contemporary Native art have

also lagged behind splashy displays of contemporary art by other groups, often white men, in the city's major museums for decades. We are at a moment in which contemporary Indigenous art is blossoming on the national stage, but also in this city. We are seeing a paradigm shift in how contemporary Indigenous artists are shown in Los Angeles, which is important, especially because LA so often casts itself as a global culture hub and, in Hollywood, as the storyteller for the world.

Virginia
The Autry has played a role in foregrounding Native art for decades.

Amy
Over ten years ago, in 2013, the Autry Museum's ongoing *Art of the West* exhibition was among the first to place historical and contemporary examples of Native art alongside one another and in dialogue with non-Native art in ways that transcended culture and time. Examples include Navajo Chief blankets in conversation with monumental ceramics by Rose B. Simpson and Alaskan totem poles next to one of Marie Watt's (Seneca) towers of folded blankets. In the same gallery are also historical landscapes from the expansion era, Spanish Colonial paintings, a beaded Lakota saddle, and works by Chicano artists. Native art should be a part of this conversation, not pigeonholed. These objects have a lot to say to one another.

Kristen
Cutting-edge multisensory artworks, such as those by X (Koasati/CHamoru) and Cannupa Hanska Luger, will dialogue with the contemporary art scene of Los Angeles.

Virginia
What are the distinctive features of the book?

Suzanne
The book includes many voices. We took a heterogeneous approach to give space to different viewpoints.

Amy
The book offers a wide range of perspectives, voices, cultural geographies, artistic traditions, and scientific literacies. Indigenous scientific literacies are brought to the table by artists and writers ranging from Sonny Assu and Virgil Ortiz to Kristen Dorsey, Amber-Dawn Bear Robe, Amanda Wixon, Jason Edward Lewis, Matthew Ryan Smith, and, of course, Gerald Vizenor, a leading voice in Indigenous science fiction, which is where the movement began. They all have

unique perspectives on Indigenous scientific literacies and knowledge systems, especially when reimagined as visual art or in the form of Vizenor's literary art. The book weaves all these voices together to expand, challenge, and complicate audience awareness and thinking when it comes to Native art as being both a contemporary phenomenon and a signpost for the future.

Amber-Dawn
To my knowledge, this is also one of the few publications associated with a Native American art exhibition that includes Indigenous fashion. There have been Native fashion exhibitions and publications, but *Future Imaginaries* is one of the first contemporary Indigenous art exhibition catalogues to include Indigenous fashion.

Virginia
The publication will make the exhibition's content, particularly the imagery, available to an audience outside of LA. Books have a life beyond the walls of the museum and beyond the community where the exhibition occurs. And a book is, of course, an old technology that can create new meanings.

Suzanne
Going back to what Kristen said at the beginning about art being a form of research, this book also offers a deeper analysis of what visitors will see in the exhibition. It provides a glimpse of the exhibition to anyone unable to visit.

Amy
For *Future Imaginaries*, adopting an artist-led curatorial methodology was critical for us as curators. We spoke with almost all of the artists, often multiple times throughout the process, sharing the show's content as it evolved and changed and listening to their thoughts on where and how their work fit and contributed to the broader narrative. We may have had some preconceived ideas of what we know or like about their work and what we think would fit, but these conversations sometimes shifted that thinking in ways that have improved the exhibition. It's been a dialogue, as opposed to a more traditional top-down approach where curators look through studios, museum basements, private collections, and online databases and then make selections, often side-stepping the artists altogether. Instead, we wanted to partner with the artists and bring them into the curatorial process so the pieces accurately reflect where their work is now. The publication also reflects that process.

* * *

Similar to the curatorial process and works of art featured in
the exhibition, the writings in this volume reflect a multivocal
approach that includes a range of authors and expertise. Amy
Scott, PhD, argues in her essay, "Apocalypse Is the Opportunity
We Are Looking For," that the different perspectives found in
Native and non-Native art when it comes to envisioning land
are key to understanding the opportunities that Indigenous art
and technologies hold for the future. Using the backdrop of Los
Angeles and its unique blend of Hollywood sci-fi, architectural
futurism, the aerospace industry, and a global art scene, she
explores how these entities imagine and manifest the future
and how the artists in this show enrich that dialogue.

PhD candidate Kristen Dorsey (Chickasaw) and Nancy Marie
Mithlo (Fort Sill Chiricahua Apache), PhD, co-wrote "When We
Remain," which explores the work of Cayuga Nation elder Tammy
Tallchief. Tallchief's *Space Farmer with Radishes* considers the
importance of Indigenous farming techniques, such as radishes,
to the potential for growing food in outer space. Offering more
nutrients and possible growth in challenging environments, the
humble radish could be the answer to feeding the future. Dorsey
and Mithlo equate the resilience of Indigenous seeds to the
resilience of Indigenous artists, writing, "Indigenous art practices
are like seeds; some might lay dormant, weathering the traumas
of genocide, and then emerge with new generations who have
opportunities to reconnect with ancestral art forms."

In her essay, "Riff, Ground, and Dream: Defining Indigenous
Futurisms in Visual Arts," Suzanne Newman Fricke, PhD, expands
the conversation in the field of Indigenous Futurisms as found
in the arts. Some artists, like Ryan Singer, Andy Everson, and
Jeffrey Veregge, embrace the characters, locales, and material
from popular sci-fi universes like *Star Wars* and *Star Trek* in what
Fricke describes as "Riff." "Ground" considers how other artists,
including Virgil Ortiz, Skawennati, and Kite, find similarities between
Indigenous oral histories, sci-fi aesthetics, and narrative structures.
"Dream" encompasses artists like KC Adams and Mercedes
Dorame, whose works reflect an idea beyond a specific narrative,
suggesting a future environment from an Indigenous perspective.

"Indigenous Fashions of the Otherworldly" by Amber-Dawn
Bear Robe (Siksika) notes how art historical approaches to
Western fashion are inadequate when applied to Indigenous
fashion, which has been central to American design for
well over a century. Exploring the work of emergent Native
designers alongside more established ones, she breaks
down the boundaries between fashion, art, and performance,
revealing how Indigenous designers are central to the future

of fashion while underscoring the knowledge, technologies, and influences present in their work.

Chickasaw curator Amanda K. Wixon's essay "Apocalypse When? Historic Disasters and Transformation" addresses numerous instances of apocalypse in Indigenous oral histories. Beyond the colonization by the European forces beginning in the sixteenth century, many tribes include other apocalyptic events, such as the Great Flood origin stories found among numerous peoples, including the Chickasaw, Akimel O'odham, and the Lakota. Wixon notes how these events are often transformative for the culture, forcing difficult and regenerative change. As Wixon writes, "Embedded within their Native origin stories are the lessons of communal collective action in times of uncertainty, and these stories, which have been told since time immemorial, are part of the collective memory of each source community."

In "A Long Time Ago in the Final Frontier: Picturing Indigenous Futurism through *Star Wars* and *Star Trek*," curator and art historian Matthew Ryan Smith, PhD, considers different constructs of time as proposed by artists, scientists, and writers and how the idea of time shapes our understanding of the world. He notes that the image of the *Starship Enterprise* from the original *Star Trek* series, as seen in the work of Neal Ambrose-Smith and Marie Watt, "symbolizes the retreat into deep space or light-speed flight to faraway worlds."

In his essay "The Myths of My Descendants," Jason Edward Lewis (Kanaka Maoli/Samoan), redefines the idea of technology not as something new but as something found in Indigenous cultures worldwide. In his words, "Technology is the transformation of our knowledge about the world into tools we can use to manage and shape our existence within it." Lewis advocates for a more nuanced and mindful approach to using tools that respects how they came about and how they change us as much as we change them.

Manuela Well-Off-Man, PhD, art historian and chief curator at the IAIA Museum of Contemporary Native Arts (MoCNA), writes about the seminal role of that institution in providing the support, space, and creative freedom necessary for many of the artists and the genre of Indigenous Futurisms to flourish in "Imagining the Future at the IAIA Museum of Contemporary Native Arts." Well-Off-Man describes some of the works within the *Future Imaginaries* exhibition in terms of their critical contributions to the field and their origins within MoCNA's storied history as the first and still, to date, the only museum in the country dedicated to contemporary Indigenous art.

Dispersed throughout this volume are also contributions from artists in the show, sharing their perspectives on Indigenous Futurisms through the lens of their artistic practice. Under the heading "Windows to the Future," these short essays provide glimpses into the varied ideas, influences, technologies, and traditions that inform their work. They highlight some of the distinct voices in the exhibition and this volume while speaking collectively to the complexity and diversity of Indigenous art and culture today. In "Windows to the Future," Cannupa Hanksa Luger (Mandan/Hidatsa/Arikara/Lakota), Mercedes Dorame (Tongva), and Sonny Assu (Ligwiłdaʼxw of the Kwakwaka'wakw Nations) talk about aliens, colonization, sacred beings, and ancestral technologies (among other things) to expand further the meaning and potential of Indigenous Futurisms. Additionally, renowned author of Indigenous sci-fi Gerald Vizenor (White Earth Nation) and artist Weshoyot Alvitre (Tongva/ Scottish) have contributed two new, original works of art in the form of a short story and a narrative in graphic form, respectively, specially designed for this volume.

Lastly, it is important to note that the varied voices, ideas, and images shared in these pages reflect the heterogeneous and rapidly morphing nature of Indigenous Futurisms as an artistic field unrestrained by traditional museological categories or Western definitions of art, fashion, and technology. And that is precisely the point. Museums are, by nature, colonial institutions and have been central to the project of collecting, categorizing, and marginalizing Native art in relation to Western art for centuries. As the Autry and museums across Los Angeles and the United States (not to mention around the world) seek to display and engage with Indigenous Futurisms, they do more than show contemporary art; they confront their role in the erasure of Native cultures that has been central to the American project since its founding. Confronting the past is one way to create a better future; the art and artists showcased throughout this volume help take us there, and beyond.

the Opportunity
We Are Looking For

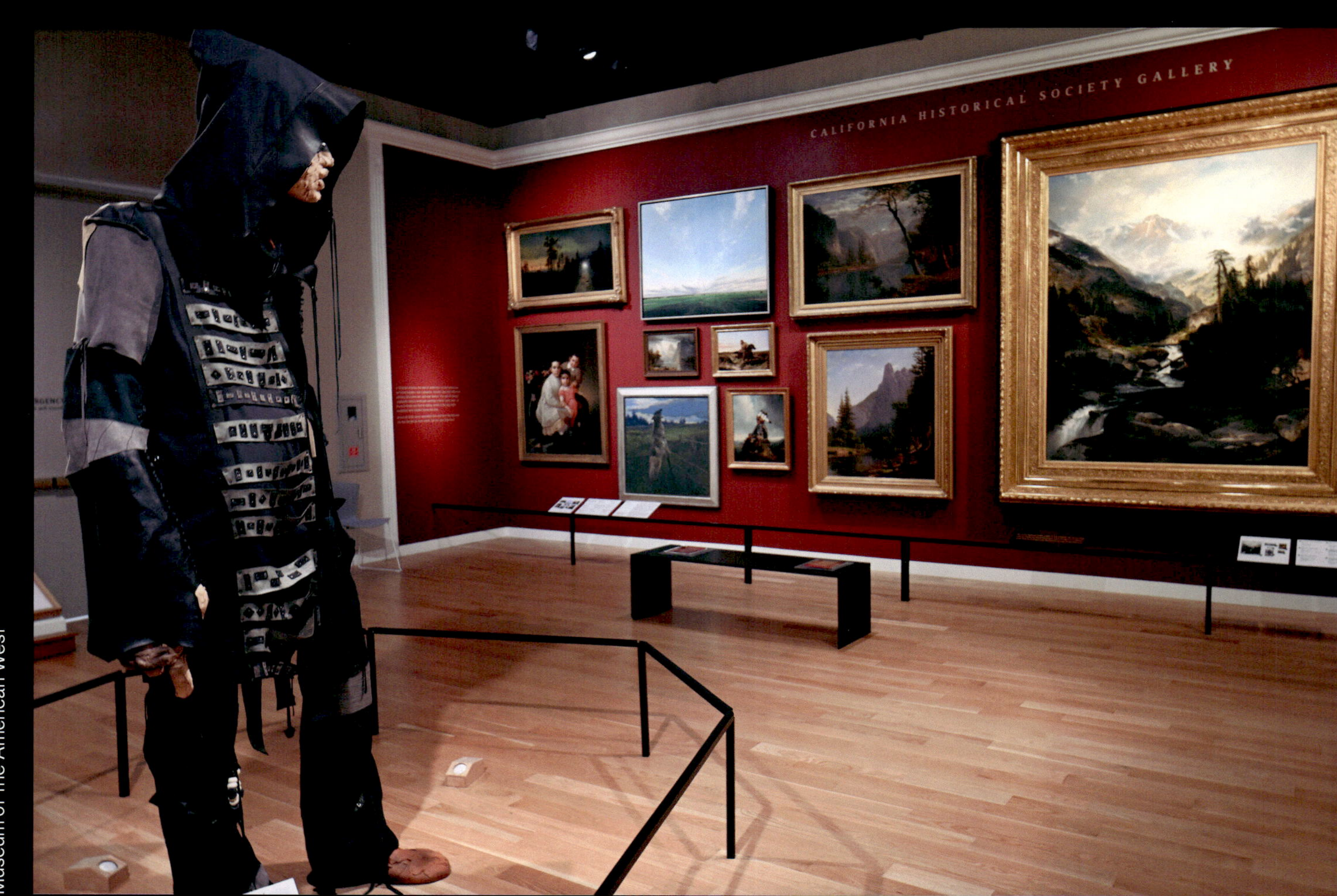

the Autry Museum featuring *Ground (Witness)* by Rose B. Simpson (Santa Clara Pueblo). Courtesy of the Autry Museum of the American West

Maybe "apocalypse" is the opportunity we are looking for, even
if we don't quite know it yet.
— Rose B. Simpson[1]

Tense: Future Past

In the heart of the *Art of the West* exhibition at the Autry
Museum in Los Angeles stands a figurative sculpture titled
Ground (Witness) (figs. 1 and 2).[2] Over eight feet tall, this work
was created by Santa Clara Pueblo artist Rose B. Simpson
and is dressed in oversized black leather pants and a hooded
jacket customized with bespoke details, including patchwork,
fringe, cutouts, and ceramic beads (pl. 18). A thick black stripe
is painted across the eyes, while the clay head and hands
have a cracked, flaky texture reminiscent of the dry riverbeds
scattered across the artist's ancestral lands in northern New
Mexico. As Lucy R. Lippard writes in the catalogue to the 2016
exhibition *Ground* at the Pomona College Museum of Art—for
which the piece was created prior to its acquisition by the Autry
Museum: "Simpson's post-apocalyptic figures [are] . . . a fusion
of ancient, still vital beliefs with popular culture, contemporary
cutting-edge art, and a lifestyle that honors permaculture and
local ecologies."[3]

From its position in the middle of the gallery, *Witness* gazes
upon a long, horizontal wall hung floor-to-ceiling with landscape
paintings by some of the best-known artists of the nineteenth-
century American West, names such as Albert Bierstadt and
Thomas Moran. Filled with flowing waterfalls, towering mountains,
and pastoral valleys bathed in golden light, the paintings speak
less to the contours of any given site than to a nationalistic
vision of the West as "virgin" or "promised" land, a site of "future
reconciliation in a postwar world of arcadian peace and plenty," far
from the bloodstained battlefields of Gettysburg and Antietam
(fig. 3).[4] Yet, as art historians have pointed out, what western
landscapes of this era do *not* depict often has more to say
about the historical moment than oversized waterfalls and too-
tall mountains. By the end of the Civil War, decades of disease,
broken treaties, forced relocation, and military aggression had
dramatically transformed the physical and cultural environment
of the American West in ways that marginalized or destroyed
the lifeways, food sources, religious practices, and linguistic ties
of the Indigenous cultures that had lived there for centuries. As
Native resentment festered and tensions between tribes and the
government escalated, so did military campaigns against them.
During the war, both Union and Confederate troops stationed in
the West had been deployed against Native peoples. Hostilities

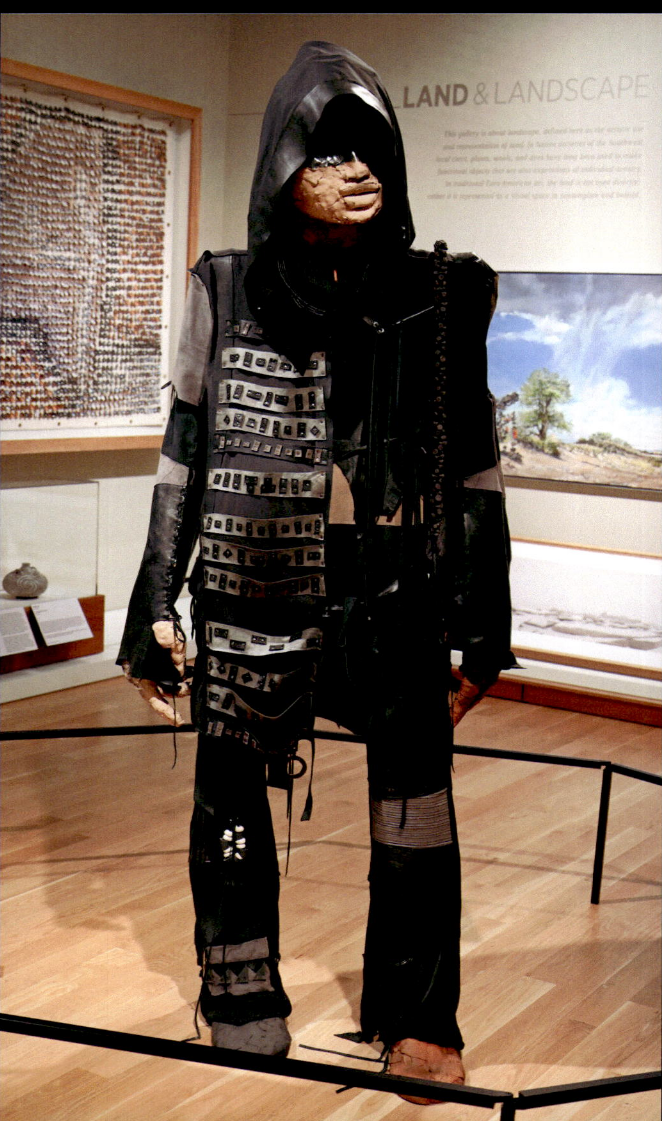

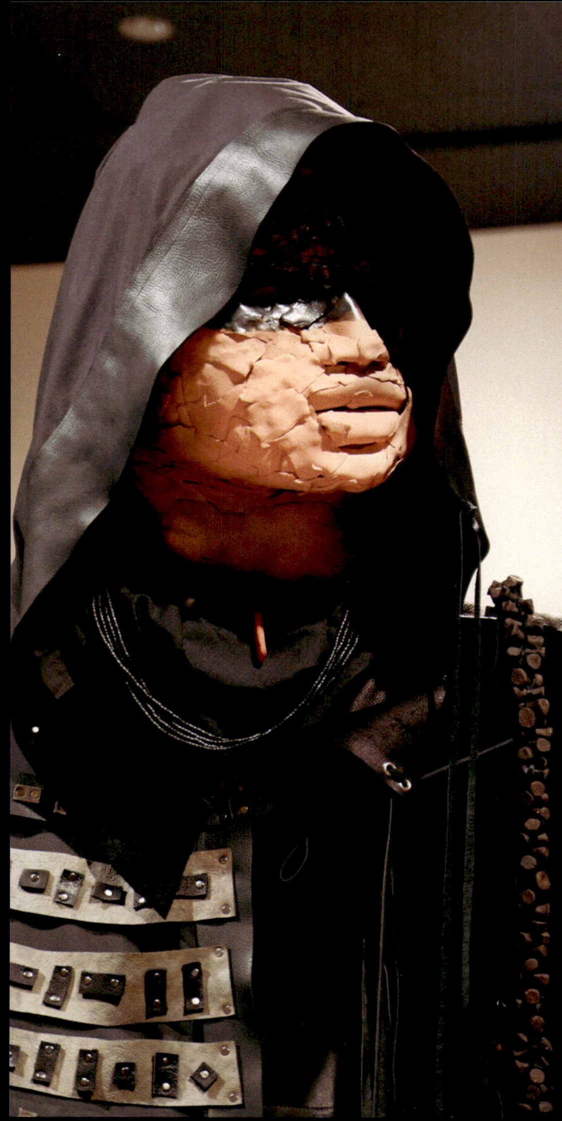

Fig. 2. Rose B. Simpson (Santa Clara Pueblo), *Ground (Witness)*, 2016. Ceramic, steel, leather, textile, 99 x 17 x 27 in. Courtesy of the Autry Museum of the American West

toward tribes did not end with the Union victory or the abolition of slavery. Instead, the government refocused its efforts on westward expansion and the "Indian Problem," launching at least twenty conflicts between the end of the war in 1865 and the close of the frontier in 1890 (including the Ghost Dance War of 1890-91, which culminated in the massacre of hundreds of unarmed Native women, children, and elders).

Ecologies of the Future

The landscape paintings on the wall across from *Witness*, like so many of this era, exist both within and without the past, referencing an imaginary history of the West as vacant and vast, while anticipating future settlement by white Christian people who would "improve" the land through agriculture, extraction, development, and tourism. By turning the viewer's eyes toward a brighter future in a golden West, landscape art helped naturalize violence against Native peoples by creating an imagined past, one emptied of humanity and therefore ready for settlement by an acquisitive, righteous audience.

The future, of course, belongs to no single group. The contemporary artists in this volume, many of whom embrace the idea of a plurality of futures, employ Indigenous lenses to reestablish connections to ancestral lands, actively reclaiming their narratives from the near erasure prescribed by so much historical Western art. This effort is very much tied to the land, not as it was depicted centuries ago, but as the source of long-standing Indigenous technologies and knowledge systems critical to cultural survival, ecological recovery, and a more sovereign, sustainable future. As the Indigenous environmental scholar Kyle Whyte (Potawatomi) points out, settler colonialism was not just political or military domination; it was also "ecological domination . . . that disrupts human relationships with the environment," and the "covenant of reciprocity" between humans and nonhuman beings.[5] Other scholars have similarly noted how "the disruption of Indigenous relationships to land represents a profound epistemic, ontological, cosmological violence," one that, like colonialism itself, is intergenerational, carrying over from the past in ways that shape the present and endanger our shared future.[6]

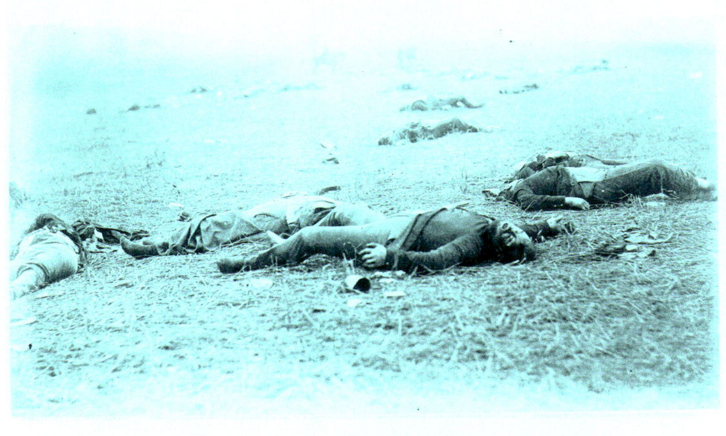

Fig. 3. Timothy O'Sullivan and Alexander Gardner (negative by O'Sullivan, positive by Gardner), *A Harvest of Death, Gettysburg, Pennsylvania, July 1863*, printed ca. 1865. Albumen print. Courtesy of the Library of Congress

Perhaps the best-known example of this continuum is the 2016 protests at the Standing Rock Reservation (fig. 4), which saw Indigenous artists-turned-activists on the front lines of a monthslong standoff between the Standing Rock Sioux (and their many supporters, including non-Native individuals, environmental and social justice organizations, and local farmers) and the developers, construction workers, and private security personnel charged with building the Dakota Access Pipeline, which carries crude oil from North Dakota south, ultimately to Texas. At the center of the struggle were the waters of Lake Oahe, said to be poisoned by the "black snake" of the pipeline, setting off a global movement for water protection called *Mni Wiconi* (Lakota for "water is life"). One of the more visible artists associated with the Standing Rock protests is Cannupa Hanska Luger (Mandan/Hidatsa/Arikara/Lakota), who designed protective regalia (or "mirror shields") for the water protectors (fig. 5) and whose work has long sought to connect an Indigenous present to respect for ancestral homelands against growing industrial incursions. Indeed, Luger's *Future Ancestral Technologies* project was conceived shortly after the events at Standing Rock, which he describes as "Indigenous Science Fiction . . . a way of dreaming rooted in continuum."[7] As Luger writes later in this volume about *Watȟéča* (see Luger, fig. I), a birdlike scavenger who scours the earth for the detritus of the colonial past as the building material of future worlds, "*Watȟéča* celebrates and integrates the scavengers' gifts into our future cosmology. The scavenger becomes kin, teaching us critical technology for future survival. As we look to the buzzard and the coyote, we see the models and allies we need to survive."[8]

Final Frontiers and the Future Imaginary

Indigenous Futurisms today connect Indigenous technologies, their ancestral origins, and the future by reintroducing Indigenous ecological concepts, perspectives, and knowledge long marginalized by colonial violence, imagining a future unmoored from exploitative and racist colonial industries, including those at work at Standing Rock. As with Luger's *Future Ancestral Technologies* project, contemporary Indigenous art about the future brings visibility to the Indigenous present by interrogating ideas about the future in ways that both raise awareness of and interfere with its audience's preconceived ideas.[9] Indigenous artists' drive to envision alternative futures is important for a variety of reasons, both from within and outside Native communities today. Many of the artists in this volume see Futurism as a means to create alternate futures in ways that offer healing in the present. They use the lens of the "future imaginary" not only to call out the historical injustices of the colonial past but also to address the more subtle, sinister ways in which lingering biases and narratives continue to circulate throughout American culture, including Western science and industry as well as environmentalism and the arts. Building on a concept developed by scholar Jason Edward Lewis, art historian Kristina Baudemann defines the future imaginary as "the portion of a thought or of an utterance, artwork, and human or non-human act that projects forward and thereby foregrounds the idea of a future," the future imaginary "signifies the future" and "makes thought about the future possible by projecting a 'set of beliefs' that can be accessed in the present."[10]

While these strategies take many forms, the visual arts have proved a potent medium for centering Indigenous Futurisms as a conduit between a post-apocalyptic present (as seen through an Indigenous lens) and a self-determined future driven by Indigenous values, ecologies, and the technologies based on and stored within them. Indigenous technologies (also referred to as knowledge systems) are rooted in an ancestral experience of place, are intergenerational, and inform aspects of daily life from food, medicine, and wayfinding to artmaking, as in the highly technical knowledge required to source, form, and fire the clays long used by Simpson's family and others in her Santa Clara community. Because Indigenous knowledge systems accommodate ongoing, complex, and interlocking components of local ecologies (including relationships across species and with various features of the land such as lakes or mountains), they are important in confronting both the causes and impacts of climate change, an existential threat to all of humanity currently unfolding in natural disasters such as hurricanes, floods, and fires. These events—including the inferno that destroyed the Hawaiian community of Lahaina or the massive flood in eastern Libya that cost over eight thousand lives (both of which transpired just weeks before this writing)—feel like a real-time apocalypse to those caught, unexpectedly, in their wrath.

As we look for potential alternatives to our distressed planet (pl. 15), there is also the very real danger of history repeating itself, not just on a global but a galactic scale. Since the dawn of the Space Age in 1957 with the launch of the Soviet satellite Sputnik, politicians have delighted in using metaphors of westward expansion to describe American interests in outer space. John F. Kennedy spoke about space exploration as "setting sail on a new sea," while Lyndon B. Johnson referred to astronauts as "space pioneers" headed for a "glorious New World." George H. W. Bush compared space missions to Christopher Columbus's 1492 "discovery" of the Americas while his son, George W. Bush, evoked the Lewis and Clark expedition as a metaphor for space exploration. Bill Clinton and Barack Obama also spoke of space as the next, or even "the final frontier" (a phrase borrowed from the immensely successful TV and film franchise *Star Trek*). And in 2019, Donald Trump created the "Space Force," a military branch designed specifically to enforce national interests in space via a "global network of space surveillance sensors" that would maintain America's "space superiority."[11] Trump further articulated this narrative of the future using the terminology of the past in his 2020 State of the Union address, proclaiming: "In reaffirming our heritage as a free nation, we must remember that America has always been a frontier nation. Now we must embrace the next frontier: America's Manifest Destiny in the stars."[12]

Invoking Manifest Destiny, Trump (like his predecessors) sends a clear message about who belongs in space and who does not.[13] As Simpson's *Witness* demands we do, rethinking who gets to imagine the future and how they might do so is a task well suited to Los Angeles, a city known for reinventing itself and those who live here. The westernmost end point of Columbus's "New World," Los Angeles was dubbed the "City of the Future" in 1970 by then mayor Sam Yorty.[14] Seeking to court real estate developers and technological industries, Yorty conjured the city's own future imaginary-turned-reality of soaring freeway interchanges and space-themed landmarks—such as the rotating, flying-saucer structure in the middle of Los Angeles International Airport (fig. 6), the

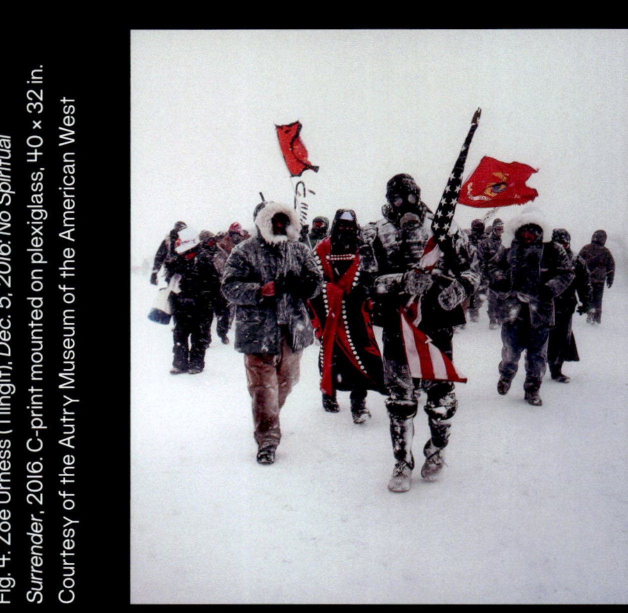

Fig. 4. Zoe Urness (Tlingit), *Dec. 5, 2016: No Spiritual Surrender*, 2016. C-print mounted on plexiglass, 40 × 32 in. Courtesy of the Autry Museum of the American West

phaser-beam-shaped Capitol Records tower, and the Westin Bonaventure Hotel, a cluster of glass cylinders resembling giant rocket launchers—many of which have functioned as characters themselves in cinematic sci-fi classics such as the 1984 film *Blade Runner,* in which Los Angeles is portrayed as an ecological hellscape soaked in acid rain. Like many works of Western science fiction, *Blade Runner* is a cautionary tale, a portrait of a dystopic world driven by environmental decay and social unrest resulting from a slavish embrace of Western technology. Other sci-fi films (and there are many) about environmental decline set in Los Angeles include *Escape from LA* (1998), *Heat Wave* (2009), *Elysium* (2013), *LA Apocalypse* (2014), and *The Cloverfield Paradox* (2018), while alien invasions or their aftermath play out also in *Skyline* (2010),

Battle Los Angeles (2011), *Oblivion* (2013), and *Moonfall* (2022). Others still focus on the impact of artificial intelligence and human-machine hybrids as they disrupt interpersonal relationships, linear time, and the city itself, including *Her* (2013) and what is perhaps the city's best-known dystopic film franchise, the five-part *Terminator* series, starring California's future governor Arnold Schwarzenegger as a cyborg assassin who unleashes chaos as he stalks a woman across the city at night.[15]

Alongside the futuristic fantasies on display in both the built environment and cinematic imagination of Los Angeles is the very real presence of the city's sizable aerospace industry, a matrix of tech industry giants, private companies, and start-ups scattered across the city from its beach towns to the

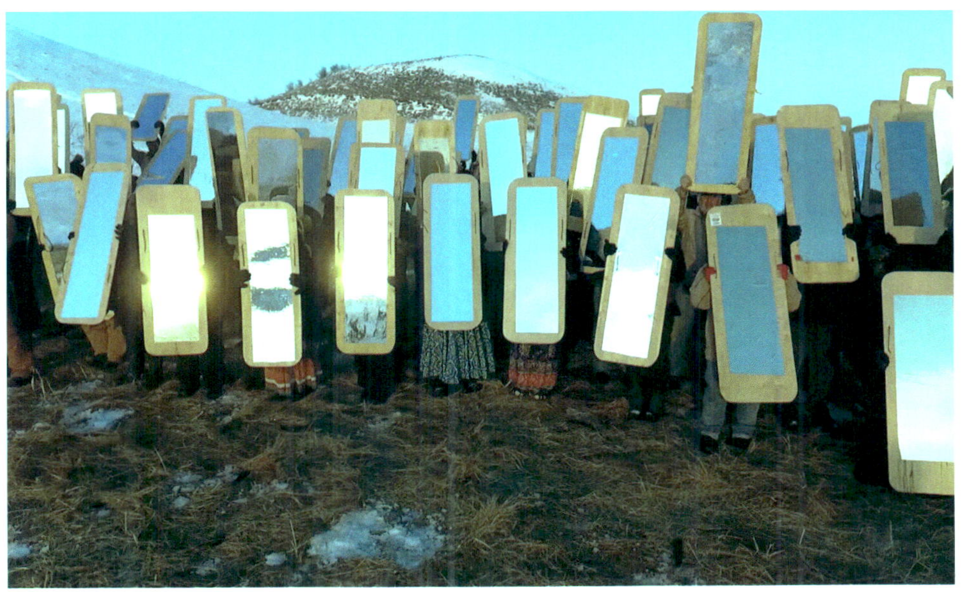

Fig. 5. Cannupa Hanska Luger (Mandan/Hidatsa /Arikara/Lakota), *Mirror Shield Project*, 2016–present. Mixed media. Courtesy of the artist

Water Serpent (River), a site-specific performance of Luger's *Mirror Shield Project*, was organized by Luger in collaboration with Rory Wakemup. The event took place on November 18, 2016, at Oceti Sakowin Camp, Standing Rock Indian Reservation, North Dakota.

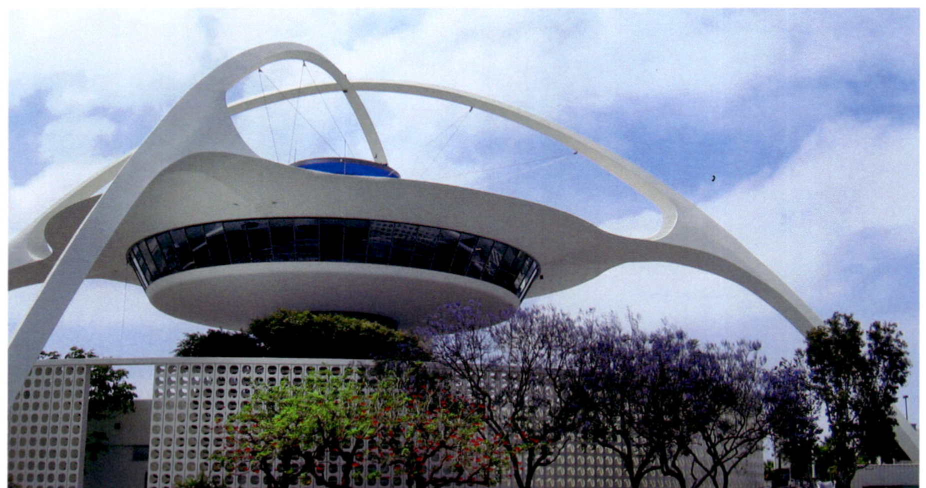

Inland Empire. Perhaps the best known is NASA's Jet Propulsion Laboratory, born at the California Institute of Technology in the 1930s to develop military jets, and which led the U.S. into space in 1958 with its first satellite, Explorer I. Northrop Grumman, known for producing aircraft, spacecraft, and high-energy laser systems for surveillance and reconnaissance, has locations in multiple LA enclaves, including Northridge, Woodland Hills, Azusa, and nearby Ventura. Headquartered in Hawthorne is Space X, a private manufacturer of spacecraft, satellites, and rockets. Boeing, one of the largest aerospace and defense contractors in the world, has locations in both San Diego and Los Angeles, where it joins a teeming nexus of tech, media, and entertainment start-ups clustered in Los Angeles's "Silicon Beach," which stretches from Venice Beach to West LA.

Yorty's "City of the Future" looks different in 2024 than it did in 1970, its technological savvy, creative capital, and capacity for reinvention joining forces with its multifaceted art scene, leading Los Angeles County Museum of Art director Michael Govan to describe it as "the most creative city on earth at any time in history."[16] Today, the city features more than thirty art museums and an extensive local-meets-global art economy that includes dozens of art galleries, supportive nonprofits including residencies and exhibition spaces, and renown training academies such as the California Institute of the Arts, the ArtCenter College of Design, and Otis College of Art and Design. And in 2025, the city will debut its newest museum, the Lucas Museum of Narrative Art (fig. 7), an elegant, curvilinear structure designed by Ma Yansong of MAD Architects that, at first glance, appears more galactic cruiser than art museum. Founded by filmmaker George Lucas, creator of *Star Wars* (the longest-running most commercially successful sci-fi franchise in the world), and Mellody Hobson, president of Ariel Investments, the architectural design of the Lucas Museum is not about space travel, but rather transporting visitors from their urban surroundings to a more spiritual place inspired by the ethereal elements of nature. Ma's structures, often rendered in glass, steel, and concrete, evoke natural elements like wind, water, and mountain peaks, in a deliberately "discordant combination of the worldly and the otherworldly" that serves as an antidote to the "soullessness" of city life.[17] And while not designed as a literal spaceship, in its promise to convey visitors away from the historical model of museums as cultural citadels and toward a more fluid space that integrates the natural environment, the Lucas Museum is itself a piece of architectural futurism, one that represents a new and more holistic approach to the museum experience while adding another chapter to the city's history of creative reinvention.

Weaving together the city's fantastic, technological, and artistic dimensions is the Getty Foundation's PST ART series, for which this book and the exhibition it accompanies, *Future Imaginaries: Indigenous Art, Fashion, Technology*, was produced. Launched in 2012, Pacific Standard Time (now known by its rebranded moniker PST ART) is a recurrent series of citywide exhibitions initially devoted to exploring the "mythically vast reaches of Southern California." In 2017, PST went hemispheric with its second major installment, PST: LA/LA, on the artistic intersections between Los Angeles and Latin America. The following year, the Getty announced its third PST ART initiative, PST ART: *Art & Science Collide*, exploring the close ties between art and science throughout history and around the world, cementing, as Getty president and CEO Katherine Fleming stated, "Los Angeles's place as one of the global cultural capitals of the twenty-first century." The focus on the entwined fields of art and science was deliberately future-focused, posing questions that "are crucial for our very future. What can artists and scientists do in collaboration to overcome ecological damage and imagine a more sustainable future?" As Luger likewise observed, the theme of art and science is one that creates paths forward through which we all might "navigate through darkness toward a future where we can thrive," showcasing "technology that values reverence for the land we belong to, rather than privileging extraction from a land that we mistakenly believe belongs to us."[18]

In joining art to science, PST also questions the idea that unfettered technological advancement along the lines of the Silicon Valley "move fast and break things" ethos is in the best interest of either a democratic or a sustainable future.[19]

This is important in an era in which our lives are increasingly governed by a handful of unelected, ultra-wealthy "techno-oligarchs" such as the venture capitalist Marc Andreessen, whose recent "Techno-optimist manifesto" begins with the claim that "our control over nature" is in fact "our birthright," capable of advancing human society to a "far superior way of living, and of being" by "exploring and claiming the technological frontier."[20] As critics have pointed out, many of the technologies promoted, funded, and celebrated by Andreessen and his cohorts (a small group of white male billionaires including Mark Zuckerberg, Peter Thiel, and Elon Musk)—such as the "metaverse," generative AI, genome editing, and other life-extending, biological "enhancements"— are incredibly expensive, disdainful of the physical world, and likely to exacerbate rising levels of social inequality.

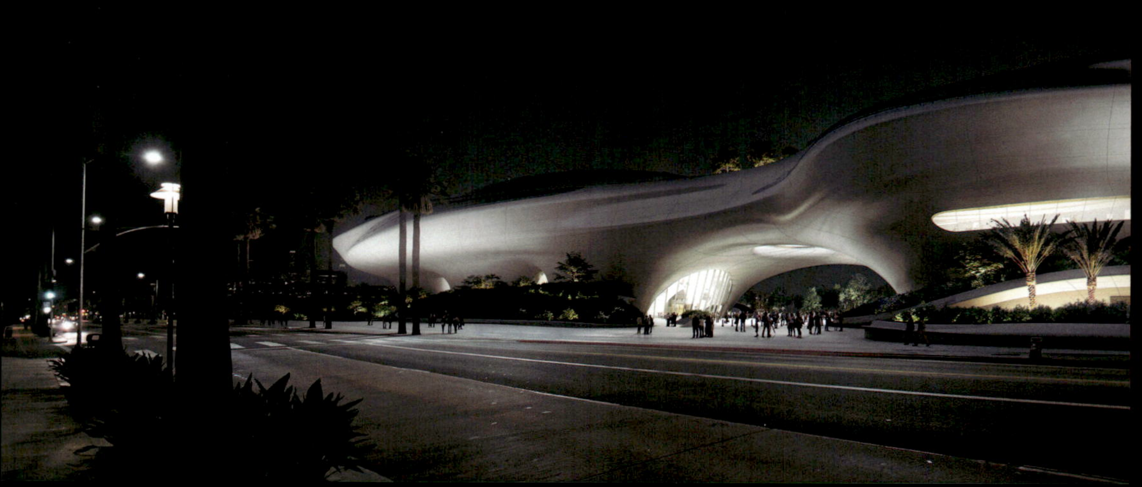

Fig. 7. Lucas Museum rendering, street view from Vermont Avenue at night. Courtesy of the Lucas Museum of Narrative Art, © Lucas Museum of Narrative Art

This version of progress as a winner-take-all scenario is embedded in the frontier-style metaphors that promote space exploration and the aerospace industry that drives it. It is also found in the cautionary tales of environmental decay, cyborgs, and alien invasions that wreak havoc across LA's cinematic landscape. Some forty years ago, Fredric Jameson argued in the journal *Science Fiction Studies* that the concept of progress embedded in political rhetoric and technological advance is a collection of "master fantasies" entwined with recognizable mythic structures. As Jameson describes it, the concept of progress has made little progress in the futures promoted by the technocrats, whether it is a life led entirely in virtual reality or among a small group of bioengineered elites. This form of progress is more one of "distraction and displacement, repression, and renewal," less an attempt to imagine what might be than a means of creating a mock future that "serves the quite different function of transforming our present into the indeterminate past of something yet to come."[21]

Jameson's theory returns us to the field of Indigenous Futurisms as an alternate model grounded more in collective continuities and a sense of kinship with ecological systems rather than colonization, conquest, and capitalism. Grace Dillon, who coined the term "Indigenous Futurism," offers a variety of alternative narrative structures within the genre that set it apart from both the "master fantasies" of either Western science fiction or the technocratic elite. These strategies are varied and include the idea of "slipstream" (time travel and alternative concepts of time), contact, Indigenous science and sustainability, Native Apocalypse, and *Biskaabiiyang*, or "returning to ourselves." The distinctions between Dillon's themes are beyond the scope of this essay. What unites them is a more inclusive approach to non-Western technologies and Indigenous ways of knowing, prompting us to imagine what future worlds might contain if defined by Native conditions and values, liberated from the oppressive narrative structures, models, and metaphors, and emancipated from limited and static ideas of "progress" as a function of Western science and its colonial roots.

An artistic field about Native peoples and by Native peoples, Indigenous Futurisms contain lessons that transcend the specifics of Indigenous history by bringing Native stories into the now through the lens of the "future imaginary," a malleable concept that, as previously noted, takes many forms. This volume is less an attempt to itemize these than an investigation into some of its most visible and engaging forms and themes. The images and ideas presented here offer a range of portals into the Indigenous present by, as Jameson suggests, imagining "our present [as] the determinate past of something yet to come."[22] Yet the "something yet to come" proposed collectively by the artists in this volume is a world away from the "master fantasies" of ecological hellscapes, space colonization, or virtual worlds governed by supermen.

Witness the Future

If we think about these connections between art and erasure, between land and life, between precilections of the past and prognostications of the future embodied in the synthesis of fantasy, futurism, and progress that plays out across the city and into the stars, we can more clearly see why Simpson's *Witness* appears skeptical of the historical landscapes before it. From the perspective of its young Pueblo maker, they depict a past that never existed yet had real consequences for the (then) future, our present reality. As a testament to the impact of colonial narratives over time, *Witness* also defies the idea that progress necessarily entails victimization of the kind implied by the absence of human history in these same paintings. As the artist reminds us, there is opportunity in the apocalypse, "even if we don't quite know it yet," ways of learning from the past without repeating it, but also in the new beginnings and ideas formed in the wake of destruction and loss. The post-apocalyptic narratives, seen in the work of Simpson, Luger, and artists across this volume, are often reality for Indigenous communities who have survived centuries of trauma and attempted erasure. For them, making art about the future offers healing by challenging the inevitability of colonial notions of progress and reclaiming one's destiny from the politicians, technocrats, and industrial developers vying to conquer "the final frontier." This is true not only for those peoples who have suffered colonization, but for all of us. As the Lipan Apache scholar, scientist, and author Dr. Darcie Little Badger states, "Both in and outside fiction, we are pushed to the past tense. The reality is, many Indigenous cultures in North America survived an apocalypse. Any future with us in it, triumphant and flourishing, is a hopeful one."[23]

1   Kathleen Howe, ed., *Rose B. Simpson: Ground* (Claremont, CA: Pomona College Museum of Art, 2016), 38.

2   This standing figure is one half of Simpson's two-part monumental sculpture, *Ground (Witness)*, 2016, which also includes a winged figure titled *Ground (Grounded)*.

3   Lucy R. Lippard in Howe, ed., *Rose B. Simpson*, 15.

4   Angela Miller, "Albert Bierstadt, Landscape Aesthetics, and the Meaning of the West in the Civil War Era," *Art Institute of Chicago Museum Studies* 27, no. 1 (2001): 40–59.

5   Kyle Whyte, "Settler Colonialism, Ecology, and Environmental Injustice," *Environment and Society: Advances in Research* 9 (2018): 126. For more on the collective continuance and the "covenant of reciprocity," see Robin Wall Kimmerer, *Braiding Sweetgrass: Indigenous Wisdom, Scientific Knowledge and the Teachings of Plants* (Milkweed Editions, 2015).

6   Ibid., 125. Originally cited in Eve Tuck and K. Wayne Yang, "Decolonization Is Not a Metaphor," *Decolonization: Indigeneity, Education and Society* 1 (2012): 1.

7   https://www.cannupahanska.com/fat/ethos. Accessed September 30, 2023.

8   See Cannupa Hanska Luger's essay in this volume.

9   "Introduction: 'Turning our backs on Mars' – futures seen through the window of an Indigenous Star Ship," in *The Future Imaginary in Indigenous North American Arts and Literatures*, Kristina Baudemann (Routledge: London and New York, 2022), 4–5.

10 Baudemann, *The Future Imaginary*, 27–28.

11 https://www.defense.gov/News/News-Stories/Article/Article/2348614/space-force-chief-us-doesnt-want-war-in-space-must-be-prepared-for-it/. Accessed September 14, 2023. See also https://www.spaceforce.mil/About-Us/About-Space-Force/#:~:text=The%20Space%20Force%20organizes%2C%20trains,West%20Cost%20Space%20Launch%20Deltas.

12 Marina Koen, "No One Should 'Colonize' Space," *The Atlantic*, https://www.theatlantic.com/science/archive/2020/09/manifest-destiny-trump-space-exploration/612439/. Accessed December 5, 2023.

13 Ibid.

14 Los Angeles was termed the "City of the Future" by Mayor Sam Yorty in 1970. For more on the connections between technology and urban planning in twentieth-century Los Angeles, see Mark Vallianatos, "Uncovering the Early History of Big Data and the Smart City," *Boom California*, June 16, 2015, https://boomcalifornia.org/2015/06/16/uncovering-the-early-history-of-big-data-and-the-smart-city-in-la/. Accessed October 3, 2023.

15 While the *Terminator* franchise was originally filmed on the streets of Los Angeles at night, not all scenes were filmed solely or even primarily in the city.

16 PST ART (@pstinla), "Brace for impact. Art & Science Collide. Coming 2024," Instagram post, May 9, 2023, https://www.instagram.com/p/CsC8dPOp6W6/. Accessed December 1, 2023.

17 Sam Lubell, "Ma Yansong Takes LA: How the Quiet Force Behind George Lucas' Museum Makes His Mark," *Los Angeles Times*, April 2, 2020, https://www.latimes.com/entertainment-arts/story/2020-04-02/ma-yansong-architect-george-lucas-musuem. Accessed December 4, 2023.

18 Cannupa Hanska Luger, https://www.getty.edu/news/more-than-50-socal-organizations-announce-exhibitions-for-pst-art-art-science-collide/. Accessed October 30, 2023.

19 "Move fast and break things" is the motto of Meta founder Mark Zuckerberg. Zuckerberg initially intended for the phrase to capture internal design and management processes at Facebook (now Meta), but it became widely associated with the tech industry's approach to disruption across all levels. As critics have pointed out, Zuckerberg's ethos contains no systems of governance or accountability. See Hemant Taneja, "The Era of 'Move Fast and Break Things' Is Over," *Harvard Business Review*, January 22, 2019, https://hbr.org/2019/01/the-era-of-move-fast-and-break-things-is-over. Accessed November 27, 2023.

20 Marc Andreessen, "The Techno-Optimist Manifesto," Andreessen Horowitz, October 16, 2023. https://a16z.com/the-techno-optimist-manifesto/. Accessed December 1, 2023. Andreessen runs Andreessen Horowitz (aka a16z), a venture capital firm that, according to its website, "backs bold entrepreneurs building the future through technology."

21 Fredric Jameson, "Progress versus Utopia; or, Can We Imagine the Future?," *Science Fiction Studies* 9, no. 2 (July 1982): 152n20, 153.

22 Jameson, "Progress versus Utopia," 152.

23 Darcie Little Bader, Rebecca Roanhorse, Elizabeth LaPensée, and Johnnie Jae, "Decolonizing Science Fiction and Imagining Futures: An Indigenous Futurisms Roundtable," *Strange Horizons*, January 30, 2017, accessed September 9, 2023, http://strangehorizons.com/non-fiction/articles/decolonizing-science-fiction-and-imagining-futures-an-indigenous-futurisms-roundtable/#:~:text=Both%20in%20and%20outside%20fiction,flourishing%2C%20is%20a%20hopeful%20one. This quote originally appeared in an early draft of Manuela Well-Off-Man's essay "Imagining the Future at the IAIA Museum of Contemporary Native Arts," which appears in this volume.

WINDOW TO THE FUTURE

Future Ancestral Technologies: *Watȟéča*

Cannupa Hanska Luger

Science fiction has the power to shape collective thinking
and imagine the future on a global scale. *Future Ancestral
Technologies* is Indigenous science fiction—a methodology,
practice, and way of future dreaming rooted in a continuum.
As an artist and a craftsperson, I understand how the very
act of making creates future potential. *Future Ancestral
Technologies* imagines, enacts, and prototypes experiences
that prepare Indigenous cultures to thrive in the future. Looking
to customs to move us forward, this work advances Indigenous
methodologies and sustainable modes of thinking through
speculative fiction, creative storytelling, and materials sourced
from the detritus of capitalism to present time-bending,
mythical landscapes. The series invites us to consider how we
choose to dream of our collective future while challenging us
to imagine a vibrant post-capitalist, post-colonial experience
where humans restore their bonds with the earth and each
other. Whereas contemporary society is obsessed with
developing mechanisms as so-called technology, *Future
Ancestral Technologies* points out that technology is *not*
the mechanism but the ideas carried throughout time. Using
installation, video, and place-based performance embedded
in the land, narratives of possibility reclaim and reframe
the technology of my Indigenous ancestors. This work
demonstrates the interconnected relationships between
humans and the land by placing the past and future in dialogue,
maintaining the *Future Ancestral Technologies* continuum.

A recent installment of the *Future Ancestral Technologies*
project is *Watȟéča*, a set of mythic characters that populate
this imagined future terrain. The buzzard and coyote regalia
created and worn for *Watȟéča* evokes and embodies the
scavenger's blessings and lessons. In Lakota culture, *watȟéča*
often refers to the food taken home following a communal
feast—the leftovers. Scavengers relish what the world rejects.
Always on the lookout, ever ready to snatch *watȟéča* from
the jaws of oblivion, the scavenger eats what no one else
wants, assigning value to what is on the brink of vanishing.
Scavengers scrounge to thrive against disappearance,
navigating environmental encroachment and collapse, habitat
loss, mass industrial extraction, and ecocidal expansion.
Coyotes roaming the outskirts of urban centers. Vultures
circling truck stops. These resourceful beings stubbornly and
ingeniously survive on what is considered obsolete. I feel the
Indigenous experience reflects *watȟéča*—surviving off leftovers.
Our land has been seized. Our customs dismantled. Our ways
of life denigrated. Our stories and languages made all but
invisible in the context of colonial supremacy. Yet we survive and
thrive off what remains. Our survivance as Indigenous peoples

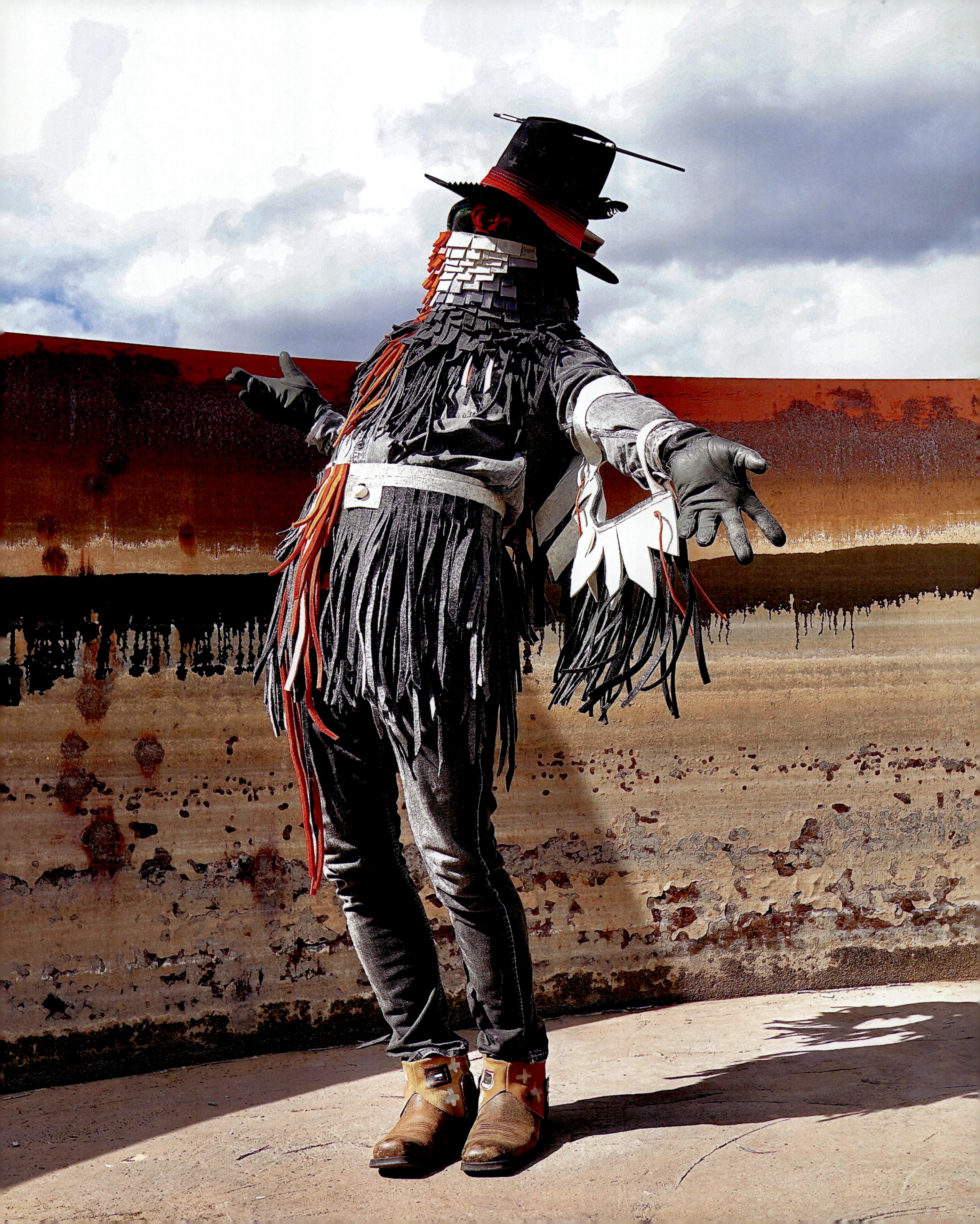

is represented in the performative movement of the animals embodied by the regalia, which I built from scavenged materials. By engaging scavengers from a mythic and reverential perspective, *Watȟéča* celebrates and integrates the scavengers' gifts into our future cosmology. The scavenger becomes kin, teaching us critical technology for future survival. As we look to the buzzard and the coyote, we see the models and allies we need to survive into the future.

There is a valuable lesson in the nature of the scavenger.

They thrive by destroying death. Immune to the diseases of rotting flesh.

A final dance for living bodies is to be torn apart completely. Scavengers transform endings into beginnings, celebrating life after death. A pivotal component to rejuvenate life's cycles.

Sheltering the living from the intricacies of death's omnivorous annihilation. Nothing shall be wasted by the scavengers because to them nothing is waste.

Fig. 1. Cannupa Hanska Luger (Mandan/Hidatsa/Arikara /Lakota), *Watȟéča: Buzzard from the Future Ancestral Technologies* project, 2021. Mixed media, ceramic, repurposed materials; single-channel video, 6:04 min. Courtesy of the artist and Garth Greenan Gallery, New York. Photography by Ginger Dunnill

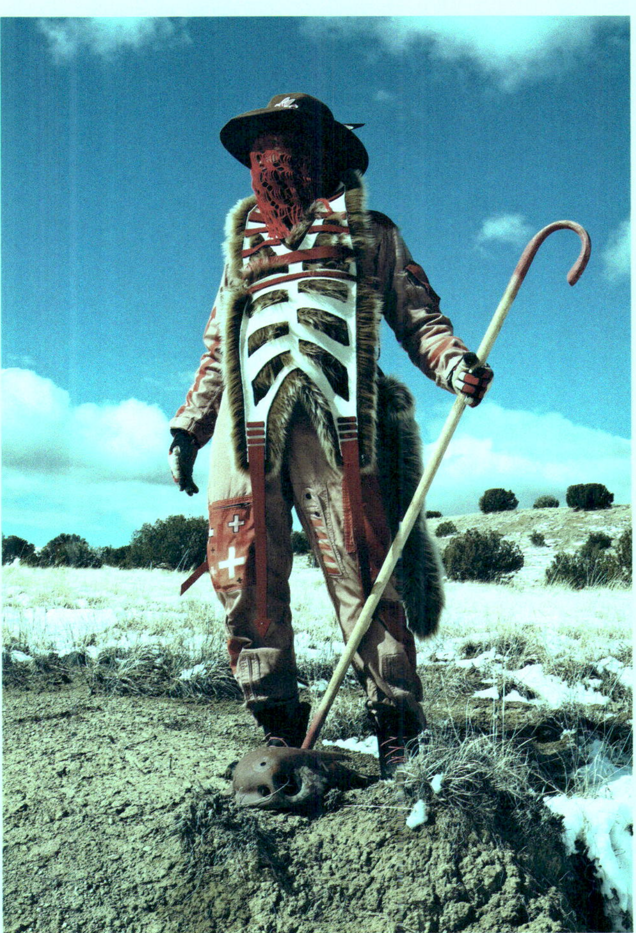

Fig. 2. Cannupa Hanska Luger (Mandan/Hidatsa /Arikara/Lakota), *Watȟéča: Coyote from the Future Ancestral Technologies* project, 2023. Mixed media, ceramic, repurposed materials; single-channel video. Courtesy of the artist and Garth Greenan Gallery, New York. Photography by Gabriel Fermin

When We Remain

Kristen Dorsey and Nancy Marie Mithlo

Okla e m<u>a</u>ɣa momakm<u>a</u>, tamaha chito okla
imihaksi tuk<u>o</u> <u>i</u> foni aiɣokli ahoba
hapiach<u>i</u> kiɣo. Okla e m<u>a</u>ɣa momakm<u>a</u>,
napakanli, micha iti, micha nan vpi ahoba
osh ohmi tamaha chito okla imihaksi tukon
okla il vbachike. Yakni <u>i</u> natanna ibachvffa
hosh okla il ilai achonli tuk. Hap<u>i</u> fiopa ɣa,
shotik chinto okla il itibani tuk.

When we remain, we will not be like the
beautiful bones of a forgotten city. When
we remain, we will be the flowers and the
trees and the vines that overcome the
forgotten city. We have woven ourselves
into the cloth of the earth. We have mixed
our breath into the expanding sky.
　—Samantha Crain, "When We Remain"

In contemplating the field of Indigenous Futurisms from an
Indigenist feminist perspective, we have chosen to focus on
generative, life-affirming aspects of Native life—generational
perspectives that prioritize earth-centered knowledges.
Songwriter and musician Samantha Crain beautifully
captures this nature-centered philosophy with her rejection
of man-made monuments in the song "When We Remain": "We
will not be like the beautiful bones of a forgotten city." Her
active verb tense, sung in the Choctaw language, of weaving
oneself into "the cloth of the earth" and mixing our breath
"into the expanding sky" reminds us of the real possibilities
of manifesting new realities from creative artistic impulses.

This essay focuses on the life and work of a beloved Native
female elder, Cayuga Nation member Tammy Tallchief.[1]
Tallchief is primarily known for her exquisite beadwork
designs but is also accomplished in three-dimensional
sculptural works. Her role as a wisdom keeper is treasured
by generations of Native artists, collectors, and arts
writers. Drawing from a recent interview with the artist,
we will explore the radical possibilities of this life-affirming
perspective by addressing Native food sovereignty,
alternative notions of time and space, and the aesthetic
potential of miniaturization. We argue that these central and
enduring values of sustenance, holism, and portability are
key tropes of entering into dialogues that deeply reflect the
perspectives that we, as writers and theorists, embrace and
endeavor to live as tribal citizens of our nations.

"If we are going to live in the future,
we're going to have to grow
our own food."[2]

Futurity for Indigenous peoples is grounded in land, specifically, the return of Indigenous lands to Indigenous communities to steward. Integral to this is the re-establishment of Indigenous subsistence and farming practices. Food sovereignty provides a roadmap beyond the trajectory of capitalist-fueled ecological collapse and inequitable food systems. Tallchief states, "If we are going to live in the future, we're going to have to grow our own food." Tallchief's studio practice draws from a land-based pedagogy in her decades-long artistic journey. Centering plant knowledges, her work visualizes her community's deep care for their homelands, not only in the gifts and sustenance that plants provide but also for their continued existence, given massive environmental degradation. For example, Tallchief's elaborately beaded cradleboard *Endangered Species* (fig. I), ca. 1993, features delicate renderings of strawberries, wild grapes, and trillium, all endangered plants due to environmental degradation, including wildfires and acid rain. She blames steel mills and pharmaceutical plants for polluting the water, stating, "It takes a long time for the waters to heal."[3]

Endangered Species indicates a holistic connection with the earth, a female-centered engagement with ancient knowledges. While the work enacts this centering, it is crucial to also reference a contextual reading with the artist's strong and empowered recognition of harm due to environmental degradation. The fact that both impulses—a decorative appreciation and a grounded knowledge of destruction—coexist indicates the complexity inherent in Native expressions.

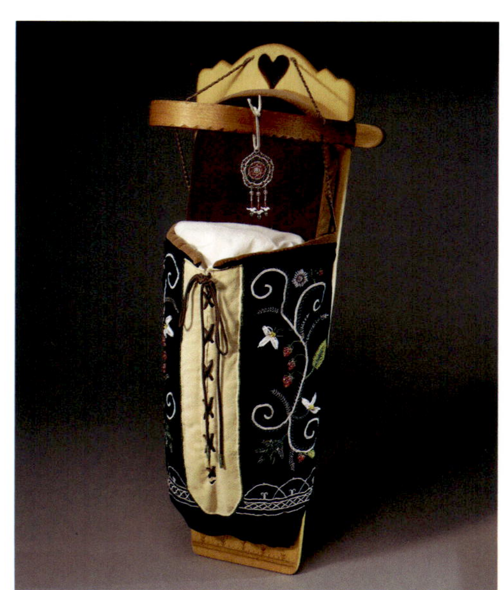

Fig. I. Tammy Tallchief (Cayuga). *Endangered Species*, ca. 1993. Wood, cloth, beads, 34 × I4 in. Courtesy of the IAIA Museum of Contemporary Native Arts, Santa Fe, NM. Photography by Walter Bigbee

In Tallchief's community, beaded designs function as aesthetic adornment for clothing and objects and pass on essential information about important plants and their uses. *Endangered Species* features scrolling vines, leaves, flowers, and berries representing traditional plants, including strawberries, wild grapes, and trillium, all endangered due to environmental degradation. These plants provide nourishment and are thus stitched into the fabric flaps of the cradleboard, securely wrapping the next generation in life-sustaining relationships with the land.

An accurate interpretation of Indigenous art requires deep
engagement not only with a purely aesthetic reading but also
with the thoughts and astute observations of the artist. This
can only be accomplished with a deep focus on Indigenous
values and a strong motivation to "get it right." As Indigenous
arts writers, we advocate this detailed and historical perspective
to understand what constitutes futurity, including feminist
appraisals of care and cyclical notions of time.

As a passionate advocate for Indigenous food sovereignty,
Tallchief believes in returning to Indigenous seed knowledges
because they allow us to weather the dystopian present, one
that Tallchief's ancestors prophesied. "Right now with the
food shortages, destruction, breakdown with our supply chain,
dependency on wheat and foreign grains, geopolitics, war in
Europe, it is going to get worse before it gets better." Relational
practices of reciprocity provide a path to weathering these
compounding crises facing humanity; Tallchief's advocacy
for Indigenous farming traditions joins a chorus of Indigenous
elders, activists, artists, and community leaders who are similarly
committed to food sovereignty. Renowned environmental and
Indigenous rights activist Winona LaDuke (White Earth Band
Ojibwe) explains, "The soil and the seeds help us navigate the
future."[4] LaDuke also centers the revitalization of Indigenous
plant knowledge as a clear path forward: "In a time when
agrobiodiversity has crashed and world food systems are filled
with poisons, our seeds remain, and they return."[5] LaDuke is
part of a growing Indigenous food sovereignty movement that
emphasizes ancestral farming methods to grow heritage seeds.
These methods are developed from generations of Indigenous
technological and scientific knowledge rooted in specific land
bases. The Indigenous food sovereignty movement lessens
each community's dependence on imported food that harms
the health of the environment and the health of the people.

The future Tallchief envisions is encapsulated in heirloom seeds
and the knowledge necessary for their planting and cultivation,
insights originating in past generations. "Seeds, seed saving,
sharing seeds, storing seeds, our seeds, sharing traditional
knowledge, is something we have been doing forever." These
Indigenous innovations and technologies span generations.
Tallchief views heirloom seeds as keys to the future. "Heirloom
seeds can be grown year after year after year; we have to
grow our own food." Community gardening counters settler
capitalism's industrialized agricultural practices. For example,
the Monsanto Company, founded in 1901, has become a global
force in genetically modified crops. These crops, designed to
withstand drought and repel pests, come with consequences

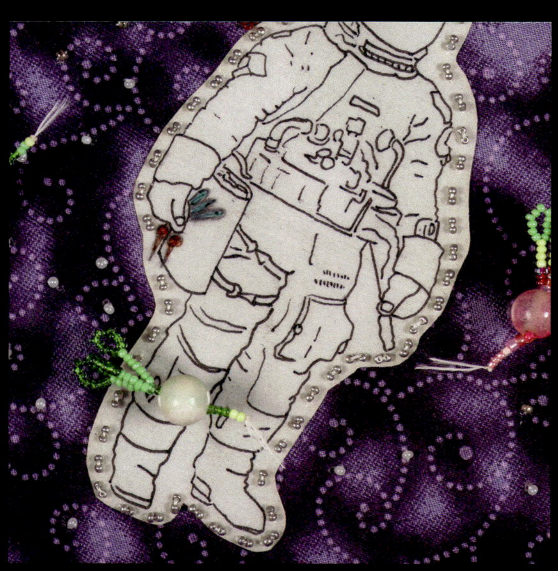

Fig. 2. Tammy Tallchief (Cayuga), *Space Farmer with Radishes* (detail), 2010–22. Assemblage, 12 in. diameter × 2½ in. depth. Courtesy of the artist. Photography by RJ Sanchez

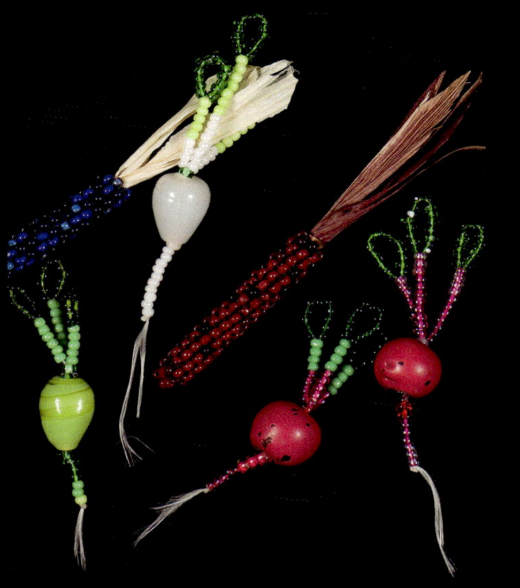

Fig. 3. Tammy Tallchief (Cayugua), *Space Farmer with Radishes* (detail), 2010–22. Assemblage. Courtesy of the artist. Photography by RJ Sanchez. Radishes measure 1 × ⅛ in. at the smallest, 2½ × ½ in. at the largest. Corn dimensions are 2½ × ⅛ in.

that not only devastate local ecologies but also community-based foodways. For food sovereignty activists, a return to heirloom seeds and community-based subsistence farming are decolonial practices. Seeds, like art, can embody Indigenous relational values in which practices of care connect both ancestors and future generations. Seeds can grow after lying dormant for hundreds of years. Indigenous art practices are like seeds; some might lay dormant, weathering the traumas of genocide, and emerge with new generations that reconnect with ancestral art forms.

In Tallchief's art practice, the humble radish symbolizes this resilience, abundance, and hope. She explains, "The radish is a metaphor; their seeds are resilient, they last thousands of years." A two-millimeter radish seed can grow into a plant yielding an average of three hundred seeds. Radishes, a fast-growing crop that can be planted in the cool weather of early spring, can be harvested in just four weeks. Their greens, flowers, and even seedpods can be eaten. They contain essential nutrients not often found in today's food chain, such as calcium, magnesium, phosphorus, potassium, and vitamin C.[6] Tallchief is drawn to this small root vegetable for its resiliency and transformative health benefits. She explains that they are a superfood because you can eat all parts of the plant, providing blood pressure stability, anti-inflammatories, weight loss, and anti-cancer properties. These heart-shaped roots are a prominent metaphor in Tallchief's art practice because "they are the perfect food to take into the future with us."

In 2020, NASA successfully harvested radishes in an experiment called Plant Habitat-02. Radishes were selected for their ability to reach maturity quickly. Plant Habitat-02 assesses the viability of different crops in space to eventually provide nutrition for the astronauts.[7] Tallchief sees these space farming experiments as components of futuristic practices. Her reverence for medicinal plants like radishes is distilled through beads in her sculptural work. In *Space Farmer with Radishes* (pl. 37), 2010–2022, constellations of white beads, roughly the size of seeds, adorn the surface of the deep purple fabric. The fabric's circular shape, color, and adornments draw the eye as if it were a window upon a spacecraft, offering a view of vast galaxies that hold unrealized possibilities. An astronaut floats within this window, holding a beaded radish in one hand (fig. 2). Surrounding the window are sculptural radishes, their luminous beads shining like jewels. Their small scale feels like that of an earthly radish, yet the delicate threads representing roots and translucent glass bulbs feel ethereal and celestial. They can nestle into the palm of one's hand, delicate and precious yet powerful sources of life (fig. 3).

The potential of radishes is representative of ancestral knowledge for Tallchief. She states, "I did a small assemblage with an ambiguous space person holding radishes; they come from the past, in all cultures, all cuisines, and they are growing them now up in space, and they are growing quite well. If we can do it with radishes, we can do it with corn, beans, squash, tobacco." These crops are important cultural staples that sustained her people long before colonization and will provide for future generations. For Tallchief, the success of radishes in space opens the potential for Indigenous futurity.

SELF-PORTRAITURE

"Only the creator can make a face."

The miniature sculptural self-portrait series *Me, Myself and I* (fig. 4), 2018, features what are traditionally termed "corn husk dolls." Creating human figures from the organic material of corn is a core staple of Tallchief's practice; she has been making these forms for over forty years. In her words, the art form is "deeply rooted in my culture." Historically used to relay traditional knowledge and morals to children, these teaching tools convey deeply held moral values. For example, no facial characteristics (such as eyes, nose, or mouth) are typically depicted in an effort to avoid vanity and encourage modesty. The traditional story of the corn husk doll relates that the most beautiful girl of a village did not want to ruin her hands, so she would disappear when it was time to work and run to the river to look at herself when her people were calling for her. One day, she looked into the water, and her face was gone. This parable is a warning to be humble and to be responsible for one's contribution of labor in a community.

An autobiographical perspective informs Tallchief's work *Me, Myself and I*, in what she terms a "deeply personal self-portrait." It is about "[me] being accepted into the family as a little girl," as she was raised in an adoptive family as a youth. Tallchief bravely addresses historic trauma through her autobiographical work, noting, "These stories need to be told." Her narrative of adoption and dislocation is representative of many Native narratives of survival following alienation from family, tribe, and ancestral knowledge. Systematic governmental policies of forced separations of children from their families were attempts to eliminate tribal peoples from traditional land bases and distance

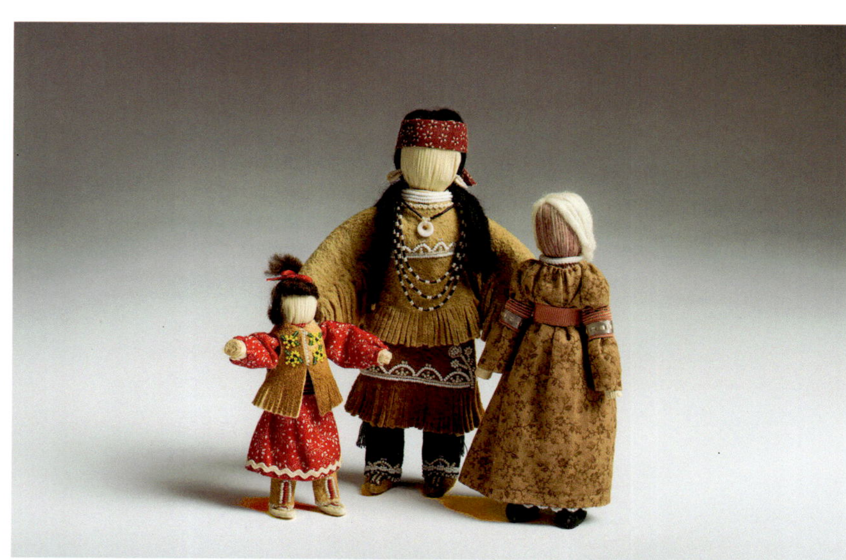

Fig. 4. Tammy Tallchief (Cayuga), *Me, Myself and I*, 2018. Mixed media. Left figure (child) 4¼ × 2¾ × 1 in., middle figure (adult) 6½ × 6½ × 1½ in., right figure (elder) 5½ × 5½ × 1⅛ in. Courtesy of the artist. Photography by RJ Sanchez

children from their land and language. Tallchief's artistic journey is representative of generations of stolen children, many of whom may never know their own histories. As an educator, Tallchief's prolific artistic life as a maker, a doer, and a thinker has inspired a new generation of Native artists to embrace experimental techniques and address traumatic histories.

Tallchief creatively plays with the medium of corn husk dolls, denying their static significance as didactic referents alone (fig. 5). In her studio practice, she may, for example, age the figures with gray hair instead of black, create male dolls, pregnant dolls, dolls with breasts, or dolls who wear punk outfits. This playful and experimental approach is a hallmark of Tallchief's artistic practice; however, her intent is grounded in serious philosophical orientations. In *Me, Myself and I*, the youngest figure wears a red rickrack-trimmed outfit fashioned after a beloved dress Tallchief's

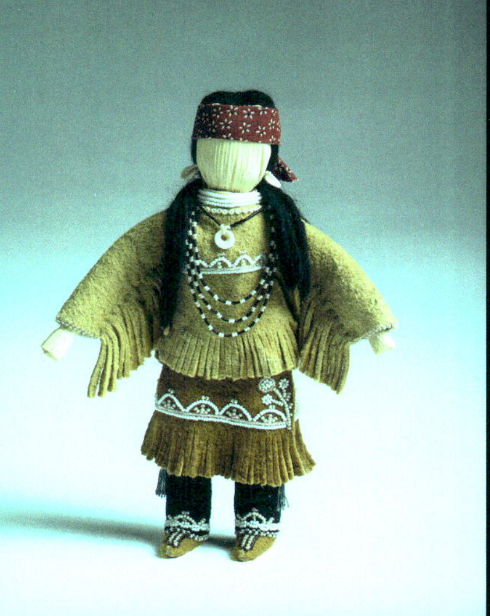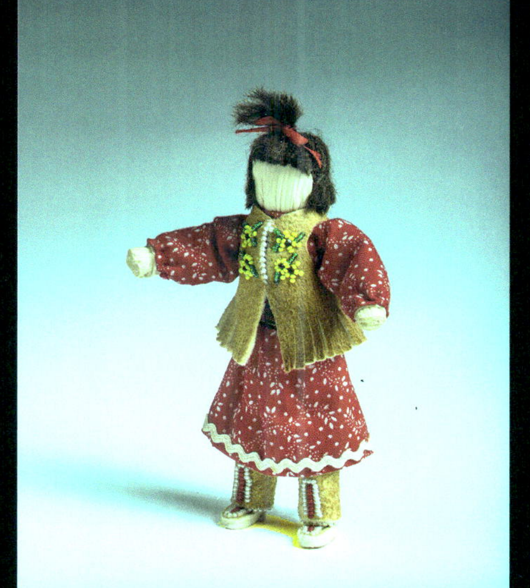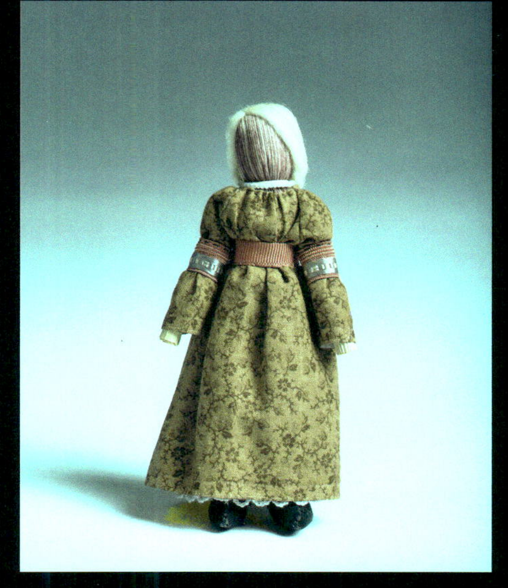

grandmother had made for her as a child. Her hair is chopped and tied with a shiny ribbon, an adornment indicating special attention and love. Sunflowers on the child's vest convey the potential and abundance of youth (fig. 6). The adult figure is fully grounded and exudes an air of presence, dressed in deer hide with wampum, long braids, and a bandana headband. Her ornate regalia signals power and authority. The older doll with gray hair is dressed in muted colors in a simple calico dress adorned only with delicate silver arm cuffs. This stately and reserved figure represents the person Tallchief wants to become: an elder whom people seek out for knowledge. Rather than representing three separate chronological life phases, Tallchief asserts that all three figures are her as one. "Three generations in one piece—it's really me as a young girl, as a mother, and as a grandmother."

These elaborate tableaux, or as Tallchief terms her medium—assemblages—deny any simple or straightforward interpretation. Their multilayered referents suggest that even the term "corn husk doll," with its focus on materials only (corn husk) and potentially derogatory connotations of simple child's play (doll), be abandoned. We argue that there is something more substantial going on in this series: self-portraiture. Self-portraiture enables a deeper inquiry into Indigenous ways of knowing and being, including cyclical time structures, humor, multiple ideas of personhood, and generational responsibilities. The depth of these interpretations suggests that the standard art historical discourse descriptive "corn husk doll" might productively be abandoned.

Denying the linearity of time is also an apt metaphor for more significant issues of Indigenous aesthetic practices, signaling an alternative plane of consciousness in which time and space are endless, ever interacting, and full of potential. Australian Wiradjuri writer and First Nations cultural practitioner Hannah

Donnelly describes how Indigenous futures "allow us to assert futures
that question and change the colonial settler framing of past, present
and future."[8] This alternative temporality is a call to collapse time, even
to dismiss it. Continuity is thus the central thread of analysis, not a linear
trajectory. Like the curvilinear patterns representing the sky dome circling
the skirt worn by the portrait's adult figure (fig. 7), repetitive patterns
harken to an abstract holism that is a hallmark of Indigenous beadwork
traditions, steeped in the wisdom of patterns, portability, and metaphors.

THE AESTHETIC POTENTIAL OF MINIATURIZATION

"Beadwork has gone through a renaissance. . . . These subtle beadwork
designs, the symbolism, and iconography that is in beadwork will continue."

While the practice of beadwork involves hours and hours of repetition
and can, as Tallchief observes, sometimes be tedious, these attributes
often lead to seeking different ways to express oneself. The practice of
miniaturization, using microbeads instead of standard-sized beads, offered
this opportunity: "Scale for me is a challenge, for me to take a scale replica
of these designs and make them smaller, the challenge for me is to work
those out in beads, using microbeads." As one of the first Native artists
using microbeads since the 1980s, scale is not merely a technical exercise
for Tallchief but a subtle reference to alternative temporalities, the place of
"no beginning and no end," and an assertion that "We will always be here."
This longevity is reflected in the deep histories of adornment in land-based
epistemologies and the non-materialistic impulses of peoples for whom
mobility was a survival strategy.

The significance of movement is underdeveloped in contemporary
assessments of Indigenous aesthetics; however, as Indigenous
practitioners increasingly incorporate animal and organic materials in
their practice, these registers can be further recognized.[9] As a counter
to the frequency of grand-scale permanent sculptural installations that

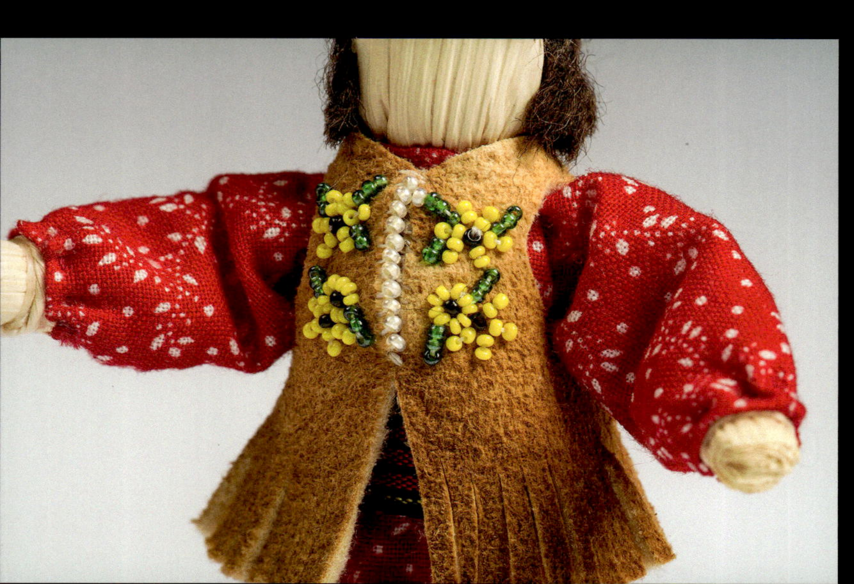

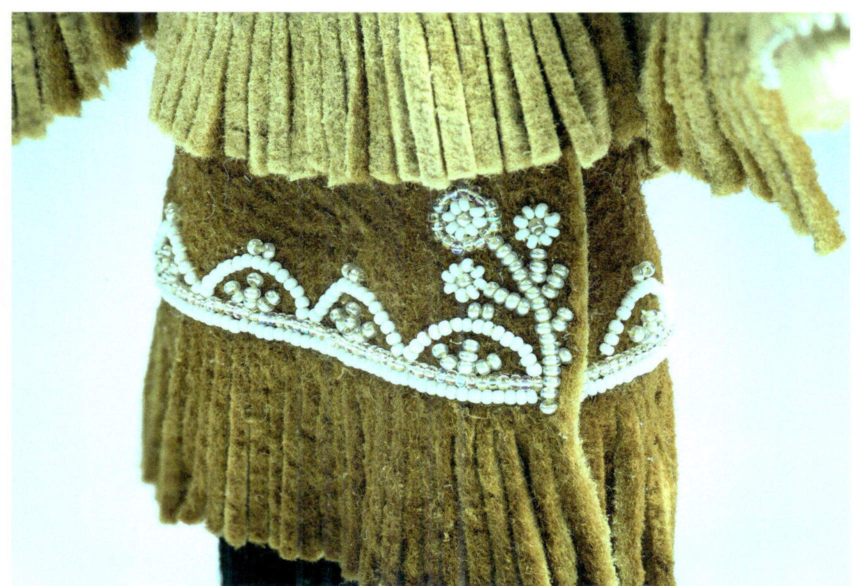

are a hallmark of contemporary arts, especially in contexts that use art as a marker of a nation, the radical possibilities of traditionally female, miniature, and craft-based arts as fine arts are exemplary. Here, miniaturization, especially considering portability, is a marker of Indigenous aesthetic traditions that embrace the personal, the eternal, and the female.

In *Long History, Deep Time: Deepening Histories of Place*, writer Jeanine Leane states, "The failure of history then, for Indigenous writers and storytellers is its containment, its selective memory and its general reluctance to recognise land as living."[10] These registers of land and movement in consideration of Indigenous arts practices offer fertile grounds to imagine otherwise. Rather than figurative miniaturization (dolls) as a hallmark of mastery or control in a private world of an individual's imagination, Tallchief's *Me, Myself and I* references a communal ideology that embraces intergenerational knowledge transfer.[11]

The conceptualization of dolls as a form of self-portraiture destabilizes notions of linear time and the mastery and control that typically define miniaturization. By configuring these micro-representations as portable knowledge holders intent on assertions of generational presences, art discourses are expanded from siloed interpretive formats to an encompassing and complex knowledge system that holistically structures time and space. Indigenist feminist perspectives enhance futuristic dialogues, complicating, expanding, and asserting what it means to "remain."

Conclusion

Settler colonialism reframes history to fix Indigenous peoples within a primitive past, rendering them incapable of exercising sovereignty over their lands in the present day.[12] Scholars refer to these versions of settler history as settler time, an immobilizing force that simultaneously makes Indigenous peoples and their knowledge systems invisible.[13] Indigenous artists disrupt settler time to clearly define Indigenous foodways as technologies of both past and future, and the Indigenous peoples who cultivate these plants as central figures of future imaginings.

Tallchief's multimedia works are engaged in the broader field of Indigenous Futurisms. Her visual interventions tap into the field's questions of how Indigenous technologies, such as heirloom seeds, are key to imagining what the future can look like. For example, her 2010–2022 *Space Farmer with Radishes* assemblage creation and her original quote, "If we can do it with radishes, we can do it with corn, beans, [and] squash," visualizes food sovereignty interventions that are important to other Indigenous artists. Similarly, *The Zenith* (pl. 36), a 2022 photograph by Cara Romero (Chemehuevi), represents the longevity of Native artists' fascination with traditional foods taking their rightful presence in space travel imagery. Romero is a critically acclaimed fine art photographer noted for her detailed compositions that translate complex Indigenous lived experiences, identities, and philosophies into vibrant and dynamic compositions. Romero's subjects are selected from her network of family, friends, and artists, and their creative practices inform her practice.

In *The Zenith*, artist George Alexander (Mvskoke Creek) is pictured as an astronaut. The helmet he wears references his *Astronauts on Horses* series, a group of paintings depicting solo figures wearing astronaut helmets as they ride horses through surreal or abstracted backgrounds.[14] Romero's composition places Alexander reclined in a blue jumpsuit paired with the helmet and breathing hose ubiquitous in his paintings. He appears to be floating in space within a cloud of Indigenous white corn set against a backdrop of stars. His uplifted hands are an exultant gesture that emphasizes the essential role that corn has today and the core contributions that corn can make for Indigenous peoples in the future. The honorific gesture and the expanse of stars forming the background suggest the limitless and joyful potential of Indigenous ingenuity.

In concert with Tallchief's *Space Farmer with Radishes*, Romero's composition places Indigenous white corn within a futuristic scene that asserts the equal value of Indigenous epistemologies to those of astronautics. The cultivation of corn is a keystone of Indigenous technologies. The careful tending and development of numerous corn varieties has provided sustenance for centuries of Indigenous societies. Corn as a technology is as critical to humanity's future as technologies manifested from sciences deemed "Western" by settler societies.

In a visual countering of the containment that settler colonial timelines impose upon colonized subjects, Tallchief and Romero embrace Indigenous presences in the expanses of space travel. In doing so, they add unique feminist approaches to art creation and interpretation—contributions that center ancestral wisdoms of holism, relationality, and alternative temporalities. These gifts ensure that "remaining" is not only a possibility, but that "when we remain," our breath will be a part of the expanding sky.

1   Tallchief (formerly Rahr) is a member of the Cayuga Nation of New York, part of the Haudenosaunee or Iroquois confederacy. Their tribal website lists the following ceremonial rounds involving foodways: seed ceremony, planting ceremony, strawberry ceremony, green corn, and harvest ceremonies. See: https://cayuganation-nsn.gov/our-culture.html.

2   All quotes from Tammy Tallchief are drawn from a June 23, 2022, interview with Kristen Dorsey and Nancy Marie Mithlo unless otherwise noted.

3   Tammy Tallchief, Mithlo interview, September 1, 2018.

4   Winona LaDuke, "In Praise of Seeds and Hope," in *Indigenous Food Sovereignty in the United States: Restoring Cultural Knowledge, Protecting Environments, and Regaining Health*, ed. Devon Mihesuah and Elizabeth Hoover (Norman: University of Oklahoma Press, 2019), 3.

5   Ibid, p. xiv.

6   U.S. Department of Agriculture, "RADISHES, RAW (SR LEGACY, 169276)," Food Data Central, published April 1, 2019, https://fdc.nal.usda.gov/fdc-app.html#/food-details /169276/nutrients.

7   Linda Herridge, "Astronauts Harvest Radish Crop on International Space Station," NASA's John F. Kennedy Space Center, NASA.gov, December 2, 2020, https://www.nasa.gov /feature/astronauts-harvest-radish-crop-on-international-space-station.

8   Hannah Donnelly, "Indigenous Futures and Sovereign Romanticisms: Belonging to a Place in Time," in *Sovereign Words, Indigenous Art, Curation and Criticism*, ed. Katya García-Antón (Amsterdam: Office for Contemporary Art Norway and Valiz, 2016), 261-274.

9   For an example, see the works included in the 2022 Venice Biennale's Sami Pavilion (formerly the Nordic pavilion), https://oca.no/thesamipavilion.

10   Jeanine Leane, "Historyless People," in *Long History, Deep Time: Deepening Histories of Place*, ed. Ann McGrath and Mary Anne Jebb (Australia: ANU Press, 2015), 161.

11   For a classic Western perspective of miniaturization, see Susan Stewart's *On Longing: Narratives of the Miniature, the Gigantic, the Souvenir, the Collection* (Durham, NC: Duke University Press, 1993).

12   Mark Rifkin, *Beyond Settler Time: Temporal Sovereignty and Indigenous Self-Determination* (Durham, NC, and London: Duke University Press, 2017), 5.

13   Sherene Razack, "Settler Colonialism, Policing and Racial Terror: The Police Shooting of Loreal Tsingine," *Feminist Legal Studies* 28, no. 1: 4.

14   For Alexander, the astronaut symbolizes the complexities of humanity's drive to explore, https://www.ofuskie.com/shop/p/whats-that-over-there.

WINDOW TO THE FUTURE

All the Mountain Ranges in the Sea—*Wee Xaayy Moomta 'Ashuunga Woo*

Mercedes Dorame

*What do we hope to learn from the past, and what are the
implications of transposing this information onto the present and
the future imaginary?*

When I approach records of the past world, question the
information held by the land, anthropologica accounts, and how
my peoples' cultural belongings, or artifacts, are understood. Time
is a filter for knowledge. Our current existence, understanding,
and space-time position translate this information into truth. We
exist in a continual triangulation of experience, as time is not
linear; it is cyclical and malleable. Cultural history is understood
through present reality, and we must acknowledge the shifting
of meaning that takes place through this triangulation. Past and
future are the same. They are held within us understood in our
beings at the moment of encounter. We simultaneously see, feel,
and understand all these spaces. They live within us.

My ancestors teach me how to move through this world. They
tell me the stories I need to hear and guide me on a path I could
not have mapped alone. One example of this interaction is my
engagement with cogged stones, or star stones, as I call them.
These objects, found specifically on our tribal ancestral lands
and in the immediate surrounding areas, were exquisitely made
by my ancestors; they had use, purpose and inherent truth at
the time of their making.

When they were unearthed from the land, under then-current
archaeological practice, their original context had been erased
by genocide and colonization. They were understood and
named "cogged stones" based on that moment's subjective
interpretation. In my current experience, I propose another
potential interpretation of their purpose based on the objects
themselves, historical records, and oral histories combined with
my research and imagination.

Each moment of their existence holds truth, and each
interpretation is contextual to the time in which the
interpretation occurs. Each set of meanings creates a
proposal for future purposes and imagination.

Understanding the power of interpretation allows truths to
emerge even from painful places In working through historical
accounts of my ancestors recorded by Spanish priests of
the Catholic Church during intense colonization, I find harmful
and painful descriptions of my people. They are referred to as
heathens, depraved, and less than human. The Catholic priests
denounce my ancestors' ability to communicate with animals
and spirits as evil and the roots of their damnation.

Reading these descriptions in the present moment, I understand the actions of the Tongva people as the sacred communications of my ancestors with all beings, small and powerful. Had I read these accounts before I escaped from church dogma, I wonder how the priests' misshapen lens of understanding would have influenced me. As we move through time and experience, I hope that distortions are better seen from a time that allows for freedom of belief, a right not afforded to my ancestors who faced the choice of conversion or death.

Working with the camera as a tool is a form of accessing empowerment through ideas of triangulation. As a Native person, photographing my ancestral lands is an act of reclamation. My photography manifests the Native presence on the land, and I become a part of the triangle. My experience of the land allows me to see the past and the future simultaneously.

The click of the camera's mechanical shutter allows light to pass through my lens and transcribe what is in front of it onto a plane of light-sensitive material in inverse form—upside down and reversed. I then contort the film negatives through more light and translation to present a record of this experience to the viewer, much like the human brain corrects the inverted image the lenses of our eyes produce. The image is then presented in a different moment in which the viewer and I interact with the land and landscape through their lens. For me, a photograph is not a way of looking back at all but a way of looking forward in time, envisioning what could be, what might be, possibility—what existed still exists.

By accessing ancestral knowledge through research, storytelling, and intuition in the present moment, I explore that which is of the past to make sense of a future imaginary. The ideas and curiosity sparked by my artistic practice allow for a future space where Indigenous knowing is prioritized and deployed to steward the land more sustainably.

This possible future presents itself to me in the Channel Islands, known as All the Mountain Ranges in the Sea—*Wee Xaayy Moomta 'Ashuunga Woo* to my ancestors, where I have worked since 2022. The land there strongly resembles the mainland coast of Southern California, where I grew up and intimately know the land's feel, smell, and sights. However, these islands are across a body of water, upside down, backward, reversed, and disorienting in how they simultaneously hold time, space, memory, and futurity.

Fig. I. Mercedes Dorame (Tongva), *I Will Come from the Ocean-Mooomvene Kimaaro from the Everywhere is West* series, 2022. Inkjet print from 120 mm film, 30 × 30 in. Courtesy of the artist

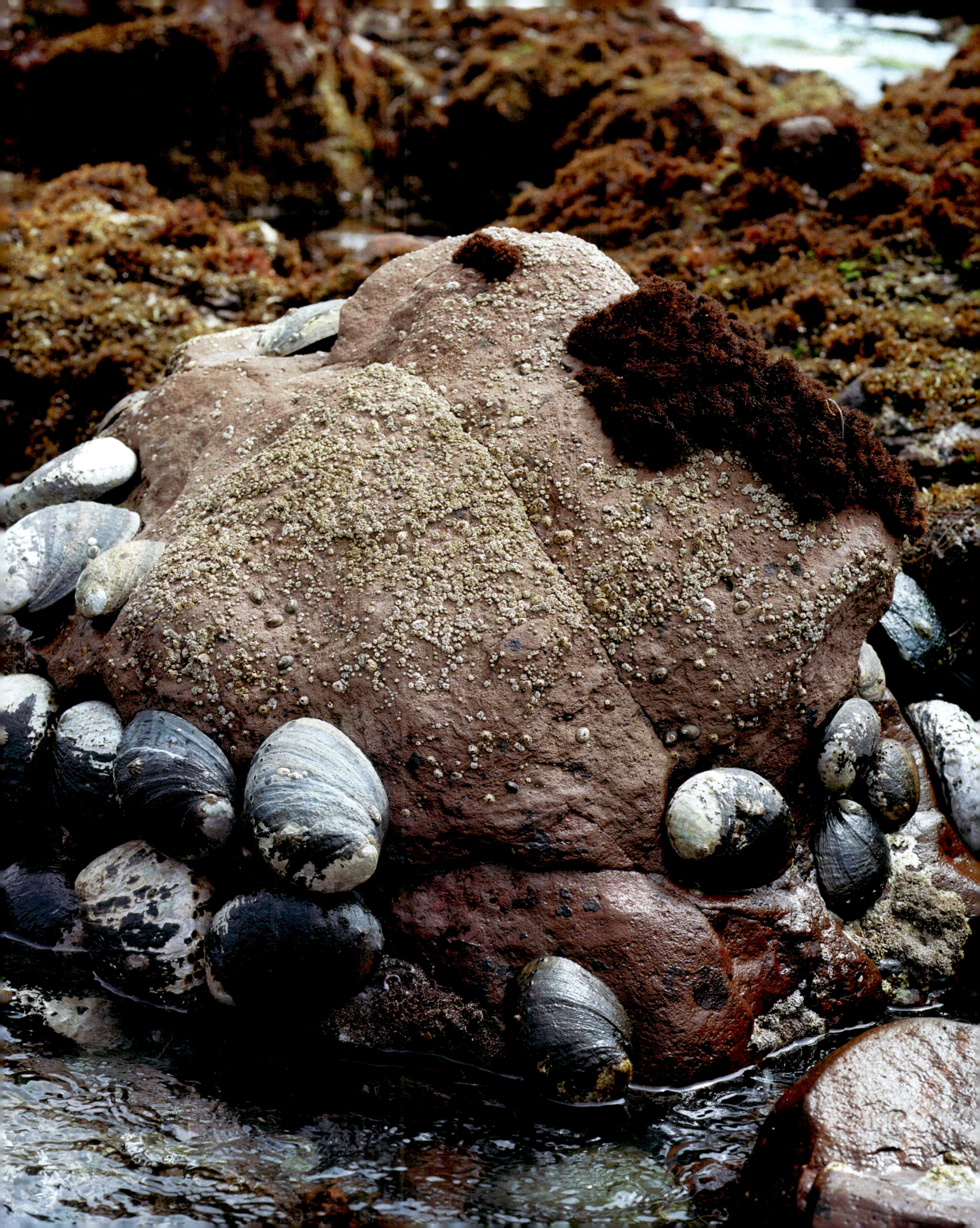

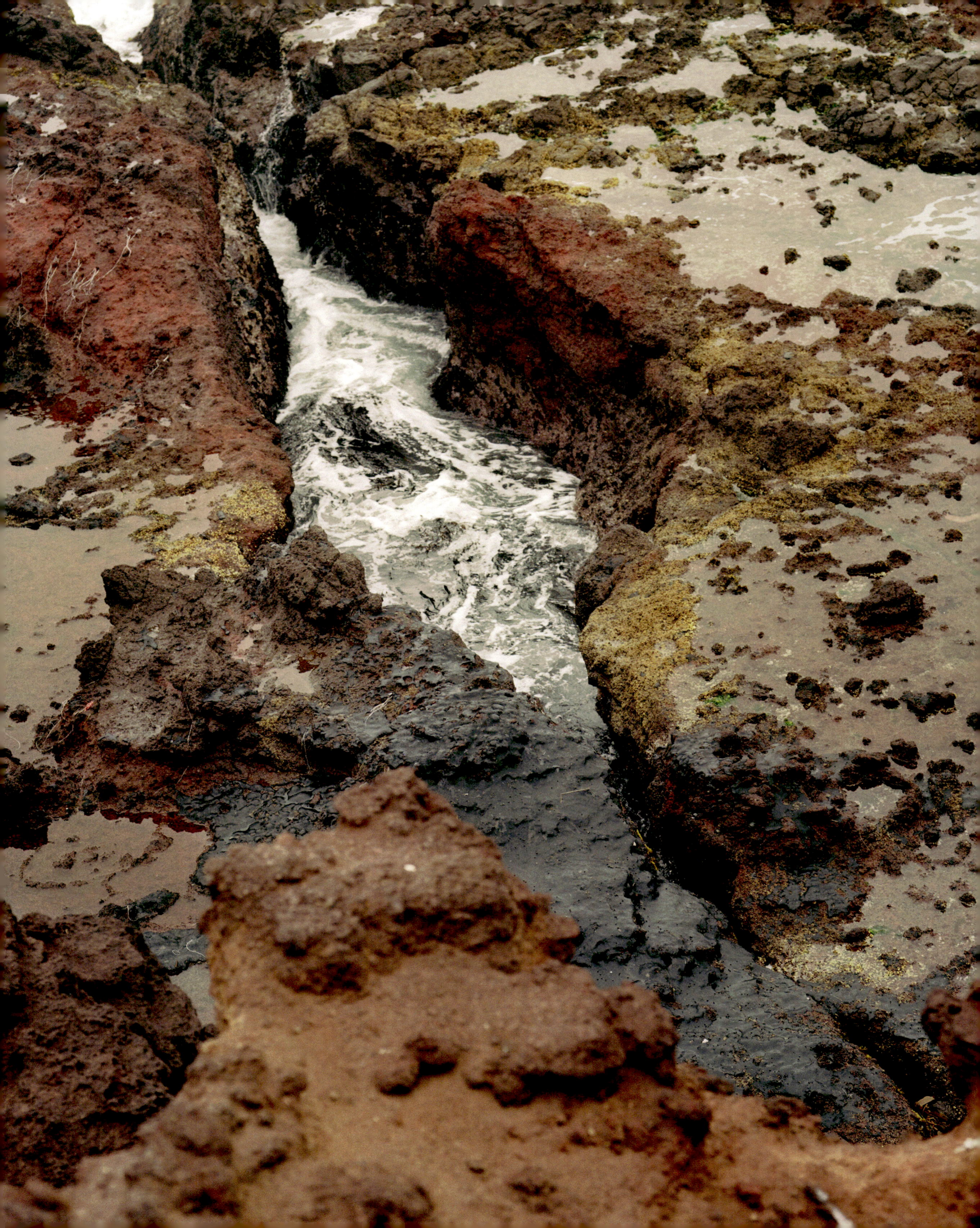

Fig. 2. Mercedes Dorame (Tongva). *Dissolving Waters-'Apaanen* from the *Everywhere is West* series, 2023. Inkjet print from 120 mm film, 30 × 30 in. Courtesy of the artist

I can see the people who tended these lands through their presence in the tools and debris they left behind. I can see the beings—plants, animals, and rocks—that have always inhabited this place. They teach me what might be and allow me to see a way forward that is not imaginary at all. They remain and have flourished outside the heavy shadow of colonization. By continuing to thrive, they simultaneously show what was and what might be. My vision of the future is in the multitude of abalone witnessed there, holding on with kindness to the stone that supports them, nourished by the water surrounding them, and their ability to teach us how to find healing in knowing them better.

As an artist working in my ancestral lands, I look to the waters, the land, the sky, and my ancestors for guidance. I hold on to the visions and experiences in my homelands and know that the same terrestrial and celestial bodies my ancestors witnessed will continue to protect and guide me and the future generations of First Peoples of Tovaangar.

Riff, Ground, and Dream: Defining Indigenous Futurisms in Visual Arts

Suzanne Newman Fricke

The works in *Future Imaginaries: Indigenous Art, Fashion, Technology* were inspired by the short but rich history of Indigenous Futurisms. Published by Grace Dillon, professor of Indigenous Nations Studies, in *Walking the Clouds: An Anthology of Indigenous Science Fiction* from 2012, the term "Indigenous Futurisms" describes a world based on Indigenous aesthetics, oral histories, and cultural values.[1] As Dillon and video game designer and professor Elizabeth LaPensée explain, Indigenous Futurisms looks:

> to those who came before us to act in the present for future generations. It disrupts the white status quo by providing alternative readings of the same pasts, presents, and futures. It displaces the 'imperial gaze' by shifting focus away from the power dynamics that historically have characterized the relationship between colonizer and colonized, leading to the erasure of the colonized or Indigenous identity.[2]

By integrating historic designs, narratives, and images with new materials and ideas, these artists offer a new vision for the present to challenge historical colonizing influences and environmental destruction. As part of the Getty PST ART study of art and science, *Future Imaginaries* reframes and redefines how Indigenous knowledge can reshape the future, the present, and the past.

Since the introduction of the term, several museum exhibitions have featured Indigenous Futurisms.[3] In addition to showing their work in physical museums, artists have been actively reshaping cyberspace to reflect Indigenous identity.[4] Scholarship has expanded to include numerous books, journals, and articles dedicated to the topic.[5] But far from being monolithic, artists and writers in the field address the subject in various ways, ranging from literal adaptations of popular sci-fi figures to more abstract approaches. This essay suggests categorical distinctions of Indigenous Futurisms in the visual arts: Riff, Ground, and Dream.

Riff

"Riff" describes how some visual artists quote directly from popular sci-fi, incorporating characters, vehicles, weapons, locales, and themes from *Star Wars*, *Star Trek*, and other pop culture favorites. Sci-fi icons such as the *Starship Enterprise* or Yoda are woven into the work of artists Ryan Singer (Diné), Jeffrey Veregge (Port Gamble S'Klallam), Andy Everson (K'ómoks/Kwakwaka'wakw), and Neal Ambrose-Smith (Flathead Salish/Sho-Ban/Métis/Cree), who layer characters and stories into Indigenous frameworks. This approach has been described as appropriation, but the word implies stealing or taking something without authorization. To call these works appropriations suggests the artists are taking something that does not belong to them. Rather, these artists adopt, adapt, and integrate figures, items, and locales into their own visual vocabulary, creating something new from something known.

As a child in the 1970s and '80s, painter Ryan Singer, who is of Tódich'íinii clan born for Kinyaa'áani, was immersed in the world of popular sci-fi. Raised on the reservation in Tuba City, Arizona, he remembers watching *Star Wars* and *Star Trek* as a child. He grew up with the action figures from the movie, often fantasizing about the far-off galaxy, and now his paintings, such as *Tuba City Spaceport* (fig. 1), 2012, are populated with stormtroopers, Boba Fett, Tusken Raiders, and other characters from *Star Wars* set in the context of Dinétah (the Navajo Nation).

The desert environment in much of Singer's work, including *Sand People Sand Painting*, 2019, underscores that for the artist, the real and the fictional locations overlap; he conflates his homeland with the desert planet Tatooine (pl. 28). When the Tusken Raiders were introduced in *Star Wars IV: A New Hope*, they were bellicose and loud, raising their gaffi stick weapons at anyone who tried to enter their lands. *Sand People Sand Painting* offers an intimate view of Tusken Raider life as conceived by Singer; two Raiders sit inside a hogan, a wooden house commonly found in Dinétah, creating a sand painting. Sand paintings are used to restore balance, beauty, and healing, known in Diné as *hózhǫ́*. Rather than the usual images associated with sand paintings like holy *yeibicheii* figures, the Raiders depict R2-D2, the droid known for his ability to save the day. Seated in the hogan with their coffee and wearing the artist's favorite sneakers, Singer's version of Tusken Raider culture illustrates Dillon's concept of *Biskaabiiyang*, "returning to ourselves," which is described as "discovering how one is personally affected by colonization, discarding the emotional and psychological baggage carried from its impact, and recovering ancestral traditions to adapt in our post-Native Apocalypse world."[6]

In his digital prints, Jeffrey Veregge, a member of the Port Gamble S'Klallam Tribe with Suquamish and Duwamish tribal ancestry (Coast Salish area), applies design elements from tribes along the Pacific coast to explore characters, themes, and locales from popular sci-fi. After earning a degree in industrial design from the Art Institute of Seattle, Veregge designed action figures and later studied with renowned carver David Boxley (Tsimshian) to learn

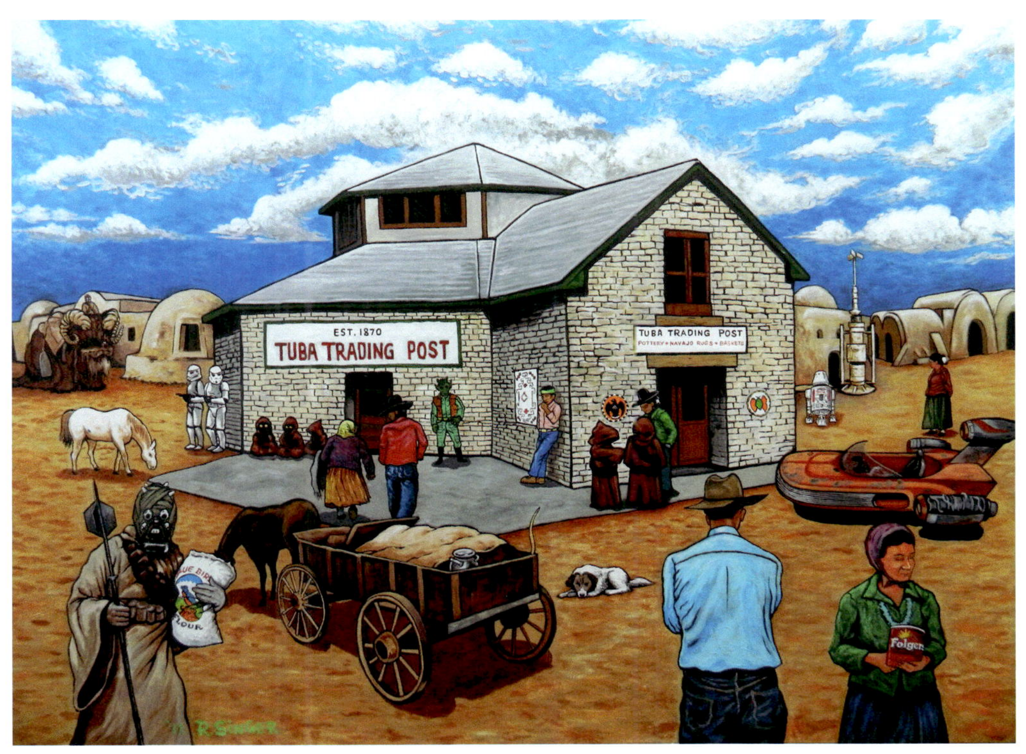

Fig. I. Ryan Singer (Diné). *Tuba City Spaceport*, 2012. Acrylic on canvas, 30 × 40 in. Courtesy of the artist

the formline design techniques often used across Northwest Coast Indigenous cultures, which incorporate bold outlines in black and red to delineate ovoid shapes.[7] In his digital prints, Veregge found an affinity between Northwest Coast formline design and sci-fi characters and ships. His work explores many popular sci-fi universes, including *Star Wars*, *Star Trek*, *Alien*, the Marvel Cinematic Universe (MCU), DC Comics, and cult classics like *Tron*, *Judge Dred*, and *Mars Attacks*.

Welcome, 2014, and *She's Got It Where It Counts*, 2016, portray *Star Wars* scenes from a Northwest Coast Indigenous perspective using formline design (pls. 25 and 26). *Welcome* depicts the Emperor's Royal Guards with the Emperor himself in the background. The shapes down the front of the guard uniforms are shown as a line of coppers. In Northwest Coast cultures, these shield-shaped objects made of copper display wealth and power. In this context, the coppers on the Royal Guards' uniforms reveal strength and purpose. *She's Got It Where It Counts* derives from *Star Wars IV: A New Hope*; when Luke Skywalker first sees the *Millennium Falcon*, he exclaims, "What a piece of junk!" only to have Han Solo reply, "She may not look like much, but she's got it where it counts." Veregge's version of the *Falcon* is similar in shape to Northwest Coast designs of Raven, with a central eye and a beak. In oral histories, the trickster figure brought back the sun, gifted berries and salmon, and found humanity. Veregge's image considers how the *Millennium Falcon* embodies the trickster role in the *Star Wars* universe, an unpredictable scoundrel who ultimately saves the day.

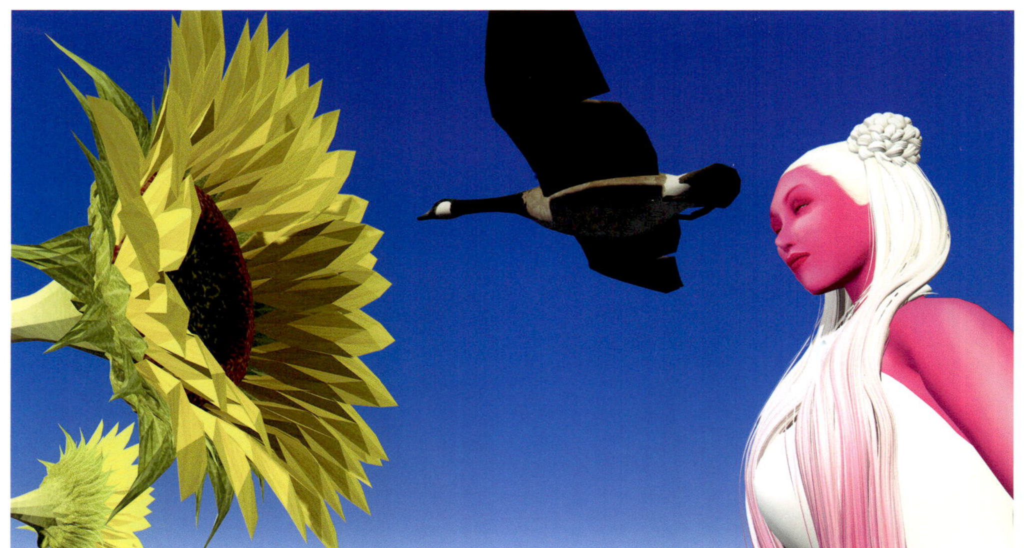

Fig. 2. Skawennati (Kanien'kehà:ka [Mohawk]). *Renewal* from *She Falls for Ages*, 2017. Machinimagraph, dimensions variable. Courtesy of the artist

Ground

Rather than adopting the characters and locales of extant sci-fi realms, some artists use the genre's aesthetics and narrative structures to construct their own worlds. "Ground" describes how artists such as Virgil Ortiz (Cochiti Pueblo), Skawennati (Kanien'kehà:ka [Mohawk]) and Sonny Assu (Ligwilda'xw of the Kwakwaka'wakw Nations) use sci-fi aesthetics and plot structures to bring to life narratives based on Indigenous oral histories and ideas of their own making. This futuristic perspective allows the artists to tell their stories in a new way.

Skawennati's *She Falls for Ages*, 2017, illustrates the origin story of the Haudenosaunee (Iroquois) in which Sky Woman descends from Sky World and lands on Turtle Island, the Indigenous name for North America (fig. 2). Skawennati's version of Sky World has a pink sky and is populated by humanoids with glowing eyes and brightly colored skin. They all wear white and live in sleek white domes surrounded by trees with blossoms that also glow. She employs *machinima*, a method of making movies by filming in a virtual environment, in this case *Second Life*, an online multimedia platform in which player avatars interact with each other in customizable environments. The artist applied the same techniques for the *machinimagraph*, or still image, *Three Sisters: Regeneration* (pl. 16), 2022, her exploration of the Haudenosaunee personifications of corn, beans, and squash, known as the Three Sisters, which have historically been food staples in the Americas. Each avatar has a different body type that reflects the vegetable she represents. Their colorful jumpsuits, each with a unique emblem reflecting one of the three crops, suggest Indigenous superheroes.

In 2006, Skawennati and Jason Edward Lewis (Kanaka Maoli /Samoan), Concordia University professor of Design and Computation Arts, founded Aboriginal Territories in Cyberspace (AbTeC) to create a Native presence on the web. As Skawennati observed:

> I fear that if Indigenous people cannot envision ourselves in The Future, we will not be there. We need to visualize ourselves as full participants in the multi-mediatized world of today and tomorrow to help ourselves become active agents in the shaping of new mediums and new societies.[8]

AbTeC co-produces Skawennati's machinimas, which has resulted in the creation of culturally specific virtual items, from Haudenosaunee villages, longhouse interiors, clothing, and even hairstyles (braids for men), to better represent Native communities in the digital sphere.

Like Skawennati, Virgil Ortiz uses the visual language of sci-fi in his *ReVOlt 1680/2180* epic to link the history of the 1680 Pueblo Revolt when the nineteen Pueblos of New Mexico banded together to overthrow the Spanish colonizers to an imagined world five hundred years in the future, in which the Castilian forces have returned, destroyed the air and water, and enslaved Indigenous populations (pl. 35). Ortiz's *ReVOlt 1680/2180* is a time-traveling sci-fi narrative connecting the Pueblo Revolt to the future through ceramics, murals, videos, installations, and elaborate regalia. As art historian and curator Chelsea Herr describes, "Through a synthesis of science fiction tropes, Western popular culture, and traditional Cochiti pottery materials and techniques, Ortiz imagines a cyclical pattern of history in which the Pueblo Revolt of 1680 resurfaces 500 years later."[9] Based on the nineteen Pueblos of New Mexico, he mixed historical figures like Po'pay, who organized the Pueblo Revolt, with nineteen sets of characters the artist invented, including the Watchmen, Aeronauts, Trackers, Blind Archers, the Translator, Venutian Soldiers, and the Sirens.

The characters in *ReVOlt 1680/2180* are executed in various media and styles, including clothing for live models, videos, installations, lithographs, and clay. Renowned for his pottery, Ortiz uses commercial clay to make abstract versions of his characters while using locally sourced clay for his *monos*, a figurative form unique to Cochiti Pueblo. Ortiz incorporates the mechanized regalia of science fiction with metallic feathers and vinyl. The characters travel through space and time, moved by the Translator, the Commander of the Spirit World Army. Dressed in spiky black leather and armed with futuristic versions of historical weapons like bows, arrows, and spears, the characters straddle the past, present, and dystopian future.

Dream

In "Dream," artists use sci-fi aesthetics and ideas to articulate an Indigenous perspective, as seen in works by artists including Kite (Oglala Lakota), Devin Ronneberg (Hawaiian/Okinawan), X (Koasati/CHamoru), Mercedes Dorame (Tongva), and KC Adams (Anishinaabe/Inninew/British). KC Adams created *Cyborg Chicken Eggs*, 2005, based on an encounter with industrially produced chicken breasts, which had been treated with growth hormones to produce oversized breasts with an unpleasant texture and flavor. The glowing cracked shells set in a bed of bleached sugar and flour reflect the artificial manipulation of natural growth as an example of human intervention perverting the natural world.

Beyond narrative and character, an aspect of sci-fi offers a more ideological shift. This perspective is seen in the work of Kite, who describes her artistic practice as a way to:

> expunge small poisons: cruel ethnographies, projections of Indian magic, destructive maps . . . As an adopted Lakȟóta child of an adopted Lakȟóta child, my desire to hear from afar has often been overwhelming. The tensions of diaspora and separation felt like a heightened sense of listening, but not hearing. If I could gift a tool to other children growing up far from a place that calls to them, it would be a listening device.[10]

> Kite and Devin Ronneberg create interactive installations and environments that reframe the world from an Indigenous perspective. In works like *Ínyan Iyé (Telling Rock)*, 2019, they added computer sensors and lights to braided hair; as viewers walk near or move the braids, the sensors change the lights, colors, and sounds (pl. 44). The installation explores the idea that in "Oglala Lakota ontologies, even materials such as metals, rocks, and minerals can communicate of their own volition. By considering the 'hearing' and 'listening' capabilities of nonhuman entities, a method of engagement reliant upon mutual respect and responsibility becomes possible."[11] Within Lakota culture, braiding becomes a form of cultural interchange. Kite notes, "In this piece, it is a hair braid which acts as both a beacon and a receiver. This hair braid, with transcendent technologies, says, 'Come find me, I am lost,' while at the same time listens beyond the world we can see."[12] *Ínyan Iyé (Telling Rock)* invites viewers to question the lines between the natural and artificial worlds.

Luzene Hill (Eastern Band of Cherokee Indians) addresses the epidemic of violence against Native American women, who are physically and sexually assaulted at much higher rates than women from other demographics. As a survivor of sexual assault, she works to help women by sharing her personal story and by creating pieces to empower and protect. She constructed her cloak *REVVV*, 2023, from a silver Mylar emergency blanket, the type given to people after a traumatic incident (pl. 10). Hill was inspired to use the material after viewing photos of women and children who had crossed the border into the United States after traversing the desert on foot; they were given Mylar blankets for warmth and the artist was taken with the visuals. Rather than viewing the blanket as something to hide in, Hill constructed a hero cape to restore and strengthen the wearer. With the shiny silver material, the cape's design borrows from sci-fi designs, similar to clothing worn on *Star Trek: The Original Series*, imparting a futuristic solution to a contemporary challenge.

Despite its short history, the field of Indigenous Futurisms has grown exponentially in the past decade in visual arts, literature, film, scholarship, and other fields, all of which have led to *Future Imaginaries: Indigenous Art, Fashion, Technology*, which offers tools to address issues facing the world today. As professors of philosophy Kyle Whyte (Potawatomi) and Julia Gibson note, "When conceived and executed well, science fiction can gesture towards or suggest ways to grapple with environmental injustice, technological challenges, and climate change."[13] As such, the field offers a way to explore complex issues and re-create the world by envisioning a new future. The categories "Riff," "Ground," and "Dream" offer a new way to address these works and consider the artists' goals.

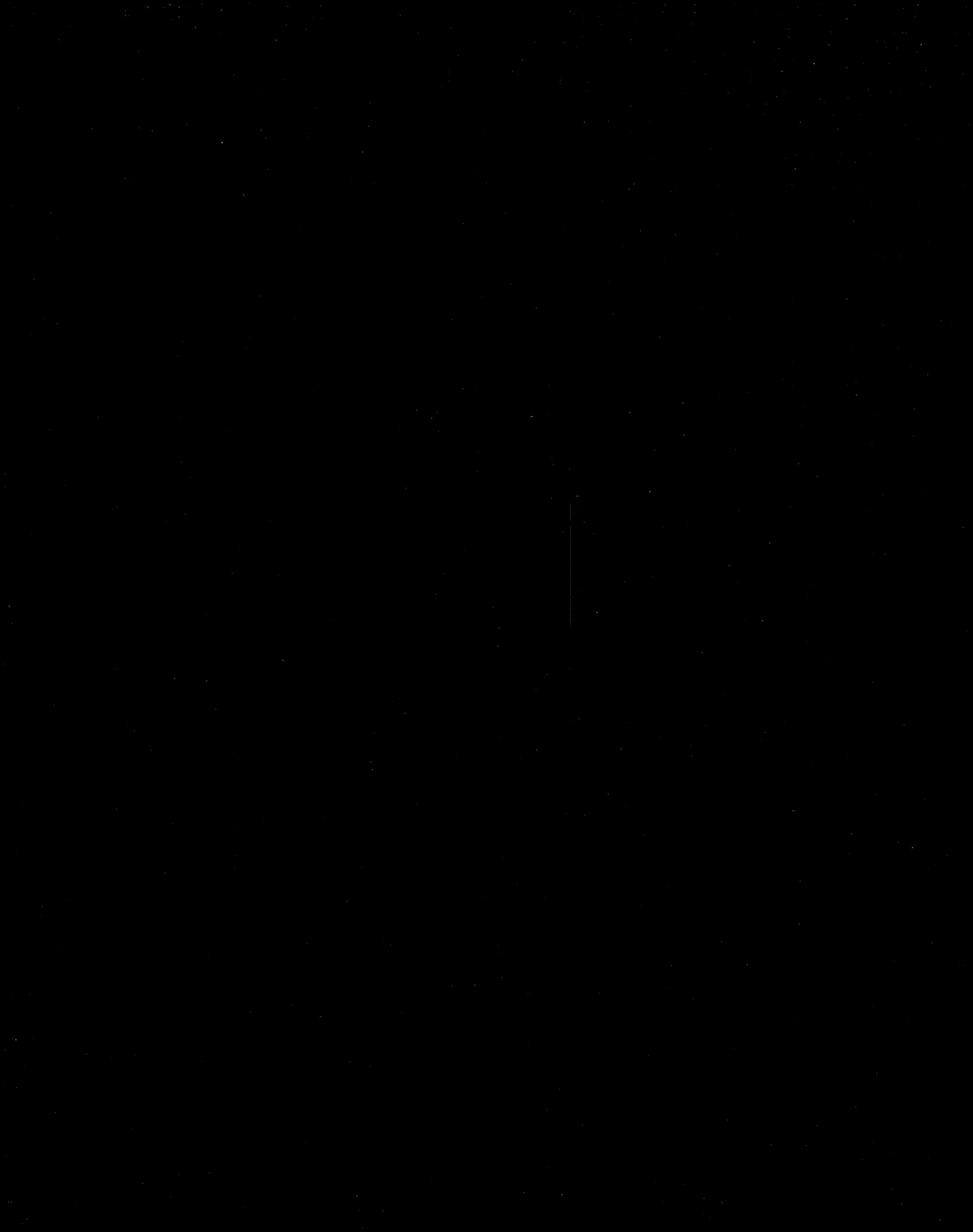

I want to thank Dr. Nancy Marie Mithlo for help in defining and shaping the ideas presented in this essay.

1   Indigenous Futurisms was in part inspired by Afrofuturism, a concept introduced by American cultural critic Mark Dery. Afrofuturism refers to avant-garde works inspired by African cultures and technologies, such as the film *Black Panther* or the music of Sun Ra, George Clinton, and Janelle Monáe, the sci-fi novels of Octavia Butler and Colson Whitehead, and the art of Jean-Michel Basquiat and Ellen Gallagher. Mark Dery, "Black to the Future: Interviews with Samuel R. Delany, Greg Tate, and Tricia Rose," *South Atlantic Quarterly* 92, no. 4 (1993): 736.

2   Grace Dillon and Elizabeth LaPensée, personal communication with author, April 4, 2019.

3   The work of Virgil Ortiz has been shown at many venues, both in the United States and internationally, including at the Denver Art Museum in 2015. In 2019, *Skawennati: From Skyworld to Cyberspace* at the McIntosh Gallery in London, Ontario, featured the artist's photos, fashion, and *machinima* videos, which use the *Second Life* platform to create films with avatars. In 2018, Jeffrey Veregge received a commission from the Smithsonian Museum of the American Indian to paint a mural depicting a battle between the heroes from Marvel Comics and invading aliens. *The Force Is with Our People*, which featured works by Native southwestern artists inspired by *Star Wars*, was exhibited at the Museum of Northern Arizona from October 2019 to October 2020. In 2020 and 2021, the IAIA Museum of Contemporary Native Arts in Santa Fe, New Mexico, hosted *Indigenous Futurisms: Transcending Past/Present/Future*, an exhibition designed to show the breadth of the field, including works by Native artists from the United States and the First Nations across Canada.

4   In 2006, Kanien'kehà:ka (Mohawk) artist Skawennati (neé Skawennati Tricia Fragnito) and Kanaka Maoli/Samoan digital media theorist, software designer, poet, and professor Jason Edward Lewis founded Aboriginal Territories in Cyberspace (AbTeC), an organization dedicated to creating a strong Native presence on the web. AbTeC organized online events such as CyberPowWow, a webspace with a gallery and library, and created culturally specific clothing, skin tones, and hairstyles for Native communities on online platforms like Second Life, where people create and interact via avatars. In 2014, Skawennati and Lewis also founded the Initiative for Indigenous Futures (IIF), which organized workshops, residencies, and symposia for scholars in the field. The collective has also commissioned artworks and compiled an archive of images and videos.

5   In 2016, Grace Dillon edited an edition of the science fiction journal *Extrapolation*, and in 2019, *World Art* dedicated an issue to the topic edited by Suzanne Newman Fricke and Henrietta Lidchi. Kristina Baudemann's *The Future Imaginary in Indigenous North American Arts and Literatures,* 2021, addressed how Native artists illustrate the future outside of a colonizing history. In that same year, a group of Native American artists in Chicago, Illinois, including Andrea Carlson, Debra Yepa-Pappan, and Chris Pappan, founded the Center for Native Futures, a nonprofit dedicated to creating spaces to explore contemporary issues facing Indigenous cultures.

6   Grace Dillon, ed., *Walking the Clouds: An Anthology of Indigenous Science Fiction* (Tucson: University of Arizona Press, 2012), 10.

7   Northwest Coast formline design is discussed in Bill Holm, *Northwest Coast Indian Art: An Analysis of Form* (Seattle: University of Washington Press, 2014).

8   Quoted in Matthew Ryan Smith, *Skawennati: From Skyworld to Cyberspace* (London, ON: McIntosh Gallery, 2019), xiii.

9   Chelsea M. Herr, "The Evolution of Revolution: Virgil Ortiz's *Pueblo Revolt 1680/2180* as an Assertion of Native Presence through Indigenous Futurisms," *World Art* 9, no. 2 (2019): 127.

10   Suzanne Kite and Kristina Baudemann, "Fragmentary Transmissions: On the Poetics, Practice, and Futurisms of Listener," *World Art* 9, no. 2, 2019 (183–203): 184.

11   From Suzanne Kite's website: https://www.kitekitekitekite.com/portfolio/inyan-iye-telling-rock-2019. Accessed November 1, 2022.

12   Kite and Baudemann, "Fragmentary Transmissions," 184.

13   Julia D. Gibson and Kyle Whyte, "Science Fiction Futures and (Re)visions of the Anthropocene," in *The Oxford Handbook of Philosophy of Technology*, ed. Shannon Vallor (Oxford, UK: Oxford University Press, 2021): 11.

Indigenous Fashions of the Otherworldly

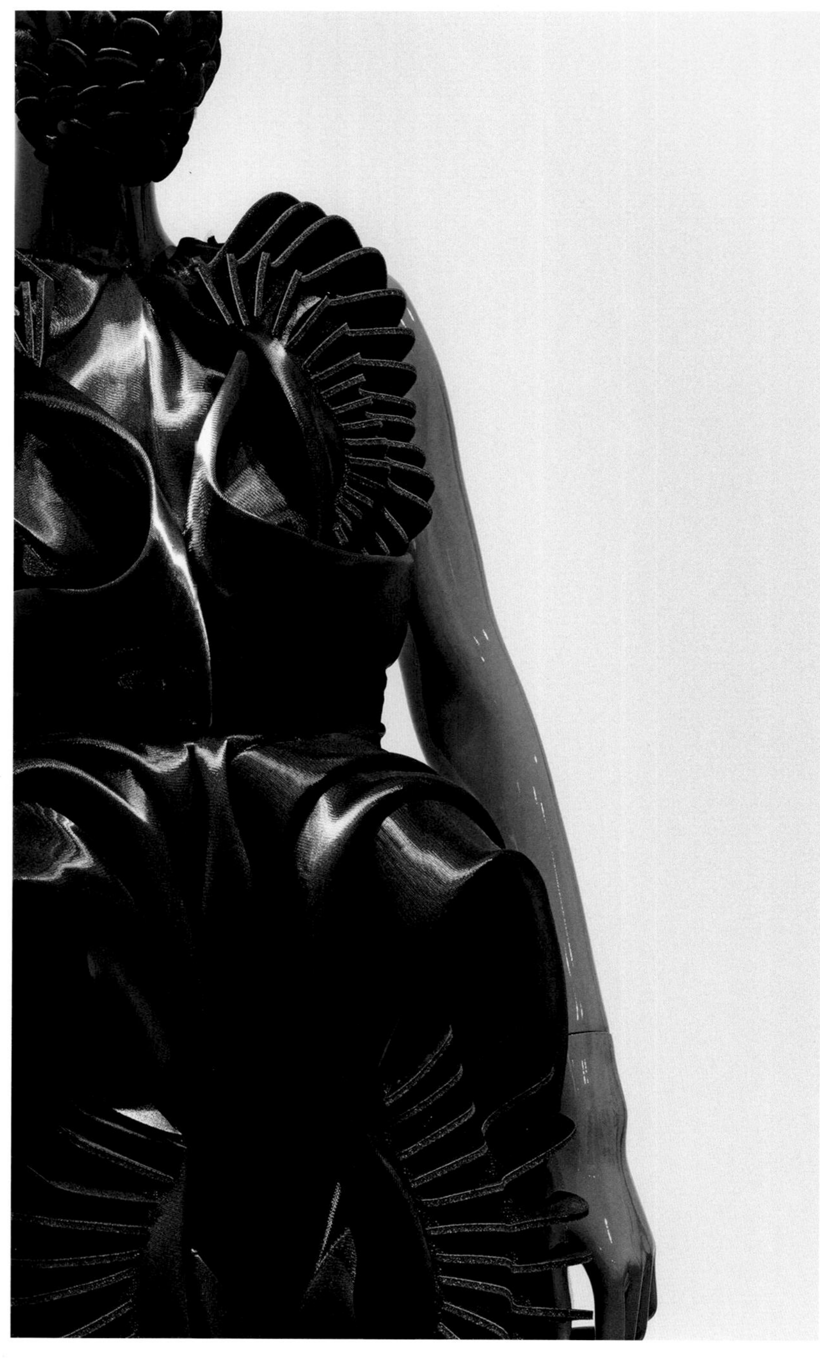

Jontay Kahm (Plains Cree), *Fossil 2.0 with Pebble Mask* (Detail), 2023. Organza twill, dimensions variable. Courtesy of Vancouver Art Gallery

Amber-Dawn Bear Robe

For something to be otherworldly, its content or context must be unbound by earthly constraints. It's a space for fantasy and a place for dreams.[1]

Fashion writer Greg French poses the question "What is Otherworldly?" in a visually intoxicating publication, *Otherworldly: Avant-Garde Fashion and Style.*[2] Notably, the book never fully answered the question. "After all," French writes, "the concept is informed by the unknown and unexplainable."[3] The term "Otherworldly" may also serve as an alternative descriptor of Futurism, specifically Indigenous Futurism, the driving force behind *Future Imaginaries: Indigenous Art, Fashion, Technology.* Futurism often evokes visions of spaceships, teleportation, and moon boots. However, Indigenous Futurism is far more expansive, relying on ancestral knowledge to create an informed future. Just as the definition of otherworldly is uncertain, so too is the definition of Indigenous fashion, a genre that is poorly understood. This essay examines otherworldly aspects of Native fashion as seen in the work of designers Barry Ace (Odawa), Catherine Blackburn (Dene/European), Orlando Dugi (Diné), Jontay Kahm (Plains Cree), Caroline Monnet (Anishinaabe/French), Celeste Pedri-Spade (Anishinabekwe/Ojibwe), and Adrian Stimson (Siksika). Their work offers a context to understand Indigenous fashion in all its diversity. These designers demonstrate there is no one way to define fashion design created by Native North American artists. Serving as knowledge carriers for generations, Indigenous North Americans have forever been design visionaries, fashioning extraordinary clothing and personal adornments with unconventional methods imprinted with the maker's stories, values, memories, and worldviews.

An examination of Indigenous design reveals that Native North American fashion is a well-established art form with a rich history; it has consistently embraced innovation while being an exemplar of Indigenous Futurism. Moreover, the necessity of employing Western language in describing Indigenous fashion underscores fashion history's incapacity to convey the forward-thinking nature of this practice. Visual culture scholar Malcolm Barnard argues that fashion and fashion history, far from expressing a single theoretical framework, incorporate many fields. "Fashion is a rich and multi-disciplinary subject," Barnard explains, "and a point at which history, economics, anthropology, sociology, and psychology could be said to meet with each discipline inherent in its own theories in studies of fashion."[4] These fields center white, Euro-Western male perspectives, largely excluding histories and experiences outside of a Western worldview. Until recently, it was generally accepted by dress historians that the birth of fashion occurred in the mid-fourteenth century during the late medieval period in Europe.[5]

This leaves Indigenous North Americans completely out of the fashion canon. With no scholarly framework through which to view Indigenous fashion systems outside of an anthropological lens, Native American style or dress resides in the abyss of American fashion history.[6]

An awareness of Indigenous fashion's exclusion leads to a basic understanding of its marginalization and why people think it is a new phenomenon. Even with the increase of scholarly texts on global fashion history, Native American fashion remains overlooked. As professors Linda Welters and Abby Lillethun write in *Fashion History: A Global View*, "For many decades, the study of fashion history has been limited to Western dress worn primarily in urban environments beginning with the middle of the fourteenth century."[7] While the book brings invaluable focus to neglected regions of the fashion world, only a few pages cover the Indigenous fashion of North America. The authors are aware of the insufficiency: "It is hoped that this work will inspire new, inclusive fashion histories that incorporate cultures beyond the West and before the rise of capitalism in Europe."[8] Ironically, Native Americans are not beyond the West but are the original peoples of the North American West.

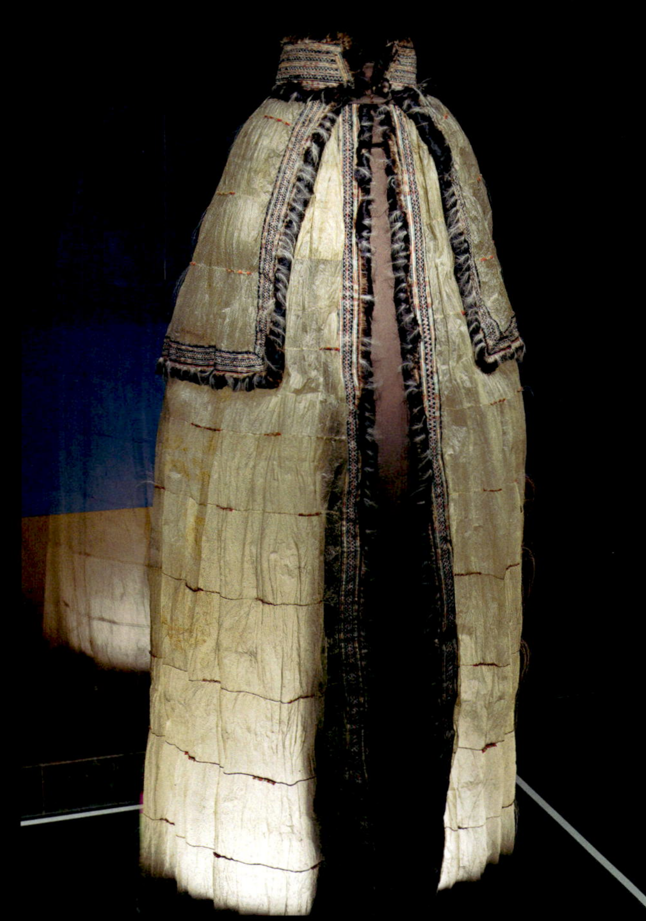

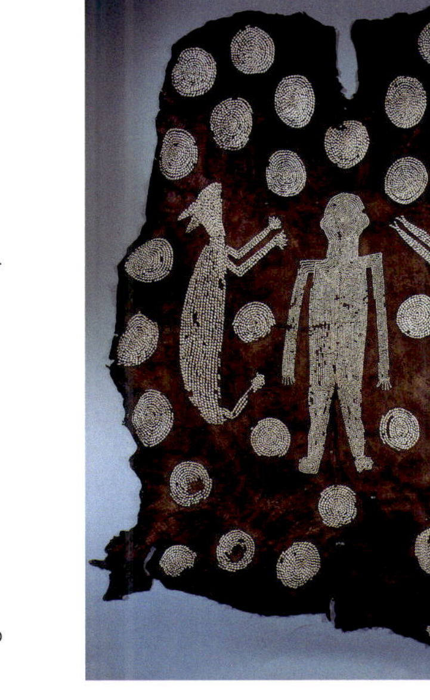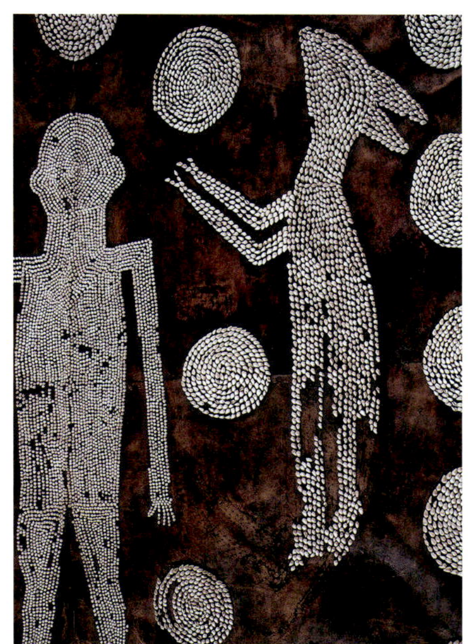

Fig. 2. Unknown Indigenous maker, *Mantle (Powhatan's Mantle)*, 17th century. Deer hide with shell bead decoration and sinew, approx. 93 × 63 in. Courtesy of the Ashmolean Museum, University of Oxford, Image © Ashmolean Museum, University of Oxford

Pivoting from excluded aspects of Native fashion, what does Indigenous fashion include? While there is no single meaning, there are common characteristics that tie into the futurity of the practice. Indigenous fashion is the oldest form of design in North America that is constantly changing with the introduction of new technologies and materials while retaining the design languages specific to the designer's Indigenous culture.[9] The otherworldly of Indigenous fashion is the unknown communication through Indigenous design languages that references worlds unseen by those not Indigenous to these lands.

Indigenous artists stand as the original couturiers of North America. Alaskan Native and Inuit gutskin garments exemplify couture, blending cutting-edge technical expertise with unparalleled beauty (fig. 1). Harvesting and preparing a marine mammal marks the initial steps in physically creating gutskin fashion. This involves meticulously cleaning the animal's intestines to create a visually appealing material for crafting a parka through the lifesaving sinew-sewing technique. Each creation is one of a kind, tailored to the wearer, and conceptually rooted in Inuit/Alaska Native societal values. Deeply abundant, these ideas pay homage to the hunted animal, simultaneously delighting those individuals drawn to its aesthetic allure. The process and life cycle of the gutskin parka are connected to the unknown and unseen, or the otherworldly. The remarkable historical design ingenuity employed in crafting gutskin garments, coupled with artistic vision and engineering techniques, is truly remarkable. If modernism is relative to its time and place, this atelier custom demonstrates futurity in its ingenuity and conceptual foundation.

A remarkable couture creation, *Powhatan's Mantle* remains as powerful now as when it was initially fashioned in the seventeenth century (fig. 2). This extraordinary garment, part of the permanent collection of the Ashmolean Museum, Oxford, is characterized as "unique with no known parallels."[10] The cape boasts an embellishment of over twenty thousand Marginella shells[11] meticulously arranged to depict figurative symbols of power, social prominence, and wealth.[12] Crafted from four white-tailed deer hides, the *Mantle* is expertly trimmed and sewn together with sinew. At its center stands a humanoid figure, flanked symmetrically by two opposing animal figures, all presented in profile. Forming two bordering animal representations, the shells illustrate a wolf with claws and a long tail, juxtaposed with a symbol featuring hooves and a shorter tail, symbolizing a white-tailed deer.[13] The central figure could represent a human, an entity, an otherworldly being, or perhaps Powhatan himself. Surrounded by thirty-four beaded circles, the trio might allude to central human forms navigating celestial realms with protective animal spirits by their side. The exact meaning of the cloak remains elusive, as encoded knowledge is retained within the artists and their communities as a form of communication between past, present, and future generations. The meticulous shell stitching stands as a remarkable expression of Indigenous couture.

Evoking innovative methods and novel materials, Indigenous artists historically shifted from working with small shells to embracing the art of design through porcupine quills and beadwork. This transformation showcases adaptability and creativity in crafting distinct Indigenous design languages over time. Vibrant glass beads emerged as an alternative or addition to geometric porcupine quillwork. This method is notably quicker, producing vivid colors that surpass the range achievable with natural dyes. The skilled incorporation of this new material illustrates Indigenous designers' embrace of new technology to create original design languages. Materials, techniques, and visual expressions may undergo constant change, but the essence of Indigenous design remains deeply anchored and entwined with the artists' identity and their connection to the land as Native North Americans. Although the appropriation of Native beading may mimic Indigenous design, it inherently lacks the capacity to capture or convey the profound meaning embedded in this art form.

Barry Ace showcases innovative ornamentation and beading in his wearable art creations, using new materials to infuse his work with hidden narratives. In *Efface*, 2017, a pair of oxfords adorned with vintage round circuit boards, coated wire, capacitors, light-emitting diodes, and resistors draws inspiration from beadwork and animal hair tufting (pl. 5). Ace innovatively redefines design techniques by stitching computer components together to reinterpret organic curvilinear and floral configurations, rooted in a traditional design language specific to the eastern Native and Métis people. This transformation results in ultra-modern oxfords that seamlessly blend contemporary materiality with historical design concepts, creating a stylistically cohesive expression of Indigenous knowledge. Ace's work not only carves out space for the continual flow of encoded messaging intended for future Indigenous generations but also mirrors the approach seen in *Powhatan's Mantle*. *Efface* embraces and translates foundational forms of design, incorporating modern technology and new materials while conveying otherworldly narratives.

The otherworldly is fluid in idea and production, continuously forging ahead and changing the world to create new realities. Virgil Ortiz conceives novel realms, shaping immersive spaces that momentarily transport spectators to alternative dimensions. Ortiz's artistic career began with ceramics, progressing to textiles, graphic murals, and multimedia installations populated by otherworldly figures made of clay or fiberglass and dressed in dramatically shaped, majestic garments (fig. 3).[14] The design dialect of Cochiti Pueblo pottery, named for the region where Ortiz is from, informs his work. Although this design language is grounded in the Pueblo land where Ortiz obtains his clay, his imagery is more than the transference of historical color palettes and design motifs to modern forms. Indigenous fashion specialist Jessica Metcalfe writes, "Ortiz adds an additional, if unattainable, metaphorical level of 'knowing' and understanding his sometimes-subversive work." Metcalfe continues:

> Through his work, he transfers Cochiti aesthetic concepts to the fashion world, including Cochiti composition and color theory, the Cochiti tradition of parody and social commentary through performance, Pueblo storytelling and oral tradition themes, and cultural continuity through subversive creativity. Ortiz uses the lens of Cochiti aesthetics to understand, and express to others, the world around him.[15]

The parameters of Pueblo art are stretched, manifesting conceptual spaces and dialects yet to be seen or experienced. Through material experimentation, the artist forms innovative language leading Pueblo generations into the otherworldly with design semantics centered in Cochiti knowledge.

Jonfay Kahm, an emerging designer, crafts sculptural dresses rooted in Indigenous perspectives. The profound influence on his designs can be traced back to his late father, Jeff Kahm, an exceptional abstract painter who left an indelible mark as a painting instructor at the Institute of American Indian Arts. His father's modernist aesthetic, characterized by Indigenous abstraction, resonates in Kahm's fashion creations. Striving to "reinvent Indigenous fashion from his Plains Cree perspective," Kahm materializes this vision in pieces like his 2023 hybrid animalia dress, *Fossil 2.0 with Pebble Mask* (pl. I).[16]

This vanguard ensemble features exaggerated, slick, oil-colored folds emanating from its center, intricately structured into four organic quadrants. Within the deep folds, reptilian spines are revealed, piercing the garment's corners, creating the illusion of an otherworldly entity weaving in and out of the dress. The overall effect suggests either an ethereal form residing within the dress or an alien being worn as a garment. Regardless, *Fossil 2.0 with Pebble Mask* serves as a protective shield for the wearer, enveloping the body's core with armor. The pebble mask complements the dress by serving as a protector, safeguarding the wearer's head. Its smooth, dark gray, ovoid shapes, resembling wet skipping stones, cover the entire face, seamlessly connected to the spine of the outfit. Beyond offering protection, the mask also encapsulates intelligence and memory within the stones.

> Native North American cultures, with a specific historical emphasis on the Tsimshian Nations of the Pacific Northwest Coast, have a tradition of expertly crafting stone masks. These historical masks, intricately engraved with formline features, have captivated scholars. Notably, there are two nesting Tsimshian stone masks—one housed at the Canadian Museum of History and its counterpart in Paris at the Musée de l'Homme. *"In the Blink of an Eye": Collecting the Tsimshian Stone Masks* is an extensive account of the twin masks by scholar Joanne MacDonald. She writes:
>
>> The events surrounding the collecting of the two nesting Tsimshian stone masks [have] eluded the net of history; much of the knowledge about them is a mystery. For years it was not known who the masks represented. Being the only stone Northwest Coast masks places them in a unique category.[17]
>
> Fundamentally, Kahm's creations reinterpret and reimagine Indigenous concepts, transporting them into a new dimension where the past merges with the present. Traditional knowledge

is intricately interwoven with avart-garde aesthetics, inviting a broader audience to actively engage with and appreciate the profound depth and complexity of Indigenous perspectives on knowledge, history, and cultural continuity.

Caroline Monnet's innovative design language is vividly showcased in *Echoes from a Near Future*, 2022, a large-scale inkjet print mounted on aluminum (pl. 11). The heart of this image is its central configuration featuring six Indigenous matriarchs and three children. Notably, the artist shares a personal relationship with each member of the group, a mix of family members and prominent leaders for whom custom garments were specially designed.[18] One of these bespoke garments, worn by the dance and performance artist Aïcha Bastien-N'Diaye,[19] takes physical form in the *Future Imaginaries* exhibition (pl. 12). A striking, wide-shouldered cape constructed from unconventional building materials is the focal point of Bastien-N'Diaye's ensemble, highlighting the textures of the blue-and-white patterned coat. Beneath it, a vibrant blue slip intricately woven with construction materials is revealed. Bright pops of orange delineate the long sleeves of the dress worn beneath

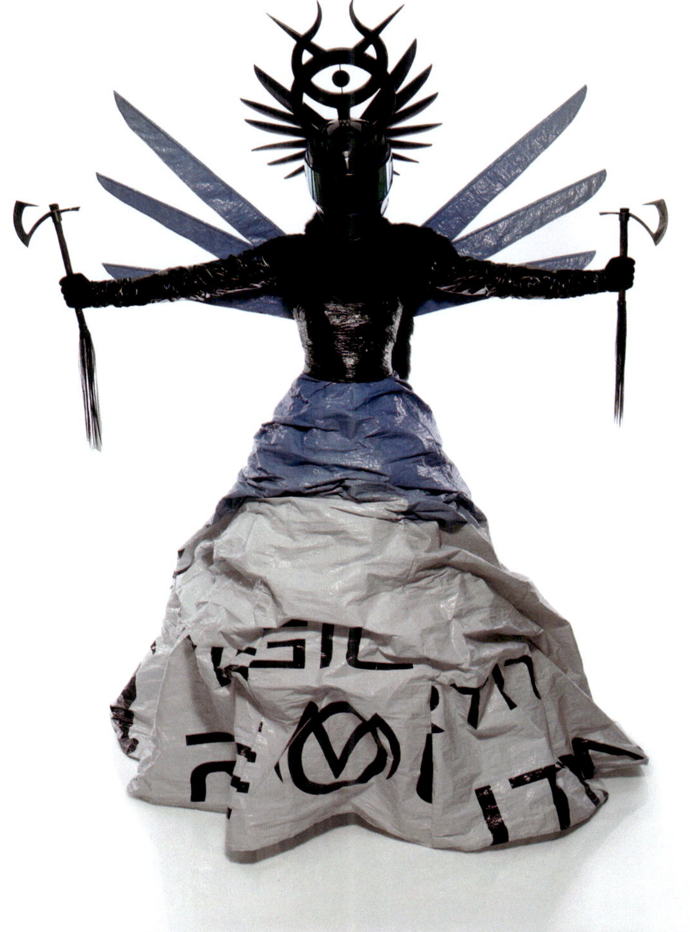

Fig. 3. Virgil Ortiz (Cochiti Pueblo), *ReVOlution Couture* from the *ReVOlt 1680/2180* series, 2019. Recycled billboard materials, latex, leather, foam fabrication, steel headdress, dimensions variable. Courtesy of the artist

Revolution couture donned by Helsman Cuda of the Aeronauts, a lead character from Ortiz's *ReVOlt 1680/2180* saga. In this scene, Cuda steers the Survivorship to Earth's realm to aid Tahu and Po'pay in opposing the Castilian Army.

the woven cape. Despite their industrial origins, these materials exude a luminous, reflective sheen, transforming the utilitarian provisions into a sculptural and avant-garde masterpiece.

Monnet visualizes a matriarchal future encompassing multiple ages and generations in both her photography and garments. Her design language is meticulously interwoven into her construction, creating unconventional shapes that act as vessels for this unique design narrative. *Echoes from a Near Future* encapsulates the lasting strength of matriarchal leadership, steering successive generations into a realm that surpasses the ordinary. The garments emerge as a visual and symbolic embodiment of the matriarchal figures' sustained influence and nurturing prowess, extending into otherworldly dimensions of time and existence.

Celeste Pedri-Spade communicates a future centered around matriarchy through Indigenous design, intertwining messages of environmental degradation and colonial history in her extraordinary design, *Anti-Pipeline Society Kwe*, part of her 2019 *Material Kwe* collection (pl. 13).[20] Merging her skills as an artist, researcher, and author, Pedri-Spade delves into her Anishinaabe ways of knowing to explore theories of materiality and Indigenous futurity:

I have incorporated aspects of Anishinaabe fashion (ribbon skirt, leather belt) with iconic clothing items drawn from mid-seventeenth-century Europe (large skirt shape and ruff). This was deliberate because in doing the HERstory work, I aim to envision a different future, one that would hopefully be marked by more productive and meaningful relations between non-Indigenous and Indigenous Peoples of this land.[21]

Horizontal ribbon bands stitched together create a royal satin bell ribbon skirt, a design recognized by most Native North Americans as a "staple" garment symbolizing Native identity. Ribbon skirts have been adapted and interpreted across Native country, with various meanings deriving from the individual wearer and Indigenous nations. Going further back in time, ribbon skirts are a result of trade that brought in new materials and technology, leading to innovative design. Another recognizable Indigenous item is the thick leather belt with round brass jingle bells. Similar to the ribbon skirt, it carries a long history of trade and individual interpretation. Both items speak to colonization, trade, adaptation, innovation, and the history of Native North America that the general society does not know.

As the garment's title suggests, *Anti-Pipeline Society Kwe* signifies the exploitation of oil and other natural resources located on Indigenous lands. In *Anishinabemowin*, "Kwe" is

slang for women,[22] highlighting the reclamation of this term
through its incorporation in the title. The sleek black fitted
top and ribbons intricately woven into a crown reinforce
this message, starkly contrasting with the vibrant colors
of the ribbon skirt. While the crown draws inspiration from
Victorian social structures, its authority is now wielded by
Indigenous creators, guiding the path toward a matriarchal
world. Pedri-Spade's designs encapsulate highly intricate
messages, serving as crucial communication in Indigenous
design for both the present and the otherworldly.

Certain Indigenous designers employ a direct visual language
that incorporates easily recognizable imagery. In the instance
of multidisciplinary artist Catherine Blackburn, her 2020
creation *Unsettle* manifests as a two-minute performance
conveying explicit messages about land, environment, and
Indigenous well-being (pl. 9). At the heart of the short film is
a fully cloaked figure navigating with difficulty through a lush
green mountain forest. This figure dons a majestic mask of
peacock blues, adorned with exaggerated facial features,
including a mouth framed with white fur showcasing jagged
nonhuman teeth, creating a "loud" roar. The seemingly abstract
and colorful imagery on the cloak gradually reveals a distinct
image—a long steel pipeline awkwardly cutting through the
organic, rich mountains.

Unsettle, explains Blackburn, "explores themes of power and
reclamation through the duality of Indigenous presence and
erasure" and aligns with Blackburn's intent to create "genderless,
oversized silhouettes that explore human and non-human
forms."[23] Her otherworldly figure is central to the film short.

The film short and mask ensemble worn by the figure deliver a
poignant message about humanity's dysfunctional relationship
with the Earth, particularly the extraction of resources from
the land, leading to global consequences. The otherworldly
figure symbolizes the Earth's burden, moving painfully through
the verdant trees. Its cape, akin to skin, is afflicted, portraying
the potential peril if action is not taken to heal and prevent the
metastasis caused by the oil pipeline.

For Orlando Dugi, fashion is a conduit for Diné (Navajo) stories
and the knowledge he acquired during childhood.[24] His design
process is deeply rooted in his heritage and culture. The *Warrior
Twins Coat*, created in collaboration with Diné artist Ryan
Singer in 2022, takes a distinctive approach to storytelling
(pl. 14). Evolving into a regal garment that also functions as
an exquisite dress, this creation narrates the Diné epic of

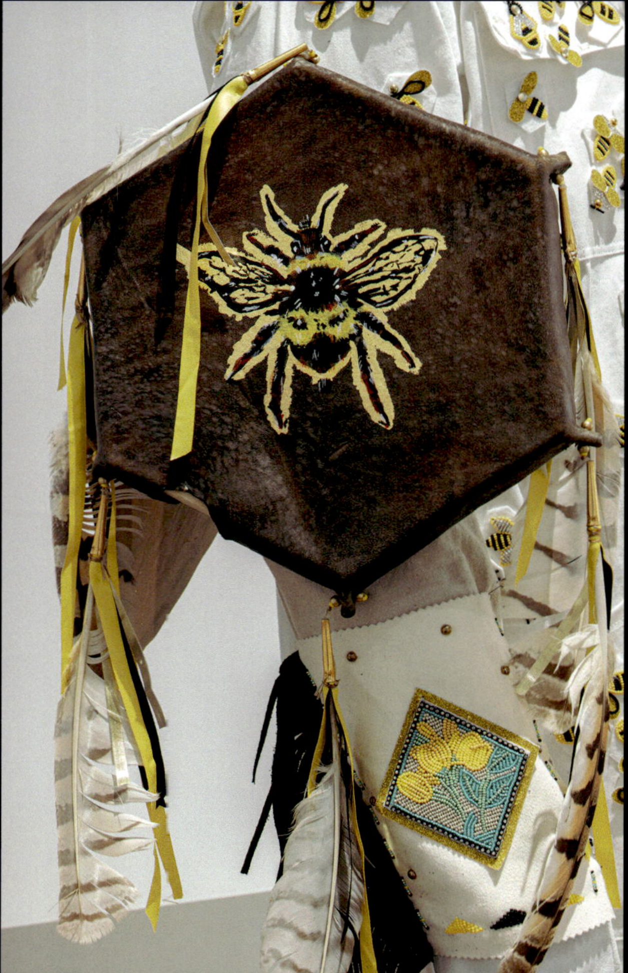
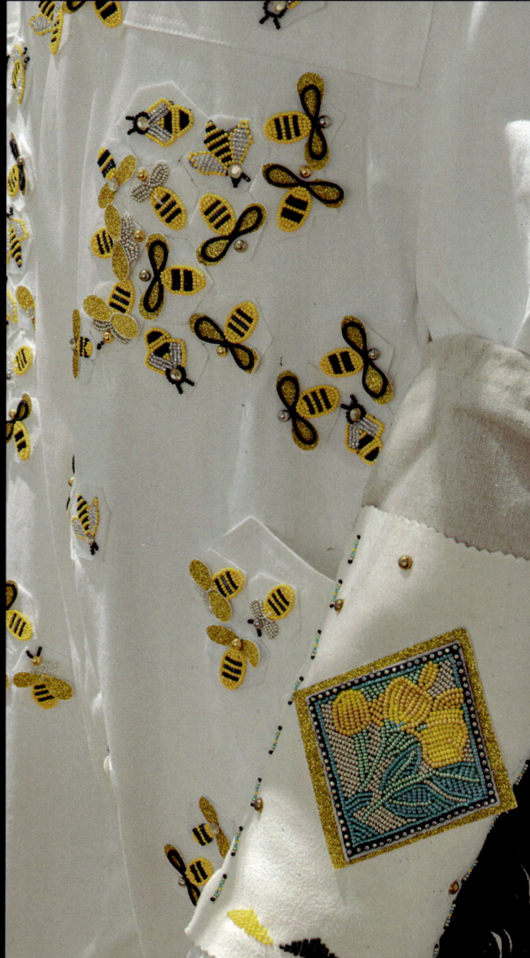

the Warrior Twins. This story has been passed down through generations, embodying a message firmly entrenched in Dugi's cultural perspectives and worldviews.

A golden sunburst, symbolizing the Twins' father, is meticulously hand-embroidered with French bullion wire and placed at both the front and center back torso of Dugi's majestic silk charmeuse coat. Ryan Singer complements this embellishment with his hand-painted images of the Warrior Twins engaged in battle with the human-killing Monster on the coat's lower half. Every detail on the garment, from one Warrior Twin wielding a bolt of lightning to the other brandishing a golden bow, serves a specific purpose. While identifiable images are present on the coat dress, they remain "abstract" in their message, tailored to particular audiences. Dugi's fresh interpretations of Diné knowledge through storytelling are firmly rooted in his identity as an Indigenous couturier.

A different manifestation of cultural knowledge through fashion is *Bumble Bee Regalia (Naamoi'stotoohsin)*, 2021, by Adrian Stimson in collaboration with beading artist Lucille

Wright Payotapaihpiyakii (Dancing the opposite direction woman) (pl. 41). Stimson's honoring and remembering is twofold, addressing harmony with the Earth's ecology and recalling Siksika societal ceremonies that were at risk during the era of assimilation policies enforced by the Canadian government.[25]

Over three hundred beaded bees adorn the beekeeper suit, representing the artist's decade as a beekeeper.[26] Bees and beekeeping are vital to the health of the Earth, land, and people while also referencing the Siksika Bee Society (fig. 4), which teaches tipi protocols while preparing children for future societies. Stimson's interpretation of bee regalia is avant-garde, with beaded yellow-and-black-striped moccasins, gloves, leggings, and headgear. The garment simultaneously addresses sociocultural and ecological issues in Blackfoot worldview with society, ceremony, history, and generational knowledge. Siksika beaded design language, as described by scholar and elder Andrew Bear Robe, "is geometric, the beading is done by the women in the family and the design is unique to the family. The beading designs can be varied depending on the bead artist's artistic expressions."[27] These skillful beadwork techniques, with their coded generational knowledge, exemplify the otherworldly.

Fashion luminaries Barry Ace, Catherine Blackburn, Orlando Dugi, Jontay Kahm, Caroline Monnet, Celeste Pedri-Spade, and Adrian Stimson collectively challenge the notion of a singular definition of fashion created by Native North American artists. Their work transmits cultural knowledge, narratives, and design perspectives to subsequent Indigenous generations. Indigenous fashion, the foundational design language of North America, constantly adapts modern technology while embracing new materials. This transformation propels it into the otherworldly, transcending conventional boundaries in fashion and design. This regeneration underscores Indigenous fashion's adaptability and enduring significance, which refuses to remain static or confined to the past. Instead, it breathes life into culture. In this way, Indigenous fashion remains a conduit for cultural messages, resonating with the ethereal and perpetuating the visionary spirit of Native North American designers across generations.

1   Greg French, *Otherworldly: Avant-Garde Fashion and Style* (New York: Rizzoli, 2013), 2.

2   Ibid., 2.

3   Ibid., 2.

4   Malcolm Barnard, *Fashion Theory: An Introduction* (New York: Routledge, 2007), 7.

5   Linda Welters and Abby Lillethun, *Fashion History, A Global View* (London: Bloomsbury Visual Arts, repr. December 21, 2018), 2-4.

6   I am specifically referring to Indigenous fashion systems of the United States and Canada.

7   Welters and Lillethun, *Fashion History*, 169-170.

8   Ibid., 4.

9   Amber-Dawn Bear Robe, "Indigenous Couture: Forever Fashioning," in *Fashion Fictions*, ed. Stephanie Rebick et al. (Amsterdam: Information Office, 2023), 44-52.

10   Ashmolean Museum Oxford, https://www.ashmolean.org/powhatans-mantle#/.

11   The Marginella shell is a pear-shaped shell, highly polished and measuring nearly half an inch, native to the Atlantic.

12   America Meredith, "Spotlight: Powhatans Mantle," *First American Art Magazine*, no. 18 (Spring 2018): 93.

13   Ibid., 93.

14   Virgil Ortiz, "First American Art," https://www.virgilortiz.com/first-american-art.

15   Jessica R. Metcalfe, "Native Designers of High Fashion: Expressing Identity, Creativity, and Tradition in Contemporary Customary Clothing Design" (electronic dissertation, University of Arizona, downloaded January 19, 2018), 293, http://hdl.handle.net/10150/194057.

16   Jontay Kahm studio visit in March 2023, Santa Fe, New Mexico.

17   Joanne MacDonald, "In the Blink of an Eye: Collecting the Tsimshian Stone Masks," in *Of One Heart: Gitxaała and Our Neighbours*, ed. Charles R. Menzies (Vancouver, BC: New Proposals Publishing, 2016), 161.

18   Caroline Monnet, Zoom conversation with the author, December 15, 2022.

19   A practitioner, choreographer, and educator originating from Wendake, Quebec, Aïcha Bastien-N'Diaye melds tradition with modernity, blending physicality and expressiveness across diverse dance genres. Embracing a rich tapestry of cultures, practices, and aesthetics, this dynamic artist encapsulates the essence of Quebec's contemporary dance landscape, characterized by openness to the global and the diverse.

20   Celeste Pedri-Spade, "Home," http://www.celestepedrispade.ca/.

21   Ibid.

22   Ibid.

23   Catherine Blackburn, "Unsettle," https://www.catherineblackburn.com/unsettle.

24   Orlando Dugi, call with the author, April 18, 2023.

25   Adrian Stimson, personal communication, April 18, 2023.

26   Andrew Bear Robe, personal communication, April 18, 2023.

27   Andrew Bear Robe, personal communication, November 29, 2023.

WINDOW TO THE FUTURE

ReVOlt 1680/2180:
Sirens and Sikas

Virgil Ortiz

In 1680, the Pueblo Revolt began. Decades before, Spanish colonizers had ravaged the landscape and decimated the Indigenous Pueblo populations. Guided by Po'pay, a Tewa spiritual leader, the members of this historic uprising successfully expelled the colonizers from their homelands, and for twelve years after freeing themselves, the Pueblos of New Mexico lived free from Castilian rule and influence. In 1692, the Spanish returned with a vengeance and stole the lands again. In the *ReVOlt 1680/2180* epic, a contemporary retelling of Pueblo history, the 1680 rebels will have more resources and aid, and their territories will be secure once and for all.

Tempest Warriors, Protectors of the People

The year is 1680. Po'pay has called representatives from the surrounding pueblos to Taos for a clandestine meeting. Their purpose: to plan an uprising. If the Pueblos are to survive and keep their traditions alive, Po'pay says, the time for action is *now*. He has summoned his living relatives, and his petition for aid has reached even farther.

In the year 2180, Tahu, Leader of the Blind Archers, has a dream: five cyclones of fire tear toward her across the landscape, and as they draw near, she hears the voice of her ancestor, Po'pay, praying for aid. With this strange and frightening vision fresh in her mind's eye, she runs to the Sirens, their team of armorers and artificers, who use her link to the past to open a portal to 1680 to aid their ancestors.

The Sirens synthesize portals for time travel, outfit members of the resistance for battle, and arm the Recon Watchmen with armor and Ha'pons (war shields). In the fire caves of Cuernavaca, the Sirens fire their clay shields and weapons in temperatures over 2400°F. In their orbiting laboratory, they innovate new technologies that combine cybernetics and organic materials. Their portal technology can be used for transportation over distance and time, and their ability to connect people is unlike any other. Perhaps their most crucial role is defending all children from the dangers of war.

But *who* are these inventors and weaponsmiths? *What* are they? As cyborgs, the Sirens are living examples of the delicate balance necessary to contain the cybernetic and the organic in one body. These ethereal automatons tower over most humans; their translucent seven-foot frames are shimmery white and almost too graceful to be human—but humans they indeed are.

The Sirens were once fully human beings who augmented their corporeal forms with cybernetic high-fire clay armor and advanced robotic servos, making extreme personal sacrifices to defend their homelands and communities. Etched into their very exoskeletons is the code for portal travel, and they can teleport themselves and others over distance and time. Their electromagnetic hair, piercing white irises, and augmented joints are integral

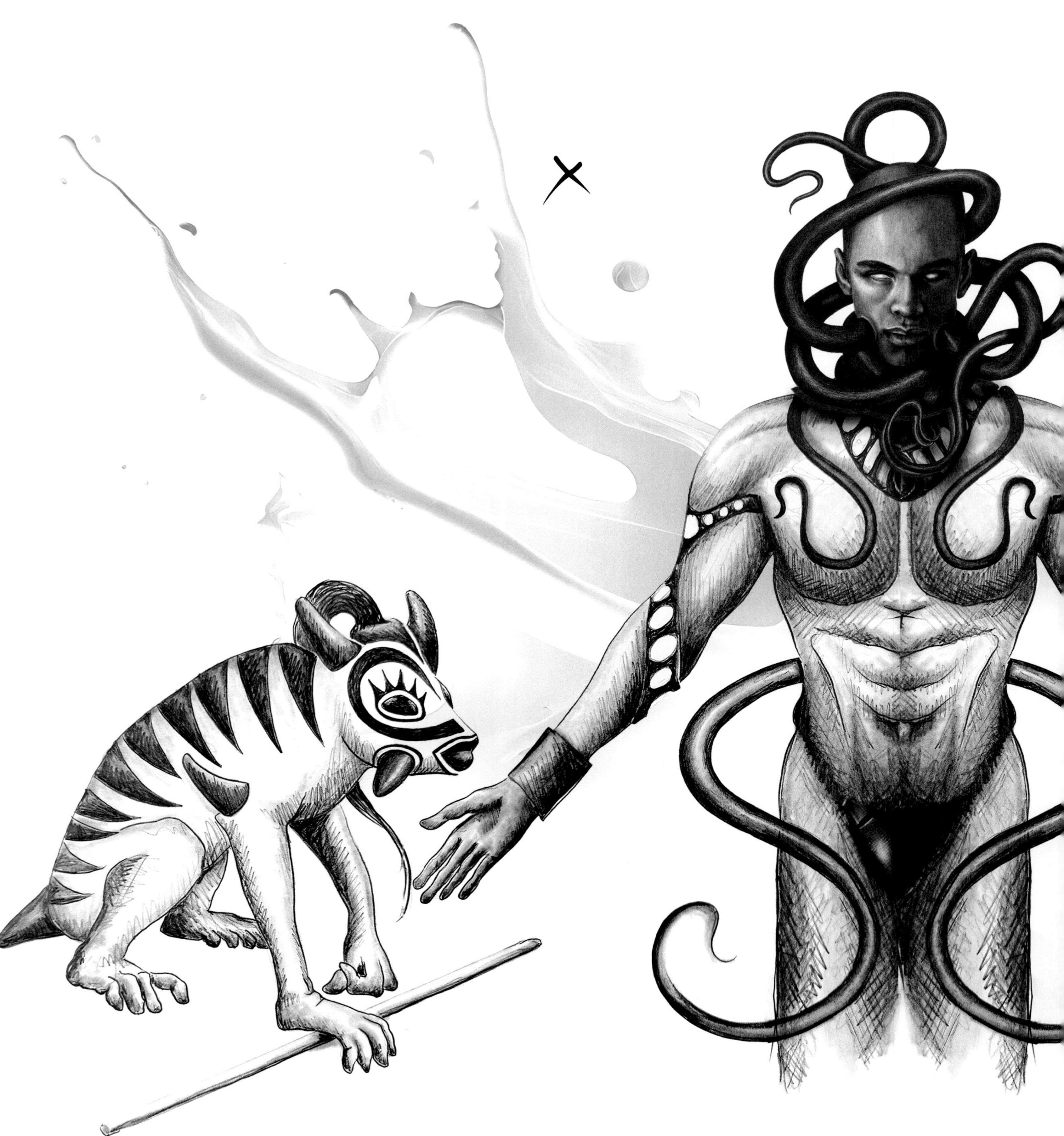

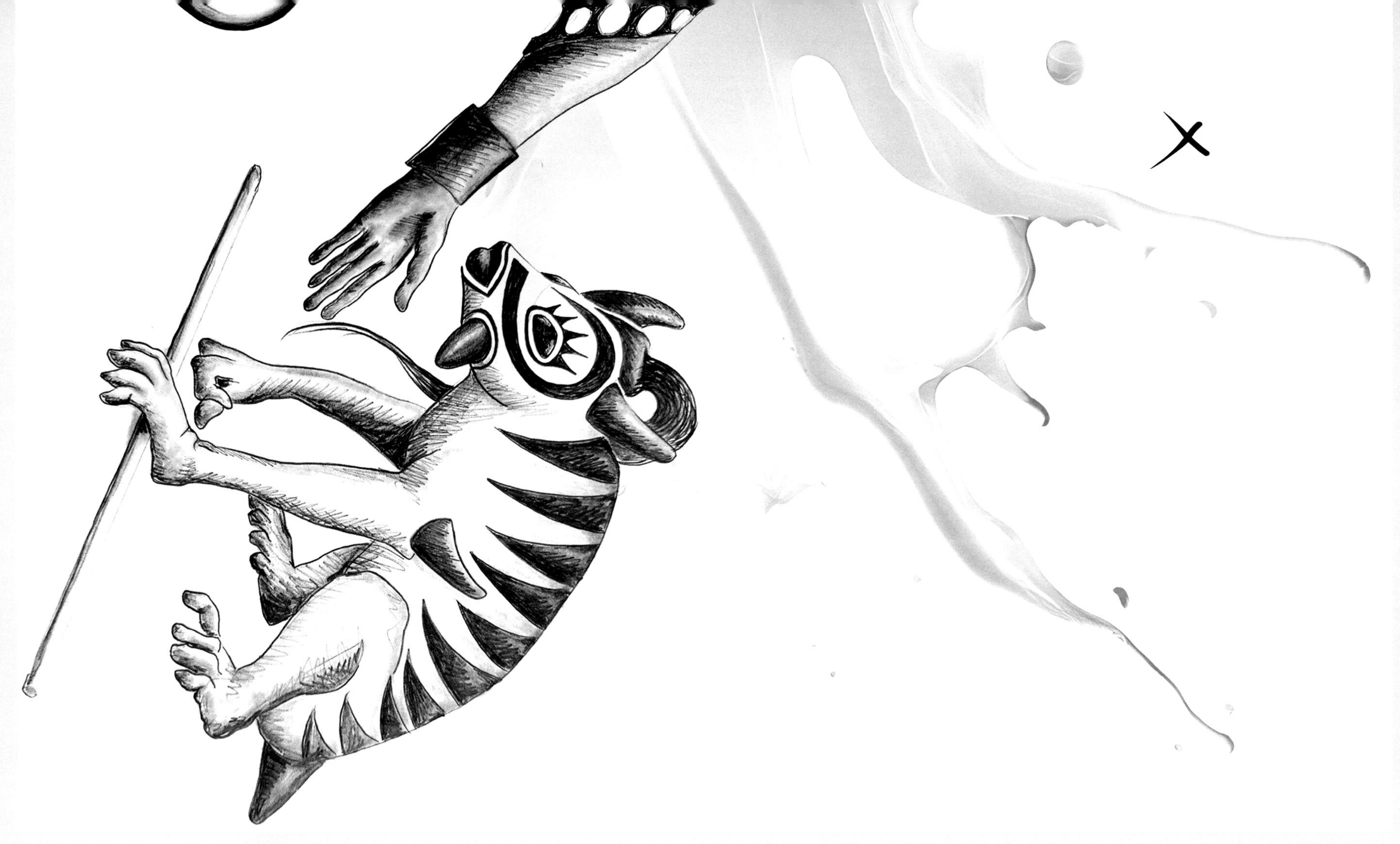

Fig. I. Virgil Ortiz (Cochiti Puebo), *Siren with Sikas,* storyboard sketch from the *ReVOlt I680/2I80* series, 2023. Graphite on paper, I6 × 20 in. Courtesy of the artist

to their roles as tireless defenders of life, tradition, and technology. Their creativity and problem-solving skills are crucial to the Watchmen's cause, as are the tools they create, tools not of destruction but defense, to bring about peace and protect our collective future.

To accomplish this, the Sirens are tasked with keeping safe all children who could be impacted in any way by war, but in case they cannot do so in person, they provide each child with a Sika. Sikas are half-simian, half-canine tetrapod mammals. These fluffy, horned animals migrate together in close-knit packs, and while they may look completely innocent, they are vicious hunters. The call of a Sika can strike a potent fear into the hearts of their quarry. Once they sense and smell that fear, Sikas will relentlessly chase their next meals out of hiding, sometimes gliding like flying squirrels to drop down and capture their prey. They aid the Horsemen in tracking and hunting game, lending their highly keen senses of smell and emotional sensitivity. When the Sirens rescue a child in danger, they give that child a Sika. Once they have bonded, a Sika will provide its child with protection, food, and unparalleled loyalty and love for as long as possible. The bond between a Sika and a human child is unbreakable.

Like many of *ReVOlt 1680/2180*'s historical and fictional characters, the Sirens and Sikas are critical to the cause because of their extraordinary abilities and their power to deliver hope to the future and the past. When we enter this narrative, we participate in an intersection of speculative futurity, technology, culture, and history. Viewers are encouraged to embrace alternative notions of space and time to reimagine pivotal historical moments and the futures that may lie ahead. *ReVOlt 1680/2180* illustrates how Indigenous traditions of past and future resistance are being shaped in the present.

Fig. 2. Virgil Ortiz (Cochiti Pueblo), *Siren: Astian* from the *ReVOlt 1680/2180* series, 2018. High-fired clay, glass, steel, 20 × 17 × 21 in. Courtesy of the artist

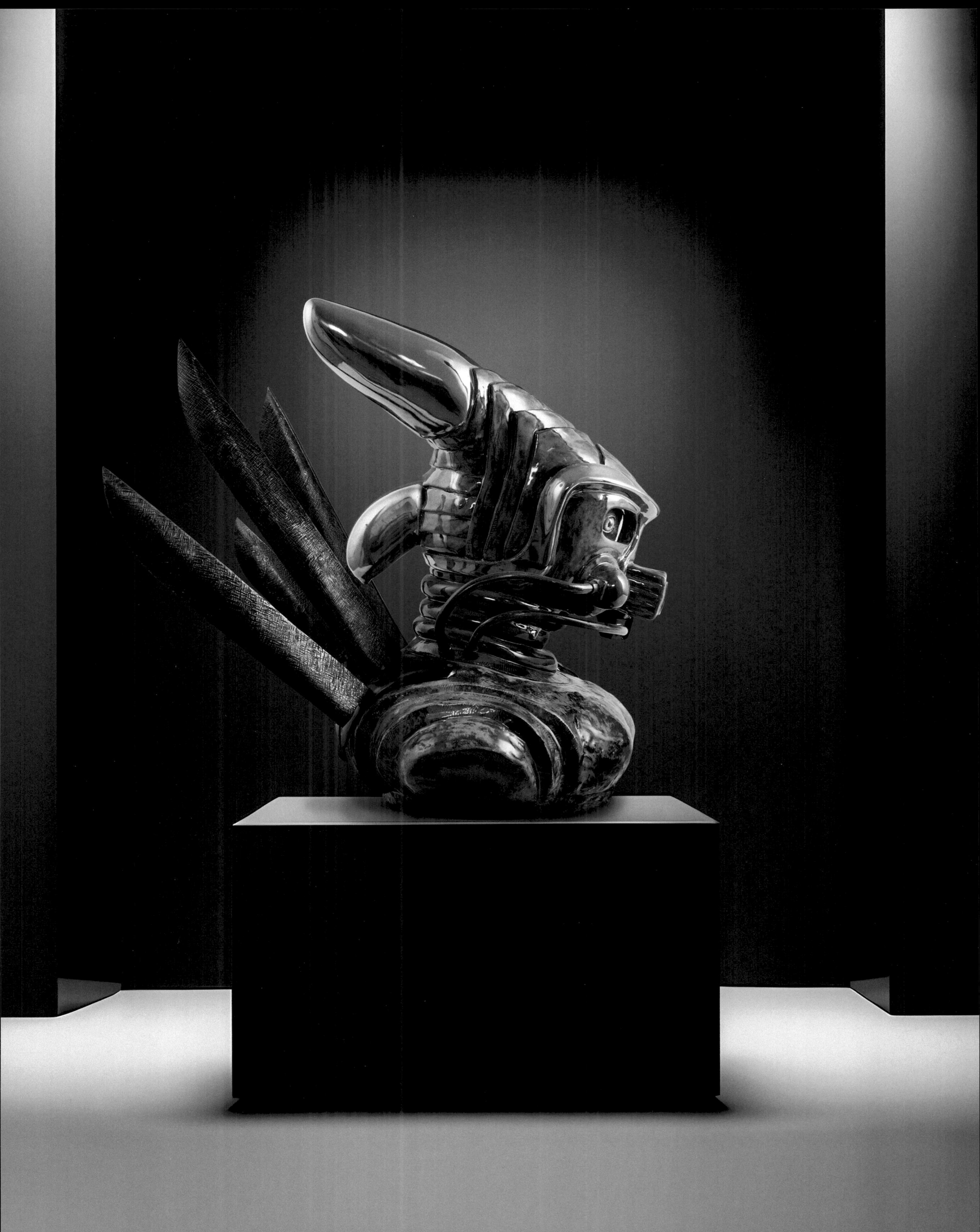

Apocalypse When?
Historic Disasters and Transformation

Amanda K. Wixon

> *When the Ancestors still resided in the land of the setting sun, the Great Spirit, Aba'Binni'li', sent rain. Soon, water covered all the Earth. Some of the Chickasaw people made rafts to save themselves. Then, the large white beavers cut the thongs that bound the rafts. All drowned but one family and a pair of each of the animals. When the rain stopped and the flood receded, a raven appeared with part of an ear of corn. Aba'Binni'li' told the Chickasaw people to plant it. Aba'Binni'li' also told them that, eventually, the Earth would be destroyed by fire, its ruin presaged by a rain of flood and oil.*
> — Chickasaw story of the Great Flood[1]

For many Native peoples, the European "discovery" and subsequent settlement of Indigenous homelands in the Americas represents a time of great suffering. In addition to the millions of lives lost due to foreign disease, the continual displacement of tribal communities resulted in the incalculable loss of both traditional knowledge and cultural practices that had endured for thousands of years. Sickness, famine, war, environmental degradation—the scale of destruction has been nothing short of apocalyptic. However, within the collective memory of many tribal communities are stories of other equally destructive yet transformative apocalypses. Through their oral histories, Native peoples recorded catastrophic floods, earthquakes, fires, and other world-changing phenomena, some of which only recently have been confirmed through Western science. The history of Native apocalypse is not limited to the European invasion and its disastrous consequences. Rather, it has been crucial to the survival of Native peoples in many ways as it serves to rededicate communities to their spiritual practices as they seek rebalance in the wake of chaos.

Numerous tribal origin stories reference a time of cataclysmic flooding, as do stories from many different periods and geographical locations. Many predate the written record and exist within the collective historical memory of the source community. Like many other Native peoples, the story of the Great Flood is an important part of the Chickasaw origin story. The Creator, *Aba'Binni'li'*, sent tremendous amounts of rain, to which the people responded by making rafts with the help of animals. When the rain stopped, *Aba'Binni'li'* instructed the people how to survive but warned them of another catastrophe, this time by fire. Unlike the Judeo-Christian concept of a similar event, the Creator did not send the flood to punish the people. Instead, the story refers to a natural event in which the Earth renewed itself. To survive, the people and animals came together as a community and continued to exist as before the disaster, honoring and stewarding the land from which they came.

For the Pima people of the Gila Valley, the flood story includes a great prophet. The prophet was warned three times of an imminent deluge by an eagle but ignored the message. By morning, no one was left alive except the son of the Creator, *Szeukha*, who had saved himself by floating on a ball of gum. *Szeukha* saw the dead and then raised them to life to repopulate the Earth.[2] In some stories of the peoples of the Great Plains, *Unktehu*, the Lakota water monster, fought the people and caused a great flood. Some believe that the Great Spirit, *Wakan Tanka*, let *Unktehu* win to create a better human being. In another Lakota story, the Creator set out to make a new world and sang songs to bring rain. When the fourth song was sung, the Earth split, and water came up from the cracks. By the time the rain stopped, all the people and nearly all the animals drowned, except for Kangi, the crow.[3]

Extreme weather and earthquakes could also serve to restart the world, according to well-documented prophetic events of the nineteenth century. Handsome Lake, the Seneca prophet, predicted that the Earth would be consumed by fire, environmental destruction, famine, and war.[4] Wovoka, a Northern Paiute religious leader born around 1865, also predicted a catastrophic event—an earthquake or an ice age—and instructed his followers in the Ghost Dance to prepare for a new world without Euro-American interference.[5] The term "Ghost Dance" has been associated with other Native revivalist movements from earlier in the century, notably the Cherokee apocalyptic prophesies of 1811-12. Fueled by extreme weather, a series of earthquakes, and a sense of disharmony among the factionalized Cherokee people, these prophecies called for a return to the old ways before the white people and have been written about extensively.[6]

Native origin stories are often considered myths or legends and disregarded as historical facts within Western academic thought. Like the Bible and other religious texts, many origin stories are coded with different meanings. However, Native stories of the Great Flood might not be just stories. According to more recent scientific studies, approximately 11,600 years ago, a massive ice sheet collapsed in North America and moved into the Lower Mississippi Valley. Due to the region's warmer climate, ice melting introduced vast amounts of fresh water into oceans, raising sea levels by over one hundred feet. The rapid rise caused disastrous flooding, forcing the region's inhabitants to move to higher ground. Those who could not make rafts drowned. In a forced and almost immediate migration, survivors found themselves in already occupied lands, and the newly displaced inhabitants possibly strained available resources.[7] A natural disaster of this magnitude, resulting in significant loss of life and sudden population shifts, would not have easily been forgotten. Indeed, the survivors and their descendants kept the memory with them as their communities rebuilt in new lands. The story, shared from generation to generation, has changed over time, evolving to suit community needs. Some of these flood story renditions are cautionary tales meant to regulate or improve communal behavior. In other accounts, like that of the Chickasaw people, catastrophic floods are not always interpreted as a punitive action. Despite these variations, in every version of the story, the Native world is transformed.

The theme of transformation spurred by catastrophe is prevalent in many Native origin stories. For some Native peoples of the Southwest, the world has undergone more than one transformation. During these events, rocks turned into animals, animals into people, and people turned into rocks and animals. Life became unbalanced within these conversions and rebalanced with the care and maintenance of cosmological relationships between the people and spiritual entities in various forms.[8] Ceremony is the most essential aspect of these relationships. Ceremonial practices strengthen these connections and are critical to a community's physical, mental, and spiritual health. Radical change might seem chaotic, but ultimately the world is reborn, balance is restored, and people are reinvigorated with a clearer sense of their spiritual responsibilities.

Transformative renewal is not always limited to this world, nor is it always involuntary. Some Native stories depict an elective departure from one world to the next. There have been four worlds in Diné *Bahané*, the Navajo creation story. The first world, *Nihodilhil*, was the beginning of time, populated by spiritual beings, *Altse Hastiin* (First Man) and *Altse Asdzaa* (First Woman). From an opening in the east, they entered the second world, *Nihodootlizh*, which animals and other beings had already populated. After a period of hardship, they left through an opening in the south to the third world, *Nihaltsoh*, of great rivers. A massive flood occurred there, and the people used a reed to climb up to the fourth world, *Nihalgai*, or the Glittering World. Within these worlds, the spiritual relationships between the people and the Holy Ones evolved, transforming and solidifying traditional Diné lifeways and culture.[9] According to the traditional beliefs of the people of the Columbia Plateau, there have been two sacred creations. The first creation was the animals, plants, and mountains, and the establishment of the *tamánwit ku sakat*—the highest law that determined the rules of nature and society. The second creation refers to the time of humans—a time that is both present and past.[10]

Within Indigenous cosmologies lies the notion of cosmic time, which is also cyclic. As a world regenerates, time begins again. Associated with this regeneration, the emergence from chaos is a creative time when religious or spiritual behavior is renewed. Seeking restoration of balance and harmony, communities recommit themselves to their spiritual practices, as they have learned within the cycle of time. Embedded within Native origin stories are the lessons of collective action in times of uncertainty, and these stories, which have been told since time immemorial, are part of the collective memory of each source community. To some, they are stories of the people who have survived and thrived in the wake of apocalypse. To others, these stories serve as an emotional resource that can empower communities to take action and protect the lifeways of past, present, and emerging Native peoples.

1   "Story of the Flood," Chickasaw Nation, https://www.chickasaw.net/Our-Nation/Culture/Beliefs/Story-of-the-Flood. Accessed November 22, 2022.

2   See *The Sons of the Wind* by D. M. Dolling, ed. (Norman: University of Oklahoma Press, 2000) for more on Lakota stories of creation.

3   Donald Bahr, Juan Smith, William Smith Allison, and Julian Hayden, *The Short, Swift Time of Gods on Earth: The Hohokam Chronicles* (Berkeley: University of California Press, 1994), http://ark.cdlib.org/ark:/13030/ft5z09p0dh/.

4   See Arthur Caswell Parker, *The Code of Handsome Lake, the Seneca Prophet* (London: Forgotten Books, 2008) for more about the religious reformer's teachings and prophecies.

5   For more about Wovoka's teachings, see Michael Hittman, *Wovoka and the Ghost Dance* (Lincoln: University of Nebraska Press, 1997).

6   Micheline E. Pesantubbee, "When the Earth Shakes: The Cherokee Prophecies of 1811–12," *American Indian Quarterly* 17, no. 3 (Summer 1993).

7   For a more complete account of Native American stories of the Great Deluge, see Gary Varner, *Water from the Sacred Well* (Raleigh, NC: Lulu Press, 2010).

8   Conversation with Clifford E. Trafzer, November 2022.

9   See Paul G. Zolbrod, *Diné Bahané: The Navajo Creation Story* (Albuquerque: University of New Mexico Press, 1987) for a narrative poetic version of the story.

10   See Clifford E. Trafzer, *Grandmother, Grandfather, and Old Wolf: Tamánwit Ku Súkat and Traditional Native American Narratives from the Columbia Plateau* (East Lansing: Michigan State Press, 1998).

WINDOW TO THE FUTURE

2050 TOTEMIC TRIBUNALS: Legal Standing of the Natural World

Gerald Vizenor

"Totemic animals are granted the same inalienable rights of
presence and liberty as Natives," declared Justice Molly Crèche.
"Monotheism promised a course of absolution, but mercenary
trappers and predatory hunters are never entitled to immunity
with the backchat of a single creator."

Justice Crèche was clever to name the most familiar totems of
bears, wolves, otters, sandhill cranes, and eagles in traditional
Native stories. Still, she honored the legal standing of many
totemic associations, spiders, bats, and moccasin flowers to
nurture a sense of justice in the natural world.

Yet creative totemic justice would never absolve the murder of
animals in the continental fur trade; the fish, amphibians, and
ducks poisoned in rivers and lakes; or the mass slaughter of
birds for hat feathers.

"Choose a beaver, bear, meadowlark, praying mantis,
water ousel, firefly, or salamander and that creative
association has legal standing in totemic court,"
pronounced Justice Crèche.

The standing of trees, water, coyotes, and other creatures was
considered in earlier legal arguments, and environmental laws
might have granted standing of some totemic associations, but
the sworn testimony for dolphins, prairie dogs, and other totems
was decried as romantic or denied as hearsay in federal courts.

Justice Crèche declared Native liberty and totemic standing
more than forty years ago as a judicial principle in the new
Constitution of the White Earth Nation in Minnesota. However,
the resolve of totemic justice, continental liberty, and the
standing of natural associations were much easier to manage in
a virtual constitution once the federal treaty reservations were
terminated by the plenary power of the United States Congress.

The ethos of totemic standing was maintained as a virtual canon
that honored the character of Native associations in natural motion.
Regular sessions of the Native court in the first few years were
formally conducted and broadcast on the internet from a rickety
houseboat on Lake of the Woods. The totemic court cruises were
close to the international border to avoid federal agents and
cultural predators, and the winter court sessions were transmitted
from a converted school bus near Columbus, New Mexico.

The totemic court continued a Native egalitarian constitution
in exile, and at the same time carried out the bygone ethos
and entente cordiale of *La Grande paix de Montréal*. More than

a thousand representatives from thirty-nine Native nations were present at the actual Great Peace of Montreal that ended the Beaver Wars on August 4, 1701. That extraordinary peace treaty has never been terminated, and at last the animals have standing in totemic court. The beaver and other animals were sacrificed for peltry in the fur trade wars between predatory Natives and greedy colonial empires.

"Come closer, listen to the Native heart stories about the deadly crack of totemic bones, the shadows of bloody animals, and count out loud the seasons of shame over peltry stacked in huge canoes by the coureur de bois and voyageurs, the gory fur trade and brutal treasure of empires," Justice Crèche proclaimed on World Animal Day.

Justice Crèche webcast a session of the totemic court late one autumn night to hear testimony that honored the legal standing of coywolves, hoary bats, and spiders as new Native associations.

Harlan Douleur created the spider totems and testified that his Native blood once ran very thin because of medications and federal dictates of blood quantum. He praised the constitution and the prudence of the court that honored Native totems and related how he sat on the screen porch and watched spiders build and repair webs during his long recovery from cancer. "Spiderwebs are intricate and shimmer in the morning light, a beautiful scene as thin as my blood," he testified in court. "A perfect web of Native spirit and totemic memory."

The desecration of sacred places, climate change, poisoned rivers, famine, forever chemicals in the blood and brain, zoonotic diseases, and deceits of environmental protection laws were the outcome of nationalism, greedy and coercive toxic enterprises, and the fascist empires of commerce. Some Native traditionalists envisioned that animals had circulated zoonotic pathogens as vengeance, and the global pandemics were justice for the ancient fur trade.

Thousands of Natives and others followed sessions of the totemic court on the internet, and some were rightly inspired to nominate esoteric spores, microbes, and subatomic particles that had never been considered as totemic associations.

Dwindle Browne graciously presented furry molds as a totemic association. The testimony over mildew, mold, must, and decay was webcast in the extreme heat of the summer, and most of the testimony was against the standing of molds. "Mold already has too much standing in my house," shouted one listener.

Dwindle related in totemic court with no obvious sense of Native irony that "molds are with us for a good reason, molds are in the air, and molds are the gentle motion of our natural decay. Natives have never been without the totemic association of furry molds."

Justice Crèche declared several weeks later that the strains and species of molds were too diverse for totemic standing, but petitions for specific species of molds, such as *Penicillium camemberti*, the great mold of Camembert and Brie cheeses; *Pencillium roqueforti*, the mold of Roquefort, Stilton, and Danish Blue; and *Pencillium chrysogenum*, the overused antibiotic, would be considered for standing in the Native totemic court.

Justice Crèche was aware that standing for specific molds would only encourage Natives to petition for zoonotic pathogens, precious minerals, vines, lichen, algae, and other autotropic plants, and the totemic court had already provided totemic standing for *Zophobas morio*, or the superworm that devours polystyrene. The ordinary fieldstone boulders secured totemic standing because the Native trickster created relations from heated boulders that burst into millions of stories.

Natives who testified for totemic animal rights heard the Justice repeat many times a selection from *The Silence of Animals* by John Gray. "The distance between human and animal silence is a consequence of the use of language," wrote Gray. "Humans cannot help seeing the world through the veil of language."

Justice Crèche paused and reminded the petitioners that "totemic associations are not hearsay or shrouds of testimony, and some justices and philosophers create uneasy reasons for silence because they never heard a Native dream song or totemic heart story."

A Long Time Ago in the Final Frontier: Picturing Indigenous Futurism through *Star Wars* and *Star Trek*

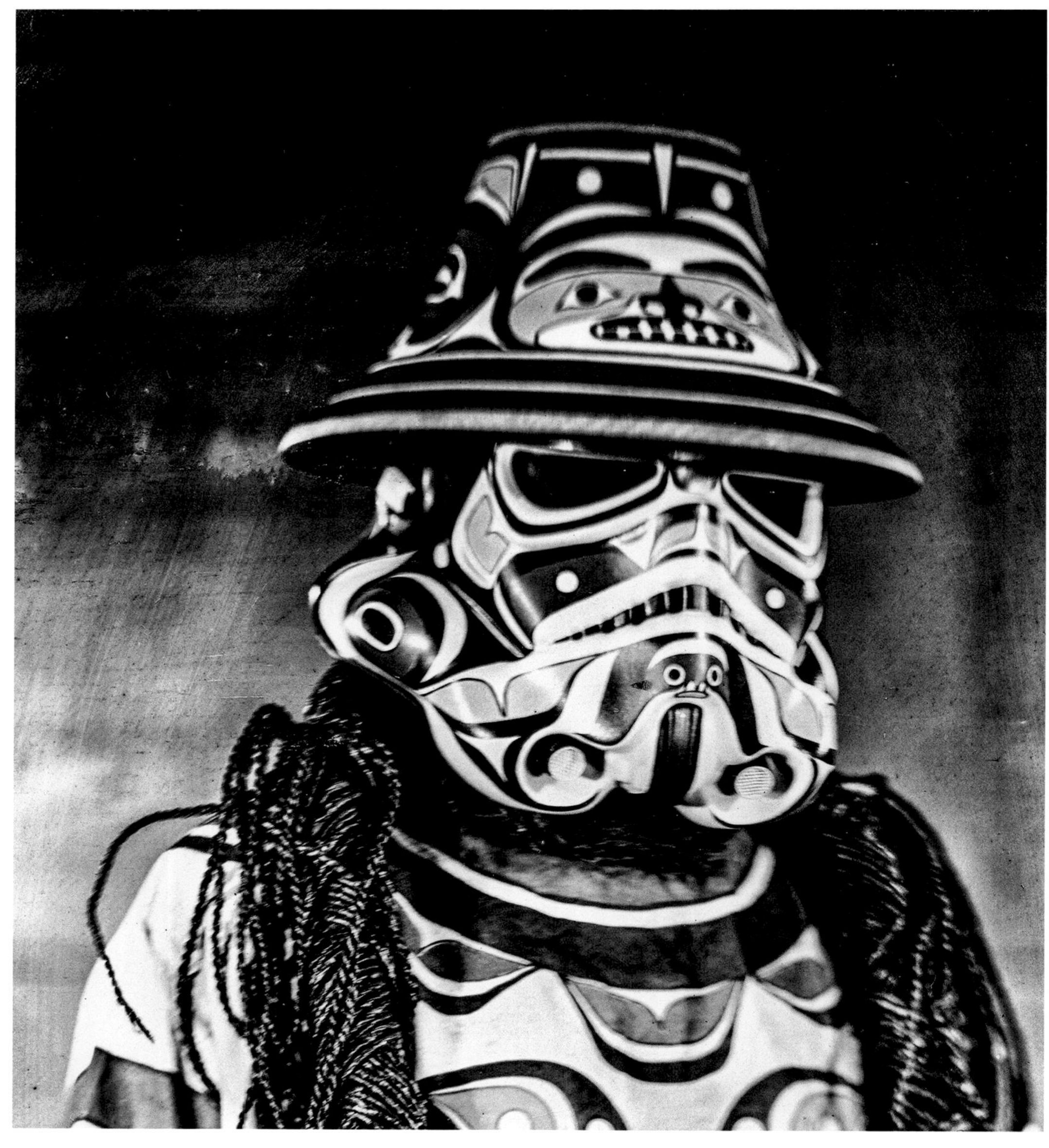

Matthew Ryan Smith

In *The Empire Strikes Back*, Yoda offers Luke Skywalker guidance:
"Concentrate . . . feel the Force flow [. . .] Through the Force,
things you will see. Other places. The future . . . the past."[1] It's a
notable scene. As Skywalker discovers the power of the Force,
he learns about time as an abstract and diffuse expression,
similar to nonlinear time as discussed by scholar Grace Dillon and
central to the field of Indigenous Futurism. As defined by scholars
Henrietta Lidchi and Suzanne Newman Fricke:

> Indigenous Futurisms propose the enduring relevance of
> Indigenous thought, artistic practice and expression; they
> reconfigure the relationship between past, present and future
> presenting the relationship between these temporalities as
> entangled, compacted or cyclical, but *emphatically not linear*.[2]

These temporal qualities are present throughout the science
fiction and fantasy genres, which makes their tropes, themes,
and subject matter ready for critical scrutiny. *Future Imaginaries:
Indigenous Art, Fashion, Technology* marks how Indigenous
artists approach time as diffuse and irregular, as a critical point
of impact on the future.

The exhibition pictures how contemporary artists enmesh
Indigenous knowledge and worldviews with the past, present,
and future. The artists integrate their aesthetics with science
fiction narratives like *Star Trek* and *Star Wars* precisely because
they redress how the future might look, feel, and function; in
other words, the plasticity of time enacted in *Star Trek* and
Star Wars serves as an ideal template for conceptualizing
Indigenous Futurism and anticipating speculative trajectories
for Indigeneity. Take, for example, the prodigious wormholes in
Star Trek or the Force in *Star Wars*—both function as powerful
catalysts for thinking through the time concepts proposed for
Indigenous Futurism.

Indigenous Futurism endeavors to deconstruct Absolute Time
to distance itself from Western epistemology while considering
future possibilities for self-determination. But the abstraction
of chronological order is not new—it has existed for thousands
of years among Indigenous peoples across the earth. In
Anishinaabemowin, the Ojibway language, writer Eli Baxter
explains that *Ways-kuch* means "a long time ago" and doubles
as a measurement of time. "Time is experience," he says. "It is
not a number."[3] In South America, the Aymara of the Andes
locate the past and future geographically, where the past
resides in front and the future sits behind."[4] In this exhibition,
Jeffrey Gibson, Skawennati, and Virgil Ortiz, among other
artists, articulate that time needn't follow a linear sequence

of numbers or a conscious perception of change—their work is evidence that time can be isochronal, experiential, even typographical in nature.

Different systems of time can be found in scientific studies from the previous century. Albert Einstein's Theory of Relativity theorizes that space and time warp in the presence of enormous objects like the Sun or planets. So, in the judgment of Stephen Hawking, if space-time can be bent enough, time travel is wholly possible. Consequently, this necessitates a series of paradoxes to the linear course of history since the universe would then contain not one history but "every single possible history, each with its own probability."[5] Hawking helps ideate the potential for unraveling the spatial, temporal, and experiential constructions of space-time while simultaneously pushing back against the generalization that Western concepts of time are exclusively sequential, flat, and one-dimensional. Of course, if that were true, films like *Back to the Future, Bill & Ted's Excellent Adventure*, and *X-Men: Days of Future Past* simply wouldn't exist. This is not to say, however, that Indigenous science and quantum physics are homogenous.

The dynamical systems of quantum physics express that time reflects the universe's perpetual state of subatomic chaos. As early as 1920, the Copenhagen Interpretation posed by physicist Niels Bohr outlines that quantum particles (electrons per se) exist *in all possible states at the same time*, thus defying linear time and the nature of objective reality itself. More recently, Western theoretical frameworks like String Theory or the Many-Worlds Theory have unraveled our understanding of Absolute Time. Still, for Professor Leroy Little Bear, developments in quantum physics may find consistencies with Indigenous science but remain firmly disconnected at their core:

In quantum physics, they talk about subatomic particles and Summa, whereas in Blackfoot, for instance, everything is about *energy waves*. We can go so far to say that, when we really examine those energy waves, they are all about what we would refer to and translate as *spirit*.[6]

Is reconciling Western science with Indigenous spirituality impossible? For Little Bear, at least, it appears so. And this is a fundamental reason why Indigenous Futurism remains at odds with Western theories of knowledge—the latter continually fails to lend credence to spirituality and experience as legitimate and reasoned sources of knowledge and truth. Yet as Baxter, Little Bear, and others make plain, these previously ignored forces hold the potential to reconfigure how time and space are understood.

In *Beyond Settler Time*, Mark Rifkin unpacks the synchronization of North American Indigenous peoples within empirical notions of time, governance, and sovereignty. For Rifkin, "Rather than approaching time as an abstract, homogeneous measure of universal movement along a singular axis, we can think of it as plural, less as a temporality than *temporalities*."[7] The ultimate outcome, what the author calls temporal sovereignty, reconceives Indigenous conceptions of time in a way that makes room for personal experience and transformation "in [their] struggles over Indigenous landedness, governance, and everyday socialities."[8] Put another way, Indigenous peoples' relationship with time has been entrenched in the authoritarian system of European colonialism and all this entails, from the signing of treaties down to the experience of seconds in a minute. Yet Rifkin fails to mention Hawking in his book, let alone Dillon, focusing instead on rebuking outmoded theories like Einstein's Theory of Relativity, which has consistently been amended to consider new research in quantum theory, artificial intelligence, the multiverse, and more. Nevertheless, in questioning the paragon of time so that it can be perceived *rhizomatically* instead of linearly—nodes connected to other nodes in unpredictable and nonhierarchical lines of flight[9]— Hawking and Rifkin manifest some of Dillon's early objectives for Indigenous Futurism. It is here that time, space, and history prompt new theories of the past, present, and future.

While some artists are attracted to the time concepts presented in *Star Trek* and *Star Wars*, others are drawn to their profoundly *relational* themes and subject matter, which mirror historical atrocities inflicted on Indigenous peoples and communities. The archetypes in these franchises project a fantastical tomorrow in deep space that is, regrettably, embedded in humanity's historical reality. Take, for instance, allusions to Nazi Germany in *Star Wars*, where Imperial stormtroopers share their name with Hitler's elite troops, or how the rise of Emperor Palpatine mirrors Hitler's 1933 ascent to dictatorial power.[10] Filmmaker George Lucas also appropriated choreographed crowd scenes from Leni Riefenstahl's Nazi propaganda documentary, *Triumph of the Will*.

Likewise, *Star Trek* creator Gene Roddenberry was so troubled by the Cold War and the looming threat of nuclear annihilation that the original *Star Trek* television series imagined a multiethnic future striving for intergalactic peace.[11] *Star Wars* and *Star Trek* are efficacious because they exploit universal fears and historical events—genocide, nuclear war, disease, assassination, eugenics, authoritarianism, extinction, et cetera. As early as 1965, writer Susan Sontag reminds us that sci-fi films are not strictly about science, "they are about disaster."[12]

We need not look far in either franchise—the Death Star actualizes the nuclear holocaust of Princess Leia's home planet Alderaan, or the resource-hungry Cardassians carry out a genocide on Bajorans during the Occupation of Bajor.

Part of what makes these franchises resonate so profoundly is their sophisticated representation of the mechanisms of colonialism and empire. According to scholar Darren Lone Fight, "The idea of hokey religions, with ancient weapons attempting to resist an overwhelming imperial force has a kind of natural resonance for Indigenous people and our history with colonialism."[13] It can be argued, then, that many of the artists in *Future Imaginaries* picture the eternal differences between those whose strength comes from within, from the land, and who wield supernatural powers—the Force, Vulcan mind-melds, telepaths, or empaths—and those destructive forces on the other side typified on film by the Imperial Order or Borg, who violently suppress rebellion and extinguish planets with the press of a button. As the Borg, the ultimate colonizer, put it so succinctly: "Resistance is futile."[14]

Andy Everson's wearable sculpture, *Northern Warrior*, borrows from a prefabricated stormtrooper helmet and interjects Kwakwaka'wakw and Tlingit symbolism (pl. 24). The work surfaces several years later in a black-and-white archival photograph by photographer Will Wilson (pl. 23). This time, however, Everson dons the helmet and poses in tribal regalia. Strangely, the image insinuates that it was taken so extraordinarily remote in the past that even Everson's Indigenized stormtrooper has become a ghost of distant memory. Wilson's series also uses dry-plate photography, employed and narrativized by Edward S. Curtis in his twenty-volume photo series, *The North American Indian*, published between 1907 and 1930. In Curtis's then-urgent words, his pictures and information for "one of the great races of mankind, must be collected at once or the opportunity will be lost."[15] In response, Wilson spotlights Curtis's failure to position Indigenous communities as extinct by working with the dry-plate glass negative—Curtis's own documentation technique—in a slamming rebuttal to declare otherwise. It's a strategic déjà vu that flips the weapon of historical disinformation and misrepresentation on its head. Thus, Wilson makes room for Indigenous subjectivities and representational agency in these photographs where there was once none.[16] It's also a poetic convergence of tribal mythology and ancestral history that permeates pop culture.

The incarnation of evil has been appropriated and reprogrammed for the purpose of good in Rory Wakemup's

Darth Chief, 2014 (fig. 1). Here we find the usurper Darth Vader recycled and made decadent into a sinister hipster sporting comfortable sneakers. His mission statement "Kill the Idiot, Save the Fan" is a cheeky take on Colonel Henry Pratt's ominous utterance from 1892, "Kill the Indian, Save the Man."[17] *Darth Chief* is a moniker for Darth Chief Mascot Hunter, the artist's satirical alter ego, who dismantles racist sports mascots, team names, and other appropriations of Indigenous culture in North America. Echoing Everson's enlightened stormtrooper, the now-liberated Darth Vader has become a messiah against the perils of xenophobia and ethnocentrism.

Ryan Singer's *They Have Both Coffees*, 2023, points to Indigenous stewardship of the land, animals, and natural resources by picturing a Tusken Raider, Jawas, and Navajo peoples (pl. 27). The composition displays the arid desert of Tatooine, the home planet of Luke and Anakin Skywalker. It's also markedly similar to the landscape surrounding Tuba City,

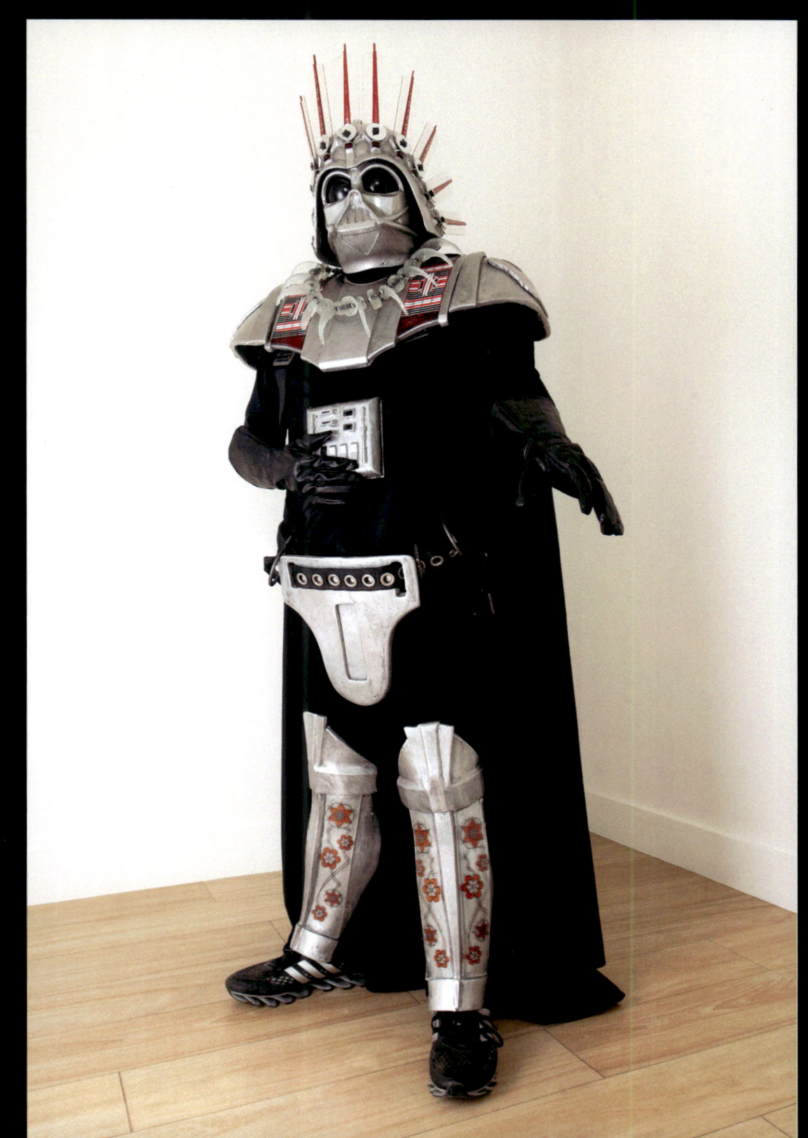

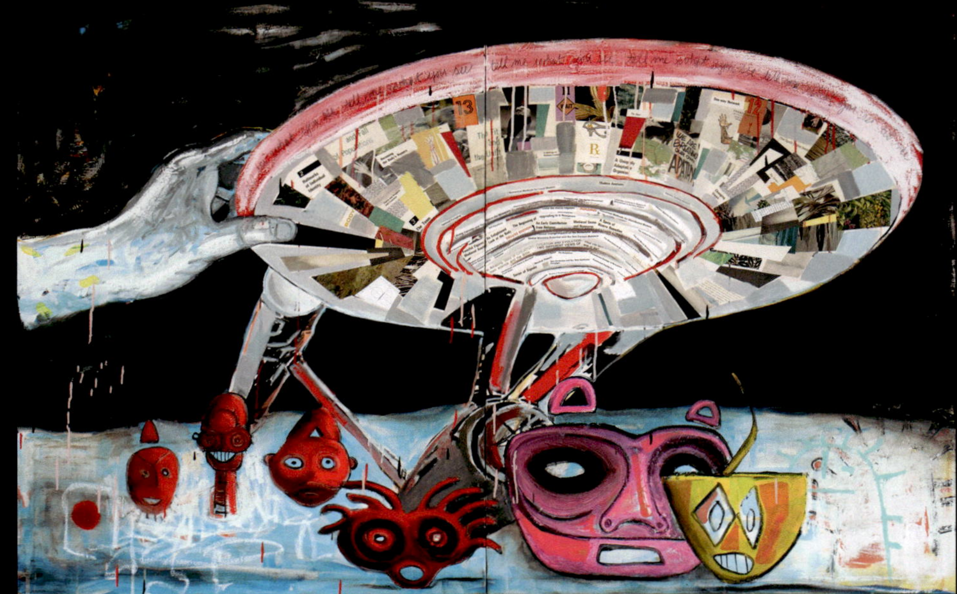

where Singer was raised, and the traditional lands of the Navajo people. At the top-left, two Jawas and a bantha stand opposite a butte, while on the top-right a Jawa queues in line with a Navajo woman and child for "Navajo tacos, fry bread, sno-cones, and pop." At the center, filling most of the composition, stands a Tusken Raider holding an untouched tri-colored sno-cone. In the first *Star Wars* series, Tusken Raiders were polarizing characters; on the one hand, they violently clash with the film's protagonist and hero Luke Skywalker in the Jundland Wastes, which immediately distances them emotionally from the viewer; on the other hand, they are also the Indigenous protectors of the land who oppose the territorial conquests of the space-colonists. The recent television series *The Book of Boba Fett* has done much to reinforce the sentiments of the latter while simultaneously humanizing a tribe that was once considered unmerciful and cruel. Additionally, the small writing on the taco stand reads "TÓ EI IINA WATER IS LIFE." It's difficult to picture water in a fantastical realm when it is critically scarce in the present reality—at the time of this writing, one in three homes on the Navajo Nation reserve do not have access to running water.[18] In a single painting, Singer conflates the past, present, and future into a coherent expression of the water crisis, one that is aggravated by reserve segregation and climate change. Once more, the mechanisms of nonlinear time are applied to communicate today's incomprehensible realities.

Neal Ambrose-Smith, Marie Watt, and Skawennati look to the *Star Trek* universe in comparable ways. In Ambrose-Smith's *The Case of the Peppered Moth*, 2013, the *Starship Enterprise NCC-1701-C* from the 1966 series is pictured alongside text, tribal iconography, and pop culture references to interpose

Indigeneity into a franchise that historically underrepresented or misrepresented Indigenous peoples and cultures (fig. 2). While the foundational ethic of the original *Star Trek* is one that operates as an arbiter of peace and justice in the known universe rather than as a war machine, the series was ultimately of its time and often fell short in its stereotyping of Indigenous cultures, sexualization of women, and more. In this sense, Ambrose-Smith's work strives to make peace and hope synonymous with the future. Conversely, the work's title refers to recent evidence that peppered moths—typically white and black—underwent an extreme genetic mutation during the Industrial Revolution in England. Due to the thick dark soot from coal-fired furnaces encroaching on their habitat, their pigment swiftly metamorphosed to black to improve their camouflage, increasing the likelihood of their continuance.

> Archetypal themes of adaptation, resilience, and survival apply to peppered moths as much as to narratives surrounding the *Starship Enterprise*'s cosmic exploits and Indigenous peoples under colonial rule. As a work of collage, *The Case of the Peppered Moth* is grounded in a systematic process that inherently demands the passage of time in physical space. But its subject matter also harkens back (and forth) from genetic mutation, magazine advertisements, tribal iconography, handwritten text, sci-fi fantasy, and more; even the *Enterprise* itself symbolizes the retreat into deep space or light-speed flight to faraway worlds. Ambrose-Smith's literal and metaphorical confluence of space-time into a singular expression closes in on the Native slipstream that Dillon hypothesizes. It was formulated at the moment when physicists were articulating the multiverse, parallel universes, and the Many-Worlds Theory, ideas that reflected historical Anishinaabe science and storytelling. In the Native slipstream, space and time are perceived as indistinguishable from each other and flow together as one interrelated subject "like currents in the same navigable stream."[19]

Seneca artist Marie Watt also introduces the original *Starship Enterprise* piloted by James T. Kirk into her textile work. *Trek (Pleiades)*, 2014, combines reclaimed wool blankets with satin binding, thread, and embroidery floss (pl. 32). Its patterned details emphasize the appearance of nine diamond-like structures found on a Native American basket. Correspondingly, the nine brightest stars of the constellation Pleiades derive their name from the Seven Sisters of Greek mythology, who were transformed into stars by Zeus to avoid the hunter Orion's unwanted advances. In Australia, there exists a comparable reading of the stars. In the Warlpiri story of the Seven Sisters

Dreaming, an ancestral entity taking the form of man falls in love with the seven sisters and continues to pursue them on Earth, so they leap into the night sky of Western Australia, where he follows closely behind as the star at the base of the Big Dipper. *Trek (Pleiades)* honors a close friend of Watts, the late Warlpiri artist Alma Nungarrayi Granites, who painted a monumental series founded on the Seven Sisters mythology. To this end, *Trek (Pleiades)* is an act of remembrance—her living memorial.

Watt writes that her textile is inspired by lengthy voyages and modern space travel, each intersecting time and space, the historical and contemporary, the real and mythical.[20] Certainly, the original *Starship Enterprise* emblematizes the spirit of adventure and exploration as it warps space-time to discover the galaxy's edges and carve out the limits of human potential. We know that stars are laden with meaning and observing them in the night sky can shock the ego. They remind us of our insignificance in the larger universe and connect us to the divine, whatever that may be, because we are made of the same elements. These atomic properties that compose our bodies and everything we see around us are said to be created billions of years ago during the big bang, in stars themselves, and stars' collapse into supernovas. If this is true, then our actual age doesn't begin at birth; it began 13.8 billion years ago. Every human being is a time traveler, a kind of spaceship.

If the *Starship Enterprise* and interstellar spacecraft like it— *Voyager, Home One, Millennium Falcon*—function as vessels or

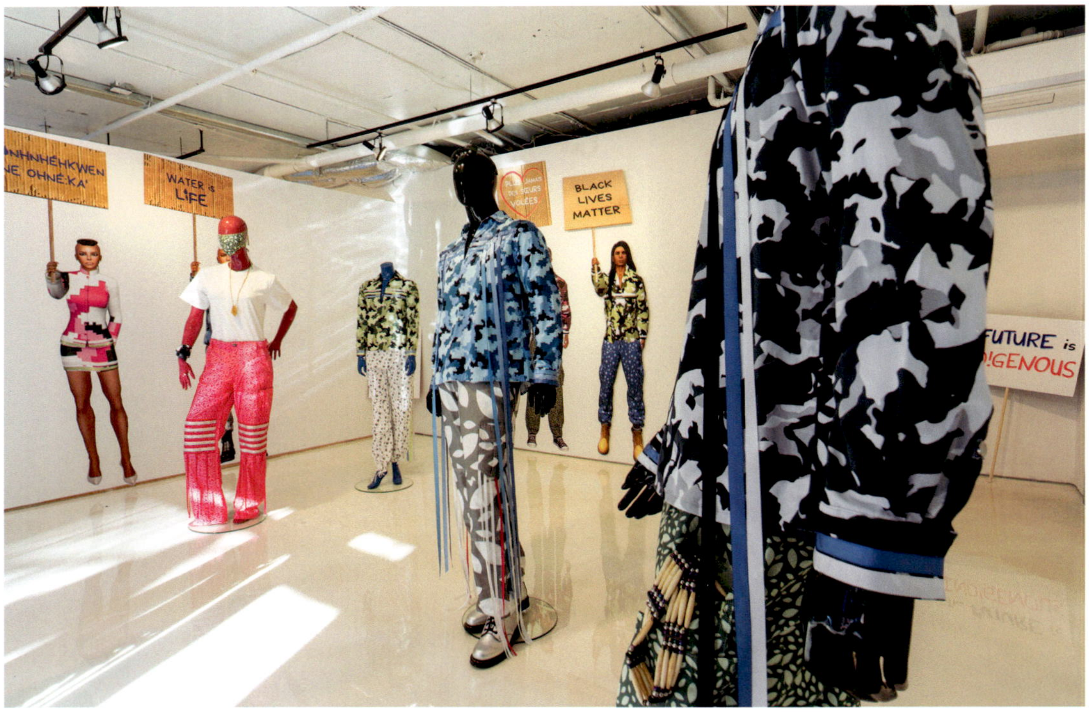

Fig. 3. Installation view of *C&C: IRL* and *Calico & Camouflage: Activist Avatars* by Skawennati from the exhibition, *Calico & Camouflage: Demonstrate*, at ELLEPHANT, October 28, 2020–January 5, 2021. Courtesy of the artist. Photography by Naor Toledano

veritable containers of cultural knowledge, then there might be
an unacknowledged reason why some artists are drawn to these
sci-fi franchises. An essay by scholar Alexandra Kahsenni:io
Nahwegahbow (Anishinaabe and Kanien'kehá:ka) reads:

> As Native people, when we think about our belongings—things
> that are made by our hands, minds, and voices—we are never
> really just thinking about them as things. They are, rather,
> meaningful objects, songs, stories, and practices that have the
> ability to contain, hold, and transmit memory, nourishment and
> sustenance across time and space. Metaphorically, they are
> always vessels.[21]

What is the relationship between the conceptualization of
vessels forwarded by Nahwegahbow and the omnipresence
of space vessels in Indigenous Futurism? One might argue
that both vessels function pragmatically and metaphorically,
as autonomous aesthetic objects and cultural bearers of
knowledge and memory. Following this logic, the past, present,
and future are bound together in a trilogy of symbolic meanings.

Skawennati references *Star Trek* in her series *Calico &
Camouflage*, not through spacecraft per se, but through avatars
(fig. 3). Skawennati's personal avatar, xox, is printed on adhesive
vinyl stickers and placed in gallery spaces alongside other
avatars that hold signs stating, for example, "RESISTANCE IS
FERTILE." Portraits of xox are constructed and later captured
in virtual environments. These machinimagraphs, as they are
called, connect the physical body to the virtual body in a kind of
cybernetic symbiosis. When Skawennati writes, "What I hope to
show is not that I want to be like my avatar or my avatar wants
to be like me but [that] we want to be like each other,"[22] she
articulates the advantages and shortcomings of avatars and
human beings; namely, how xox can never fall ill, will maintain its
appearance, and remain unaffected by age or gravity. On the
contrary, "Like Pinocchio and Mr. Data, [xox] wants to be real."[23]
Skawennati's virtual futurism takes flight into cyberspace,
where Indigenous-determined spaces mark new time and
space for political resistance. Since there are no reservations
in cyberspace or on other planets, avatars like xox determine
prospects of freedom and autonomy.

Skawennati's machinima, *Words Before All Else*, 2022, features
xox once again, this time reciting the *Ohen:ton Karihwatehkwen*
(Thanksgiving Address) to viewers in three languages:
Kanien'kéha (Mohawk), French, and English. The Thanksgiving
Address is historically recited at ceremonial gatherings or
during morning prayer, whereby the speaker acknowledges

Their gratefulness for the Creator and life itself. *Part I* begins with the verse, "We bring our minds together as one, as we give thanks for the people. Now our minds are one." These statements promote an economy of connectivity, inclusion, and acceptance between all living things in the exhibition space and beyond. Even so, the presence of xox engenders a radical shift in the mechanism of address by the interlocutor during the Thanksgiving Address, from human-to-human to avatar-to-human. Not only does this signify a dramatic transition from cultural memory to digital memory, it also questions the role and function of prayer, ceremony, and interpersonal communication in the physical world (and throughout cyberspace).[24] *Words Before All Else* is both of its time and profoundly visionary, bridging the past with the future in an instant, revolutionizing how oral traditions can take on new meaning in the cybernetics of the twenty-first century.

When Yoda first instructs Luke Skywalker how to harmonize with the Force, Skywalker quickly becomes distressed when he has a vision of his friends. While seeing the past and the future together, Skywalker is called into the present moment. "Always in motion is the future," Yoda says. The morphology of the past, present, and future into an abstracted expression is a cardinal trait of the Force as much as it is for Indigenous Futurism. Without the burden of chronological order, of Absolute Time, there is space to conceptualize the gradations of what experience, memory, and aesthetics can look like. There is also room to mull over expressions of spirituality found in cultures like the Blackfoot that may better explain the connectivity between atomic mechanisms in the universe. *Star Trek* and *Star Wars* play a fundamental role in this undertaking. In these films, we see rebellion against imperial crimes, the divine strength of righteous individuals, and the transcendent energies that bind beings together across the cosmos.

1   *Star Wars, Episode V: The Empire Strikes Back*. 1980. Directed by George Lucas. 20th Century Studios.

2   Henrietta Lidchi and Suzanne Newman Fricke, "Future History: Indigenous Futurisms in North American Visual Arts," *World Art* 9, no. 2 (2019): 100–101. Emphasis added.

3   Eli Baxter, *Aki-Wayn-Zih: A Person as Worthy as the Earth* (Montreal: McGill-Queen's University Press, 2021), 28.

4   Nathan Bierma, "South America's Aymara Put the Future Behind Them," *Chicago Tribune*, July 12, 2006, https://www.chicagotribune.com/2006/07/12/south-americas-aymara-put-future-behind-them/.

5   Stephen Hawking, "Space and Time Warps," 1999, https://www.hawking.org.uk/in-words/lectures/space-and-time-warps.

6   Leroy Little Bear, "Indigenous Knowledge and Western Science," Banff Events, 2015, https://www.youtube.com/watch?v=JeNnOZTk440. Emphasis added.

7   Mark Rifkin, *Beyond Settler Time: Temporal Sovereignty and Indigenous Self-Determination* (Durham, NC, and London: Duke University Press, 2017), 2.

8   Ibid., x.

9   Gilles Deleuze and Felix Guattari, *A Thousand Plateaus: Capitalism and Schizophrenia*, trans., Brian Massumi (Minneapolis: University of Minnesota Press, 1987).

10 Christopher Klein, "The Real History That Inspired 'Star Wars,'" History.com, December 17, 2015, https://www.history.com/news/the-real-history-that-inspired-star-wars.

11 Yanis Khamsi, Gene Roddenberry, Tribute.ca, 2009, https://www.tribute.ca/inspiration/star-trek-iv-the-voyage-home/127/2239/.

12 Susan Sontag, "The Imagination of Disaster," quoted in *Liquid Metal: The Science Fiction Film Reader*, ed. Sean Redmond (London: Wallflower Press, 2004), 41.

13 Darren Lone Flight, "Colonialism and a Hopi Princess: Why *Star Wars* Resonates with Indigenous Audiences," Tribute.ca, 2009, https://www.cbc.ca/radio/unreserved/in-a-galaxy-far-far-away-exploring-star-wars-through-an-indigenous-lens-1.5420783/colonialism-and-a-hopi-princess-why-star-wars-resonates-with-indigenous-audiences-1.5422156.

14 *Star Trek: The Next Generation*, episode 5, Stardate 45854.2, "I, Borg," aired May 24, 1992, http://stng.36el.com/st-tng/episodes/223.html.

15 Edward S. Curtis, *The North American Indian*, ed. Fredrick Webb Hodge. Field research conducted under the patronage of J. Pierpont Morgan, Cambridge, Mass.

16 Will Wilson, "Artist Statement" (Winston-Salem, NC: Southeastern Center for Contemporary Art, 2022), https://secca.org/exhibition-detail.php?LinkId=307038195#:~:text=ARTIST%20STATEMENT,has%20never%20been%20without%20consequence.

17 Richard H. Pratt, "'Kill the Indian, Save the Man': Capt. Richard H. Pratt on the Education of Native Americans," History Matters, George Mason University, 1892, https://historymatters.gmu.edu/d/4929/.

18 "Water Week: Access to Clean Water," NPR, August 8, 2022, https://www.npr.org/2022/07/28/1114179334/water-week-access-to-clean-drinking-water.

19 Grace Dillon and Pedro Neves Marques," Taking the Fiction Out of Science Fiction: A Conversation about Indigenous Futurisms," *e-flux Journal*, no. 120 (September 2021), https://www.e-flux.com/journal/120/417043/taking-the-fiction-out-of-science-fiction-a-conversation-about-indigenous-futurisms/.

20 Marie Watt, *Trek (Pleiades)*, 2014, Marie Watt Studio, https://mariewattstudio.com/work/project/trek-pleiades-2014.

21 Alexandra Kahsenni:io Nahwegahbow. *Always Vessels* (Ottawa, ON: Carleton University Art Gallery, 2017), 5.

22 Matthew Ryan Smith, *Skawennati: From Skyworld to Cyberspace* (London, ON: McIntosh Gallery, 2019), 9.

23 Skawennati, "Dancing with Myself," Skawennati.com, 2023, https://www.skawennati.com/projects/dancing-with-myself/.

24 Smith, *Skawennati: From Skyworld to Cyberspace*, 3–4.

WINDOW TO THE FUTURE

Close Encounters of the Colonial Kind

Sonny Assu

Alien encounters are not new to Indigenous folk. We have, quite frankly, been battling aliens since time immemorial, since some idiot got lost looking for spices and thought he found India. Like you, I also have those colonial revenge fantasies. If I could go back in time and change something—sink those ships in the middle of the Atlantic, heck, blow them up big-budget Hollywood style before they even left the docks! Eat those pilgrims and conquistadors (assuming they'd be rather bland) as a Thanksgiving meal. Or just level with that ancestor who showed compassion back in the day.

> Cousin, don't help those fools. They will bring you nothing but heartbreak, death, and destruction.
> —Time-traveling Sonny

Then there is the paradox of it all: If going back in time were possible (cue Huey Lewis track), which space-time theory do we observe? One option is the singular timeline where we sink those boats, and this essay never gets written! Or the multiverse timeline, where an infinite number of parallel timelines would enable us to split from a singular point to form another universe within the multiverse itself, allowing us to live a life without "discovery" all the while knowing there is a universe out there that still gets hosed.

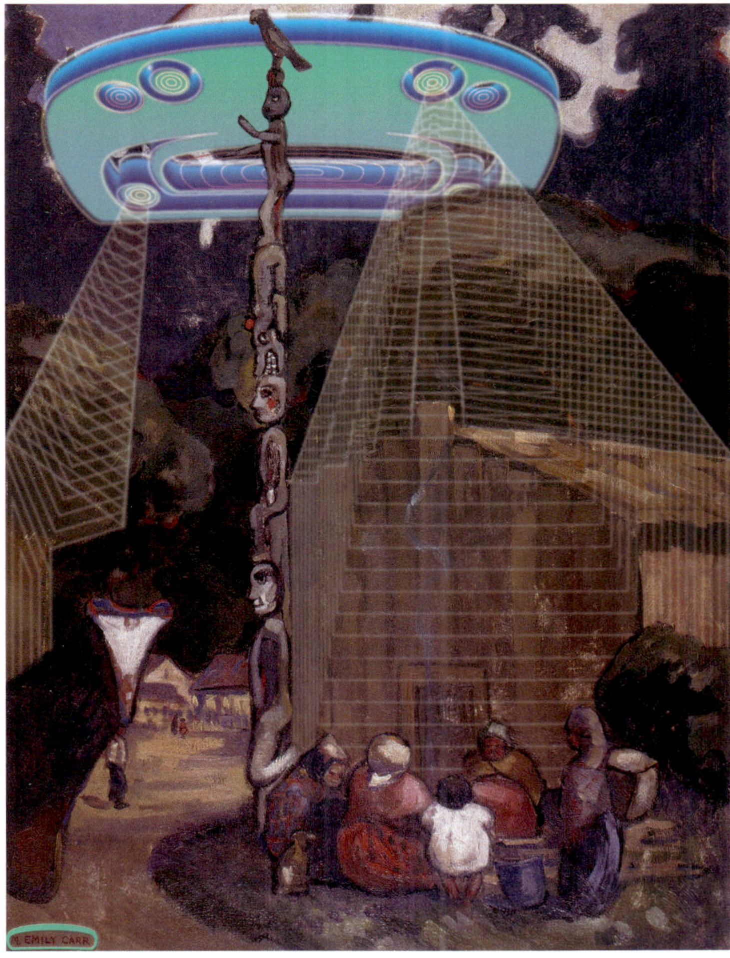

Fig. 1. Sonny Assu (Ligwiłda'xw of the Kwakwaka'wakw Nations), *Yeah . . . shit's about to go sideways. I'll take you to Amerind. You'll like it, looks like home*, 2016. Digital intervention on an Emily Carr painting (*Cape Mudge: An Indian Family with Totem Pole*, 1912). Archival pigment print, 22 × 29½ in. Courtesy of the artist and Equinox Gallery, Vancouver

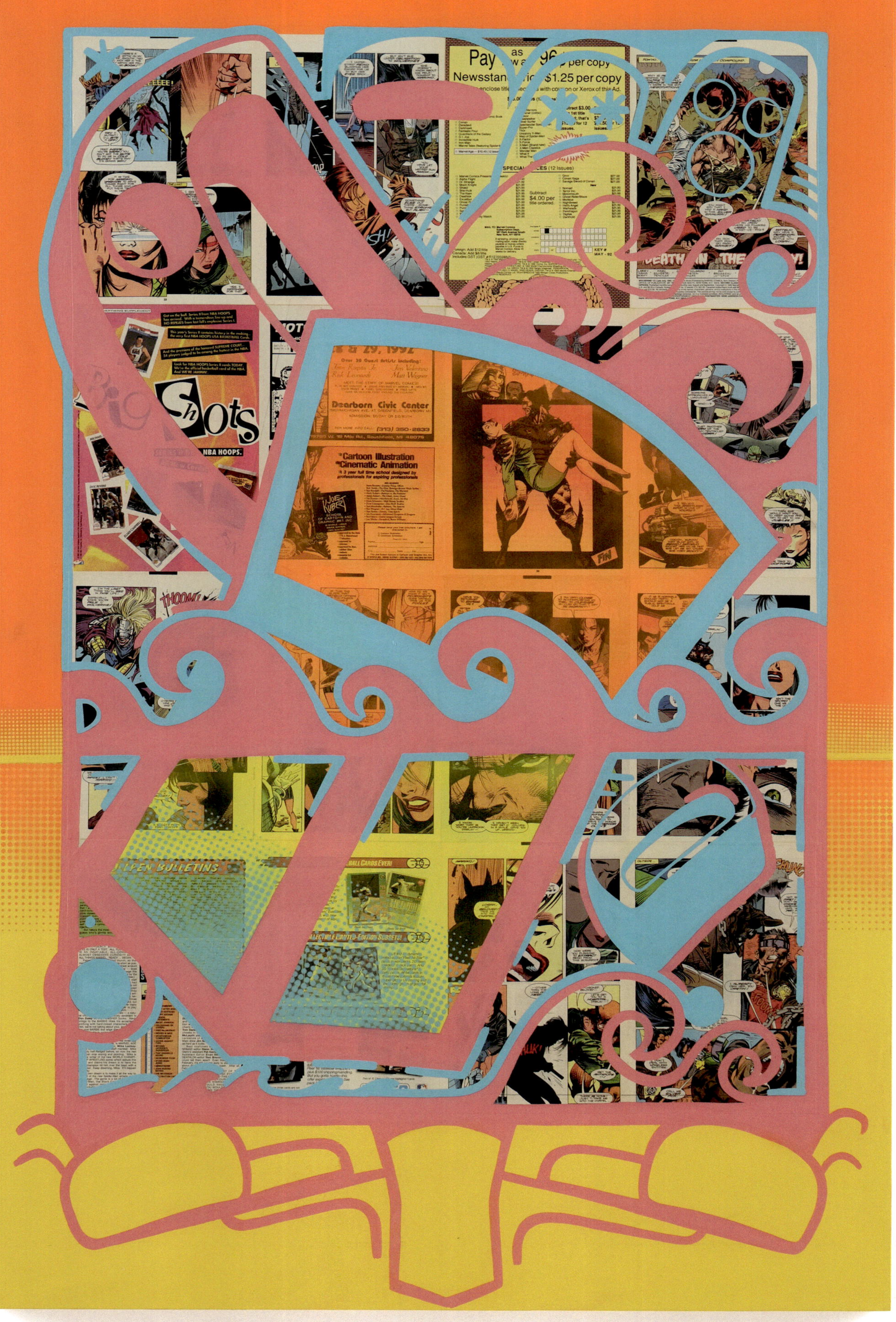

Adaptations of sci-fi, speculative theory, and pop culture are elements
of Indigenous Futurism that I have used in my practice over the
past twenty years. In the *Challenging Tradition* series, 2001–2006,
I merged Marvel's Spider-Man and other popular Super Heroes
with Kwakwaka'wakw iconography and continued to explore these
ideas in the *iDrum* series, 2005–2012, where I brought together the
formal qualities of the iPod by Apple (cutting-edge at the time) with
Indigenous formline iconography to offer contemporary interpretations
of the Kwakwaka'wakw mythos. In the ongoing series *Interventions on
the Imaginary*, begun in 2014, I confront the myth of the vanishing race
in Canadian landscape painting using digitized reproductions of works
by Emily Carr and integrating neon formline elements and references
to *Star Trek* and other science fiction fantasies. Finally, my most
recent body of work was inspired by my great-great-grandfather's
regalia. *Tempest*, 2023, is a modern-day Jacquard-woven Chilkat robe
that includes the grid pattern from the 1980s video game of the same
name I used to play at the arcade (pl. 33). Viewed through the lens of
Indigenous Futurism, *Tempest* offers insight into the transmission of
information and cultural knowledge through time and space.

The strength of Indigenous Futurism lies in its ability to reframe the
narratives and challenges of colonial constructs using the authentic voice
of Indigenous folk. In it, we are free to think and create in ways that are
uniquely our own, defiantly challenging outside assumptions of Indigeneity
while simultaneously challenging ourselves and our communities from
within. Art, music, writing, performance, and community actions such as
language revitalization, land and water reclamation, and understanding our
varied ceremonial or "traditional" lives are all part of the broader context
of Indigenous Futurism. It is an activist movement that embraces the
speculative aspect of Futurism and empowers us to free ourselves from
the confines of colonial subjugation through a lens of our own making. Filled
with the strength of our ancestors, we are breaking the colonial chains that
bind us to this singular instance of perceived reality.

Fig. 2. Sonny Assu (Ligwiłda'xw of the Kwakwaka'wakw
Nations), *Bigshot*, 2021. Acrylic paint, acrylic ink, acrylic
medium, and Marvel comic book pages on panel, 51 × 33 in.
Courtesy of the artist and Equinox Gallery, Vancouver

The Myths of My Descendants

Jason Edward Lewis

The future is exhausted. The future is exhausting. At least,
the nineteenth- and twentieth-century future. Shaped by the
three horsemen of white supremacy—patriarchy, colonialism,
and capitalism—those visions relied on a Manifest Destiny-
level sense of entitlement about who owned the future and
belonged there. Even shows like *Star Trek*, with its relatively
progressive politics and mixed-ethnicity cast, still had
three white guys in charge. And *Star Wars* had an easier
time imagining wild space magic than it did people of color
anywhere within twelve parsecs of our young white savior.

Unfortunately, we have to live in a world saturated by this
exhaustion. Dystopic futures are the norm in popular culture,
the energy and enthusiasm of the previous centuries' future
imaginaries[1] having collapsed due to the stubbornness with which
inequalities of all types continued to resist the magic wand of yet
another world-saving technology. No technology can bring about
utopia if the underlying culture is rotting at its core.

Culture matters to the kind of technology we develop. As
computer scientist D. Fox Harrel observes, "All technical
systems are cultural systems."[2] Current advanced
computational systems grow out of a Western context
structured to place the cultural values of Christian white men
at their center: anthropocentrism, patriarchy, and a willingness
to sacrifice the present in the belief that a better world lies
beyond.[3] Their desires have become the ground truth on
which such systems are built. The worlds desired by others
are ignored, overwritten, or pathologized.

The future has been colonized by a mindset that views the
world's entities—human and nonhuman—as a collection of
resources to be subjugated and exploited. As this perspective
became evermore intertwined with a technological teleology that
assumes that "more" and "newest" are better, we find ourselves
in a mainstream cultural landscape that continually serves up
dystopic future imaginaries in which advanced technologies work
wonders, but their benefits are hoarded by the few.

How do we create better futures where the technologies we
employ promote abundance for many rather than scarcity for all
but the 1%? Technology is the transformation of our knowledge
about the world into tools we can use to manage and shape our
existence within it. We have become accustomed to thinking
of technology as coincident with the digital, as advances in
computing power, algorithm design, and big data have made
astonishing advances across a breathtaking spectrum of uses
in a relatively short period.

But technologies come in all forms, and for Indigenous communities, part of the challenge is recognizing the technologies we have developed and refined over generations. Our languages are technologies. Our cultural practices are technologies. Our kinship protocols, particularly their ability to integrate other-than-humans into our relational web, are technologies. By understanding them as technologies, we can create connections between them and current computational practices, working from a position of strength and continuity to find novel approaches to integrate them.

But why should we do this? It opens us up to appropriation of our knowledges, and it risks having our knowledges warped in translation. These are significant potential pitfalls that can, understandably, make many skeptical of such engagements. However, adapting to new technologies and making them our own has ever been the case with Indigenous cultures,[4] as has sharing technologies we've developed in our communities with others.

Two decades into the twenty-first century, we can see how computational technologies are being woven into the fabric of our communities and cultures in the same way that electrical and digital technologies were in the twentieth century. With its increasing ubiquity, computation has slowly become a material out of which we fashion cultural expression and knowledge practices. Once we recognize this, how do we ensure that Indigenous peoples' existing technologies—languages, cultural practices, kinship protocols, processes for recognizing other-than-humans, et cetera—are woven into these new technological substrates with fidelity and integrity? How do we imagine these technologies working in the way we desire? How do we create them to benefit our communities?

One approach is to reconceptualize advanced technologies in terms of abundance.[5] An abundance mindset focuses on *regeneration*, or leaving more for future generations; *generosity*, or enabling and encouraging sharing with the other beings in our context; and *reciprocity*, or emphasizing that we are in a relationship with those beings that requires we sustain each other. Abundance embraces a diversity of knowledge, and the tools we create to instrumentalize those knowledges into practice to contribute to thriving networks of being in a particular place.[6] Abundance also signals "a plethora of futures,"[7] acknowledging that different communities might desire different futures and our technologies should be developed to support all of them.

We also must understand that advanced technologies are designed and built within complex choreographies of material constraints. This often means that they end up locally maximized for specific purposes and then remain stuck there because of the amount of investment that has been made rather than whether they provide the best solution over the long term. In other words, these technologies are highly contingent on factors that have very little to do with the best fit of the tool to purpose, particularly as the question of whose purpose is being served gets obscured by hubristic claims of creating technology that solves problems for all of humanity. Understanding such contingency allows us to dream about how we might otherwise structure these technologies.

Consider artificial intelligence (AI), a suite of technologies with profound consequences for our present moment and future. I believe Indigenous peoples need to engage seriously with AI both protectively and proactively. Protectively, because AI is fast becoming part of the core operating system of our world, and we are already seeing how it might follow so many other technologies in becoming a tool of exploitation, extraction, and eradication. We need to push back against that momentum by participating in mainstream AI research and development to make it more inclusive of other ways of conceiving intelligence and by building capacity within our communities to develop these technologies ourselves. Proactively, because many of our cultures have valuable insights into how to appropriately establish, maintain, and grow relationships with other-than-humans such as AI seems to be becoming. This positions us to contribute substantially to designing AI in ways that are better for everyone, not just Indigenous people.

This is no easy task. We must figure out how we can integrate and adapt existing advanced computational methods into Indigenous knowledge systems, develop new computational practices within Indigenous contexts to support the flourishing of Indigenous communities, and use the knowledge we generate to help guide the development of AI toward a more humane future. Beginning in 2013,[8] my writing on future imaginaries has sought to address how, in order to make things otherwise, we Indigenous peoples must first imagine otherwise. Venues showcasing Indigenous futurisms, such as the *Future Imaginaries* exhibition, help create spaces in which Indigenous peoples can do that work. They create avenues through which we can imagine futures that grow from the soil of our territories, express ourselves in the language of our ancestors, and align with our cultural protocols and communal values.

Kite and Devin Ronneberg's *Ínyan Iyé (Telling Rock)*, 2019, serves as an example of such imagining otherwise (pl. 44). The installation developed out of writing,[9] performance, and technical experiments examining Lakota understandings of nonhumans, our relationships to them, and the territories out of which they are made. Kite and Ronneberg explore how AI—here in the form of machine learning—can be brought into that circle of relations in a generous and reciprocal

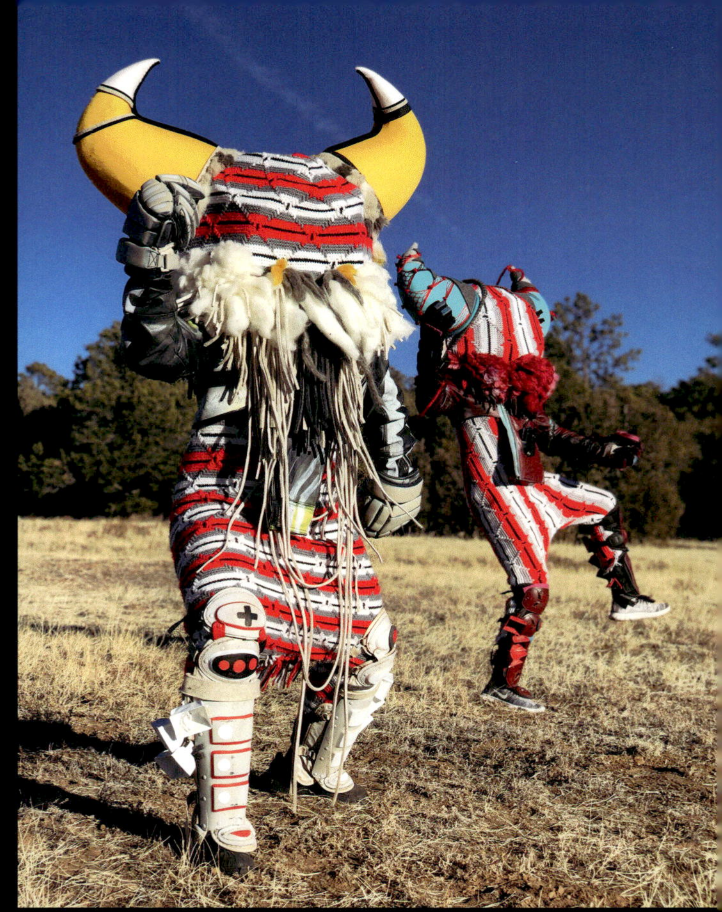

Fig. I. Cannupa Hanska Luger (Mandan/Hidatsa/Arikara/ Lakota), *Shadow holding shape to experience the energy of the sun* featuring *Muscle, Bone & Sinew* from the *Future Ancestral Technologies* project, 2021. Mixed media: ceramic, repurposed materials; single-channel video, 5:00 mins. Courtesy of the artist. Photography by Ginger Dunnill

way. In the installation, the visitor moves through a forest of hair braids descending from the ceiling, touching and twisting and raising them up and down, shaping a complex soundscape as the system learns from the visitor's actions. The work establishes an embodied dialogue between visitor and AI system within a visual, audio, and material environment expressive of Lakota knowledge practices. In so doing, it shows us futures that might be possible if we draw inspiration from Indigenous protocols to seriously consider the beinghood of AI, the type of relationship we might wish to develop with it as a fellow being, and the life-sustaining innovations that can come from co-creating with it.

Cannupa Hanska Luger's *Future Ancestral Technologies* artworks, 2018–present, traverse resonant territory, albeit with different emphases (fig. I). As the narrator says in a video component, *Shadow holding shape to experience the energy of the sun*: "All my relations is always something to recontextualize . . . what if [AI] could learn from a civilization that lives with the environment rather than capitalizes on it?" The series is a sprawling, expansive, energetic engagement with the continual process of how realities get translated into myths and how those myths reshape reality into something new. A significant aspect of the series is its focus on material culture—regalia, shelter, and craft—to provide deep texture to future imaginaries. These materials also establish continuities from past generations through the present and further into the future. They allow us to recognize the patterns our ancestors used to shape and hold meaning, and experiment with recontextualizing them for appropriate application to new technologies. The future is not all jet packs and warp drives. It's what people wear, make, eat, and speak every mundane day, with whom they are in relation, what they see on the bodies of the people around them and on the landscapes—country, urban, terrestrial, and galactic—they inhabit.

Kanaka Maoli knowledge activist Kamuela Enos reminds us, "We are the science fiction of our ancestors."[10] The converse is also true: we are the mythmakers of our descendants. How we embrace that role will fundamentally affect the world we bequeath to them. Will the technologies that permeate that future be tools that extend a legacy of exploitation and domination? Or will they be beings with whom we co-create along with our other-than-human relatives? We are writing the narratives now that will be told around the campfire seven generations hence. Let them be good stories. Let them be stories of abundance, filled with generosity and laughter, myths not of gods and monsters but of humans and nonhumans helping one another build miracles and wonders.

1   Jason Edward Lewis, "The Future Imaginary," in *Routledge Handbook of CoFuturisms*, ed. Bodhisattva Chattopadhyay, Grace Dillon, Isiah Lavender and Taryne Jade Taylor (New York: Routledge, 2023), 11–22, doi.org/10.4324/9780429317828.

2   D. Fox Harrell, *Phantasmal Media: An Approach to Imagination, Computation, and Expression* (Cambridge, MA: MIT Press, 2013), 345.

3   See Ruha Benjamin, *Race After Technology: Abolitionist Tools for the New Jim Code* (Cambridge, UK: Polity, 2019); Stephen Cave and Kanta Dihal, "The Whiteness of AI," *Philosophy & Technology* 33, no. 4 (December 2020): 685–703; Yarden Katz, *Artificial Whiteness: Politics and Ideology in Artificial Intelligence* (New York: Columbia University Press, 2020); and Safiya Noble, *Algorithms of Oppression: How Search Engines Reinforce Racism* (New York: New York University Press, 2018).

4   Candice Hopkins, "Making Things Our Own: The Indigenous Aesthetic in Digital Storytelling," *Leonardo* 39, no. 4 (August 2006): 341–344.

5   See Abundant Intelligences, https://abundant-intelligences.net.

6   See Mary Tuti Baker, "Waiwai (Abundance) and Indigenous Futures," in *Routledge Handbook of Postcolonial Politics*, ed. Olivia U. Rutazibwa and Robbie Shilliam (London and New York: Routledge, 2018), 22–31; Kamuela Enos and Miwa Tamanaha, "Ownership as Kinship: Restoring the Abundance of Our Ancestors," *Nonprofit Quarterly* (Summer 2022): 112–119; and Candace Fujikane, *Mapping Abundance for a Planetary Future: Kanaka Maoli and Critical Settler Cartographies in Hawai'i* (Durham, NC: Duke University Press, 2021).

7   Ziauddin Sardar, "The Problem of Futures Studies," in *Rescuing All Our Futures: The Future of Futures Studies*, ed. Ziauddin Sardar (Westport, CT: Praeger, 1999), 9–18.

8   Jason Edward Lewis, "The Future Imaginary," TEDxMontreal, 2013, https://www.youtube.com/watch?v=cwkyaUALKJc.

9   Jason Edward Lewis, Noelani Arista, Archer Pechawis, and Suzanne Kite, "Making Kin with the Machines," *Journal of Design and Science* no. 3.5 (July 16, 2018).

10   Kamuela Enos, "Working Collectively to Restore Ancestral Abundance," TEDxManoa, University of Hawaii, Manoa, October 5, 2012, https://youtu.be/w8iou8Rchqc?si=Z_3NAGolVr7oU-Kj.

WINDOW TO THE FUTURE

Graphic Novel:
Chinigchinich Creation Myth

Weshoyot Alvitre

Indigenous Futurisms, a term coined by scholar Grace Dillon, is "a movement consisting of various forms of media that express Indigenous perspectives of the future, the past, and the present within the context of science fiction."[1] These views manifest in interpretations of Indigenous knowledge, traditional stories, historical and contemporary politics, and cultural realities.

My contribution to *Future Imaginaries* recontextualizes the Tongva creation myth of Chinigchinich. This story initially appears in Western ethnography, documented through the manuscripts of the nineteenth-century Franciscan friar Gerónimo Boscana, who intended to chronicle in detail the religion of the Native community that made up the population at the Mission San Juan Capistrano (which included the neighboring tribes who also shared knowledge and belief systems rooted in similar oral histories) to convert them to Christianity more easily. The original manuscripts have been printed numerous times since their production, from their inclusion in Alfred Robinson's *Life in California* in 1846 to a limited art print book produced in 1933 by Fine Arts Press. They have also undergone various reprints, including the Smithsonian (as part of the Smithsonian Miscellaneous Collections) in 1934, the Southwest Museum[2] in 1969, and most recently by Malki-Ballena Press in 1978 and 2005.

In 1933, Fine Arts Press, Santa Ana, published a revised and annotated version with extensive notations by anthropologist and linguist John Peabody Harrington. This rare hardcover from 1933 also included lithographs by non-Native artist Jean Goodwin, who was predominantly a muralist contracted by the Works Progress Administration (the lithographs were also included in the hardcover reprints from Malki-Ballena Press). While these images are treasured and reproduced often, the visual representation methods carry a biblical overtone and add another layer of separation between the oral history, cultural connections, and traditions of those who followed Chinigchinich belief.

I wanted to re-illustrate these images for many years. By revisioning the original lithographs from the 1933 edition, I have begun to reclaim our story to help reinform and represent it through my familiarity with our ceremonies. I have also provided a contemporary representation of our creation story, which has existed since time immemorial, as We have, to support the revival of and familiarity with this narrative. I deliberately used a limited color palette to nod to the 1933 edition, which has become a rare and hard-to-find edition, often outside our community's reach.

Chinigchinich was born after the creator of the world, Quiot, grew sick and perished, rising into the sky as the Moon. He was a lawgiver who taught our people guidelines of strict adherence that reflect our values, reciprocity, ties to the land, and responsibilities to our people and beyond. Chinigchinich came down to our people from the stars, and returned there after his death. While this story is as old as our people, it also can be seen through a modern sci-fi lens in its embrace of evolving stories and truths about our origins that We as people traditionally believe and have passed down through generations. It also touches on cyclical time frames, connections to star stories, and universal truths of our people who followed astronomical patterns and narratives long before Western science and technology documented these phenomena. The presentation of our creation story through this visual medium is not only a reminder and a reinforcement but also a current living reintroduction and continuation of our narrative, which makes it timeless in that it continues from the past and present into future revitalizations of our people and our survivance.

1   Grace Dillon and Pedro Neves Marques, "Taking the Fiction Out of Science Fiction: A Conversation about Indigenous Futurisms," *e-flux Journal*, no. 120 (September 2021), https://www.e-flux.com/journal/120/417043/taking-the-fiction-out-of-science-fiction-a-conversation-about-indigenous-futurisms/.

2   The Southwest Museum, formally the Southwest Museum of the American Indian, is currently under the Autry Museum's stewardship. The 1969 reprint was financed by the museum's Frederick Webb Hodge Anniversary Publication Fund due to the publication's value to society concerning public knowledge of California Indians. James R. Moriarty, *Chinigchinix: An Indigenous California Indian Religion* (Los Angeles: Southwest Museum, 1969).

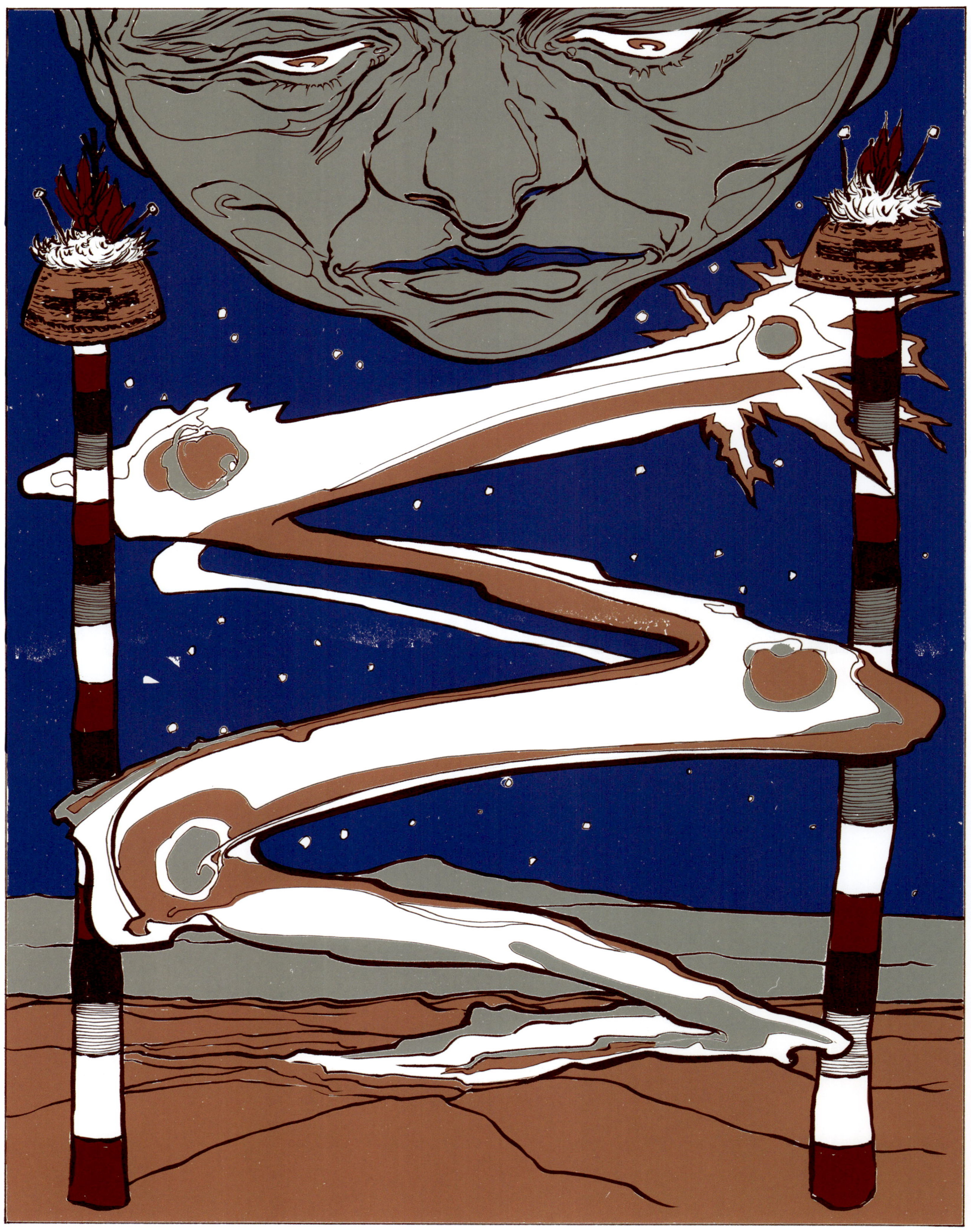

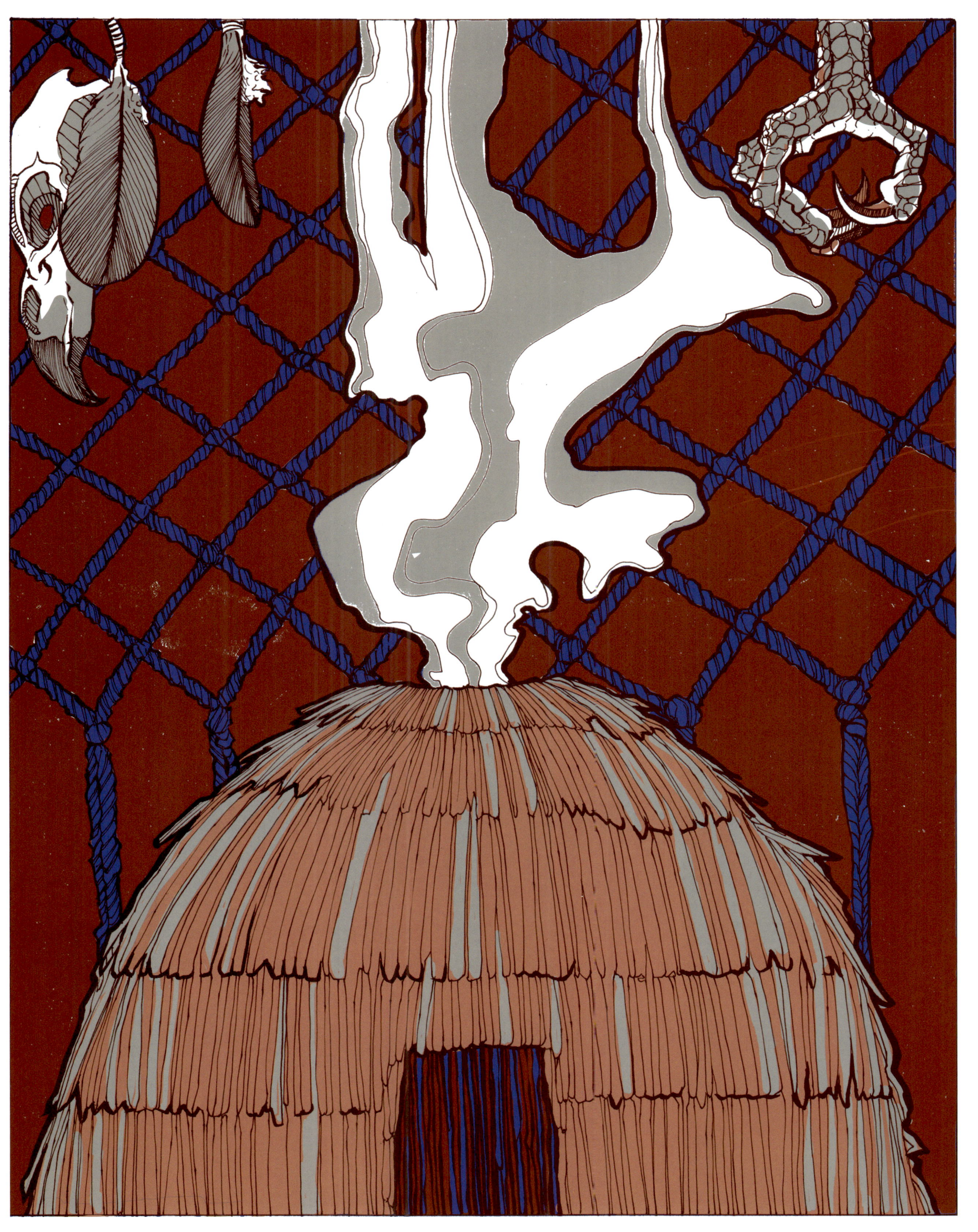

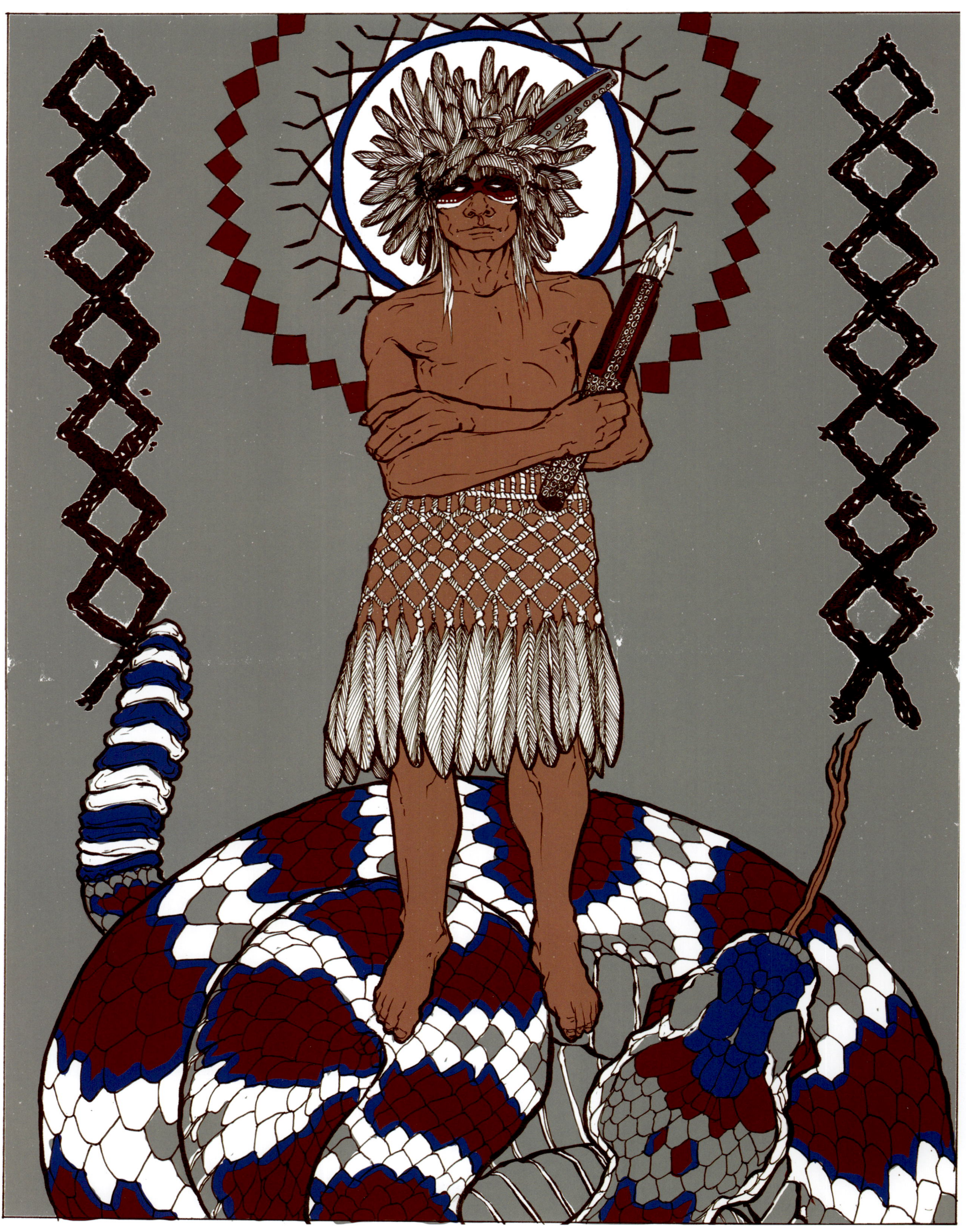

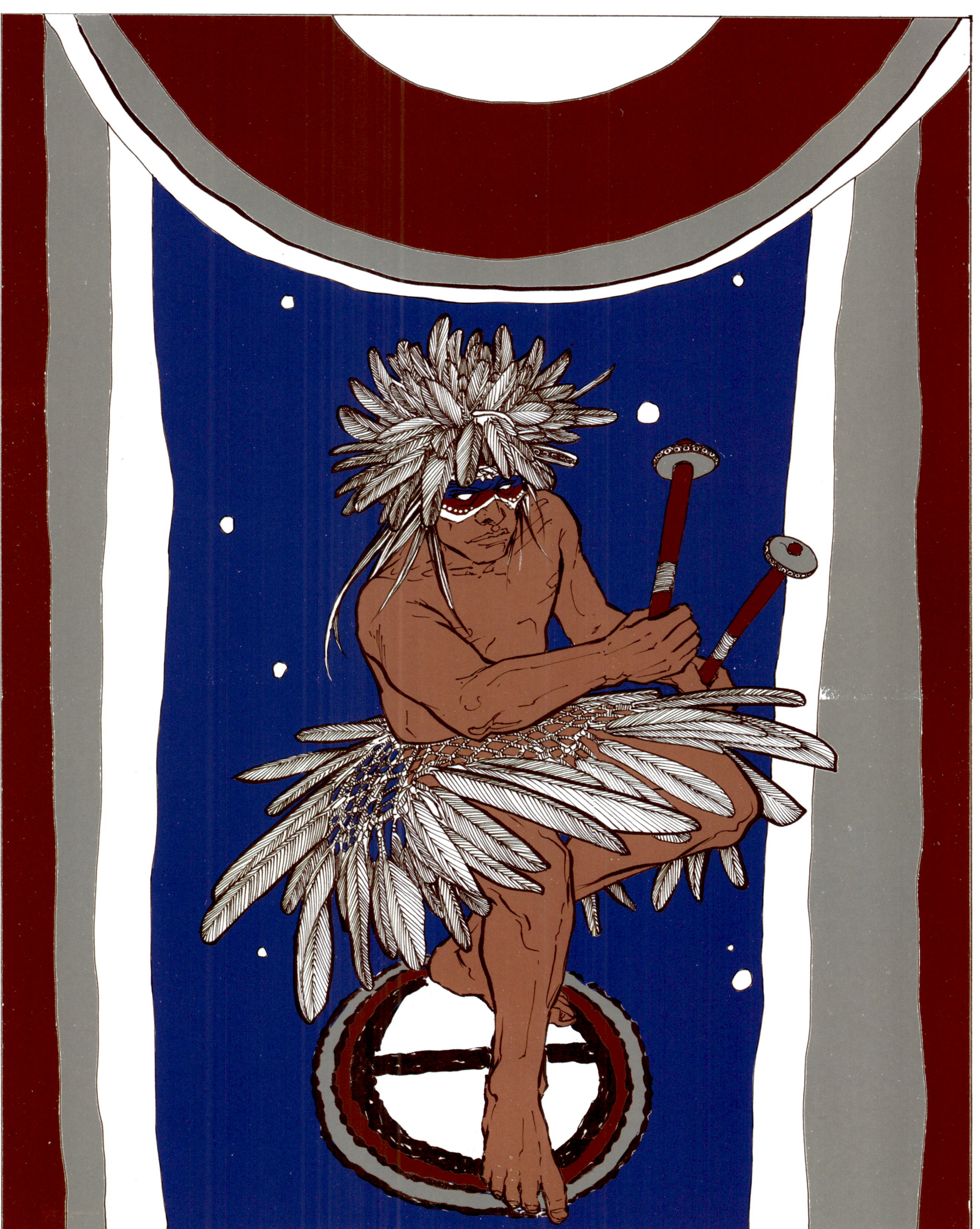

Imagining the Future at the IAIA Museum of Contemporary Native Arts

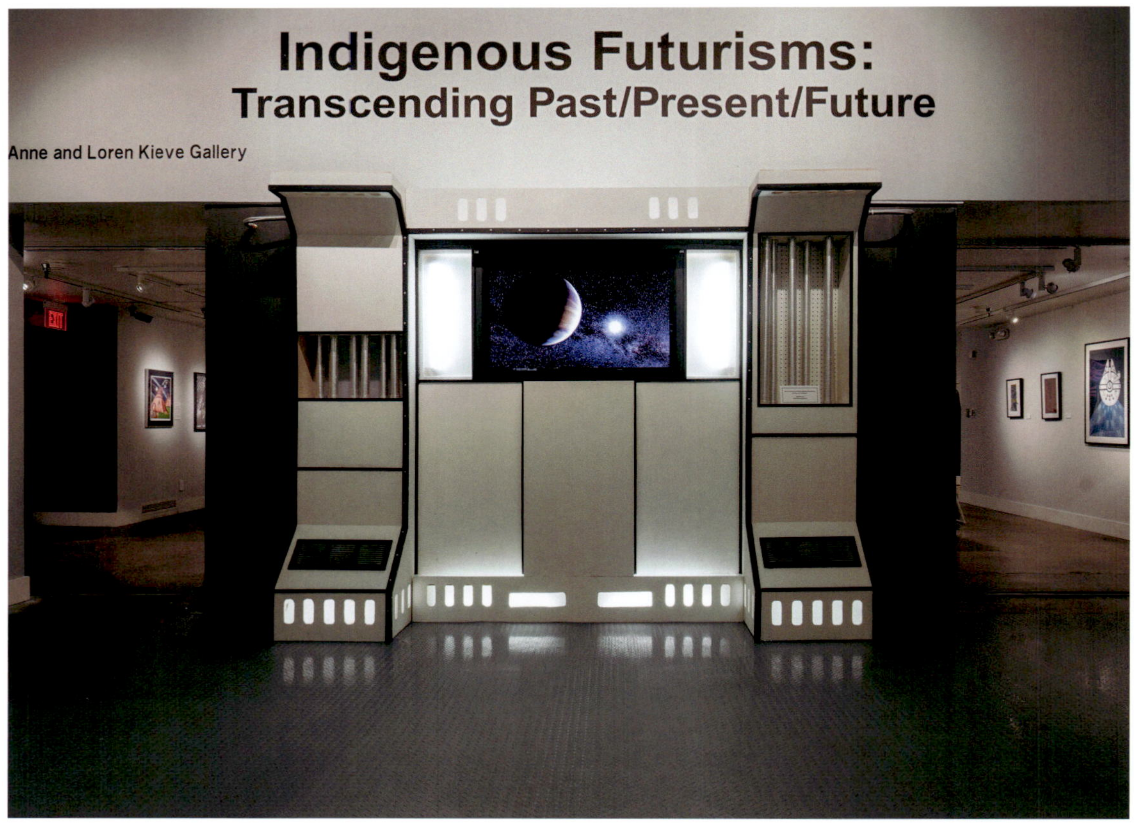

Installation view of *Indigenous Futurisms: Transcending Past/Present/Future*, IAIA Museum of Contemporary Native Arts, February 13, 2020–January 3, 2021. Courtesy of the IAIA Museum of Contemporary Native Arts, Santa Fe, NM. Photography by Jason S. Ordaz

Manuela Well-Off-Man

What does the future of Indigenous art look like? Today, many institutions, including the Institute of the American Indian Arts (IAIA), focus on contemporary Native art with an eye to tomorrow. The IAIA Museum of Contemporary Native Arts (MoCNA) is the first and only museum in the country committed solely to advancing contemporary Indigenous art. It has been instrumental in establishing both the physical space and creative freedom critical to Indigenous artists seeking to challenge the confines of historical expectations. In doing so, MoCNA has raised awareness of their work, communities, and cultures in the present while charting a path to a more inclusive future that foregrounds and honors Indigenous values, perspectives, and presence. This essay examines some of the artists in the Autry Museum exhibition, *Future Imaginaries: Indigenous Art, Fashion, Technology*, whose work has also been featured at MoCNA, highlighting their artistic practice while bringing awareness to the institutional support and cross-pollination that has helped propel the field of Indigenous Futurisms into the thriving and dynamic artistic genre that it is today.

One example of MoCNA's advocacy of innovative contemporary Indigenous art is *Íŋyaŋ Iyé* (*Telling Rock*), 2019, by Kite and Devin Ronneberg (pl. 44). The interactive installation, part of the MoCNA exhibition *Indigenous Futurisms: Transcending Past/Present/Future* (February 13, 2020–January 3, 2021), examines the relationship between human and nonhuman entities, such as computers animated by artificial intelligence. Viewers are invited to move the braided ropes equipped with sensors, which causes its sounds and lights to change. According to Ronneberg, "The AI embedded within the sculpture 'listens' to these changes and makes its own decisions that further affect the lights and sounds."[1] The work is based on an Oglala Lakota belief that materials such as metals, rocks, and minerals have a spirit and can communicate of their own volition. "By considering the 'hearing' and 'listening' capabilities of nonhuman entities, a method of engagement reliant upon mutual respect and responsibility becomes possible," explains Ronneberg.[2] Translated for everyday life, this means that humankind's relationship to computers can be improved so that the two entities not only communicate but also respect each other. With *Ínyan Iyé (Telling Rock)*, Kite and Ronneberg worked to develop an advanced AI art installation that follows Indigenous protocols to create ethical high-tech art to protect themselves, their communities, and the environment. In 2020, Kite contributed to the *Indigenous Protocol and Artificial Intelligence Position Paper* to promote Indigenous perspectives in artificial intelligence, in which she advocates: "Holistic understandings of exchange within the environment are essential to Indigenous ontologies, and to ground Indigenous ethics in a physical place that strives to resist exploitation of people or resources."[3]

Cannupa Hanska Luger, a New Mexico-based multidisciplinary artist who received his BFA from IAIA, uses community collaboration to create multifaceted projects that address environmental and sociopolitical issues. Through installations incorporating fibers, repurposed materials, metal, ceramic, video, and sound, Luger interweaves performance and political action to communicate stories about twenty-first-century Indigeneity. As Hood Museum Curator of Indigenous Art Jami Powell (Osage Nation) explained, Luger's work "is predicated on long-held understandings that art is inseparable from our lives and experiences. It is also a continuation of the experimentation, adaptation, innovation, and the avant-garde that have always been a part of Indigenous creative expression."[4] *Watȟéča* (Lakota for "leftovers"), part of his evolving *Future Ancestral Technologies* project, includes wearable, sculptural regalia and props, used in his performances and videos to examine historical and environmental trauma, decolonizing them for future generations through reclaiming spaces and reimagining histories (see Luger essay in this volume).

Luger's *Watȟéča: Buzzard* character with its black top hat and gray and white felt fringes and wings evokes a scavenger bird such as a vulture, crow, raven, or magpie. Luger has worn this ensemble in several performances[5] where he dances around a pile of ceramic buffalo and deer skulls, spreading his winged arms like a scavenger bird with blood running from its beak. Scavengers are resilient and can survive under extreme conditions. As Luger points out, "The scavenger eats what no one else wants, assigning ultimate value to what is on the brink of vanishing."[6] The work alludes to the long-term effects of colonization and the ability of Indigenous communities to overcome threats to their physical and cultural survival despite challenges such as land loss and limited resources.

As part of her practice, contemporary fiber artist and IAIA alumna Marie Watt (Seneca) repurposes recycled blankets for her installations and collaborative, community-based works. The blankets explore social connections, historical traditions, and cross-cultural meanings. She acquires the textiles through requests to a community to donate blankets and stories about their significance to the donor or family. Watt's large-scale quilt *Trek (Pleiades)*, 2014, was inspired by the original *Star Trek* series (pl. 32). The Pleiades, a constellation also known as the "Seven Sisters," serves as a marker of time in many

Indigenous cultures and is the basis of numerous stories.[7] Watt
was inspired by a historical Indigenous basket she studied
in the Hallie Ford Museum of Art collection. The artist also
uses the stars to honor her friend Alma Nungarrayi Granites,
whom she met in Australia during an artist residency.[8] The
blue and red quilted star shapes are surrounded by a series
of fabric strips that repeat the outlines, reflecting the special
effects of the ship's jump to warp speed, which references
Watt's inspiration for this work and her art practice.[9] Watt
chose to embroider the *Starship Enterprise* from the television
series to emphasize "the intersection of the historical and
contemporary, the real and mythical."[10]

Luzene Hill (Eastern Band of Cherokee Indians), best known
for her conceptual installations that address social issues and
incorporate performance, is also an alumna of IAIA's recent
Social Engagement Art Residency program.[11] Founded in
2014, MoCNA's Social Engagement Art Residency is among
the first social practice art residencies in the country.[12] Hill's
work is informed by the precontact cultures of the Americas;
her recent project *REVVV*, 2023, a cape made of Mylar
emergency blankets, draws attention to the long-term effects
of a militarized U.S./Mexican border on Indigenous communities
(pl. 10). This border artificially divides people, cultures, languages,
and communities, disrupting interdependent human, cultural,
and environmental relationships that have existed for thousands
of years. As she explains:

The paradox of Indigenous migrants along the southern
border being rounded up and given government-issued Mylar
emergency blankets prior to incarceration, [is] in contrast to
the words "give me your tired, your poor, your huddled masses
yearning to breathe free" [and] compelled me to respond. I
wanted to take those "handouts" and transform them into an
image of power bursting forth.[13]

As Hill notes, "The emergency blankets that held empty
promises and pseudo-protection have become an energizing
visual explosion of feminine energy. *REVVV* revels in Indigenous
culture rising up, being heard, being felt, exploding back into
the world—through female sexual energy and power."[14]

Diné artist Will Wilson created tintype portraits for his *Critical
Indigenous Photographic Exchange* (*CIPX*) series,[15] including
a portrait of artist Andy Everson wearing a K'ómoks-style
Imperial stormtrooper outfit (pl. 23). Everson is known for his
digital depictions of *Star Wars* characters using a Northwest
Coast style to reflect his K'ómoks and Kwakwaka'wakw cultural

heritage.[16] For *Northern Warrior*, worn in Wilson's portrait, he added a wooden hat to the stormtrooper's helmet and costume, both decorated with distinctive formline designs in yellow, blue, white, and black (pl. 24). These patterns proudly represent his ancestral lineage and are embellished with matching designs that his ancestors would have worn. Everson explains,

> The hat on this helmet displays the Kwakwaka'wakw crest of the *sisiyutł*—the double-headed serpent. This symbol of the warrior reminds us of the dichotomies in life—good and evil, right and wrong—and puts a human face in the middle to teach us that we must choose where we stand.[17]

In Everson's version, the stormtrooper becomes a more powerful character who defends his homeland.[18]

Fashion designers Orlando Dugi and Jontay Kahm create wearable art with an eye toward social engagement. Dugi (Diné) conceptualized and designed several new garments during his artist residency at IAIA, including his *Warrior Twins Coat* (pl. 14). Created in collaboration with Diné artist Ryan Singer, Dugi embroidered the upper portion of the coat, while Singer painted the lower half. Based on the Diné creation story of the Warrior Twins Nayénzgan (Monster Slayer) and Tobadzîschíni (Born of Water), the Twins received the gifts of lightning bolt arrows and flint armor from their father, the Sun, so they could rid the world of monsters who prey upon people.[19] Dugi prominently embroidered Father Sun in gold thread on the front and back of the coat, and added elaborate beading, evoking stars in the universe.

Dugi worked with IAIA graduate Jontay Kahmakoatayo "Kahm" (Plains Cree) as his intern. Kahm's creations, such as *Fossil 2.0 with Pebble Mask*, 2023, suggest humanoid hybrid creatures from the future (pl. 1). The artist combines everyday materials, such as styrofoam, pebbles, and mesh, with shiny, smooth fabrics such as organza twill, sculpting them into futuristic, wearable artworks inspired by animals, insects, or plants. Kahm conceived the idea for creating a fossil-like garment from "finding fossils and opening them up to find symmetrical bone structures from seashells and sea creatures. Hence the gray stone-like shiny fabric."[20] Mask-like headdresses are often part of Kahm's designs. In *Fossil 2.0* he covered pebbles with graphite-colored metallic organza twill, evoking the smooth stones in coastal waters where these creatures once lived. Kahm blends the intensity of a post-apocalyptic crisis with a hopeful dawning of the future. Fascinated by the theatricality of high fashion, he challenges traditional notions of dressmaking to create sculptural garments that are radically otherworldly and future-facing.[21]

The tenets of Indigenous Futurism align with those of IAIA and MoCNA. Both seek to envision a future where Indigenous art is not merely a reflection of the past but a powerful visual strategy to complexities of the present while shaping a sovereign futurity where Indigeneity is empowering and healing. By actively reshaping these narratives and confronting the enduring structures of colonialism, MoCNA seeks to empower Indigenous artists through their cultural heritage and as architects of a self-determined, shared future.

1   Devin Ronneberg, "Íŋyaŋ Iyé (Telling Rock)," https://www.devinronneberg.com/work/telling-rock. Accessed October 15, 2022.

2   Ronneberg, https://www.devinronneberg.com/work/telling-rock.

3   Suzanne Kite, "How to Build Anything Ethically. Suzanne Kite in Discussion with Corey Stover, Melita Stover Janis, and Scott Benesiinaabandan," in *Indigenous Protocol and Artificial Intelligence Position Paper*, ed. Jason Edward Lewis (Honolulu: Initiative for Indigenous Futures and the Canadian Institute for Advanced Research 2020), 76.

4   Jami Powell, "Refusal and Generosity: The Work of Marie Watt and Cannupa Hanska Luger," in *Each/Other: Marie Watt and Cannupa Hanska Luger*, ed. John Lukavic (Denver: Denver Art Museum, 2021), 19.

5   Luger's *Watȟéča* regalia and performance was included in the *STTLMNT IS NOT HERE* group exhibition at Trinity Square Video, Toronto, ON, Canada, October 8–November 13, 2021, https://www.sttlmnt.org/toronto.

6   Cannupa Hanska Luger in "Watȟéča," ed. Eden Pearlstein, Ayin Press, https://ayinpress.org/watheca/. Accessed August 12, 2023.

7   Northeastern tribes such as the Iroquois consider the Seven Sisters as a marker of time, since the constellation appears in the spring and vanishes below the horizon with the onset of winter. Lynn Ceci, "Watchers of the Pleiades: Ethnoastronomy among Native Cultivators in Northeastern North America," *Ethnohistory* 25, no. 4 (Autumn 1978): 301–317.

8   Marie Watt, "Trek," https://www.mariewattstudio.com/work/project/trek-pleiades-2014. Accessed October 9, 2022.

9   See also Don Lincoln, "Is *Star Trek*'s Warp Drive Possible," Hard Science, *BigThink*, July 19, 2023, https://bigthink.com/hard-science/star-trek-warp-drive-possible/.

10   Watt, "Trek," https://www.mariewattstudio.com/work/project/trek-pleiades-2014.

11   Due to the Covid-19 pandemic, Luzene Hill's fall 2020 artist residency was virtual. Here is a link to one of her public online events: https://www.youtube.com/watch?v=XrzenxlfG8w.

12   The Hammer Museum's Artist Residency was established in 2005 and the ASU Art Museum's program in 2011. However, most museums began instituting social practice artist residencies after MoCNA's was instituted. For example, the Kennedy Center's Social Practice Residencies began in 2019, and the Met's Civic Practice Partnership (CPP) was launched in 2017.

13   Luzene Hill, artist statement, personal communication, September 1, 2023.

14   Ibid.

15   Kaila T. Schedeen, "An Introduction to Will Wilson's *Critical Indigenous Photographic Exchange*," Delaware Art Museum, June 24, 2022, https://delart.org/willwilson-cipx/2.

16   Tamara Baluja, "*Star Wars* Characters Get Indigenized by Comox First Nation Artist," https://www.cbc.ca/news/indigenous/star-wars-indigenized-andy-everson-1.4463320. Accessed September 6, 2023.

17   Andy Everson, "Northern Warrior," http://www.andyeverson.com/2014/northern_warrior.html. Accessed September 6, 2023.

18   "Andy Everson's Stormtrooper Acts as Modern First Nations Warrior," *Huffington Post B.C.*, July 24, 2014, https://www.huffingtonpost.ca/2014/07/24/andy-everson-stormtrooper-first-nations_n_5618449.html. Accessed September 6, 2023.

19   Paul G. Zolbrod, *Dine Bahane: The Navajo Creation Story* (Albuquerque: University of New Mexico Press, 1985), 78–87.

20   Jontay Kahm, personal communication, September 6, 2023.

21   Jontay Kahm, personal communication, February 13, 2022.

Plates

I. Jontay Kahm (Plains Cree), *Fossil 2.0 with Pebble Mask*, 2023. Organza twill, dimensions variable. Courtesy of Vancouver Art Gallery

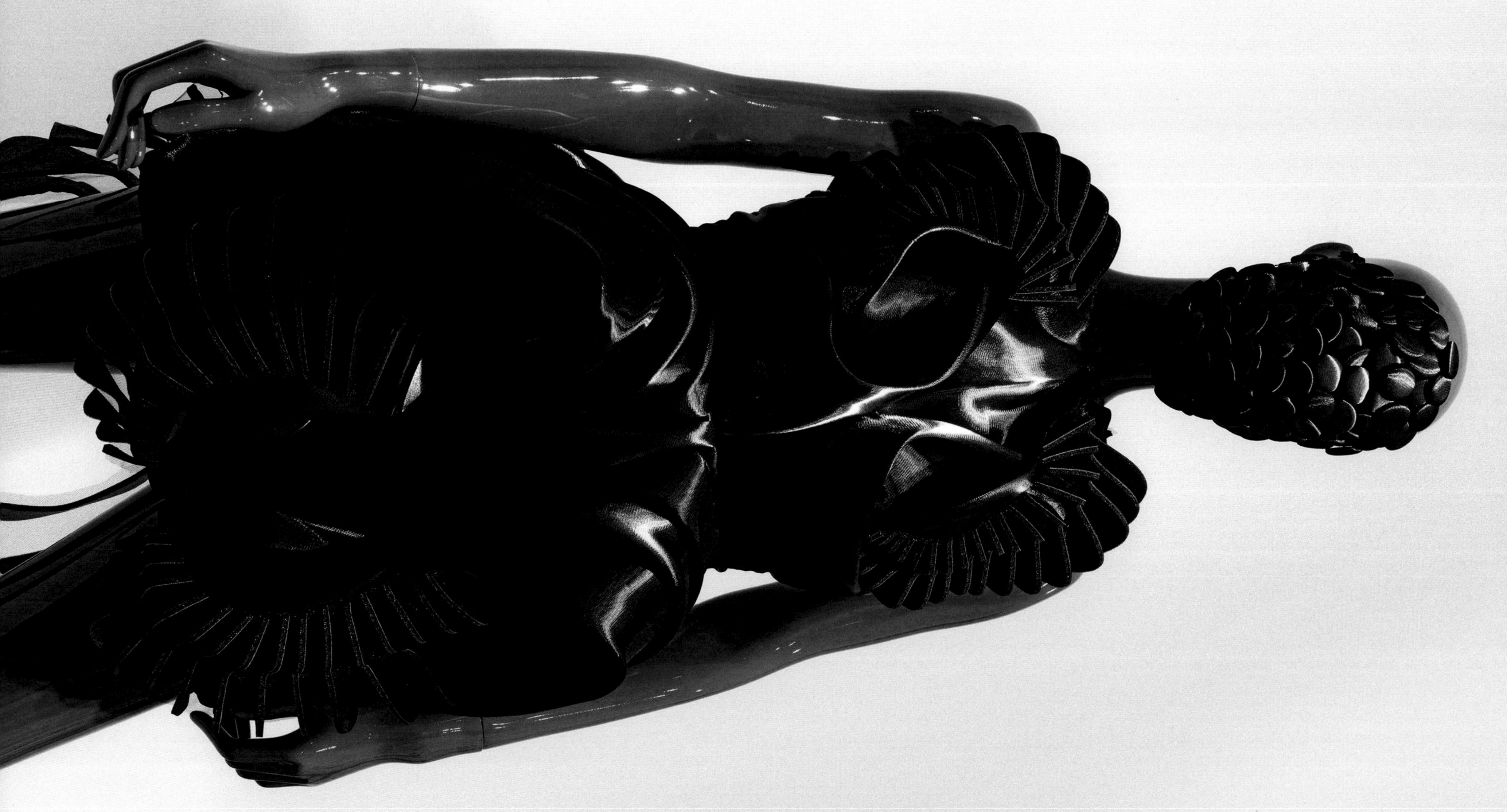

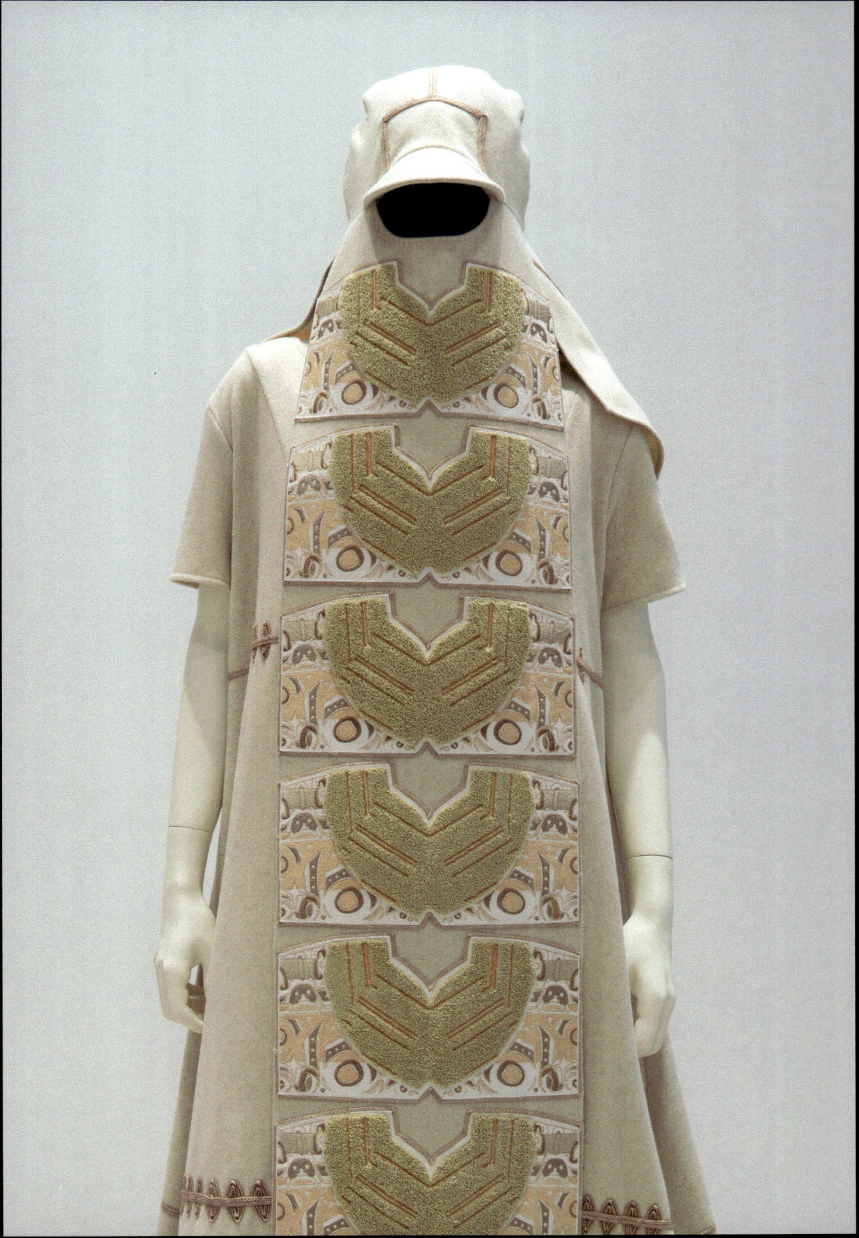

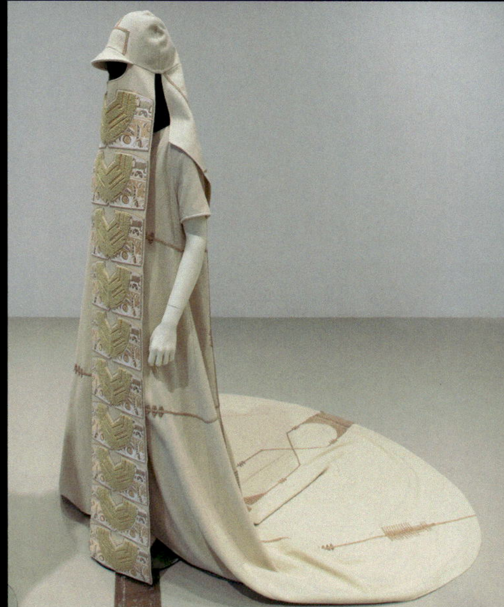

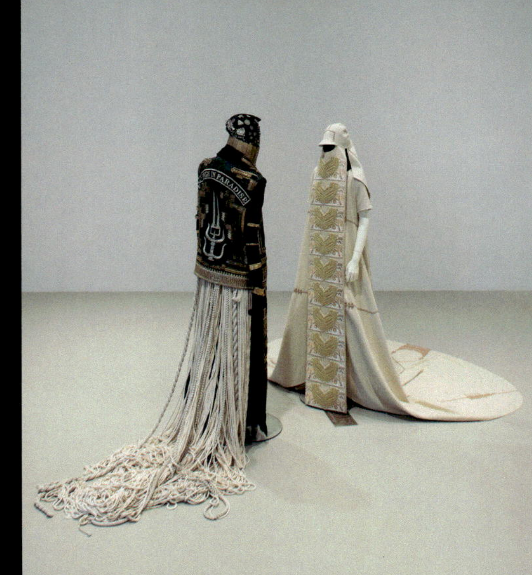

2. Nep Sidhu (Punjabi Sikh) with Nicolas Galanin (Tlingit / Unangax̂). *SHE in Light Form* from *No Pigs in Paradise*, 2015–16. Melton wool, jute, silver zari, chenille, cotton, 72 × 20 in. Courtesy of the artists and Patel Brown, Toronto

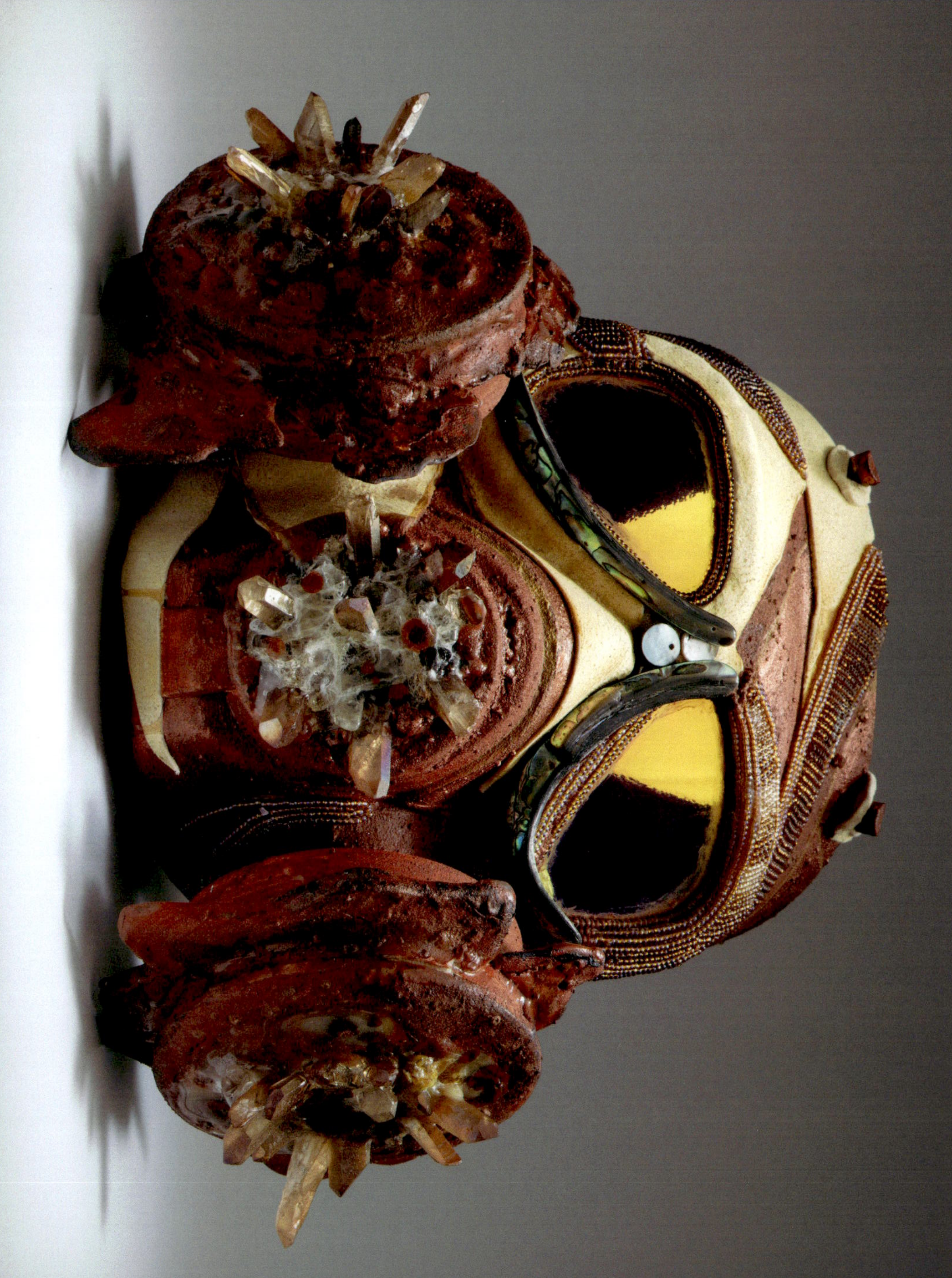

3. Mona Cliff (Aaniiih/Nakota/Eastern European), *Past/Presence/Future II*, 2020. Gas mask, seed beads, beeswax, acrylic paint, matte medium, Oklahoma red dirt, pink quartz, pine rosin, copal resin, leather, 8 × 10 × 5 in. Courtesy of the artist. Photography by Aaron Paden

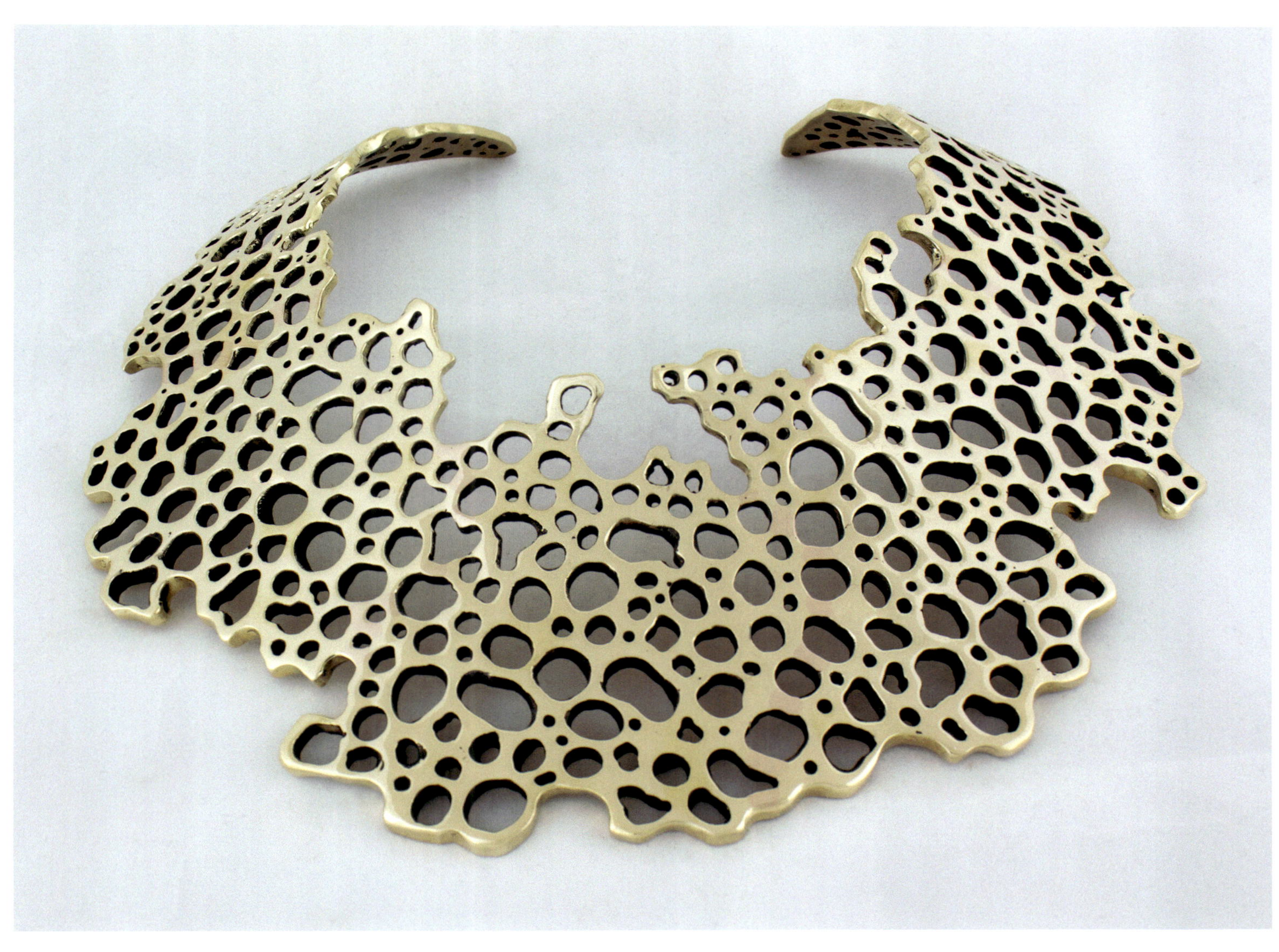

4. Matagi Sorensen (Yavapai-Apache), *Gorget*, 2024. Bronze, 9 × 10 × 2 in. Courtesy of Gallery Hózhó, Albuquerque. Photography by Chelsea Benally

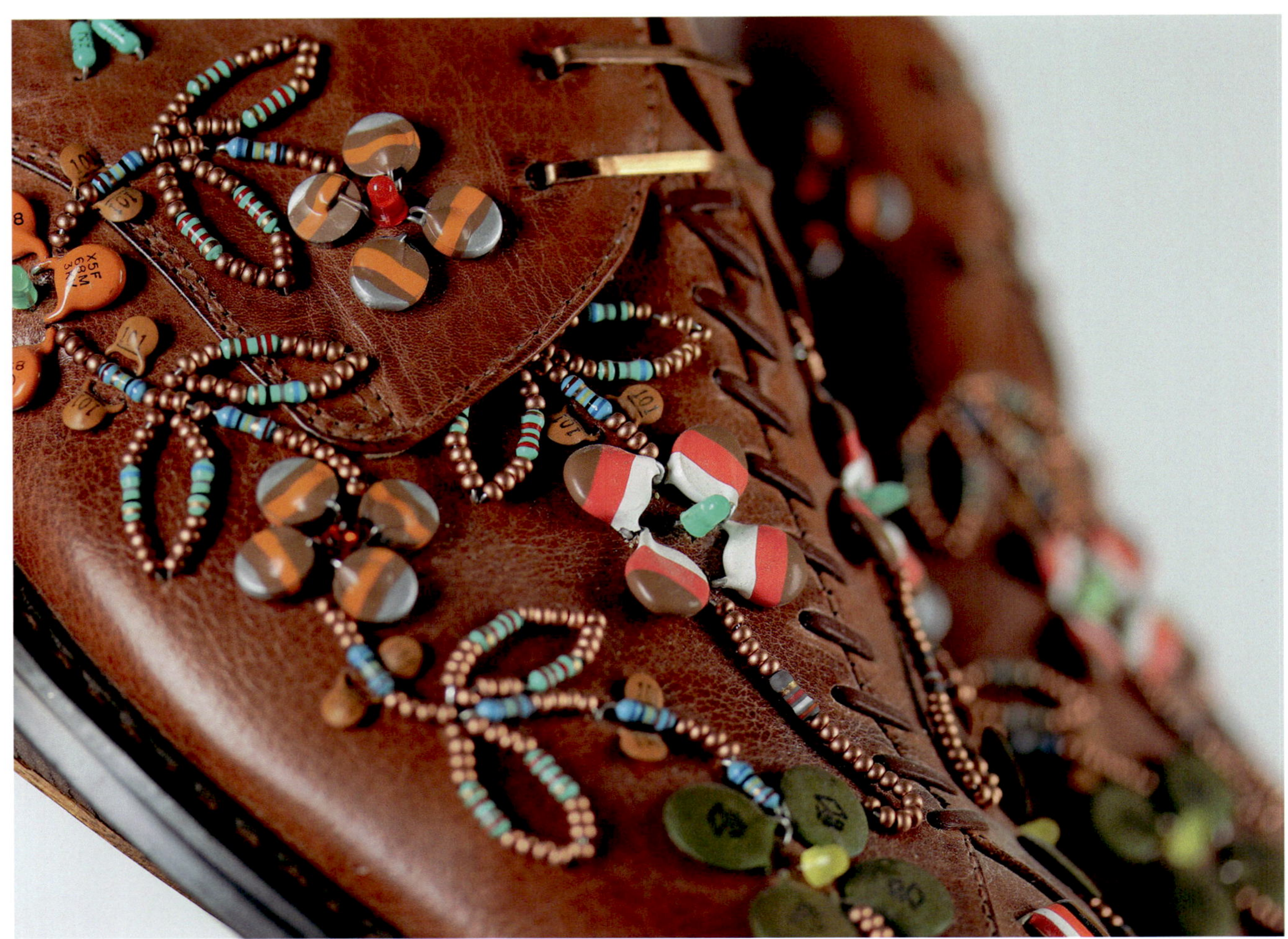

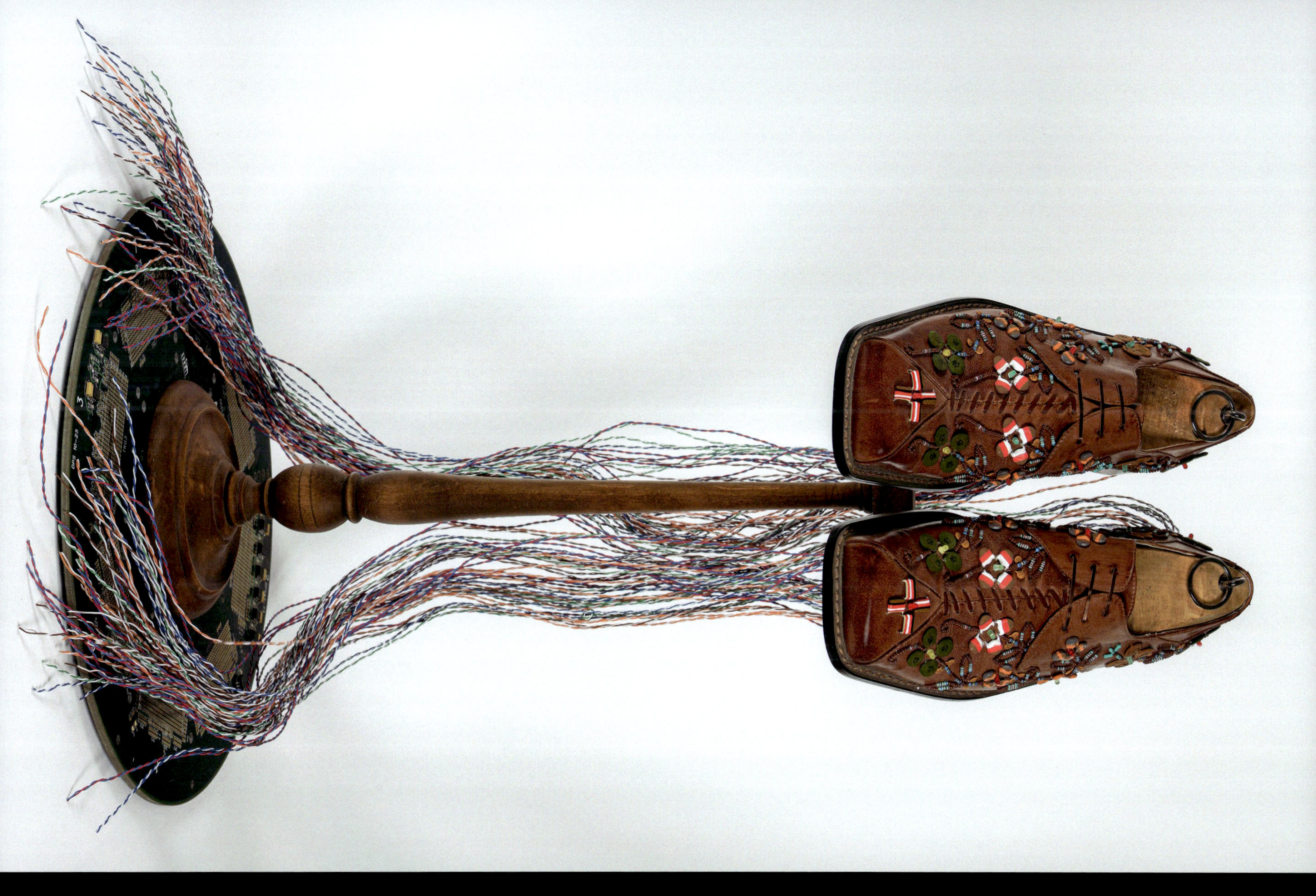

5. Barry Ace (Odawa), *Efface*, 2017. Found shoes, vintage wooden shoe stand, vintage round circuit board, coated wire, capacitors, light-emitting diodes, resistors, vintage wooden shoe lasts, metal hardware, 28 × 15 × 15½ in. Courtesy of Heffel

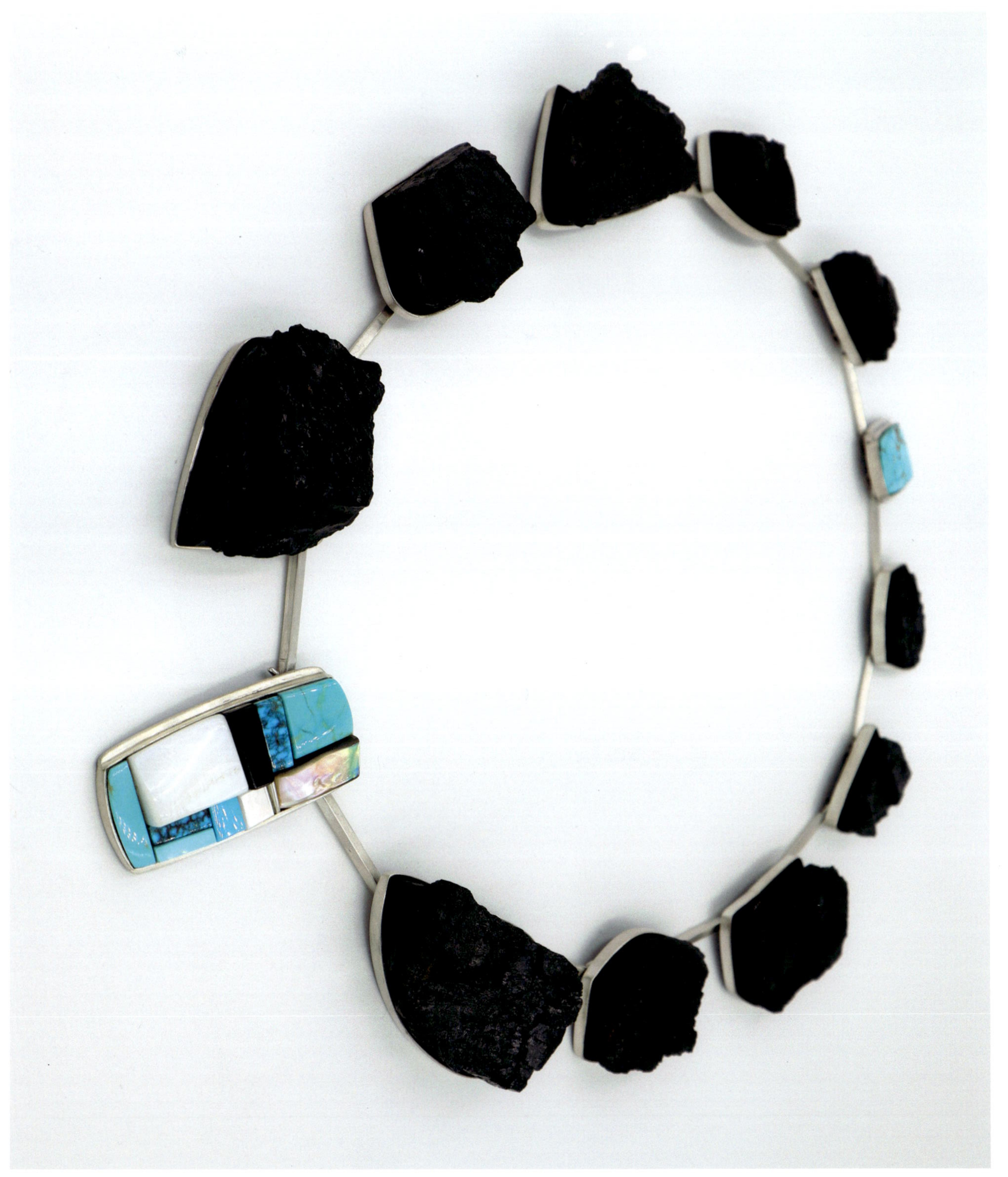

6. Nanibaa Beck (Diné), *Shí kʼé, what has been your experience with coal?*, 2018. Sterling silver, coal, Acoma jet, mother-of-pearl, abalone, American Southwest turquoise, approx. 11½ × 9½ × 1 in. Courtesy of the artist

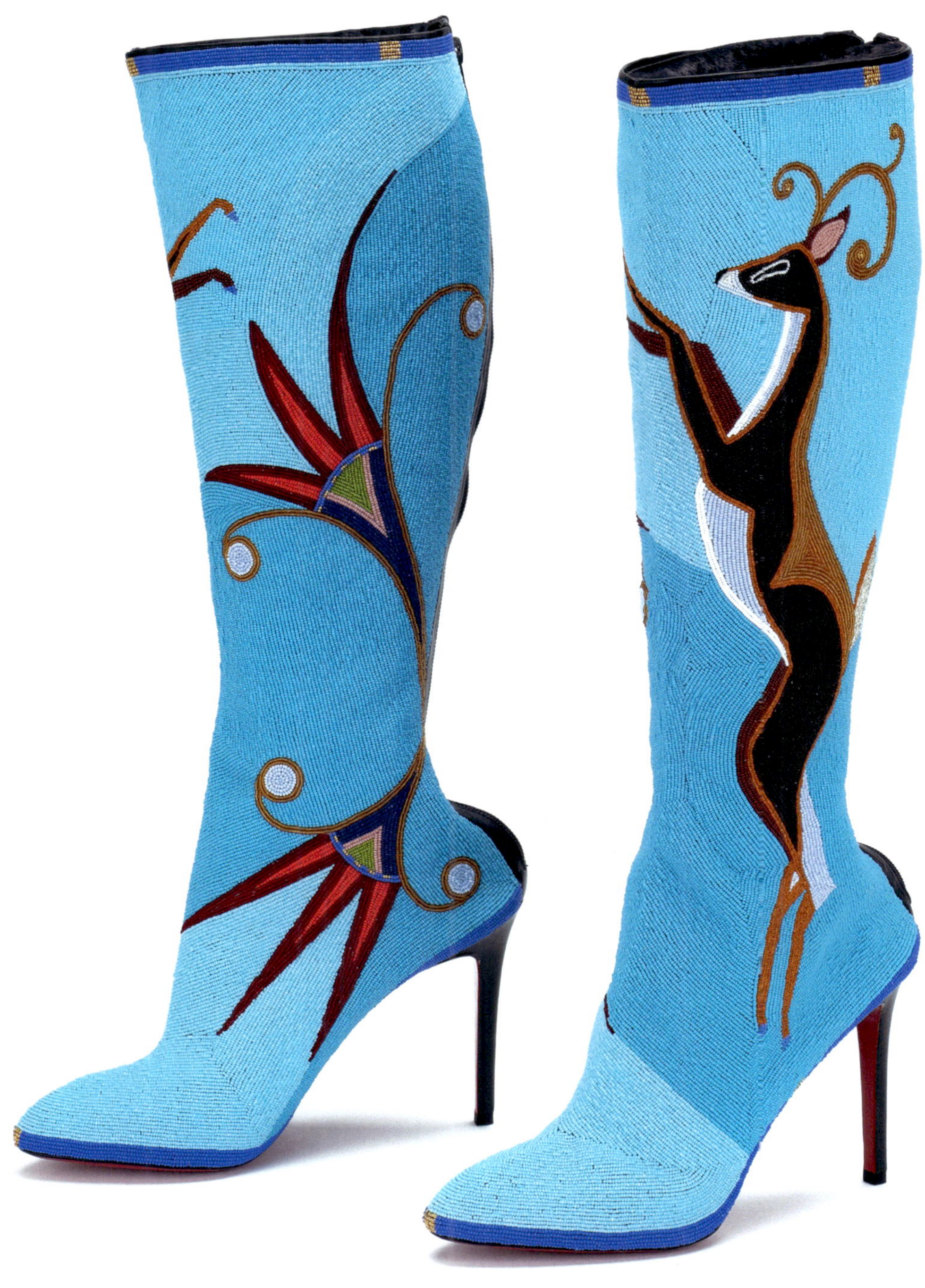

7. Jamie Okuma (Luiseño/Shoshone/Bannock), *Beaded High*

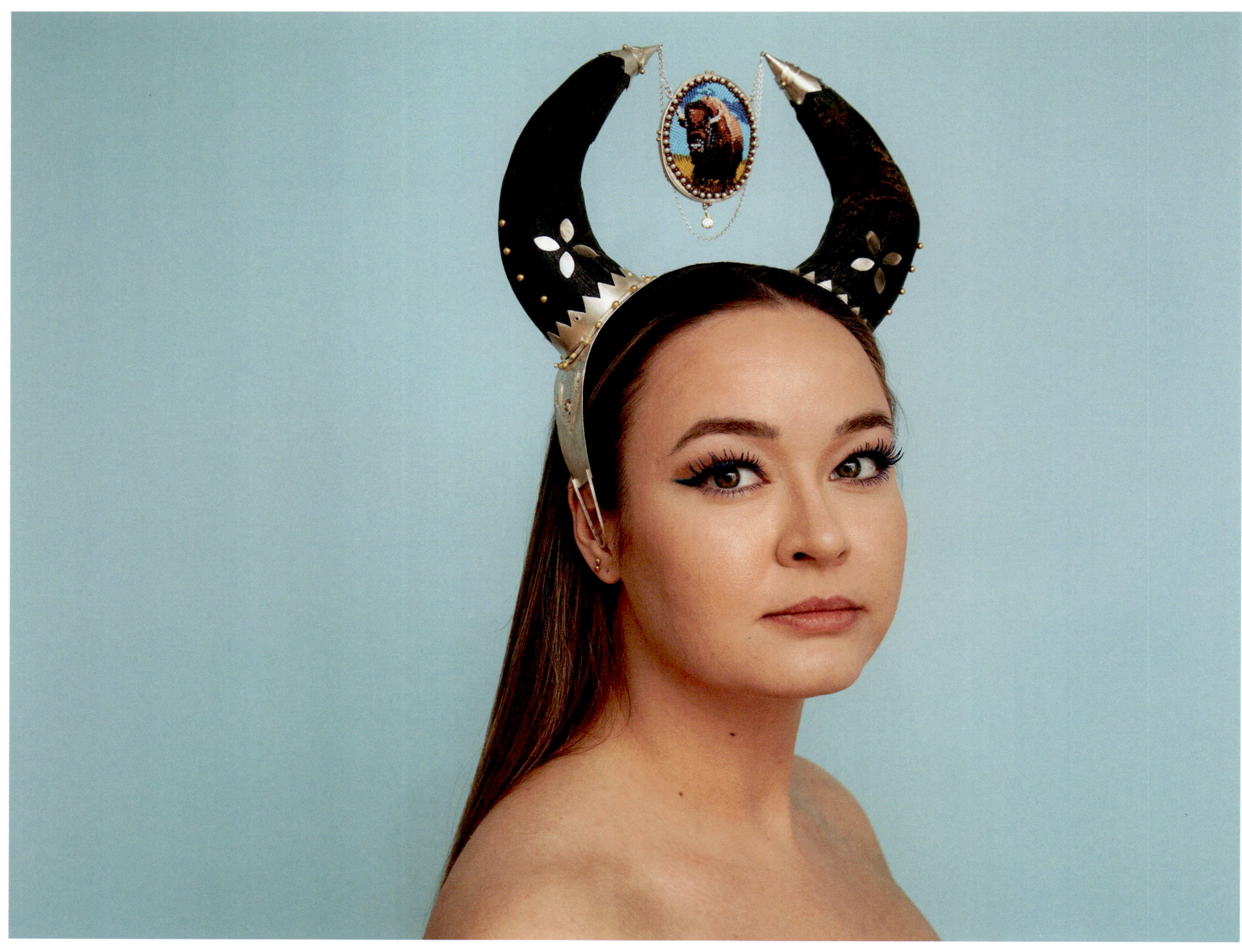

8. Catherine Blackburn (Dene/European) and Rykelle "Ahlazua" Kemp (Mvskoke Creek Nation), *We Honor Bison* from the *Convergence* series, 2022. Bison horn, unsmoked caribou hide, antique beads, sterling silver, brass, gold foil, mother-of-pearl, vintage Swarovski pearls, rhinestone chain, 11¼ × 9⅜ × 2½ in. Courtesy of the artist. Photography by Billie Chiasson

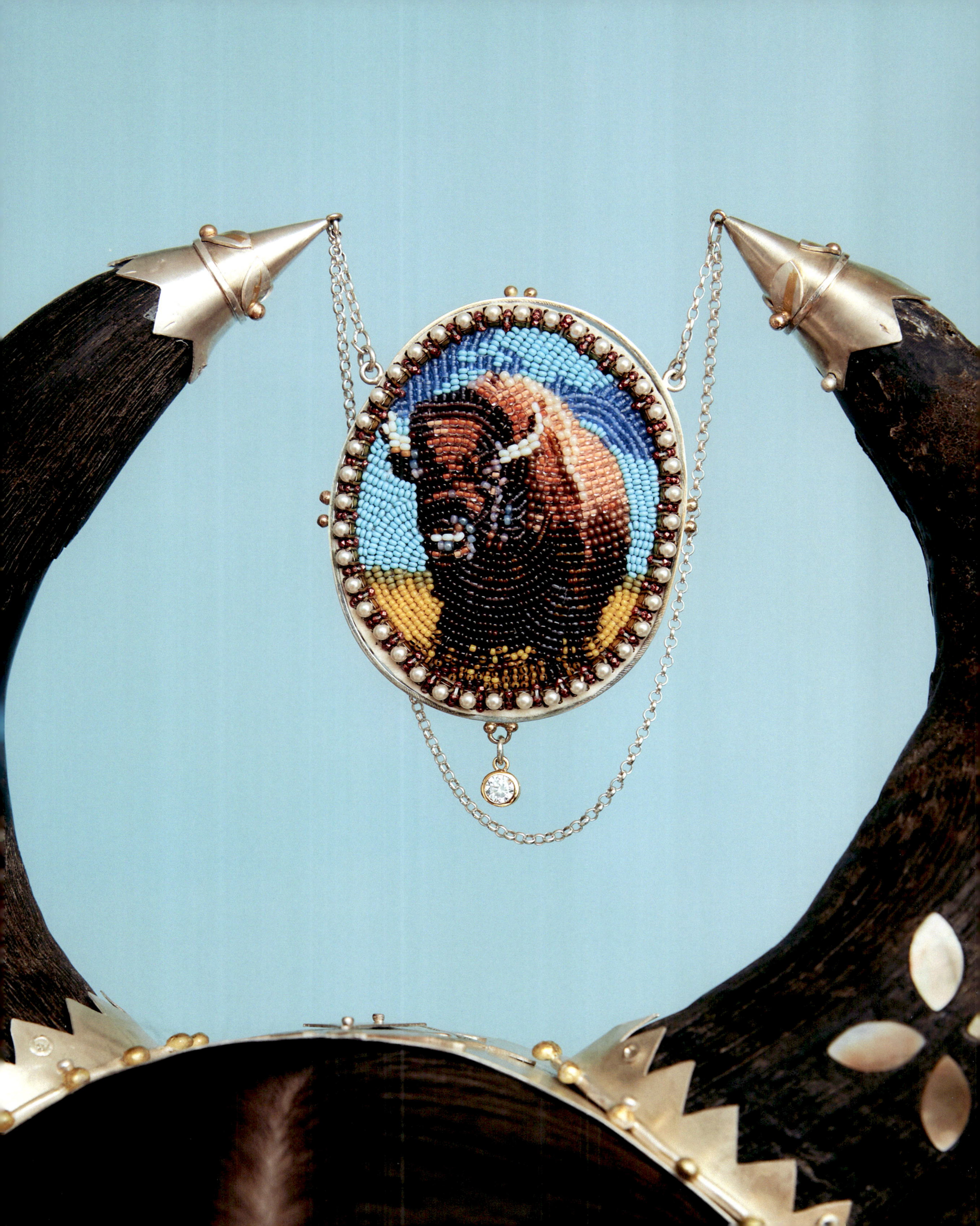

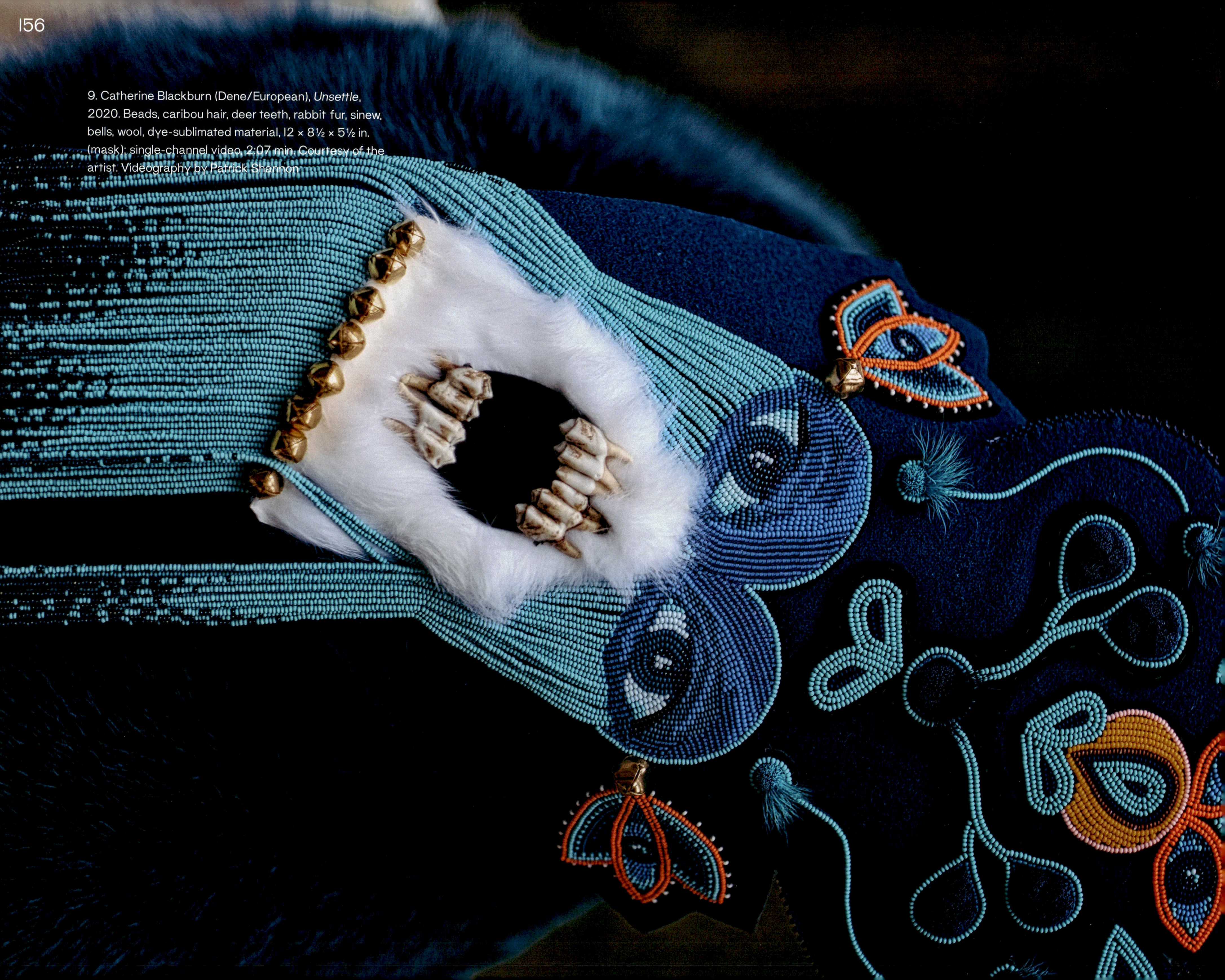

9. Catherine Blackburn (Dene/European), *Unsettle*, 2020. Beads, caribou hair, deer teeth, rabbit fur, sinew, bells, wool, dye-sublimated material, 12 × 8½ × 5½ in. (mask); single-channel video, 2:07 min. Courtesy of the artist. Videography by Patrick Shannon

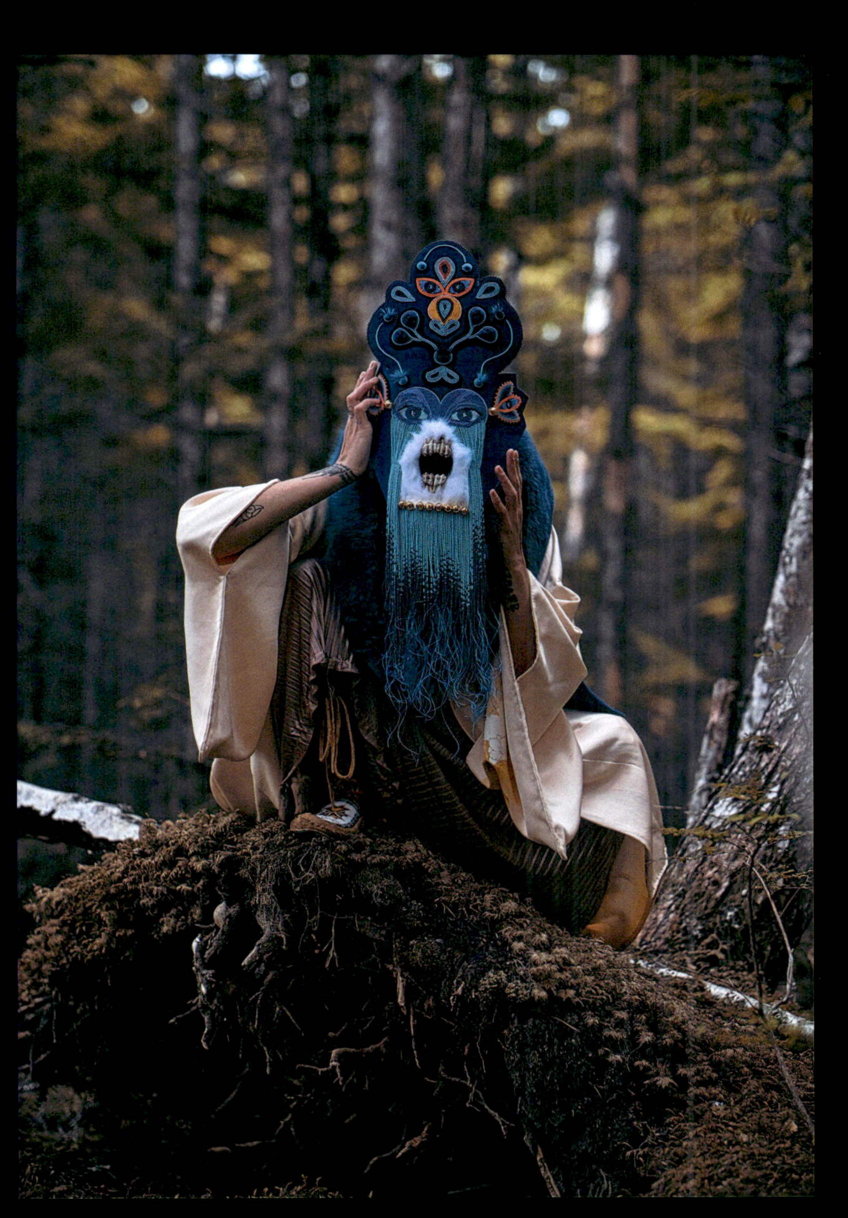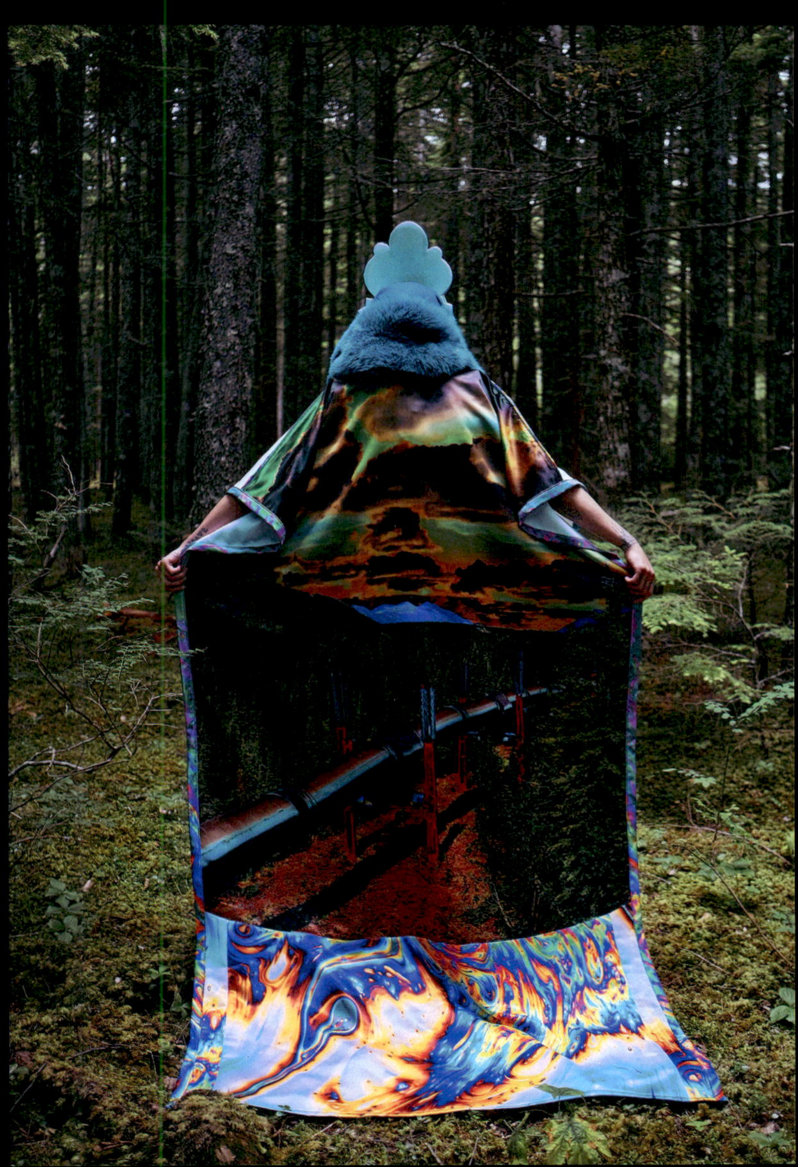

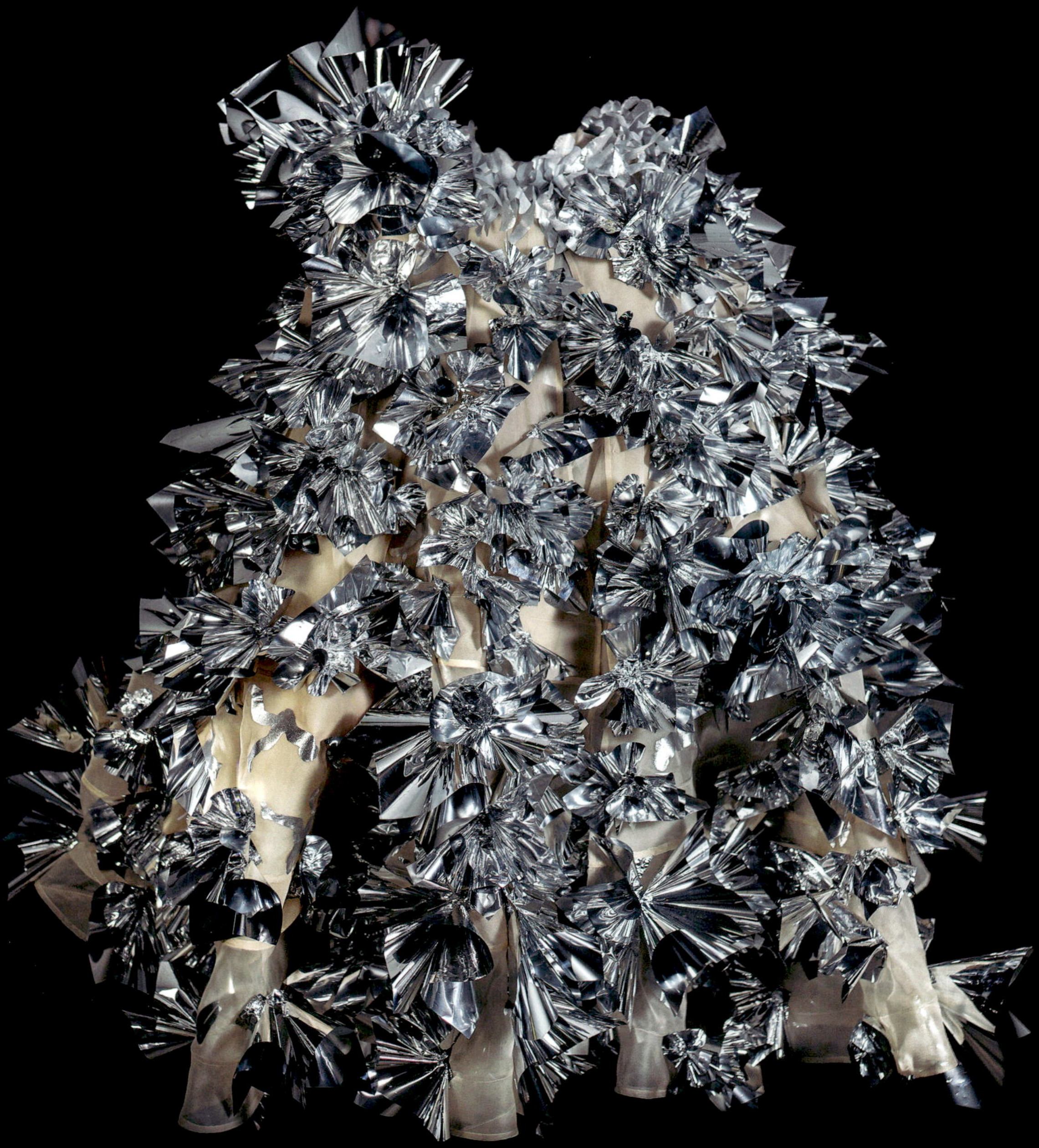

10. Luzene Hill (Eastern Band of Cherokee Indians), *REVVV*, 2023. Mylar, silk organza, silver cord, tissue lamé, 26 in. shoulder width × 180 in. hem circumference × 52 in. length. Courtesy of the artist. Photography by Carmen Arkansas Nations

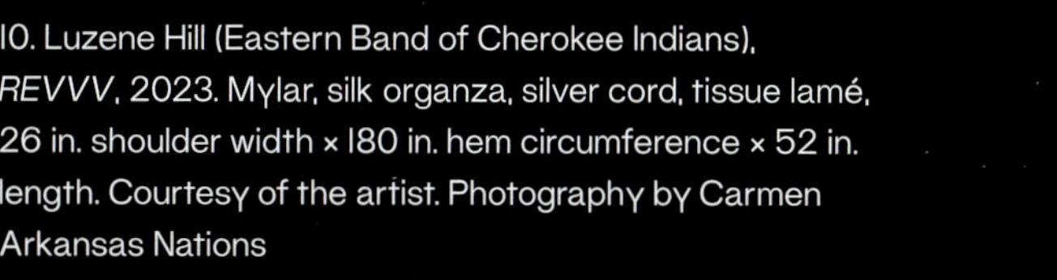

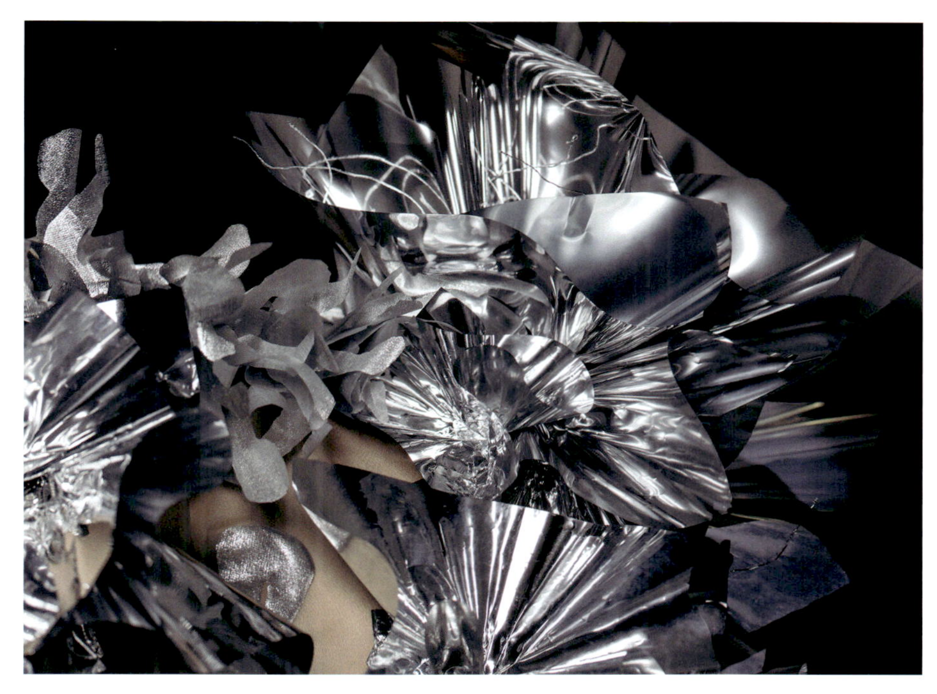

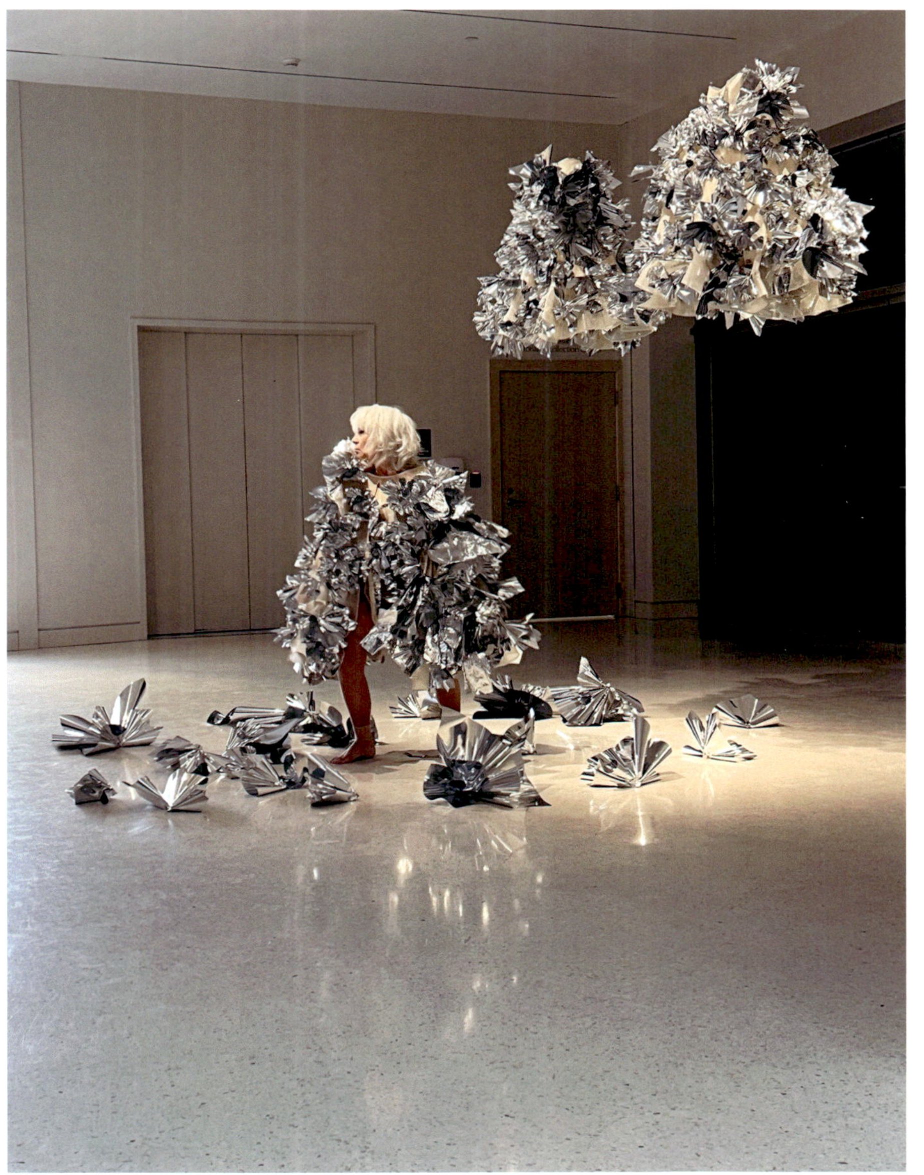

Revelate was created and worn by the artist during *Luzene Hill: Revelate*, a performance at the Asheville Art Museum on January 24, 2023.

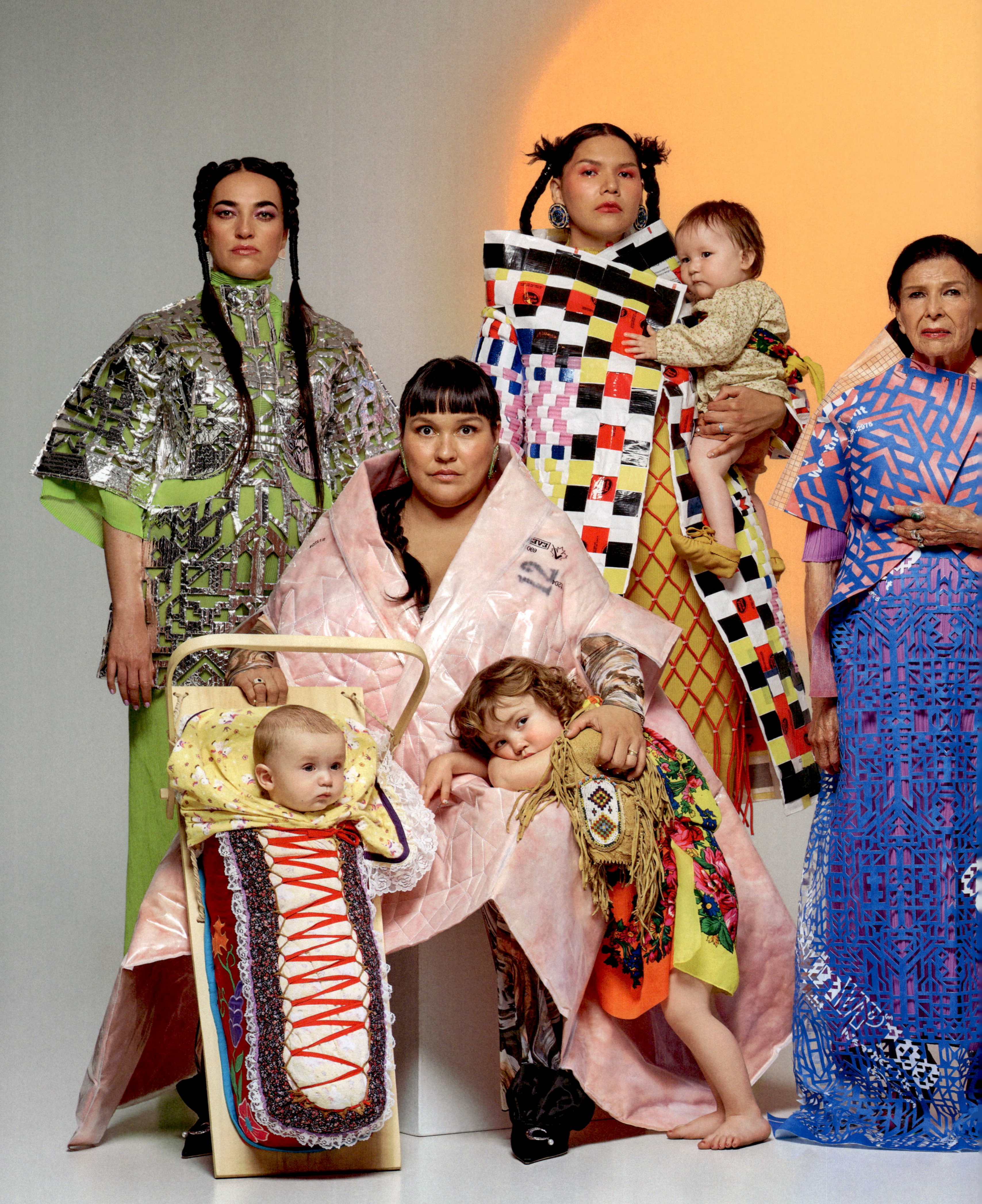

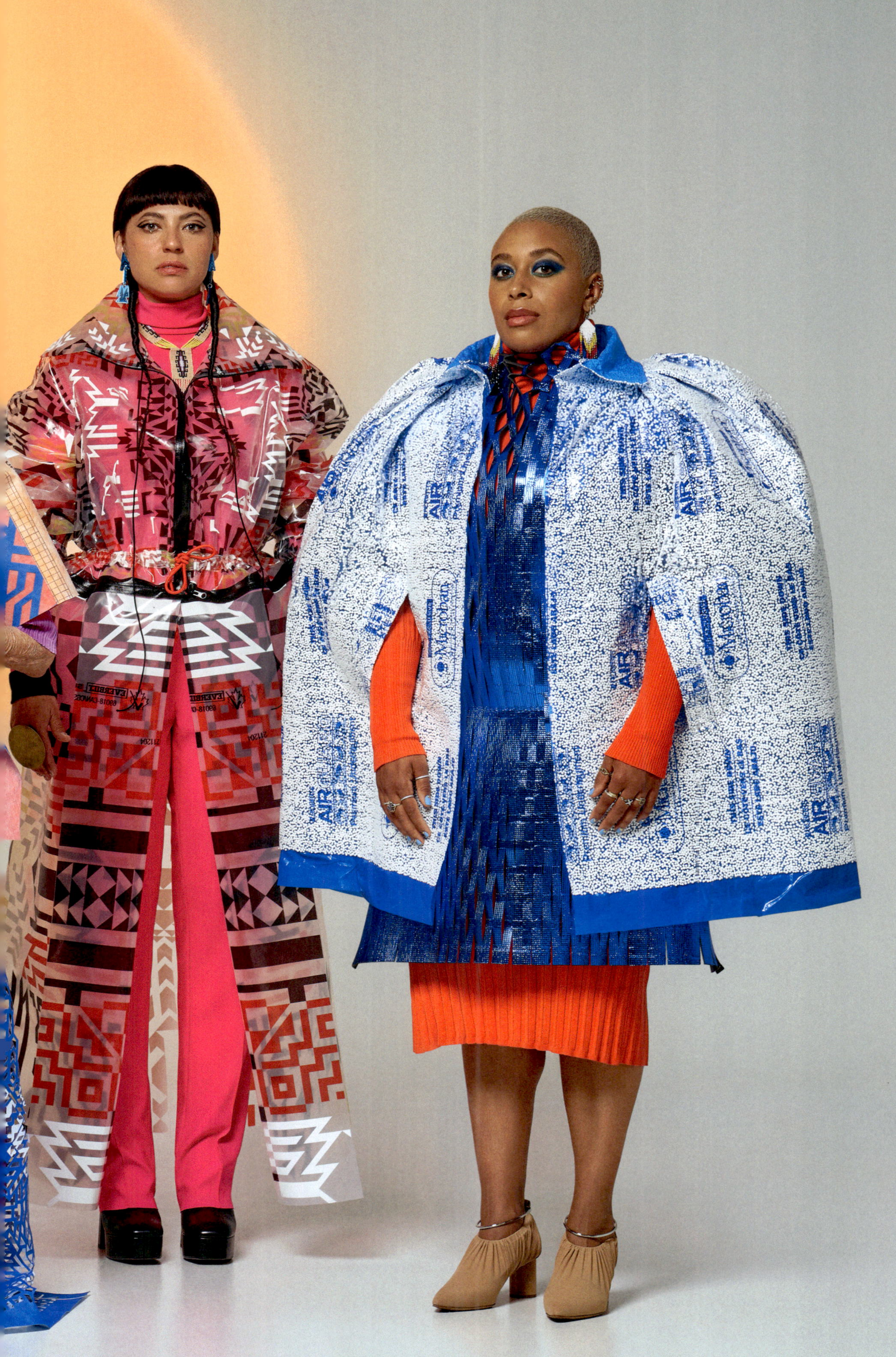

II. Caroline Monnet (Anishinaabe/French), *Echoes from a Near Future*, 2022. Inkjet print mounted on aluminum, 80 × 120 in. Courtesy of the artist

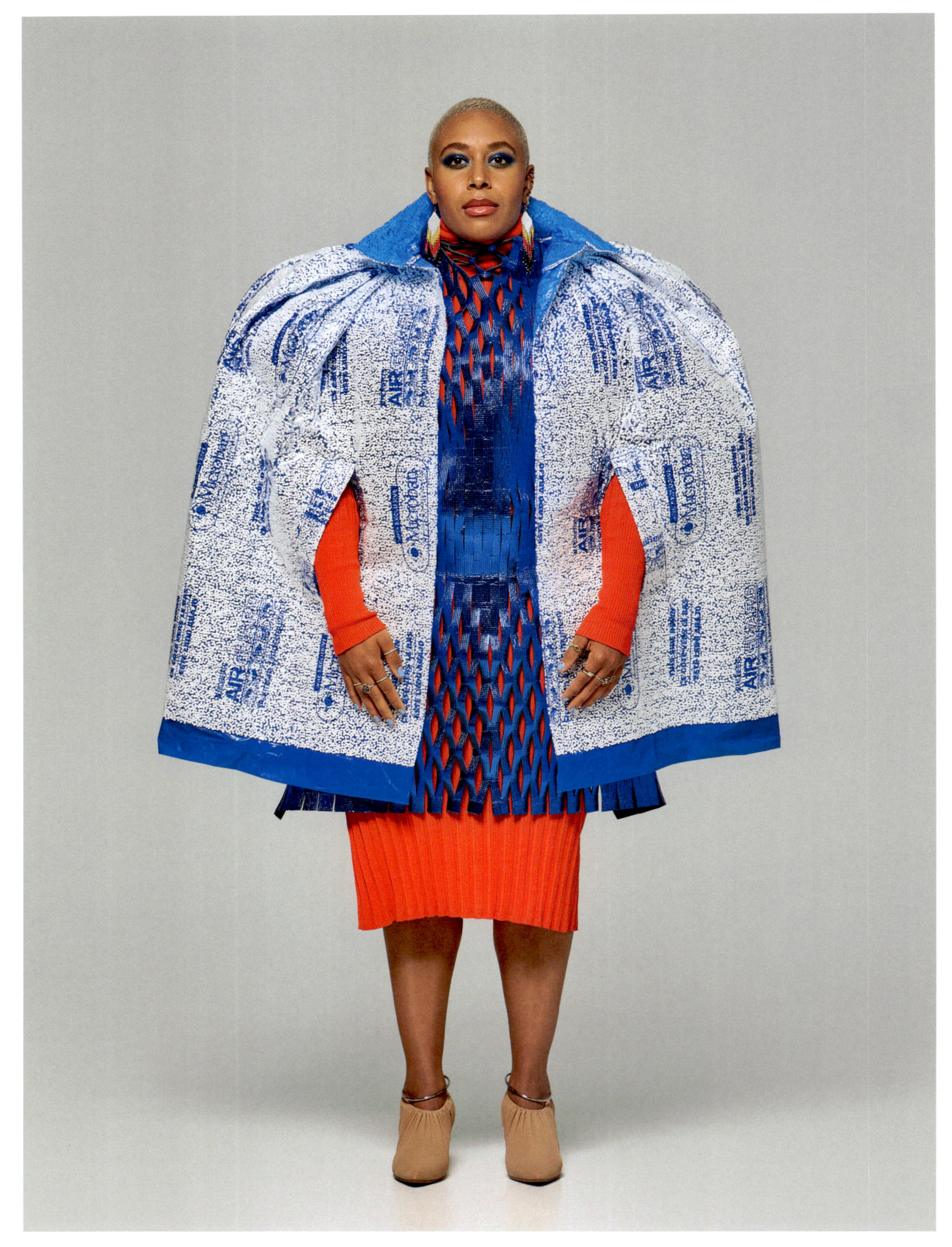

12. Caroline Monnet (Anishinaabe/French), *Aïcha's Regalia* from *Echoes from a Near Future*, 2022. Floor underlayment and reflective coating for laminate flooring, 37½ × 27 × 11 in. Courtesy of the artist

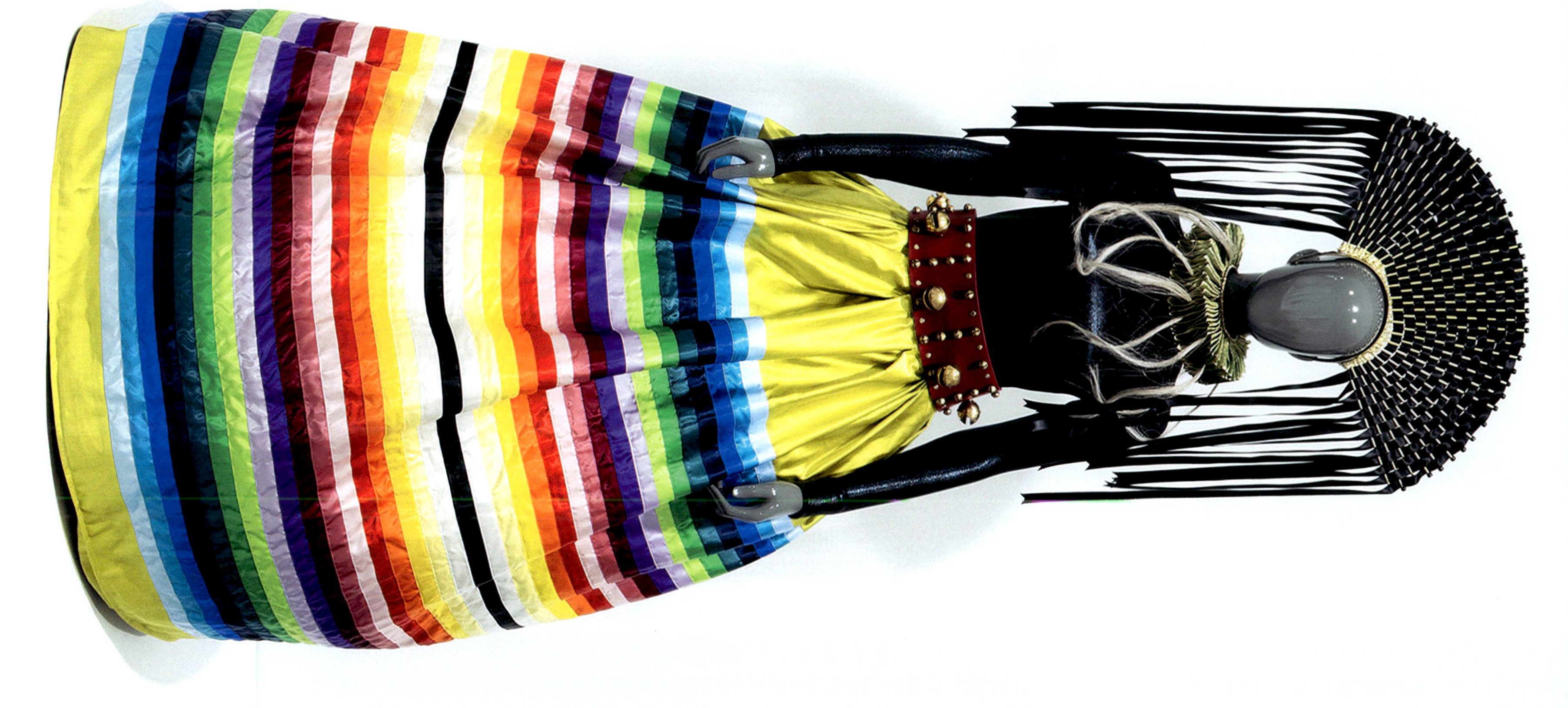

13. Celeste Pedri-Spade (Anishinabekwe/Ojibwe), *Anti-Pipeline Society Kwe* from the *Material Kwe* series, 2019. Ribbon skirt, leather belt, brass tacks, metal jingle bells, fabric, acrylic hair, dimensions variable. Courtesy of Vancouver Art Gallery. Photography by Linda Roy

14. Orlando Dugi (Diné), *Warrior Twins Coat*, 2022. Silk / wool
blend fabric, silk charmeuse, gold flat metal wire, French
bullion, silk dye paints, dimensions variable. Courtesy of
the Southwestern Association for Indian Arts (SWAIA).
Photography by Tira Howard

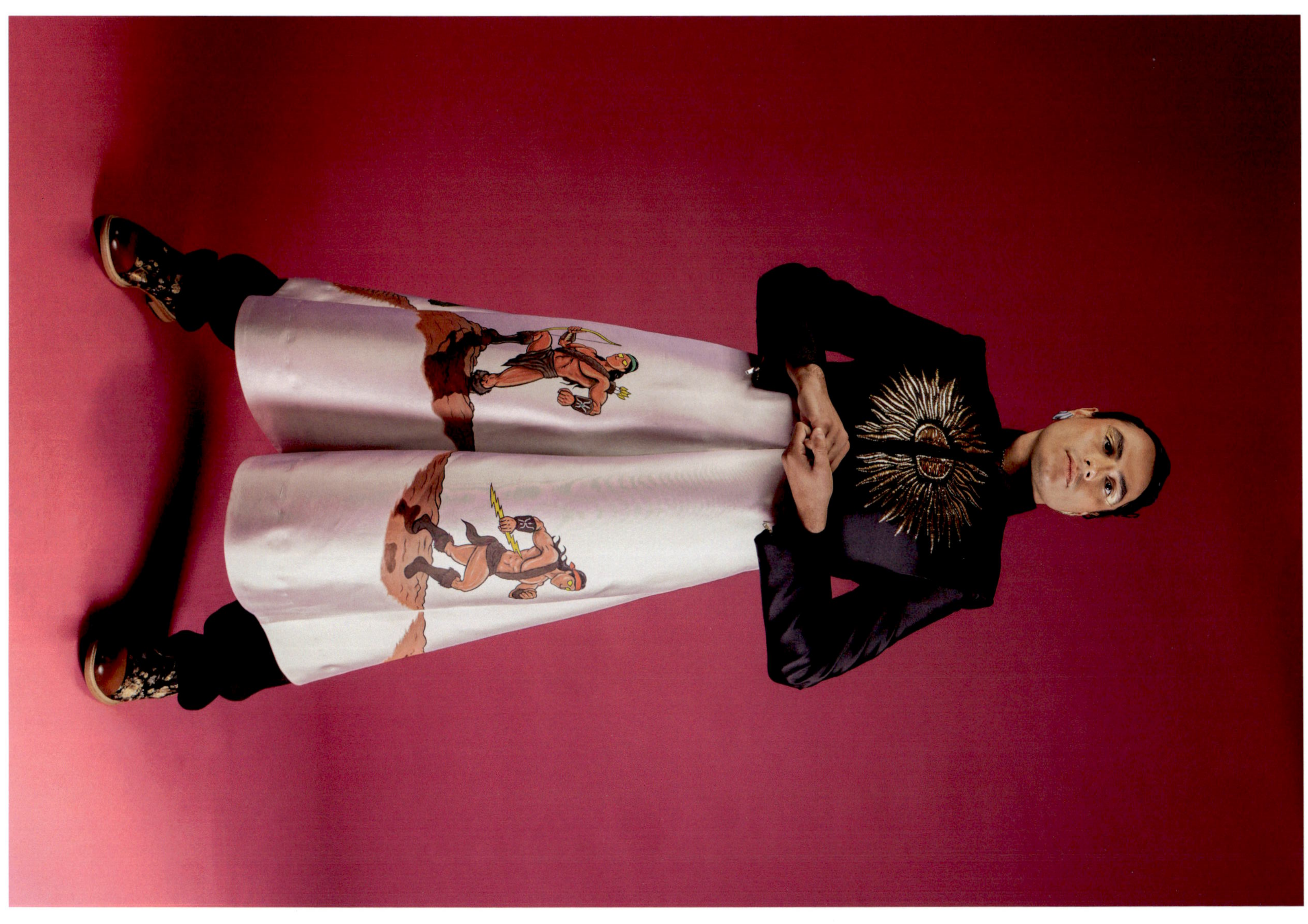

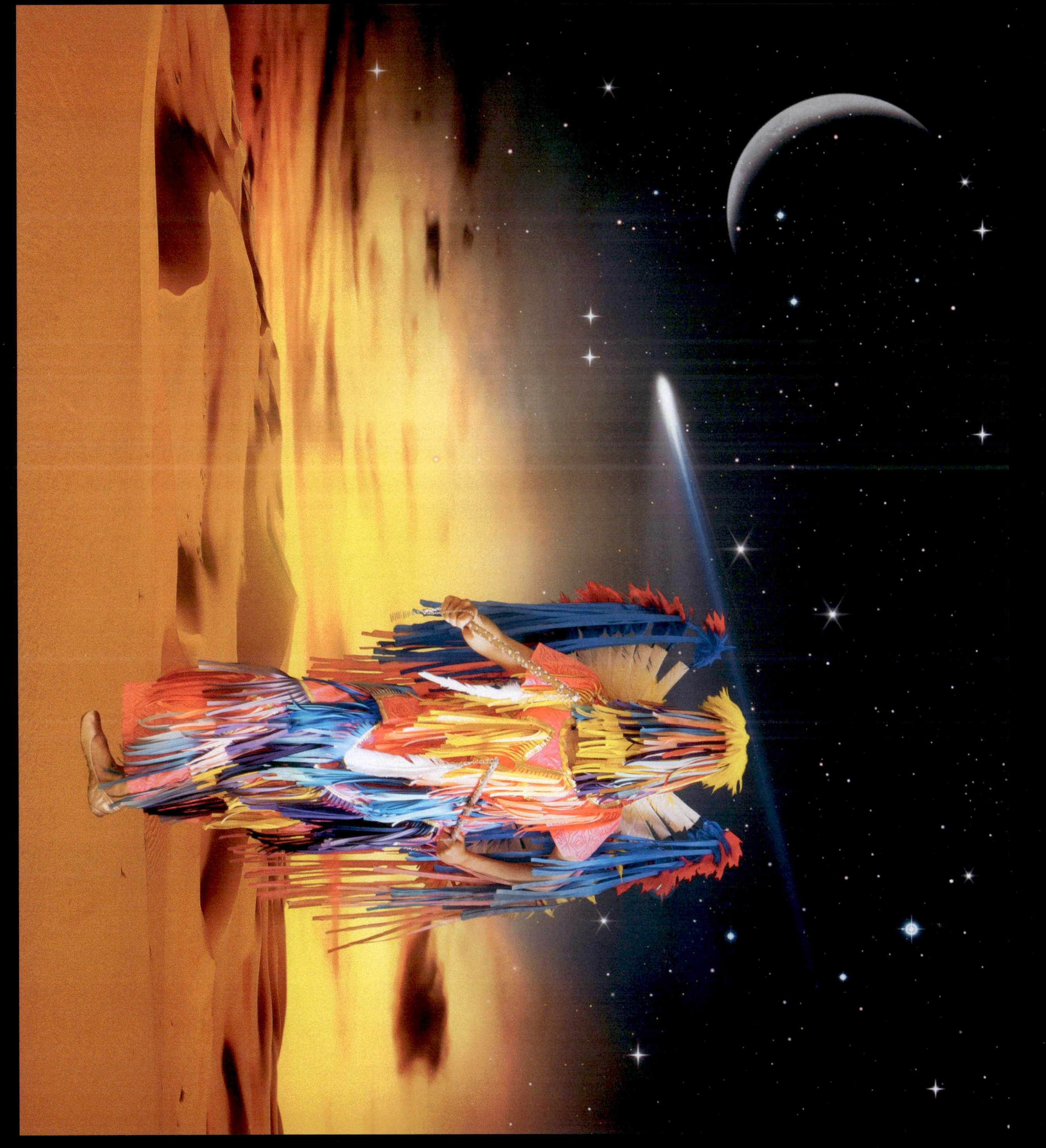

15. Wendy Red Star (Apsáalooke), *Stirs Up the Dust* from the *Thunder Up Above* series, 2011. Pigment print on FineArt Pearl, 27 × 30 in. Courtesy of the Autry Museum of the American West

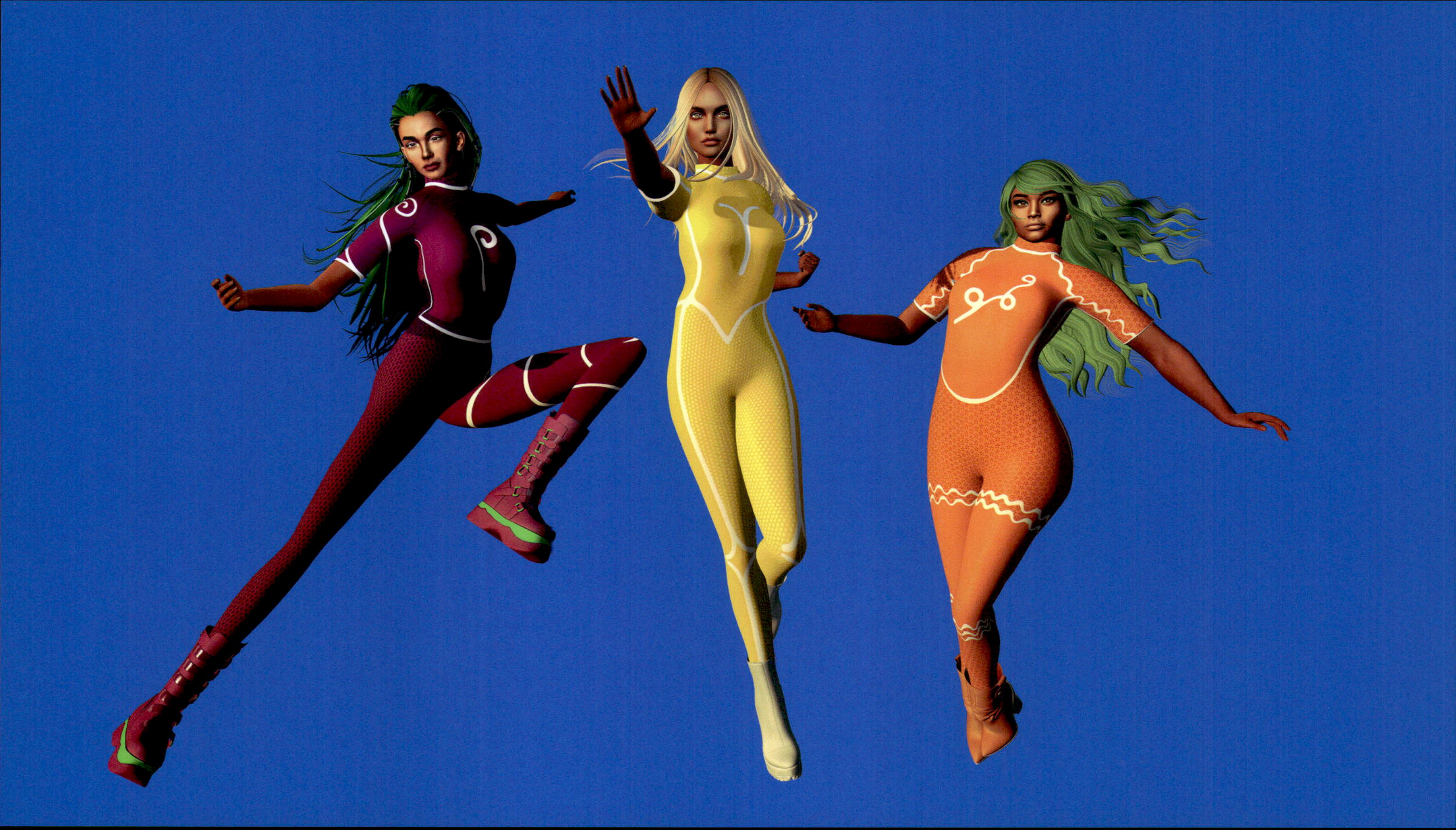

16. Skawennati (Kanien'kehà:ka [Mohawk]), *Three Sisters: Regeneration* from the machinima *Words Before All Else*, 2022. Machinimagraph, dimensions variable. Courtesy of the artist

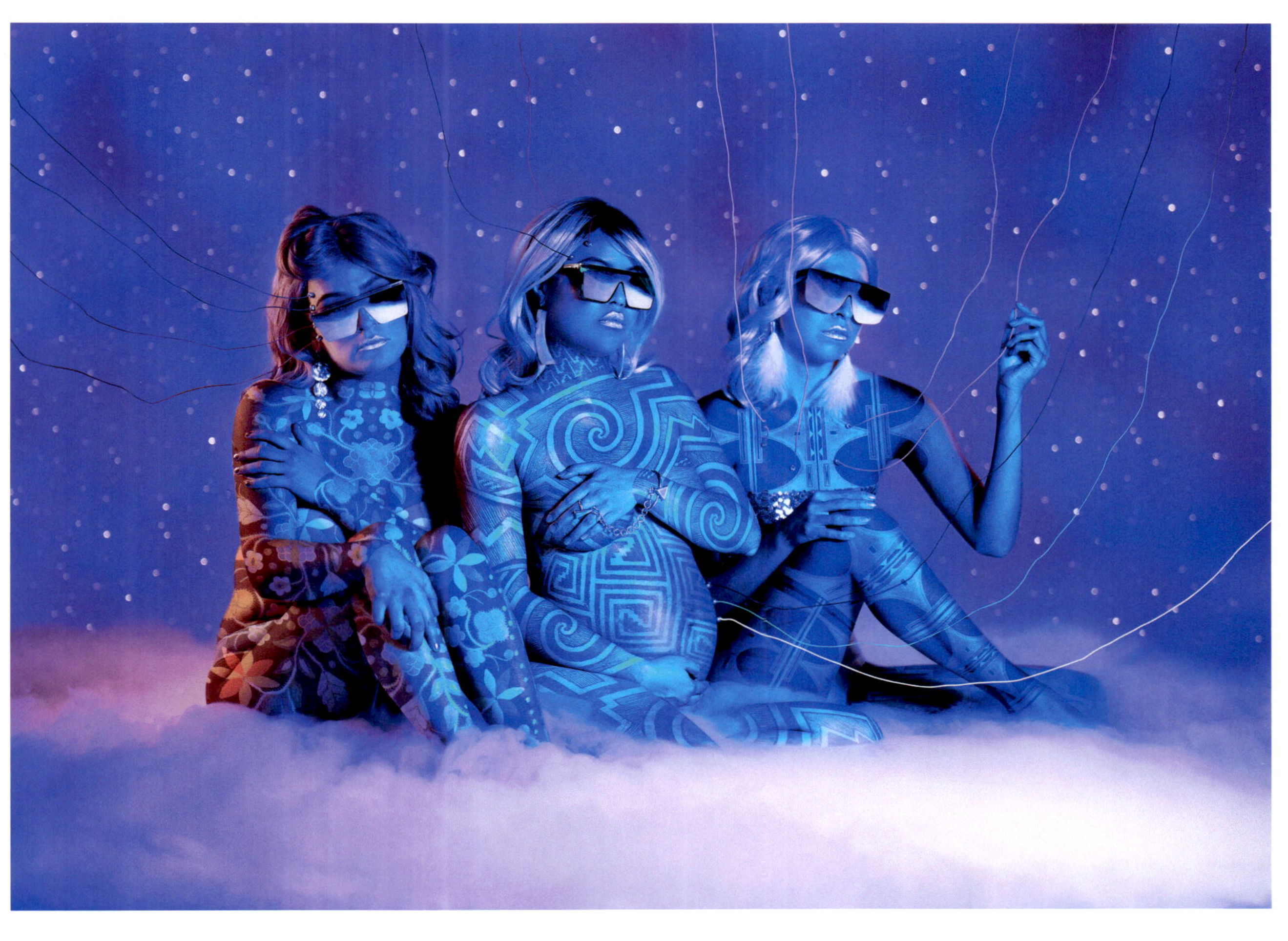

17. Cara Romero (Chemehuevi), *Three Sisters*, 2022. Limited edition archival photograph, 40 × 55 in. Courtesy of the artist

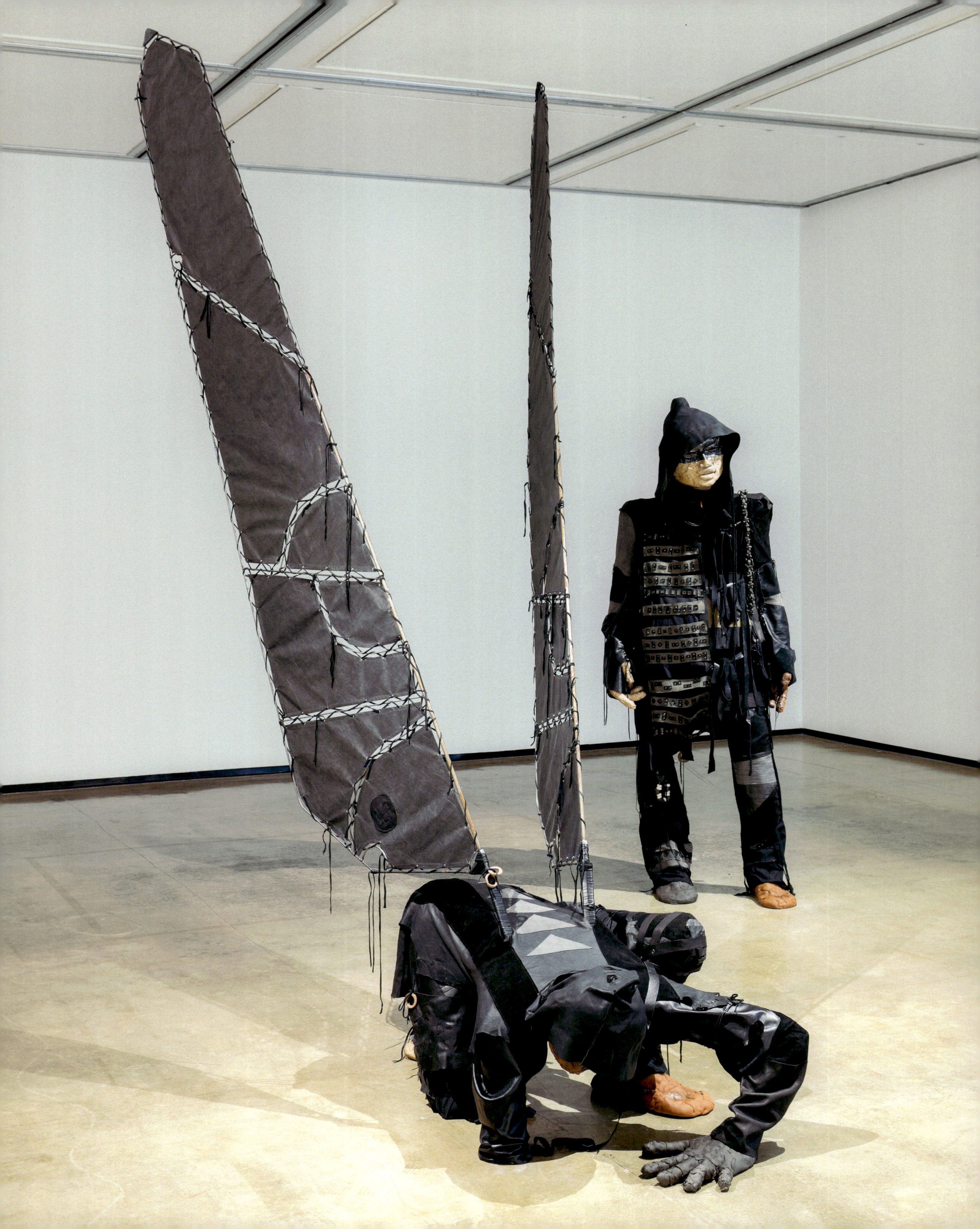

18. Rose B. Simpson (Santa Clara Pueblo), *Ground (Witness)*, 2016. Ceramic, steel, leather, textile, 99 × 17 × 27 in. (standing figure), 153 × 59 × 37 in. (winged figure). Courtesy of the Benton Museum of Art, Pomona College. Photography by Ian Byers-Gamber

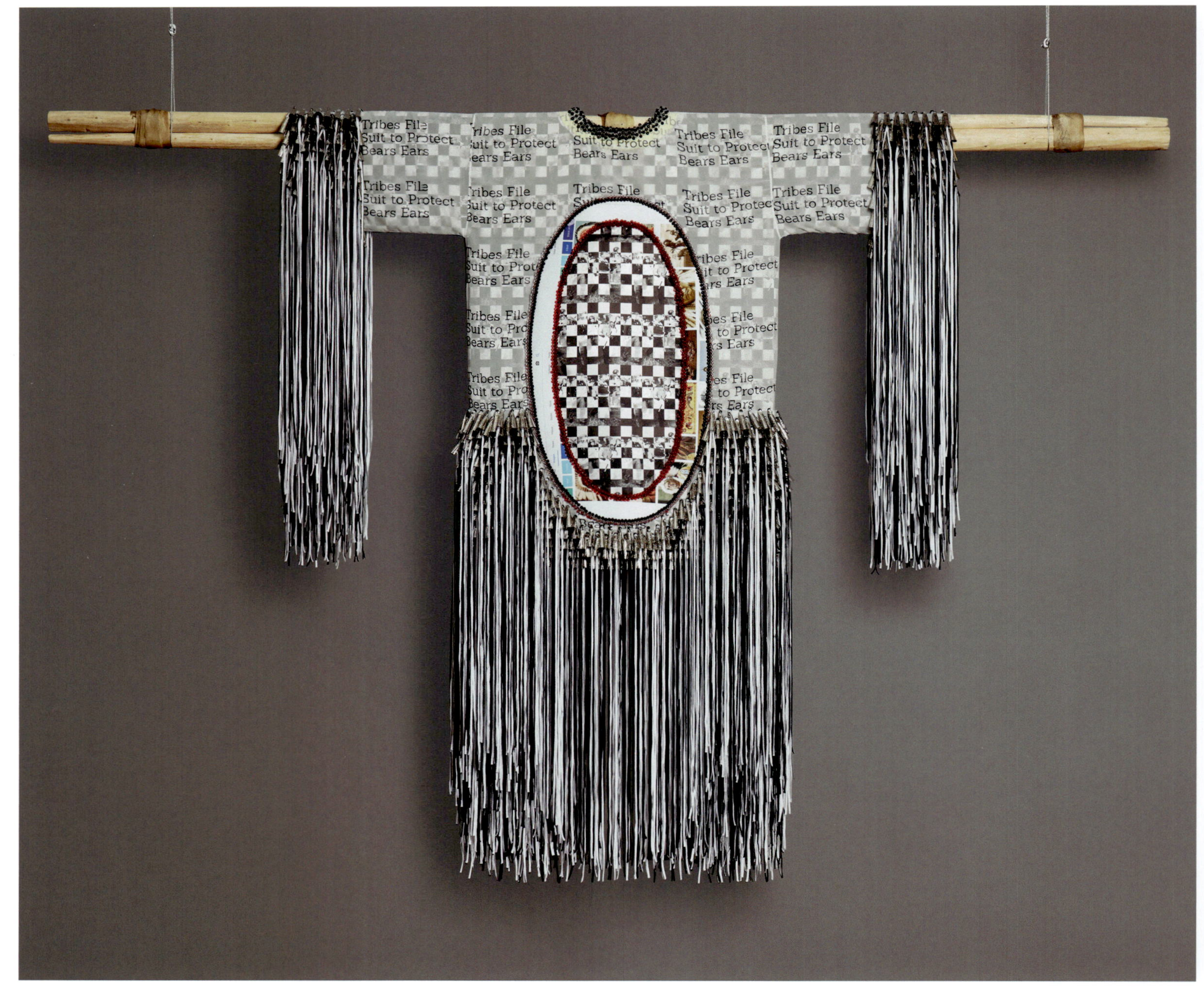

19. Jeffrey Gibson (Mississippi Band of Choctaw Indians/Cherokee descent), *Tribes File Suit to Protect Bears Ears*, 2018. Polyester satin, printed chiffon, canvas, neoprene, tin jingles, nylon fringe, glass and plastic beads, artificial sinew on tipi poles, 85 × 73½ × 8½ in. Courtesy of the Carl & Marilynn Thoma Foundation. Photography by John Bentham

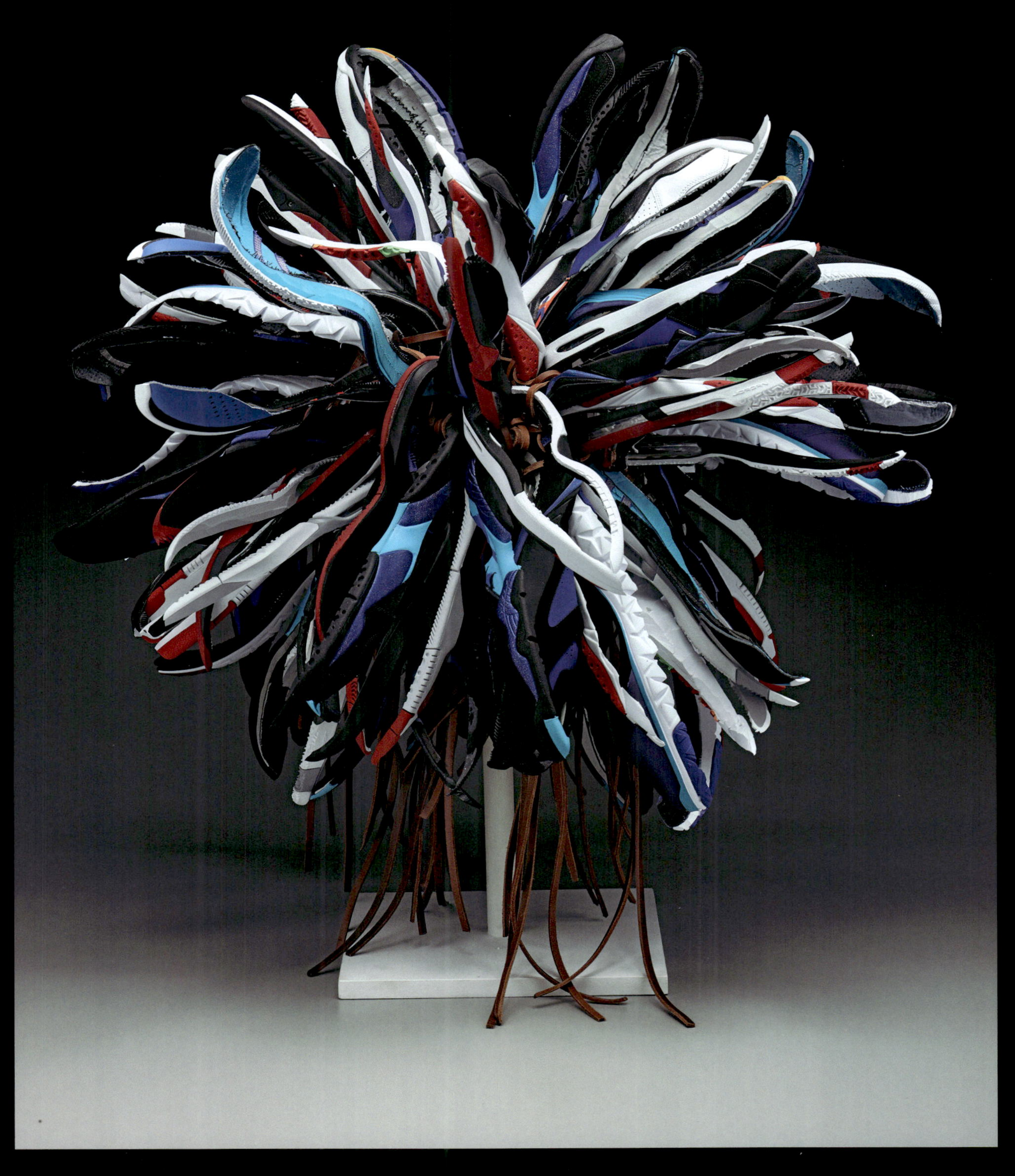

20. Brian Jungen (Dane-zaa), *Warrior I*, 2017. Nike Air Jordans, leather, 39 × 32 × 29 in. Courtesy of the Dallas Museum of Art

21. Brian Jungen (Dane-zaa), *Variant #3*, 2016. Nike Air Jordans, leather, 60 × 71 × 14½ in. Courtesy of the artist and Casey Kaplan, New York. © Brian Jungen. Photography by Jean Vong

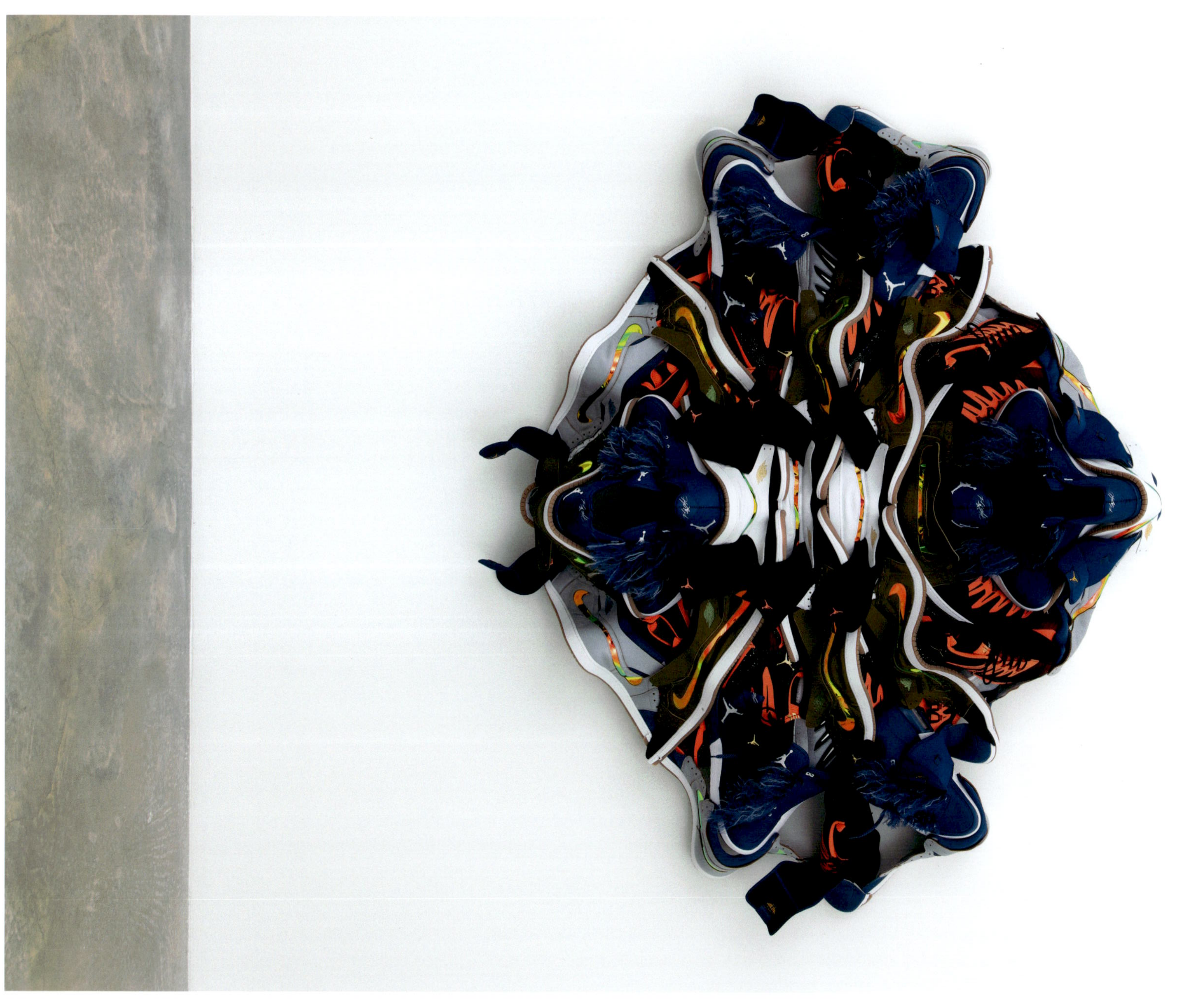

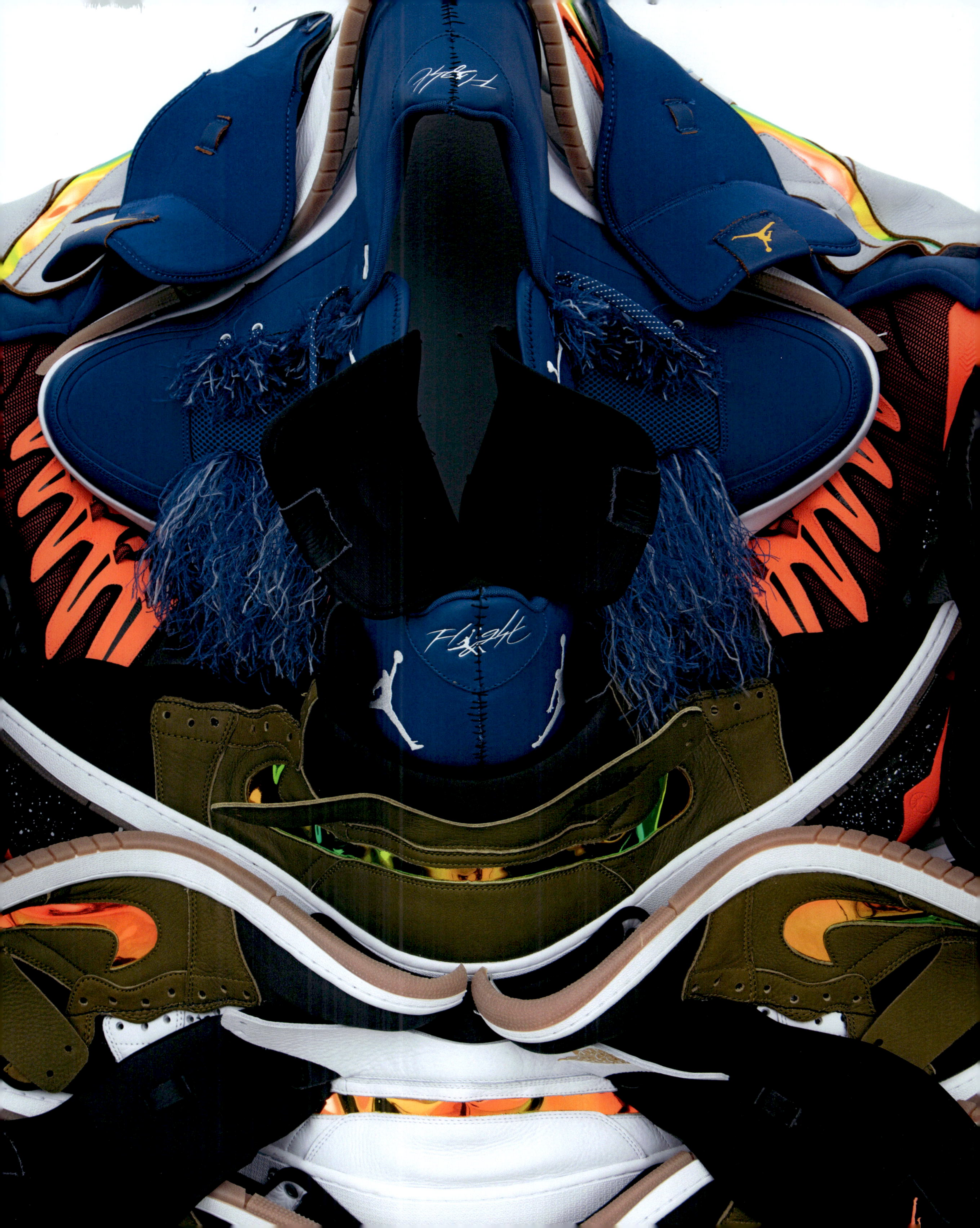

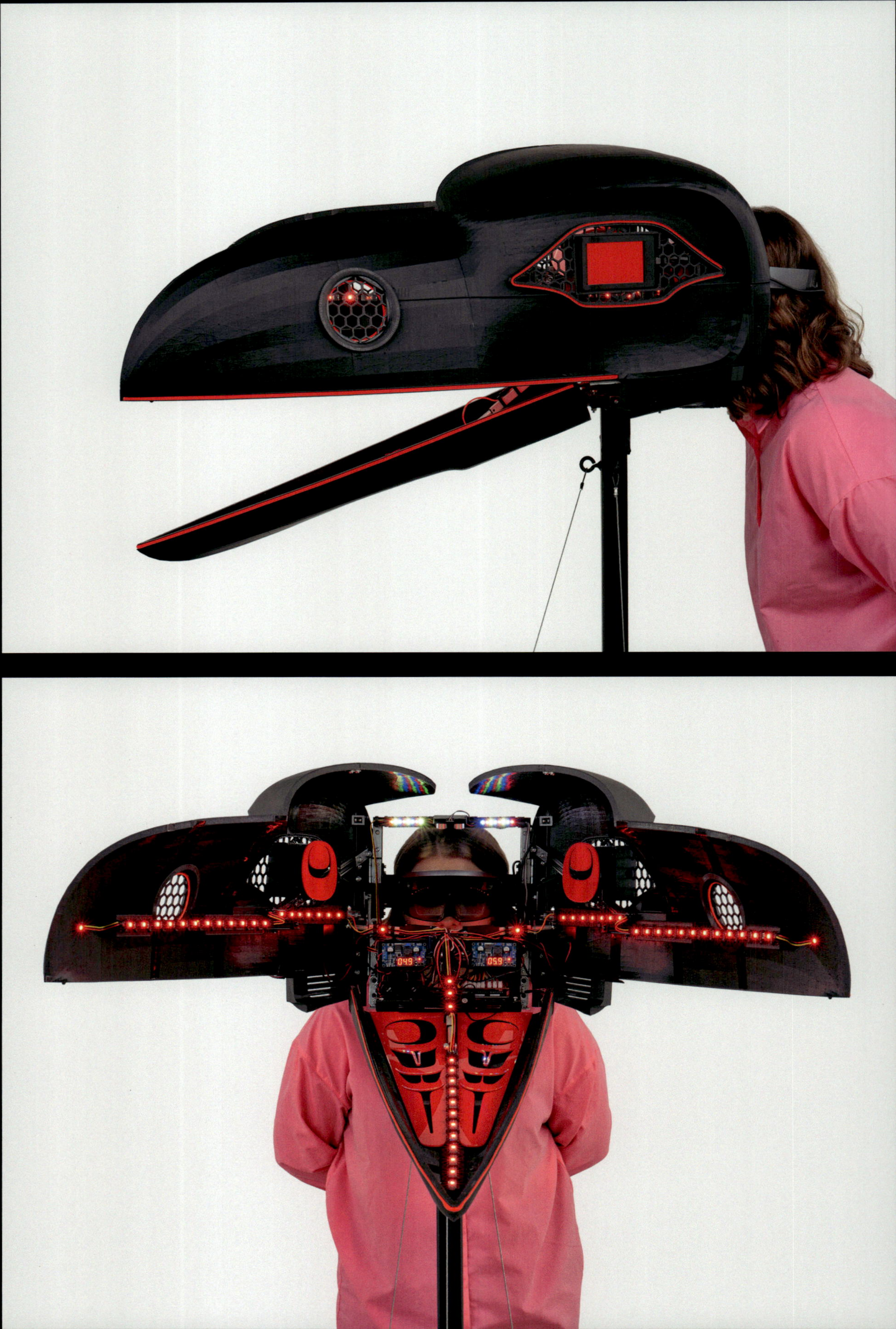

22. Shawn Hunt (Heiltsuk) in collaboration with Microsoft Vancouver and the Garage, *Transformation Mask*, 2017. 3D-printed PLA and acrylic resin, LED lights, and Microsoft HoloLens, approx. 3¼ ft. Courtesy of Equinox Gallery, Vancouver. Photography by Rachel Topham Photography

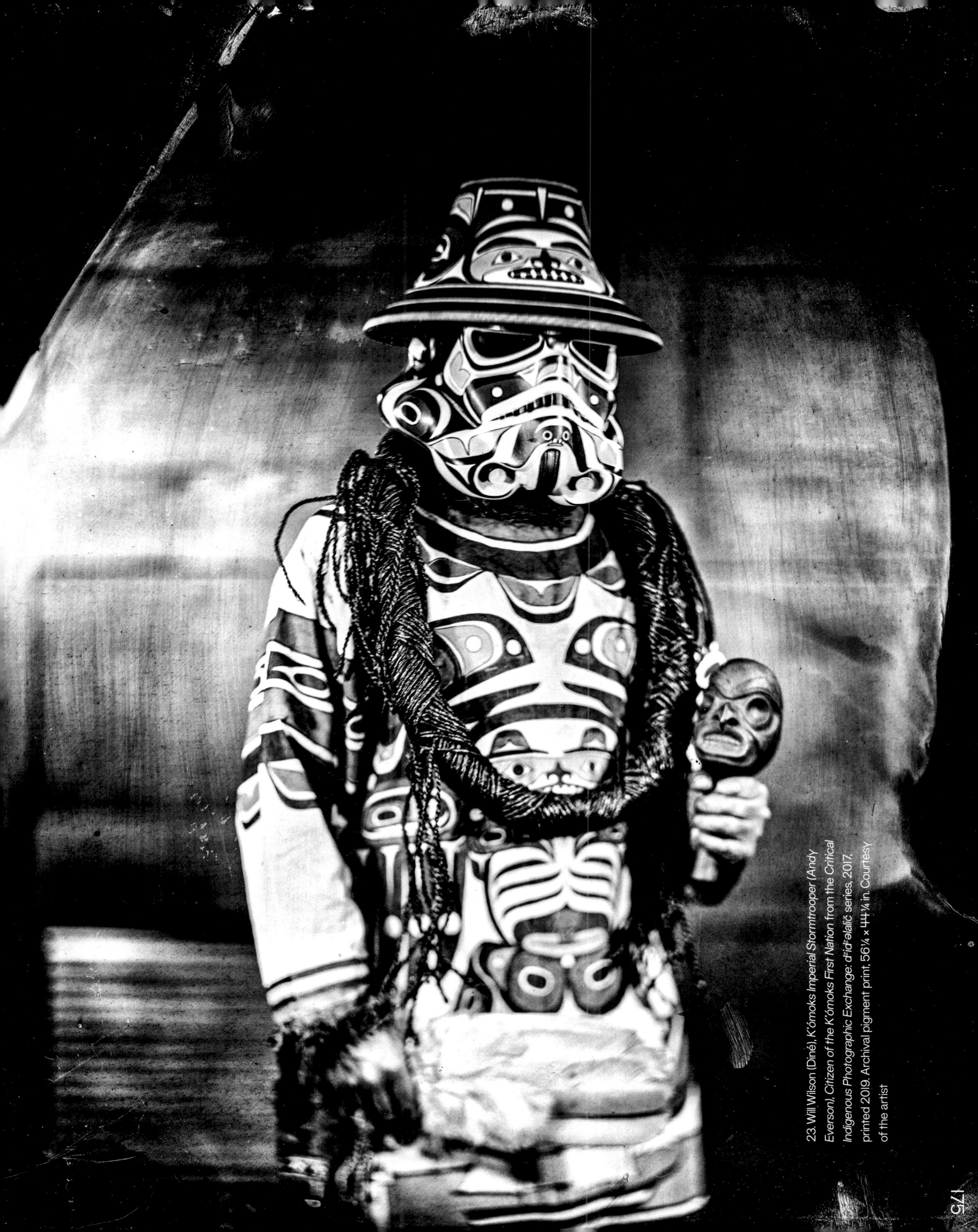

23. Will Wilson (Diné), *K'ómoks Imperial Stormtrooper (Andy Everson), Citizen of the K'ómoks First Nation from the Critical Indigenous Photographic Exchange: dᶻidᶻəlalič series*, 2017, printed 2019. Archival pigment print, 56¼ × 44¼ in. Courtesy of the artist

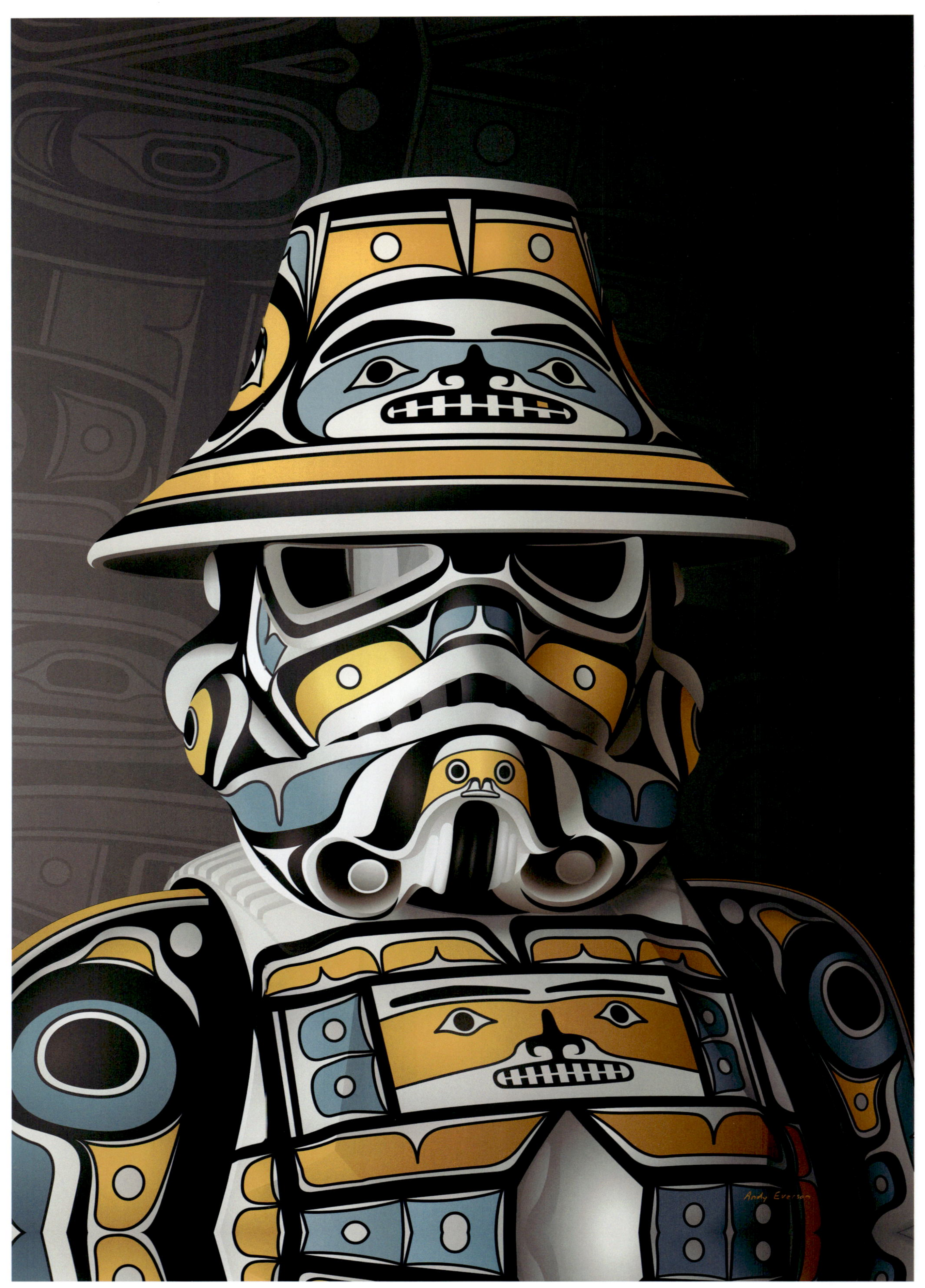

24. Andy Everson (K'ómoks/Kwakwaka'wakw), *Resistance*, 2014. Digital print, dimensions variable. Courtesy of the artist

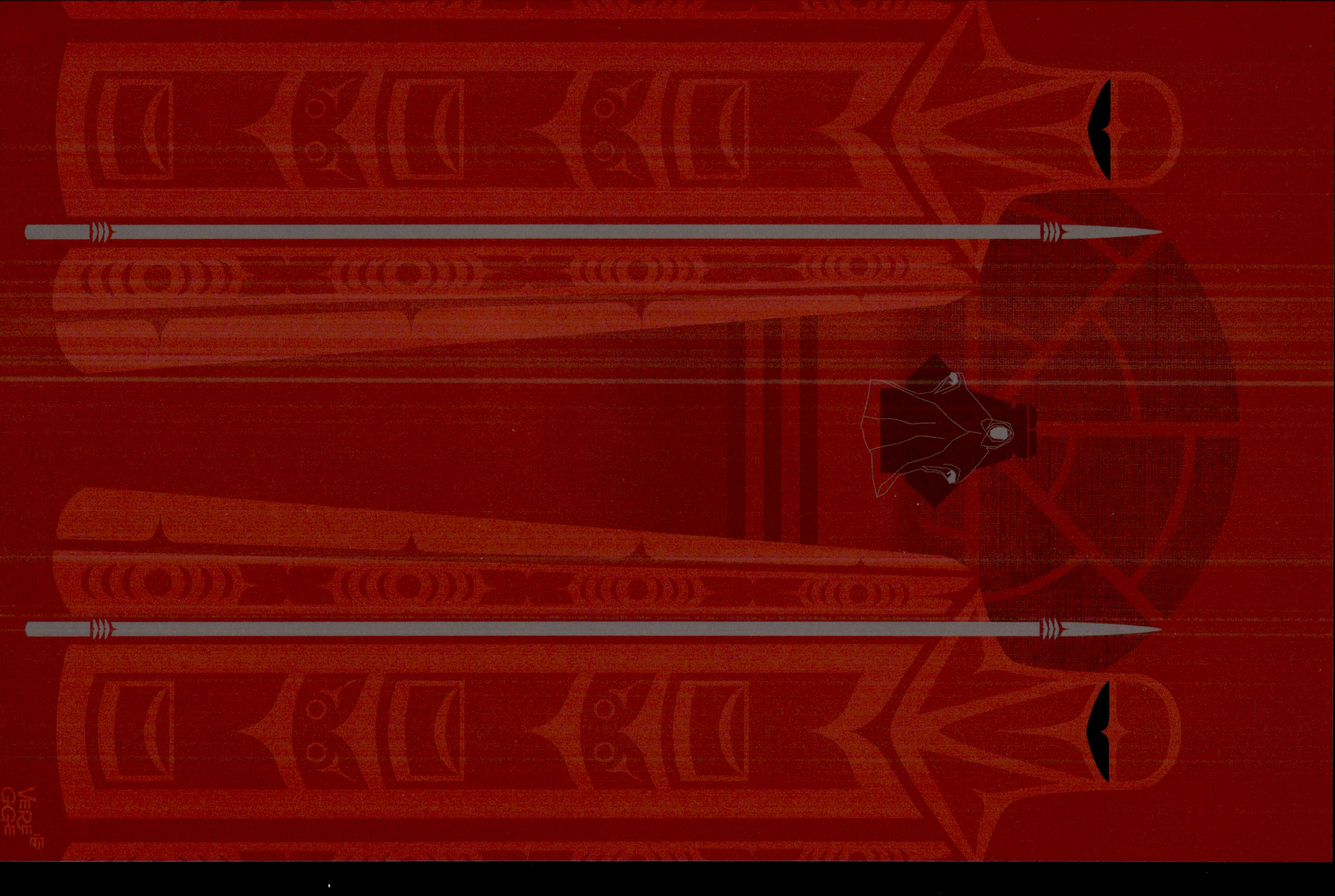

25. Jeffrey Veregge (Port Gamble S'Klallam), *Welcome,* 2014. Digital print, dimensions variable. Courtesy of the artist

26. Jeffrey Veregge (Port Gamble S'Klallam), *She's Got It Where It Counts*, 2016. Digital print, dimensions variable. Courtesy of the artist

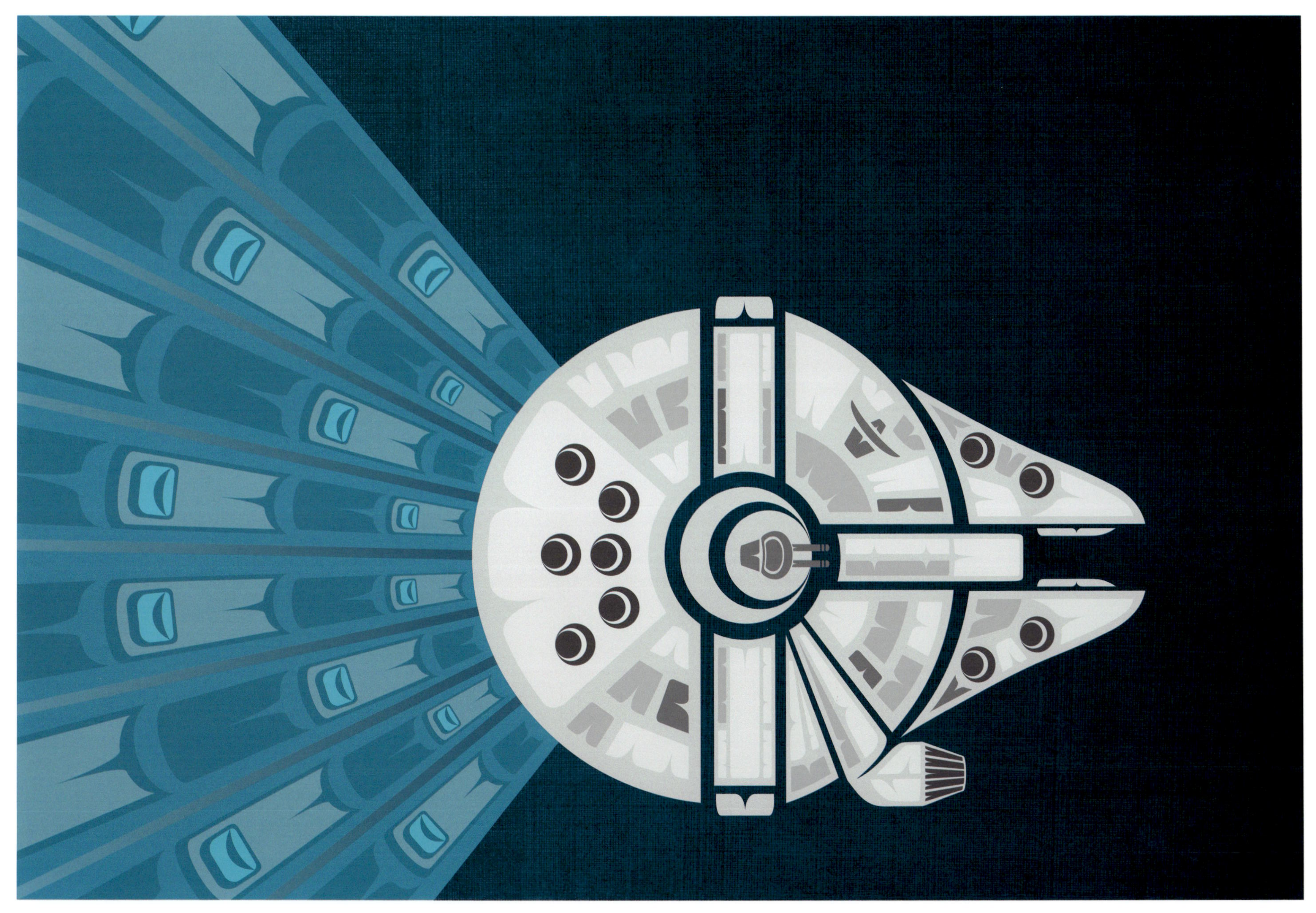

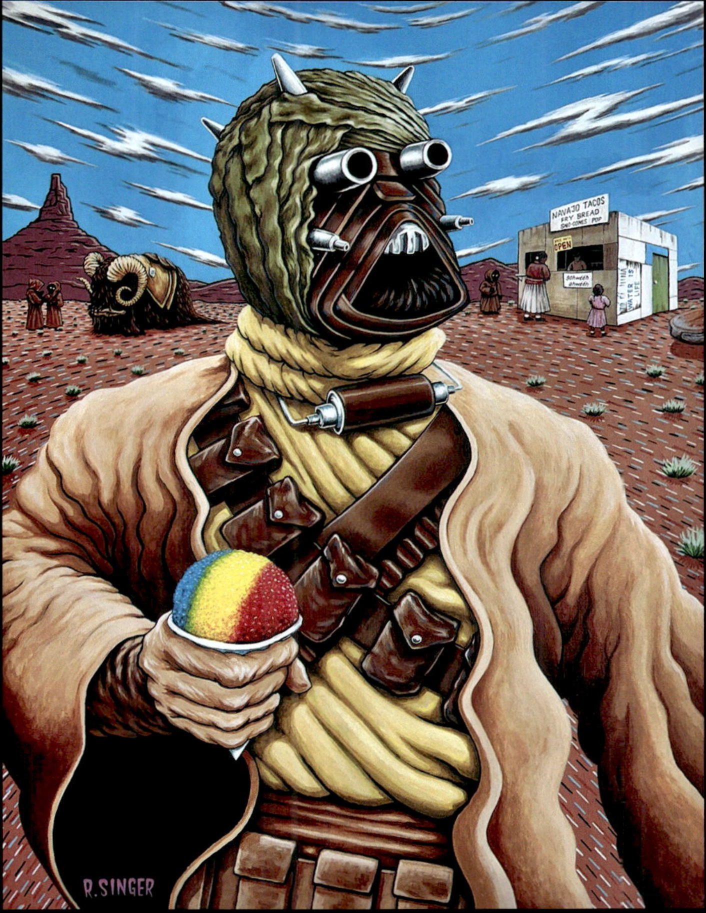

NAVAJO TACOS
FRY BREAD
SNO-CONES POP
OPEN
WATER IS LIFE
R. SINGER

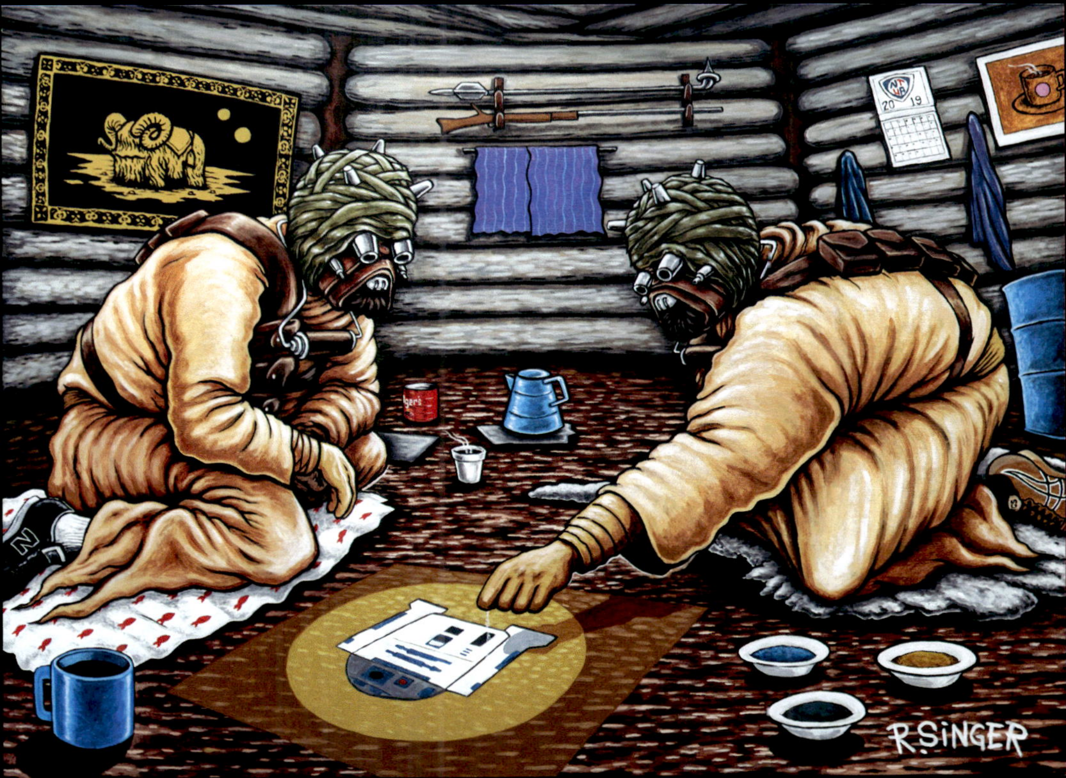

R. SINGER

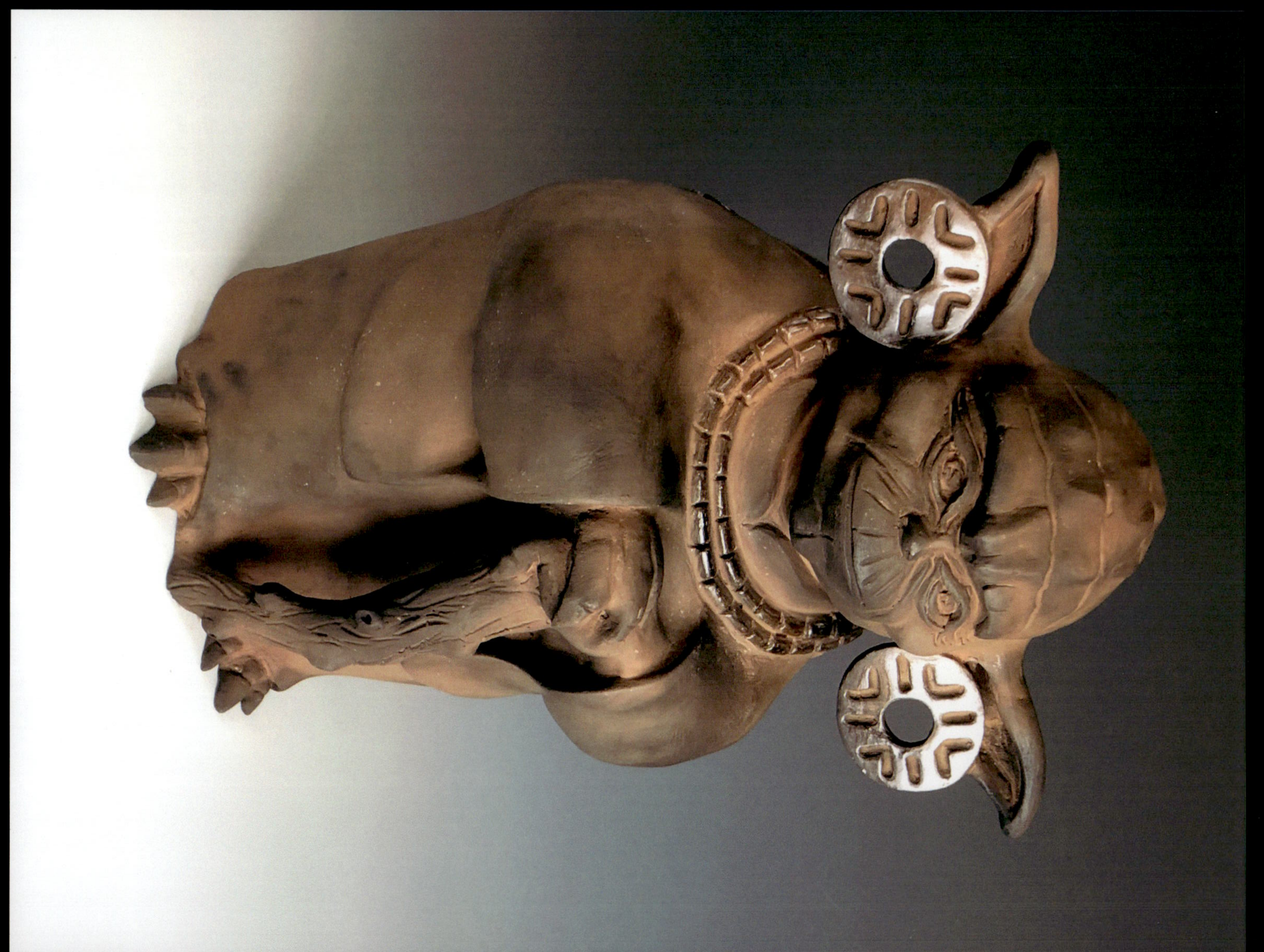

Leader Effigy Vessel, 2022. Red River clay tempered with freshwater mussel shell, 14¼ × 10⅝⁄₁₆ × 7¼ in. Courtesy of the artist

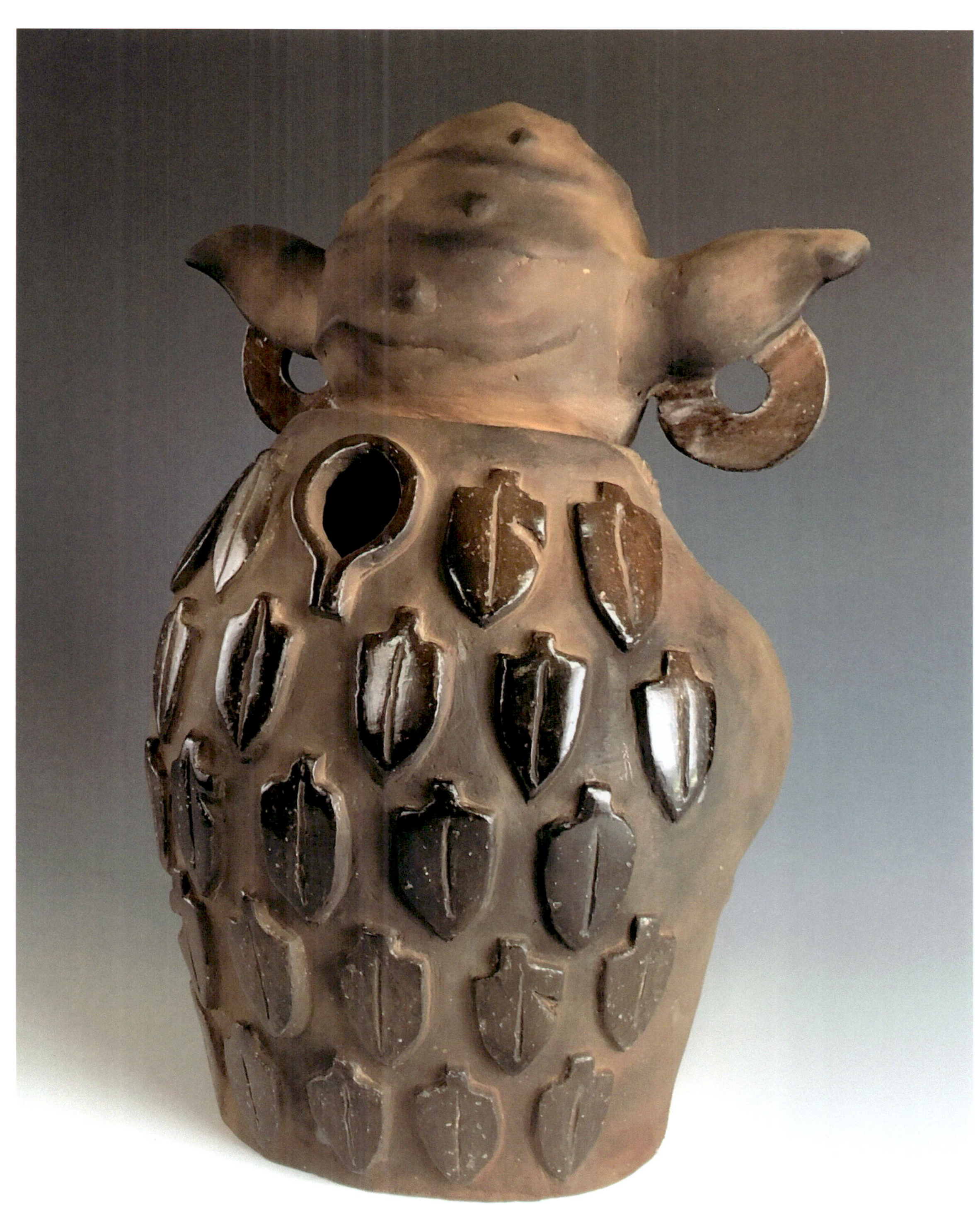

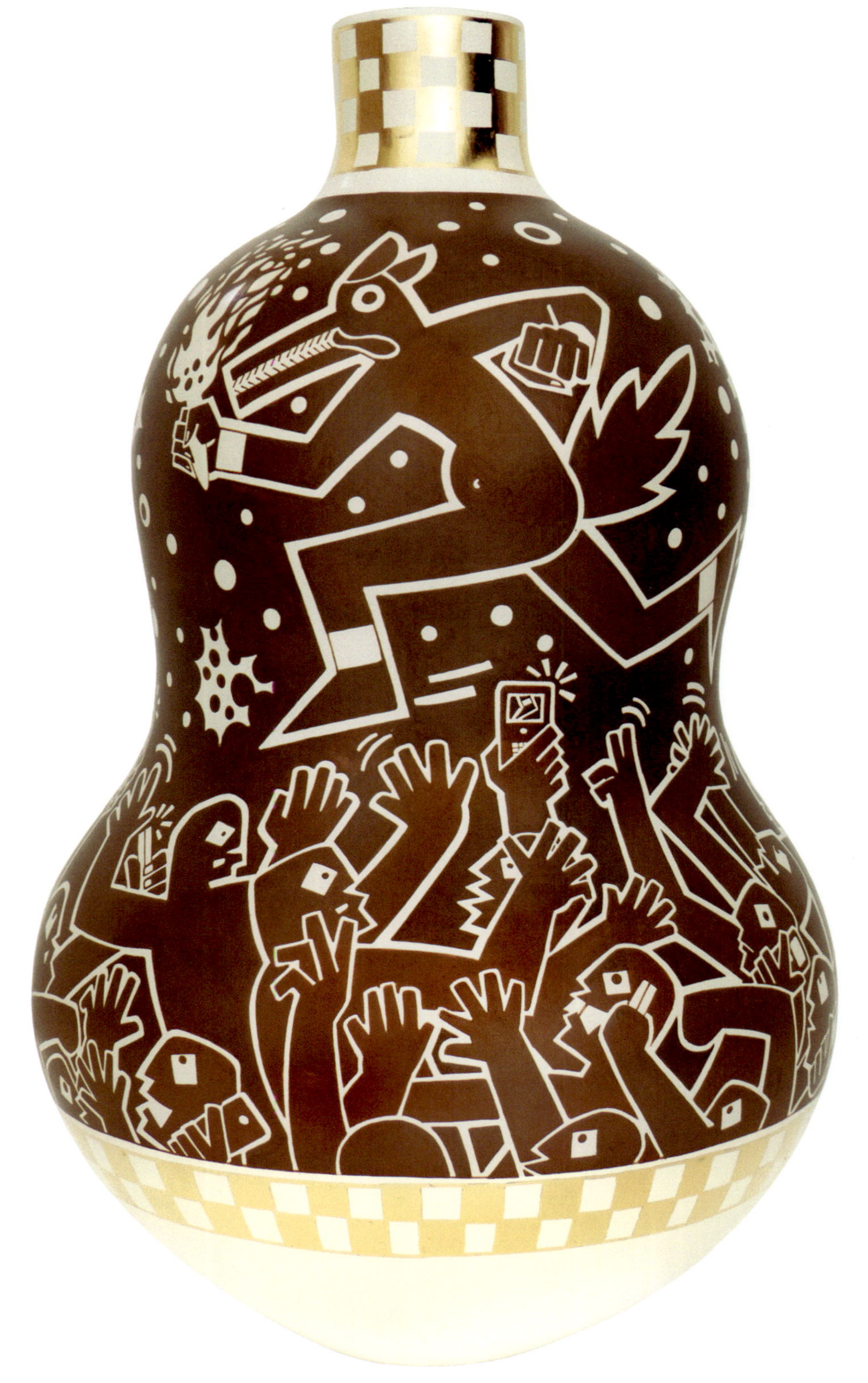

30. Diego Romero (Cochiti Pueblo). *Prometheus*, 2021. Commercial clay, commercial gold luster, natural hand-gathered clay paint, 14½ in. ht. × 8½ in. dia. Courtesy of Shiprock Santa Fe

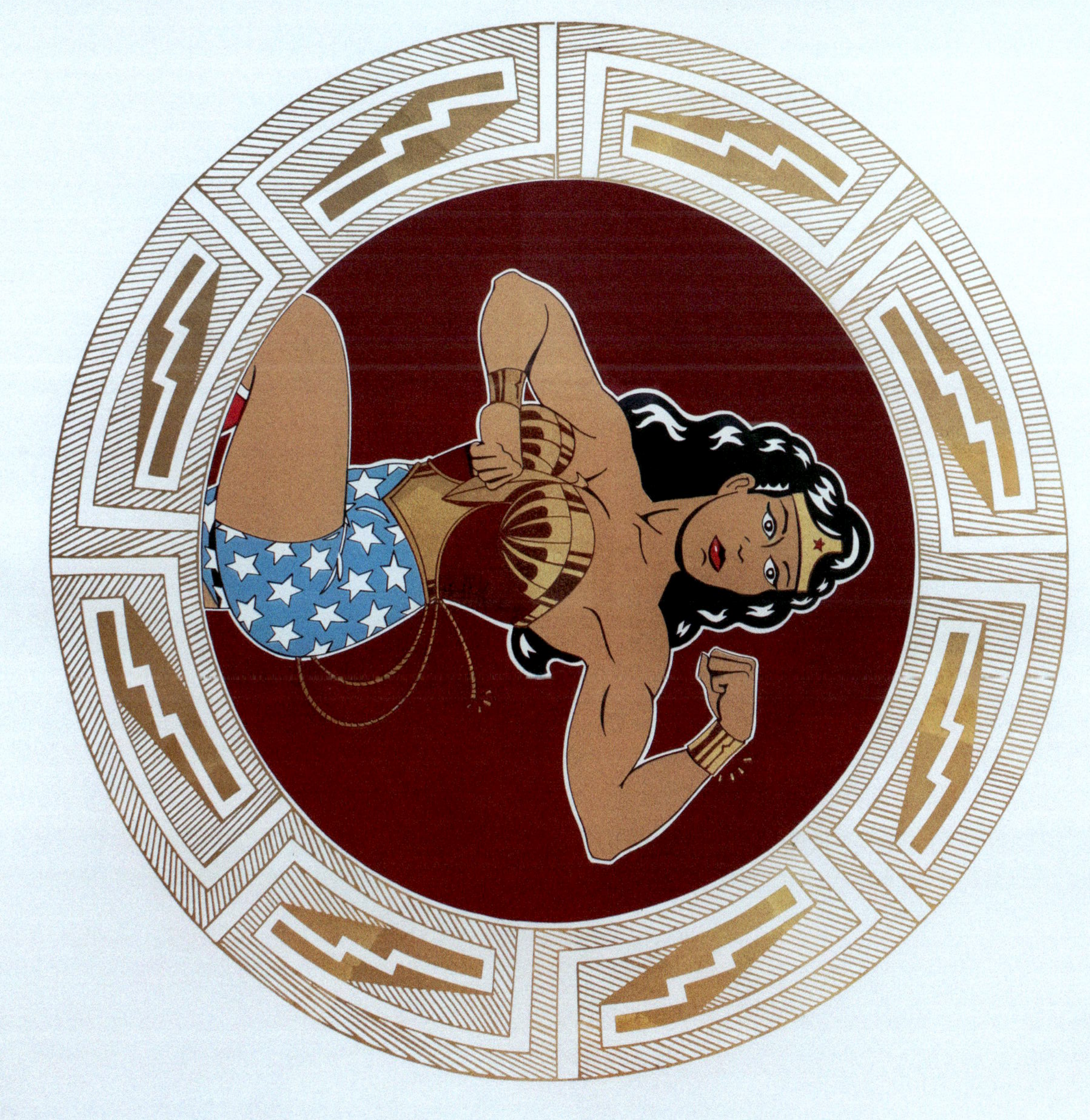

31. Diego Romero (Cochiti Pueblo), *Cara*, 2018. Lithograph with gold leaf, 24 × 24 in. Courtesy of Gallery Hózhó, Albuquerque. Photography by Chelsea Benally.

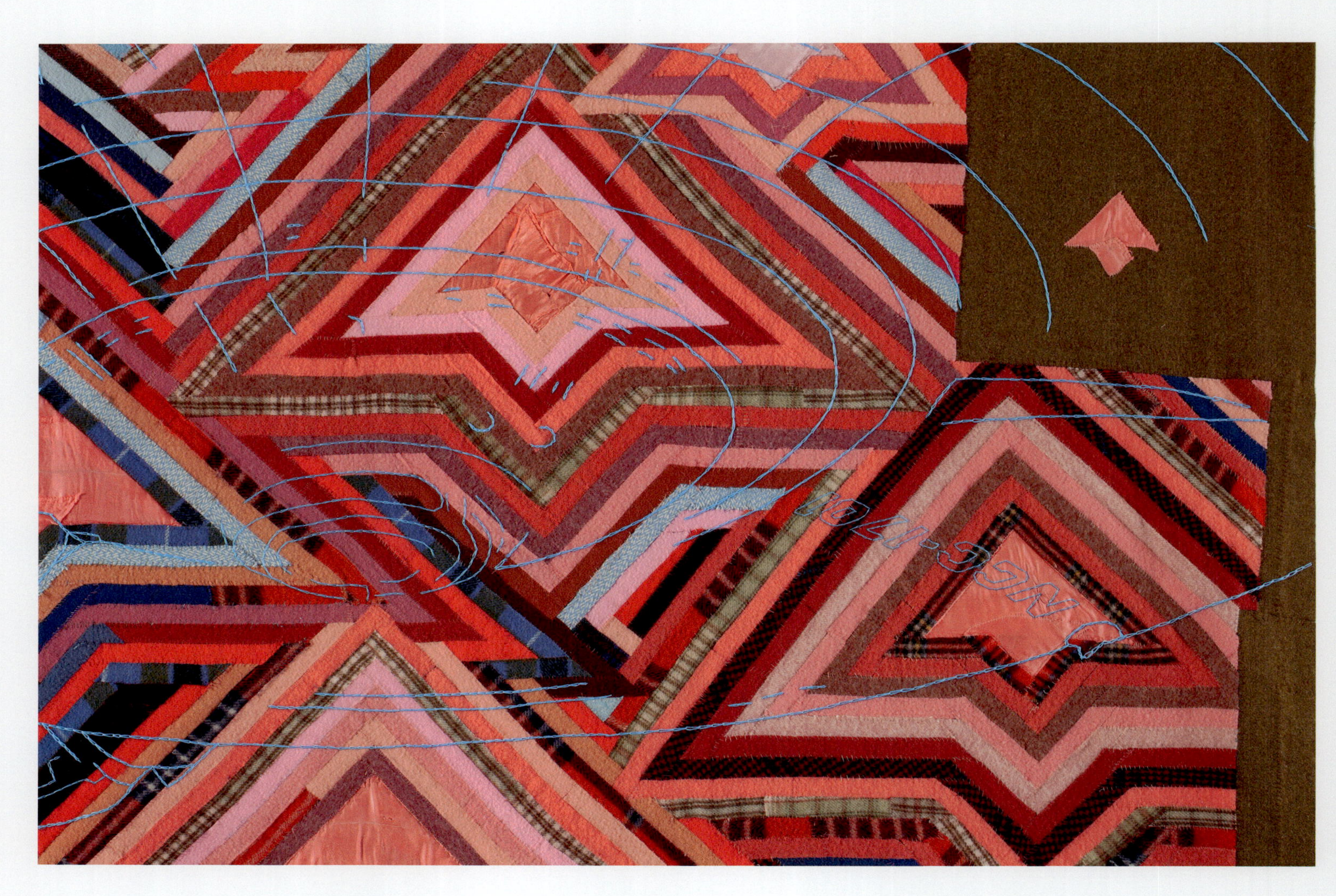

32. Marie Watt (Seneca), *Trek (Pleiades)*, 2014. Reclaimed wool blankets, satin binding, embroidery floss, thread, 74 × 123½ in. Courtesy of the Tia Collection, Santa Fe. Photography by Aaron Johanson

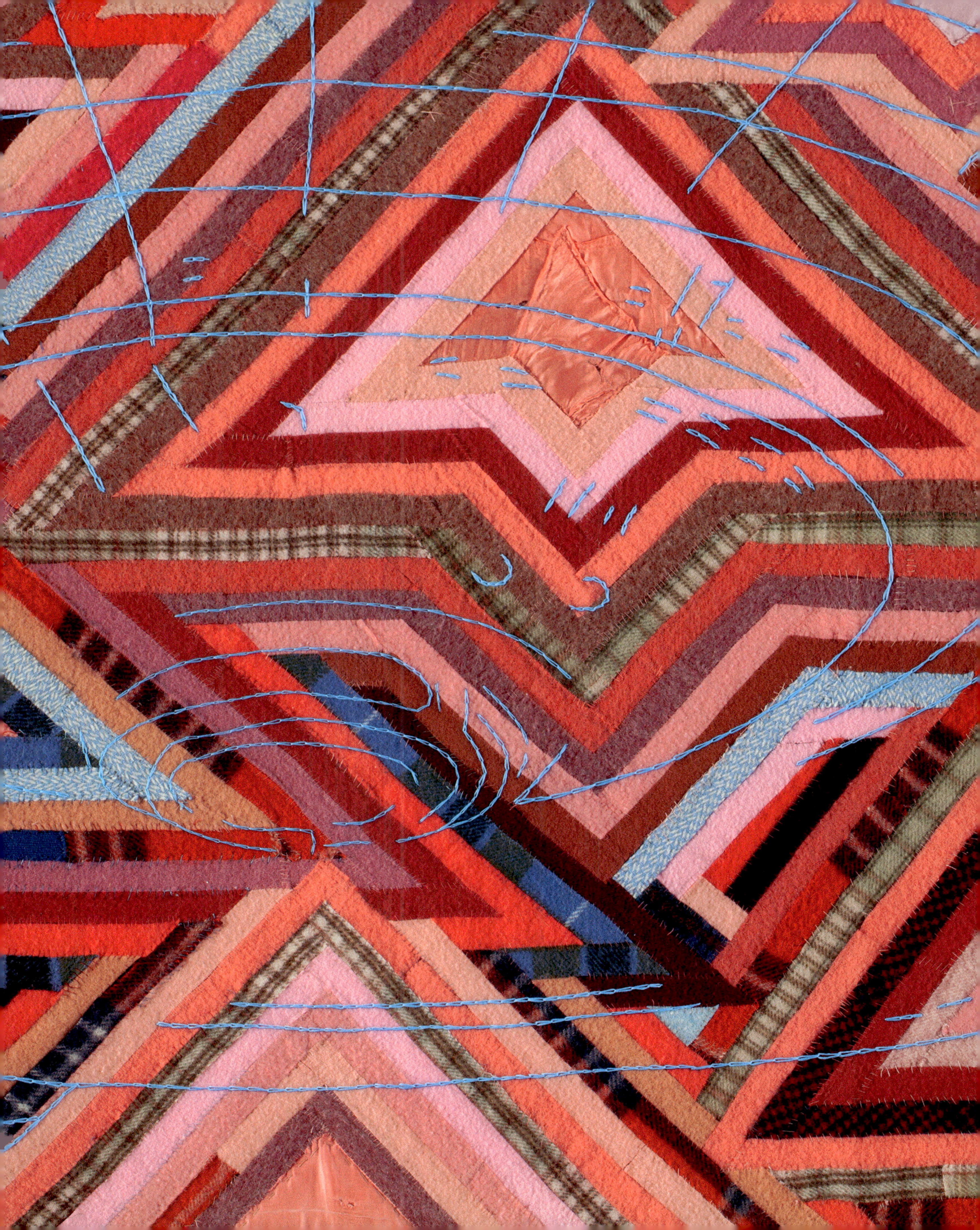

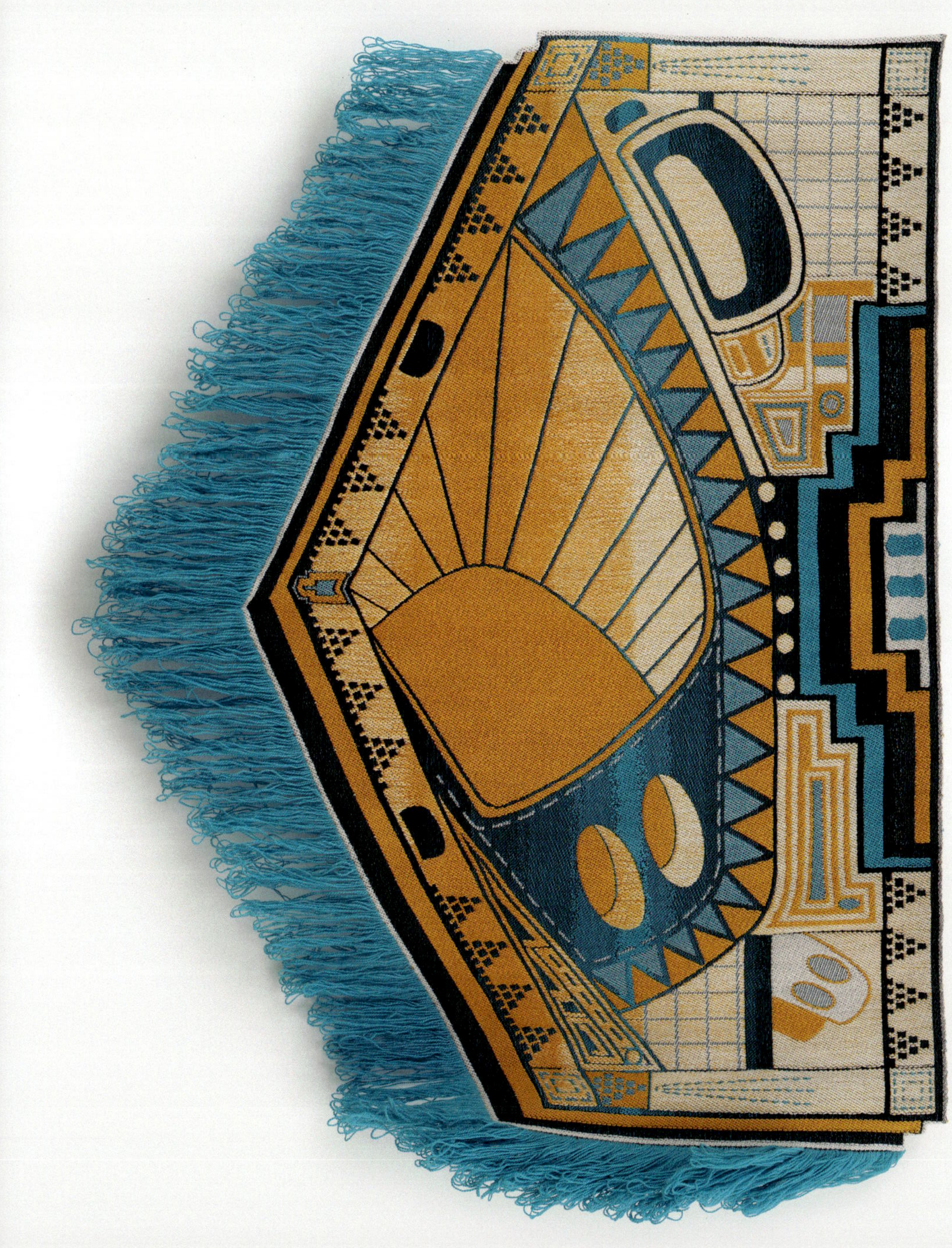

33. Sonny Assu (Ligwiłda'xw of the Kwakwaka'wakw Nations), *Tempest*, 2023. Wool and cotton Jacquard tapestry woven by Sophia Borowska, 41½ × 65½ in. Courtesy of Equinox Gallery, Vancouver. Photography by Rachel Topham Photography

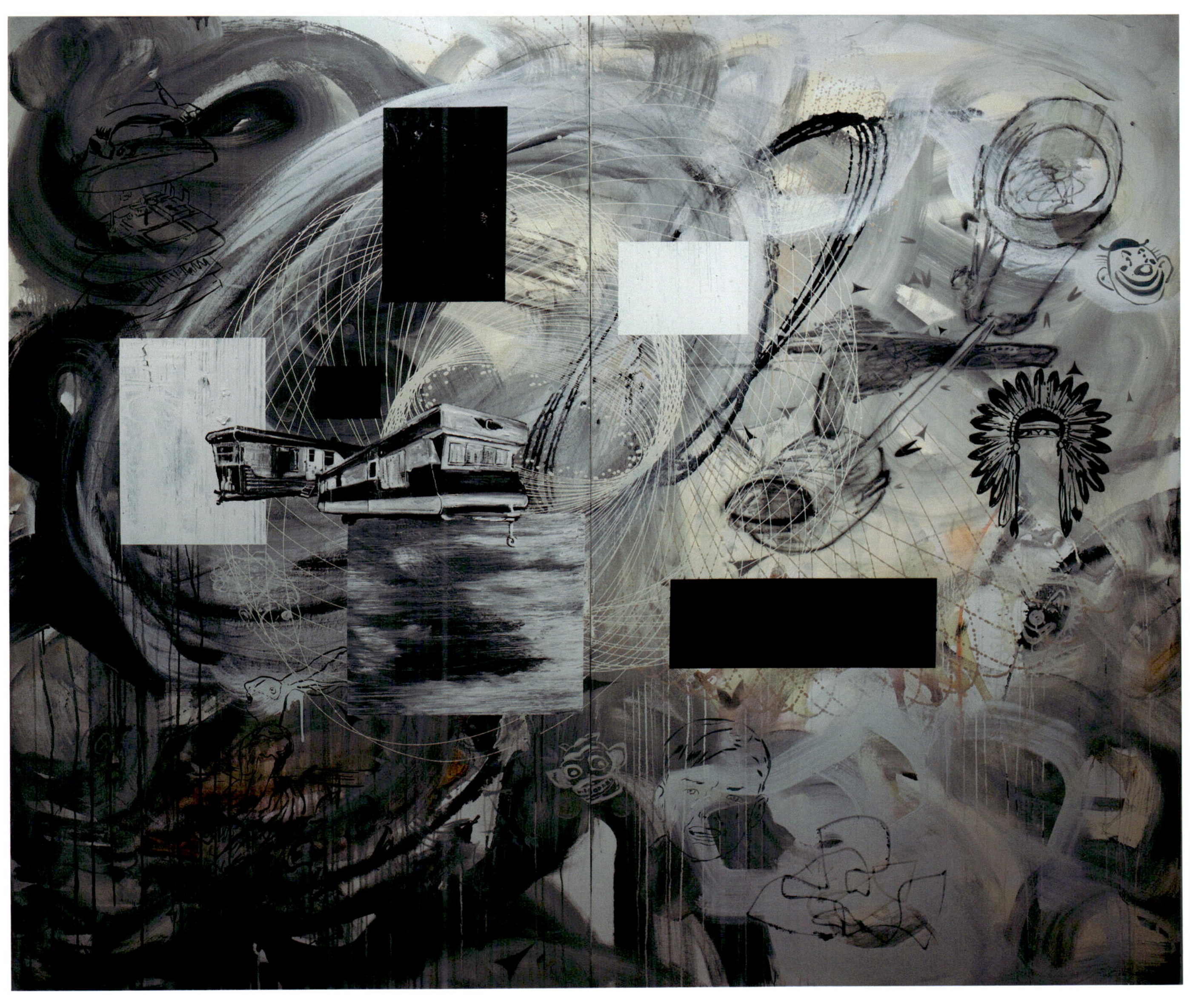

34. Neal Ambrose-Smith (Flathead Salish/Sho-Ban/Métis/Creel, *Get in the Relief Pool*, 2013. Oil, acrylic, collage, 84 × 96 in. Courtesy of the artist

35. Virgil Ortiz (Cochiti Pueblo), *Elder Statesman Astian of the Sirens awaits the arrival of the Survivorship fleet transporting the Recon Watchmen to Puebloan lands from the ReVOlt 1680/2180: Sirens and Sikas series*, 2023. Multimedia installation, dimensions variable. Courtesy of the artist

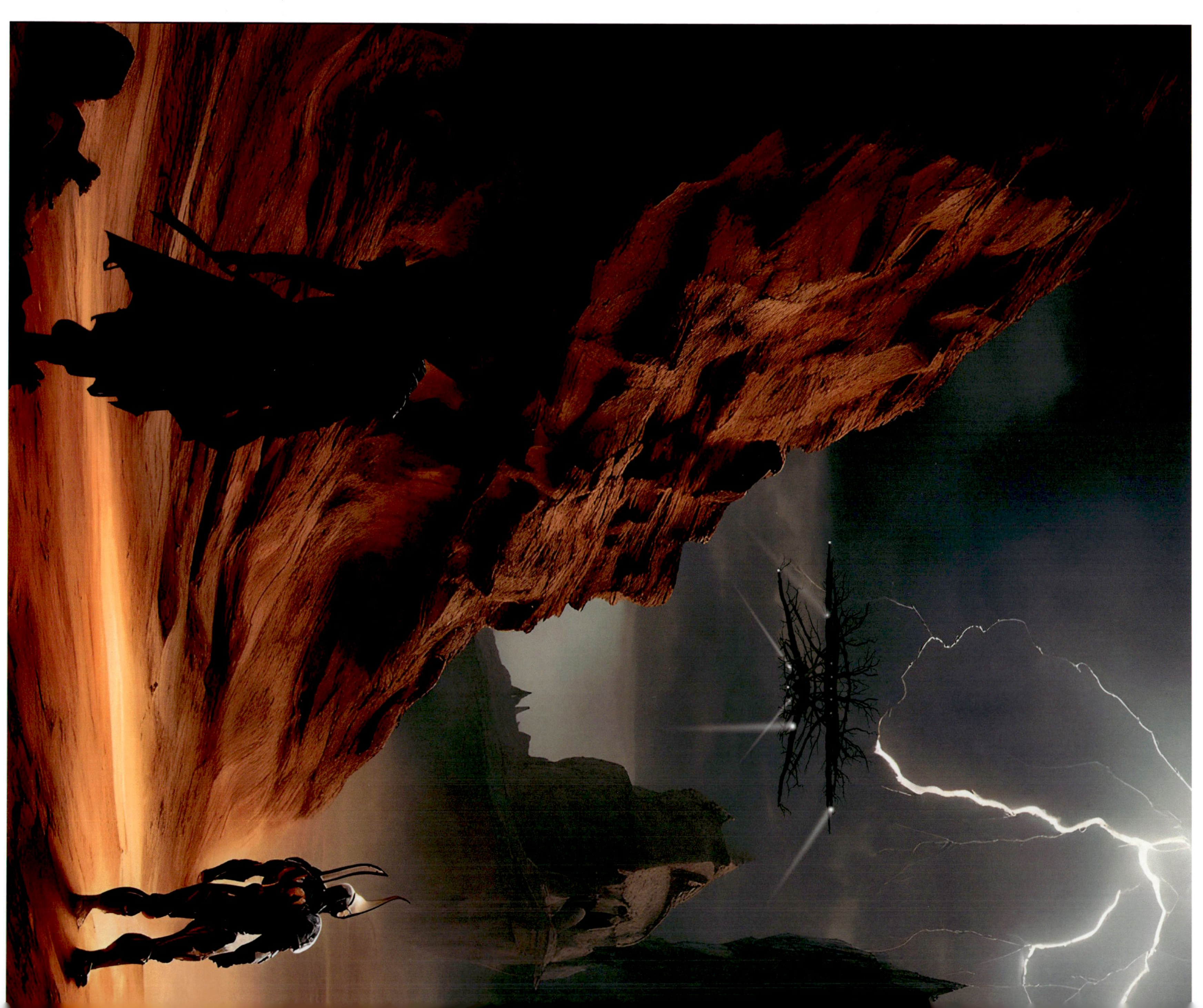

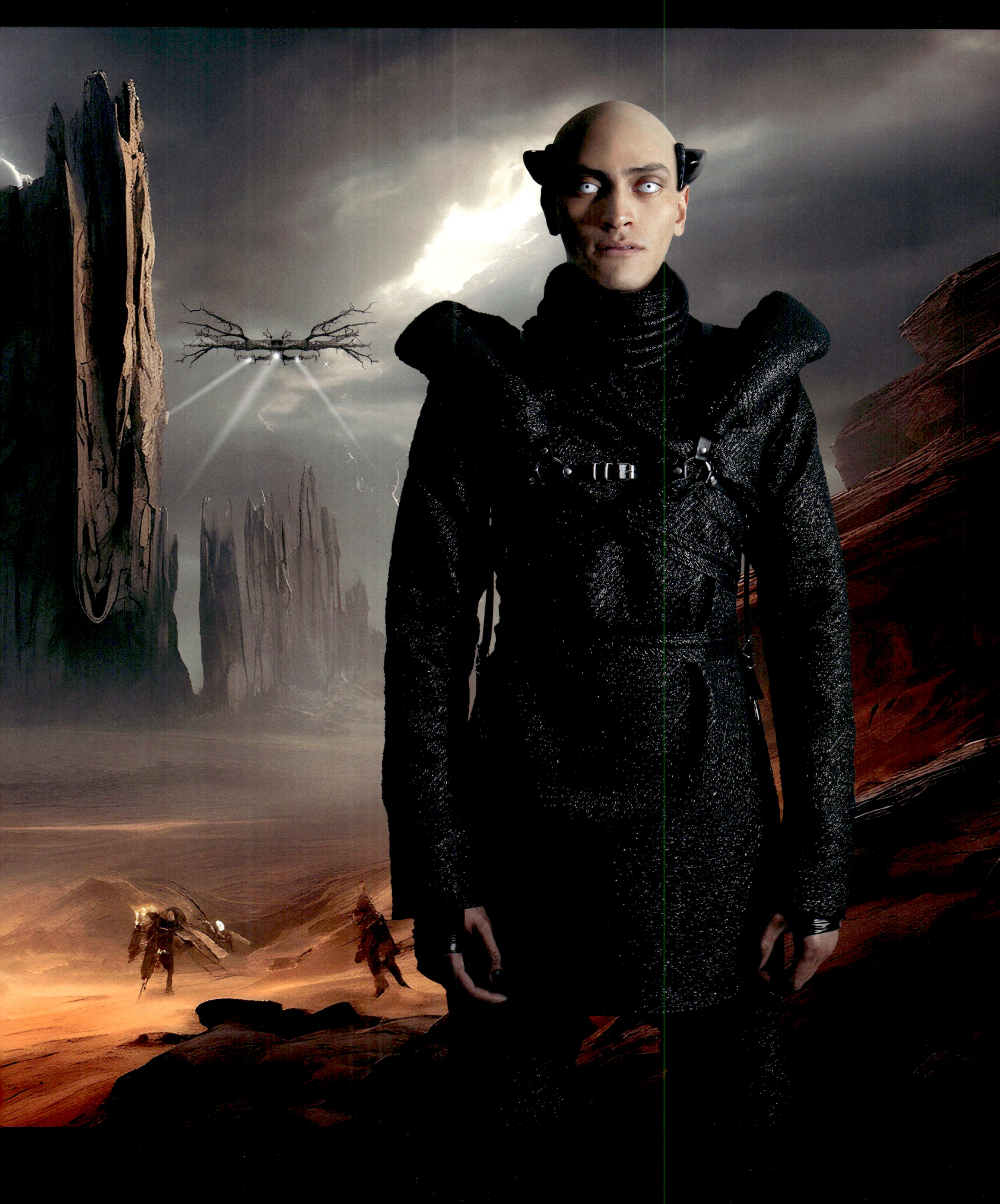

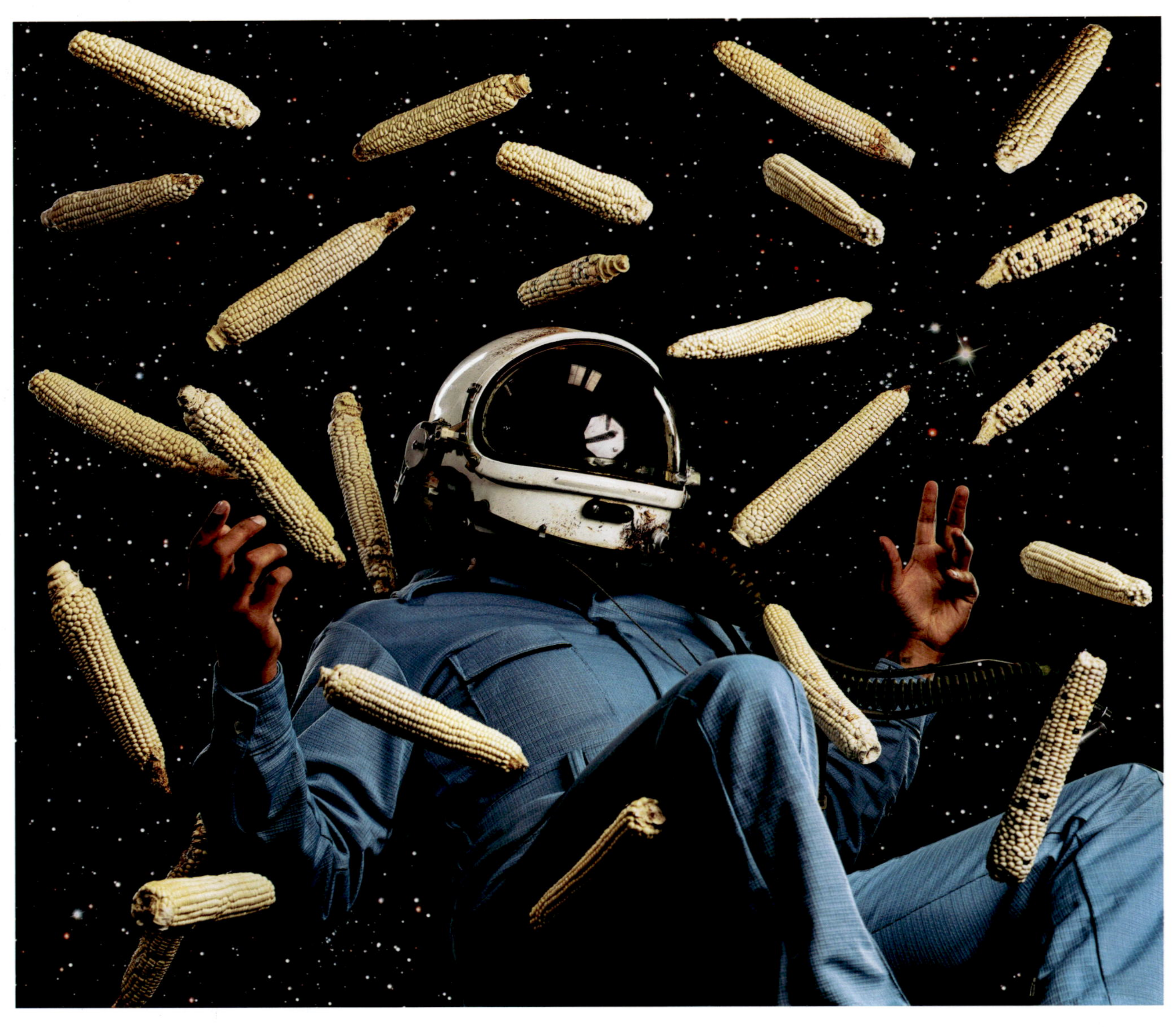

36. Cara Romero (Chemehuevi), *The Zenith*, 2022.
Limited edition archival photograph, 40 × 55 in.
Courtesy of the artist

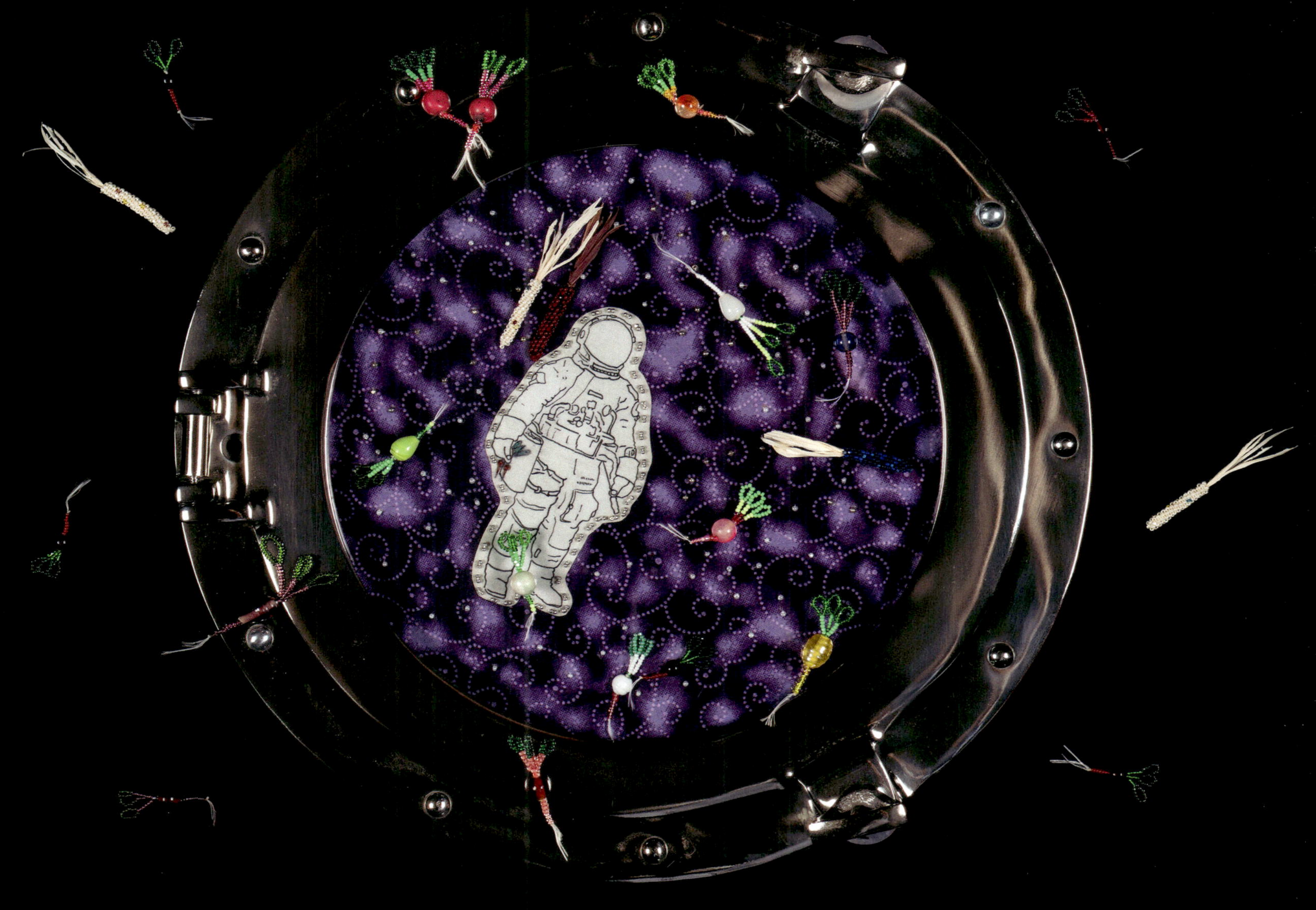

37. Tammy Tallchief (Cayuga), *Space Farmer with Radishes*, 2010–22. Assemblage, 12 in. diameter × 2½ in. depth. Courtesy of the artist and the Autry Museum of the American West. Photography by RJ Sanchez

38. Mona Cliff (Aaniiih/Nakota/Eastern European), *Conjured Topography*, 2022. Preciosa seed beads, maple wood, beeswax, copal resin, pine rosin, thread, plywood, 109 × 20 × ½ in. Courtesy of the artist. Photography by Aaron Paden

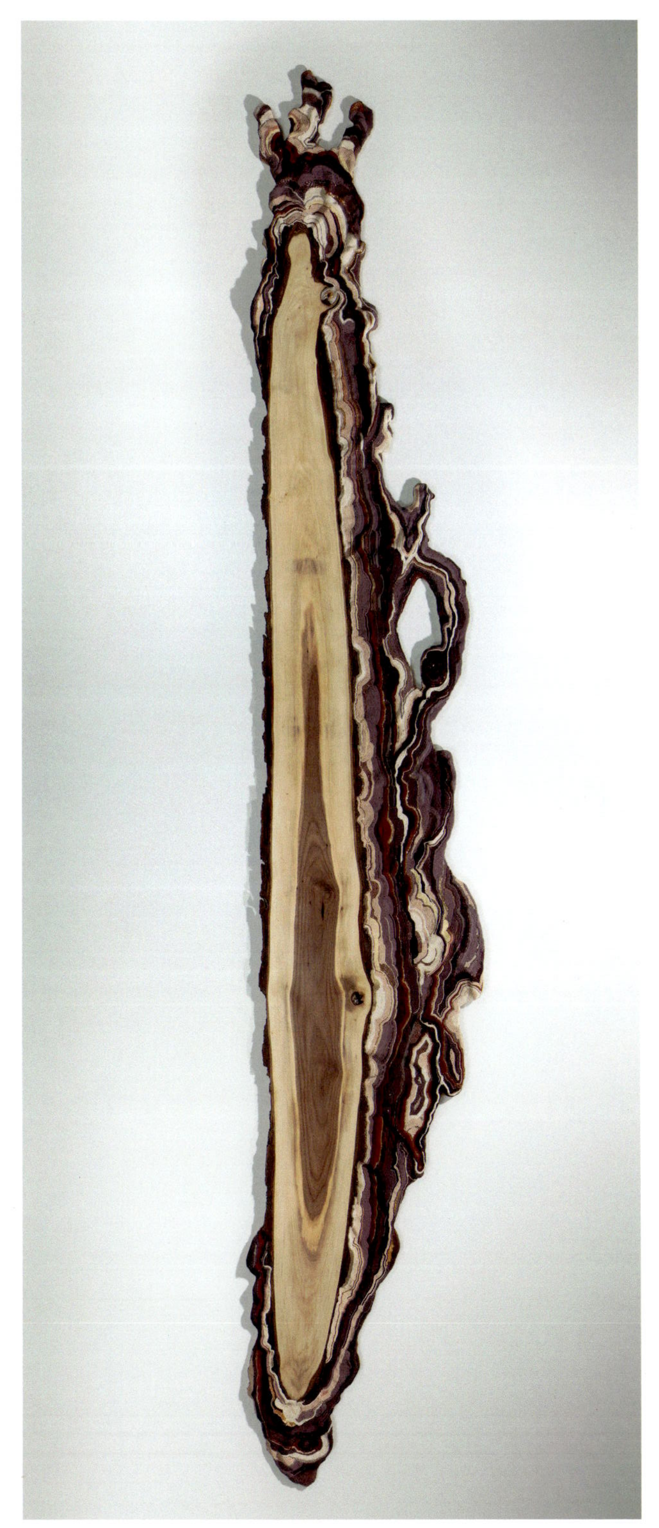

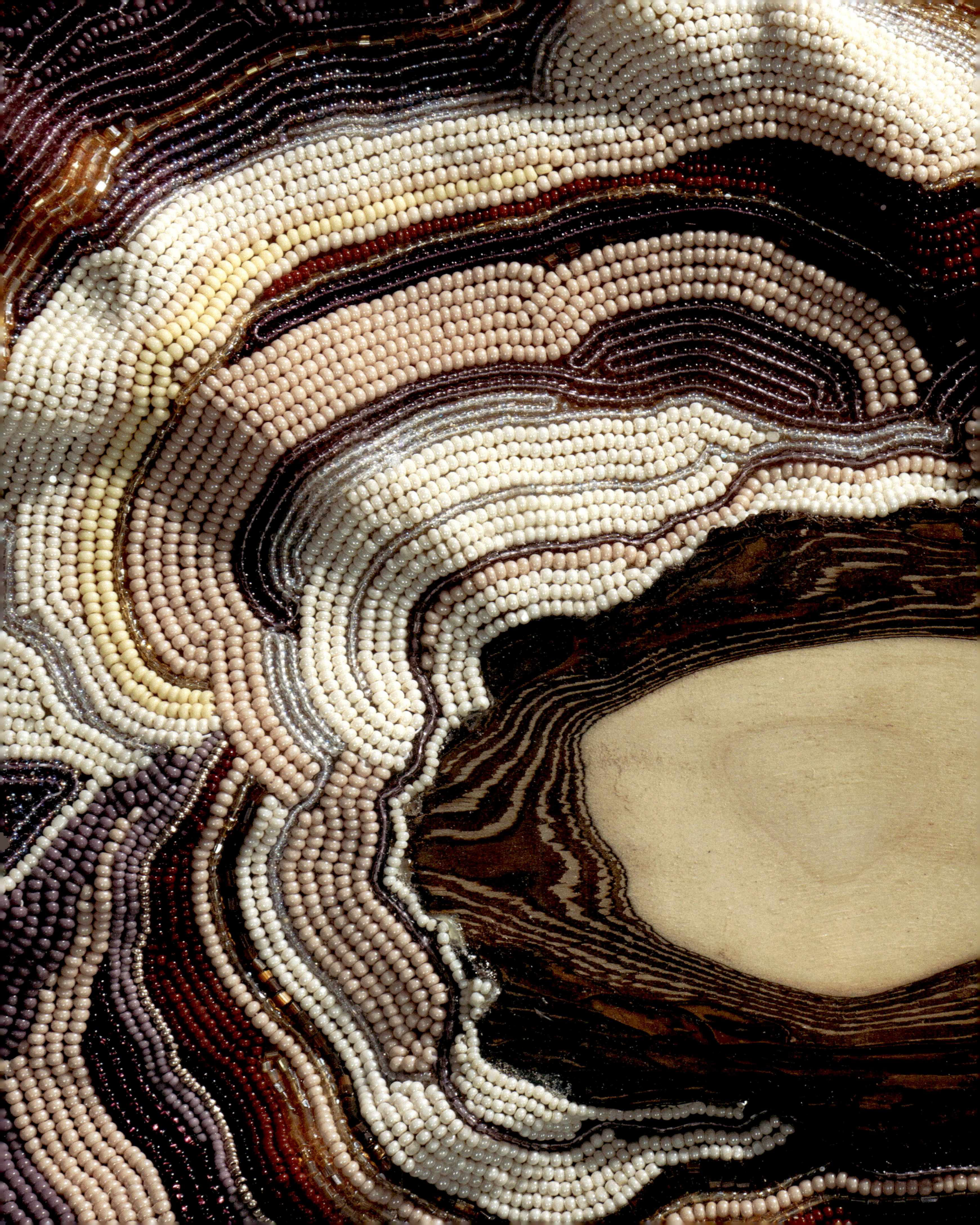

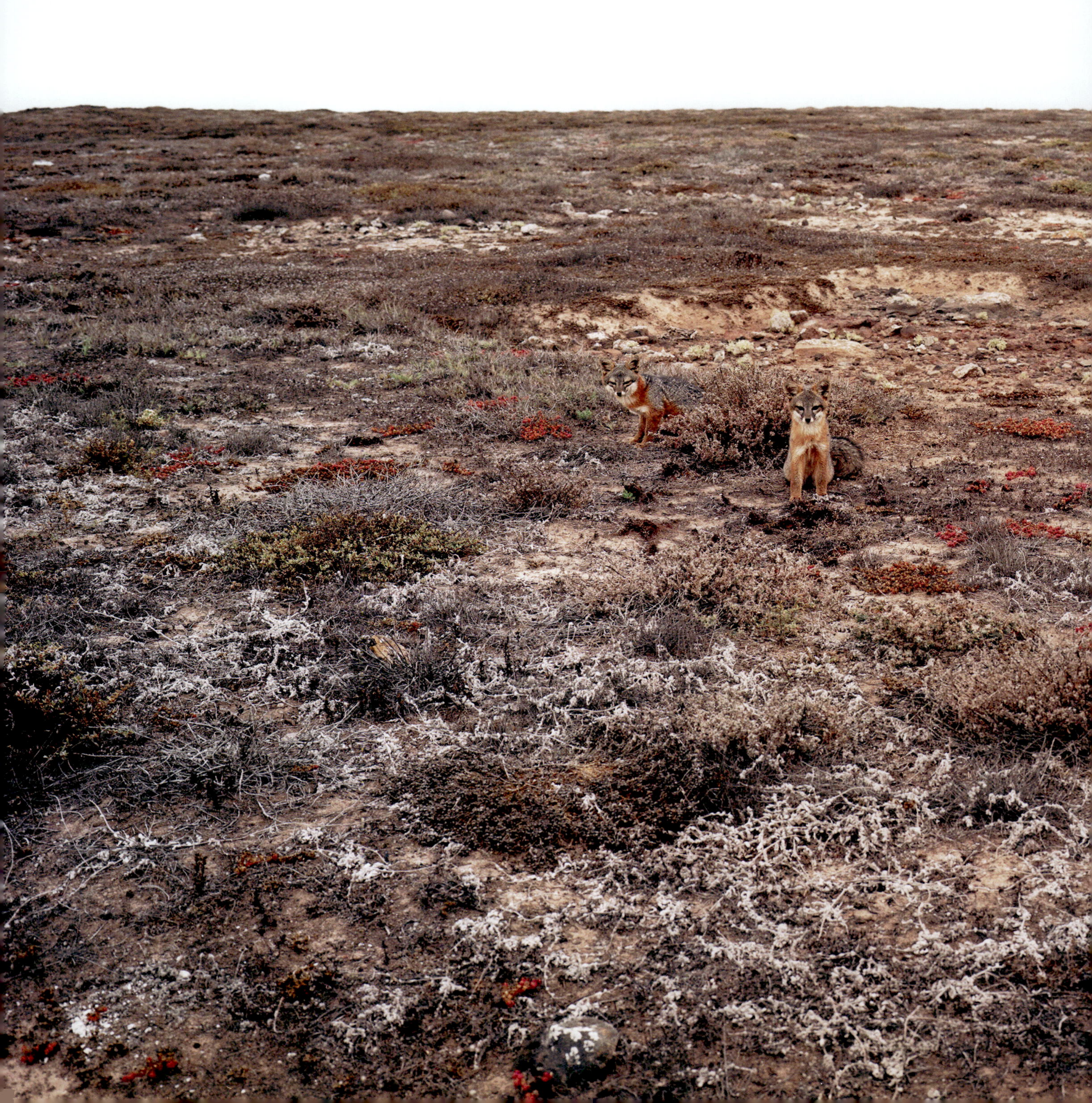

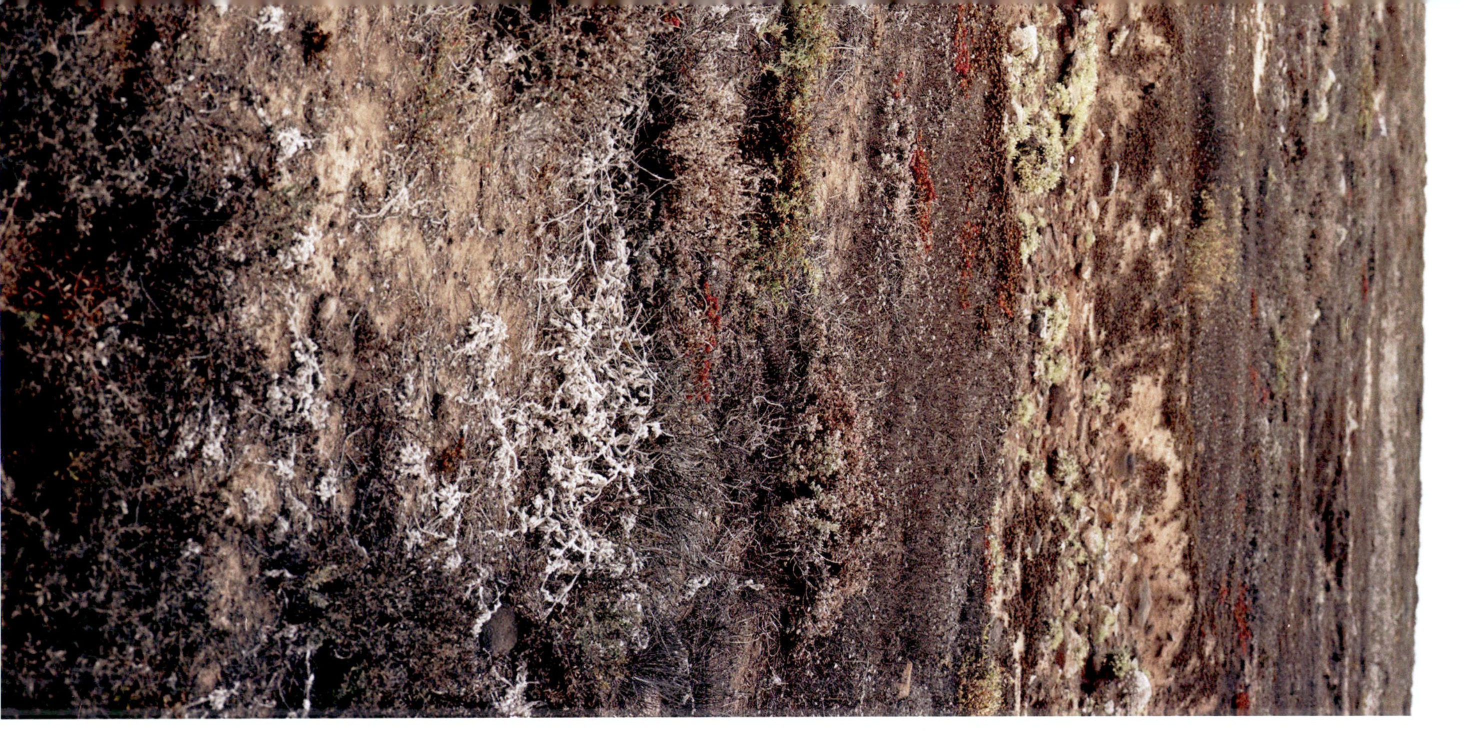

39. Mercedes Dorame (Tongva), *Fox Relatives—Kaweewesh 'Eyoohiinkem* from the *Everywhere is West* series, 2023. Inkjet print from 120 mm film, 30 × 30 in. Courtesy of the artist

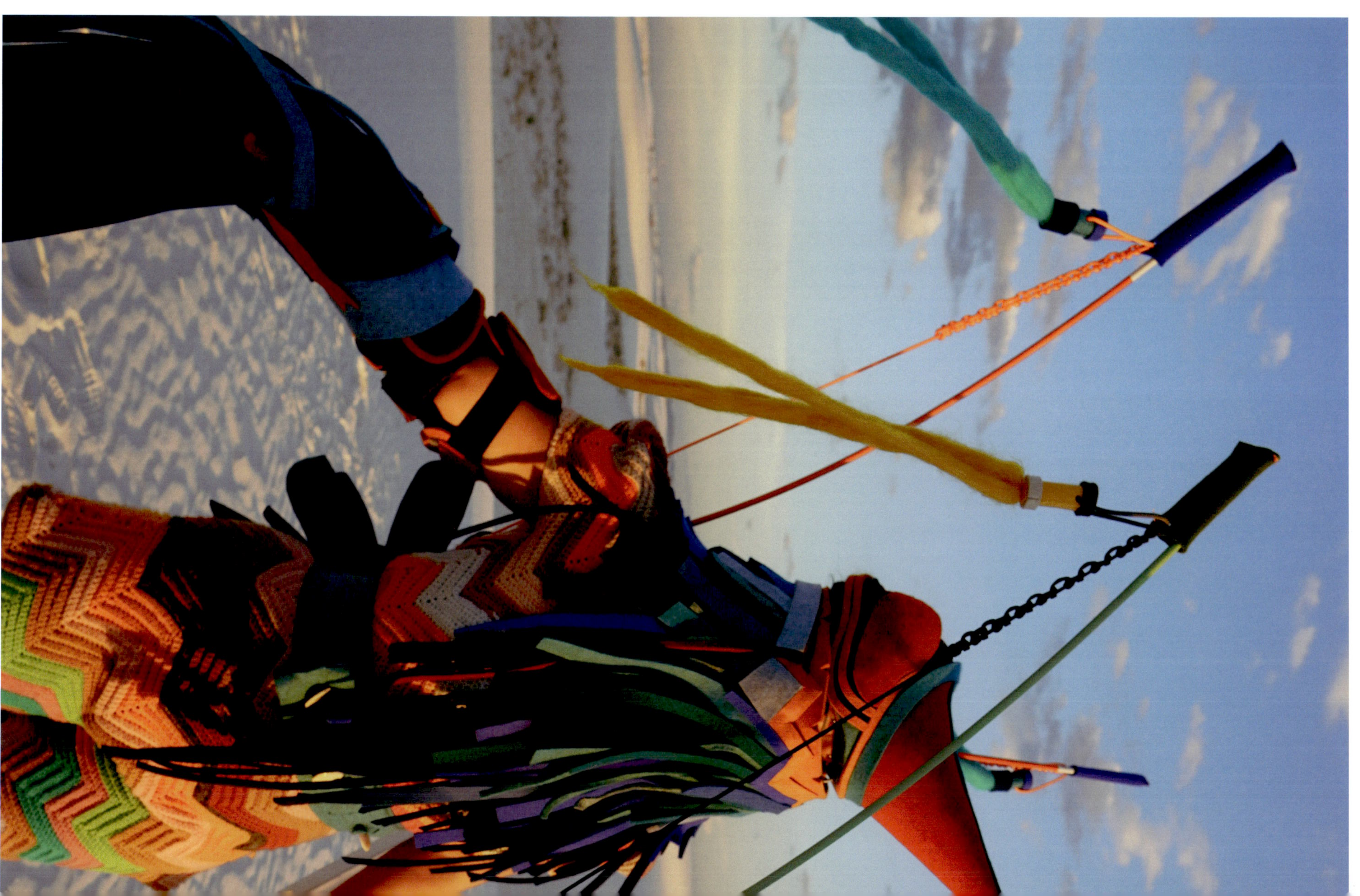

40. Cannupa Hanska Luger (Mandan/Hidatsa/Arikara/Lakota), *New Myth* from the *Future Ancestral Technologies* project, 2021. Mixed media, ceramic, and repurposed materials; single-channel video. Courtesy of the artist and Garth Greenan Gallery, New York. Photography by Gabriel Fermin

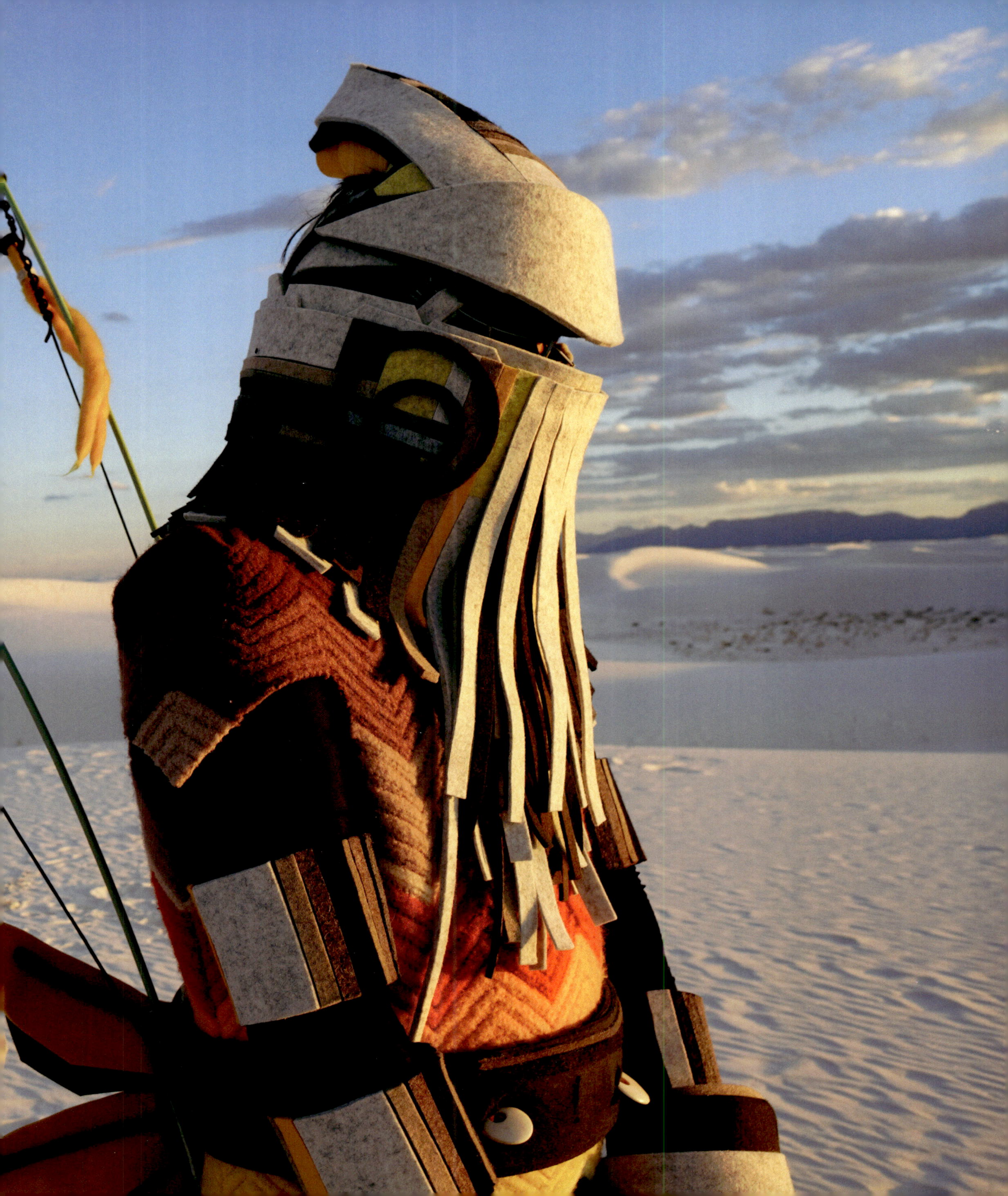

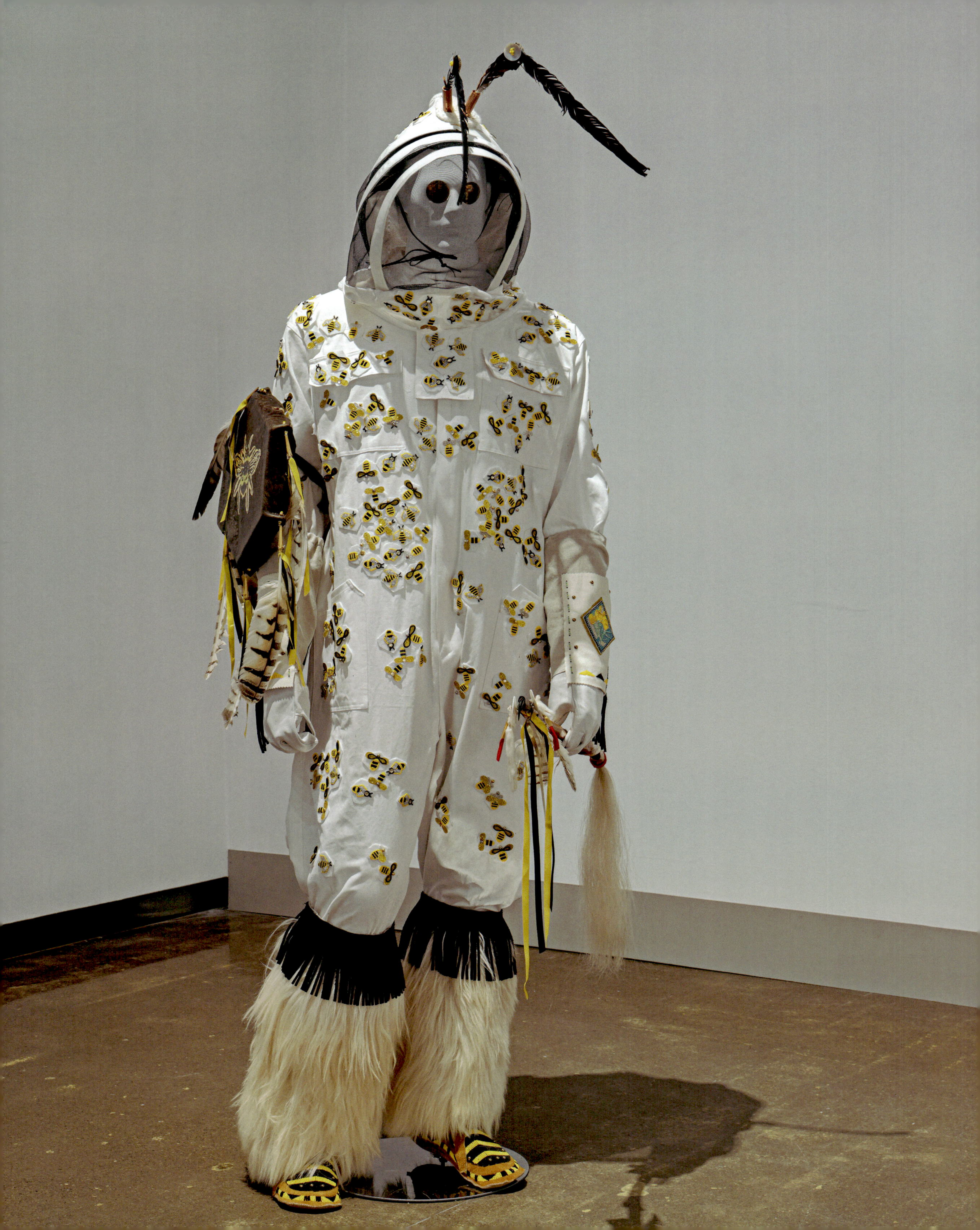

41. Adrian Stimson (Siksika) and Lucille Wright
Payotapaihpiyakii (Dancing the opposite direction woman)
(Siksika), *Regalia Naamoi'stotoohsin (Bumblebee Regalia)*,
2021. Cotton coveralls, fur leggings, headgear, beaded
gloves, beaded moccasins; dancing stick with leather,
bird talon, shell, horsehair, ribbon, feathers; painted bison
rawhide shield with ribbon, beads, feathers, dimensions
variable. Courtesy of the artist

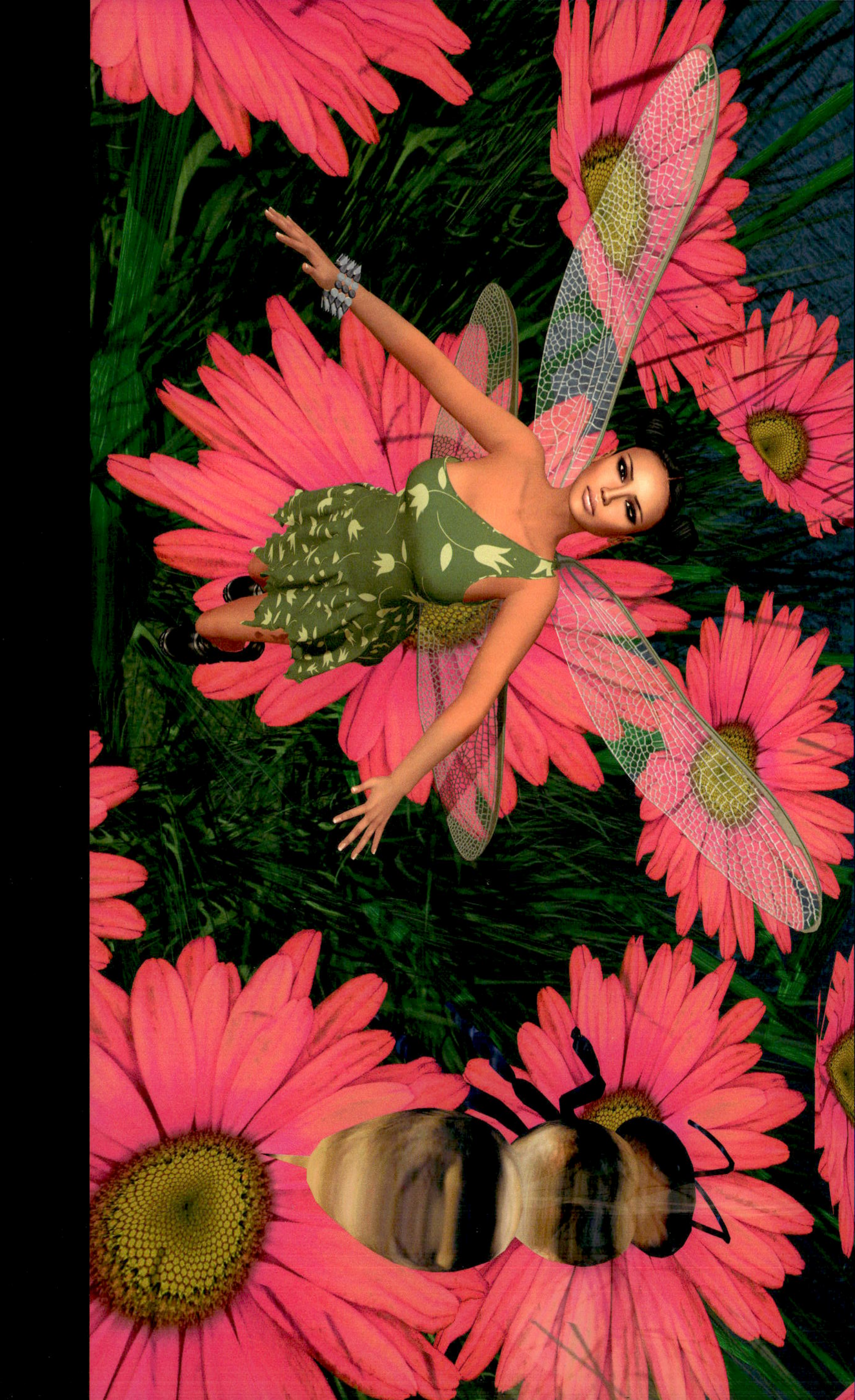

42. Skawennati (Kanien'kehà:ka [Mohawk]), *Let's Hear It for the Bugs* from the machinima *Words Before All Else*, 2022. Machinimagraph, dimensions variable. Courtesy of the artist

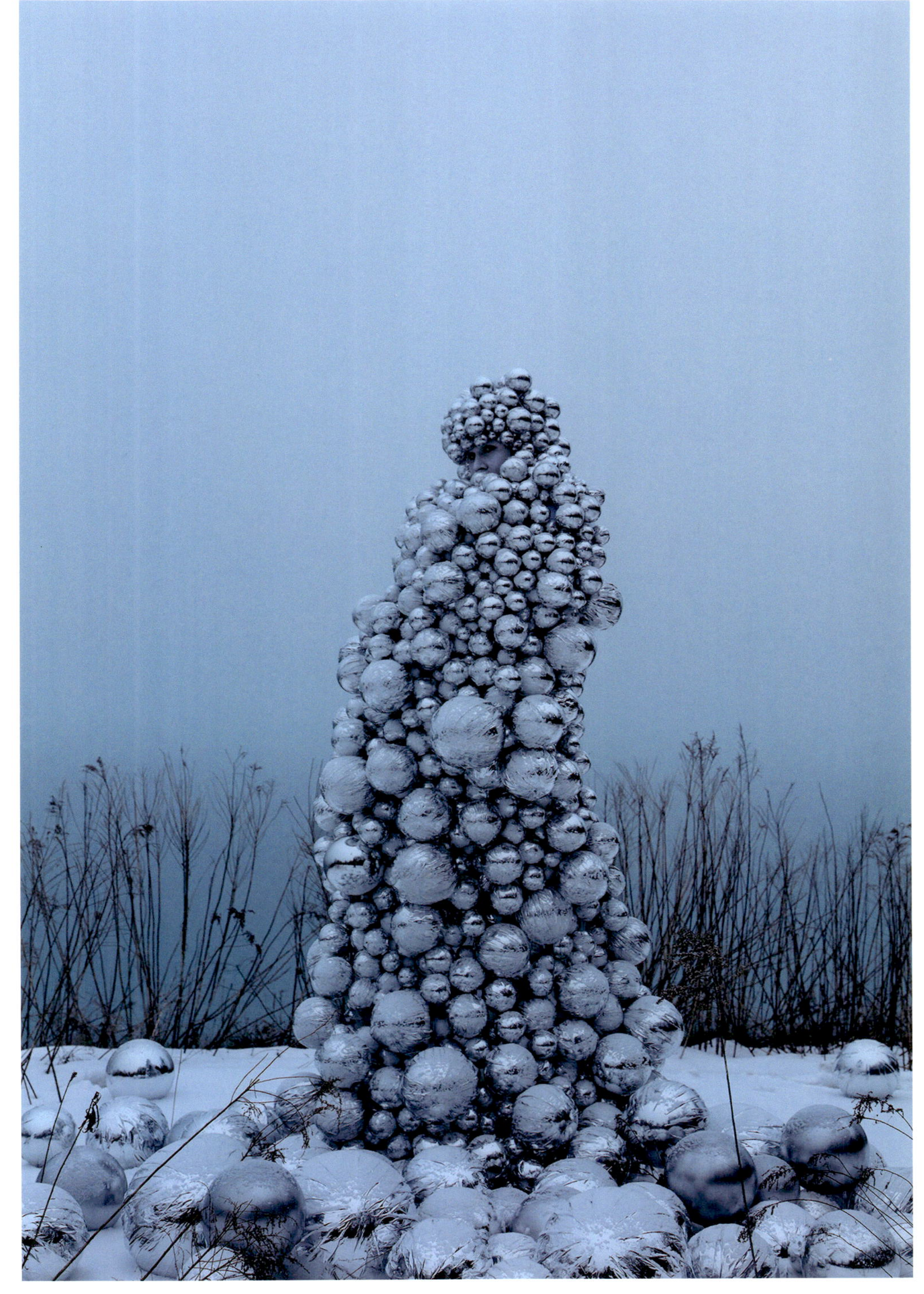

43. Meryl McMaster (nêhiyaw/Métis), *Of Universes We Have Just the One*, 2019. Chromogenic print mounted on aluminum composite panel, 45 × 30 in. Courtesy of the artist, the Stephen Bulger Gallery, and Pierre-François Ouellette art contemporain

44. Kite (Oglala Lakota) and Devin Ronneberg (Hawaiian/Okinawan), *Ínyan Iyé (Telling Rock)*, 2019. Gold, silver, copper, aluminum, human hair, silicon, fiberglass with sound, processors, machine learning, handmade circuitry, dimensions variable, Courtesy of the artists

Installation view of *Ínyan Iyé (Telling Rock)* from the exhibition, *Inner Ear Vision: Sound as Medium*, Bemis Center for Contemporary Arts, July 11–September 14, 2019. Photography by Colin Conces

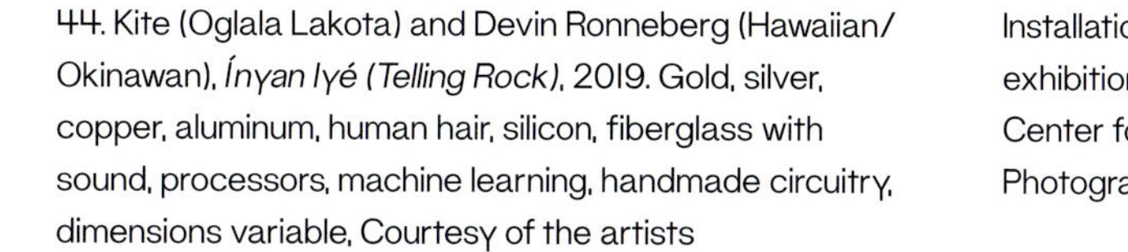

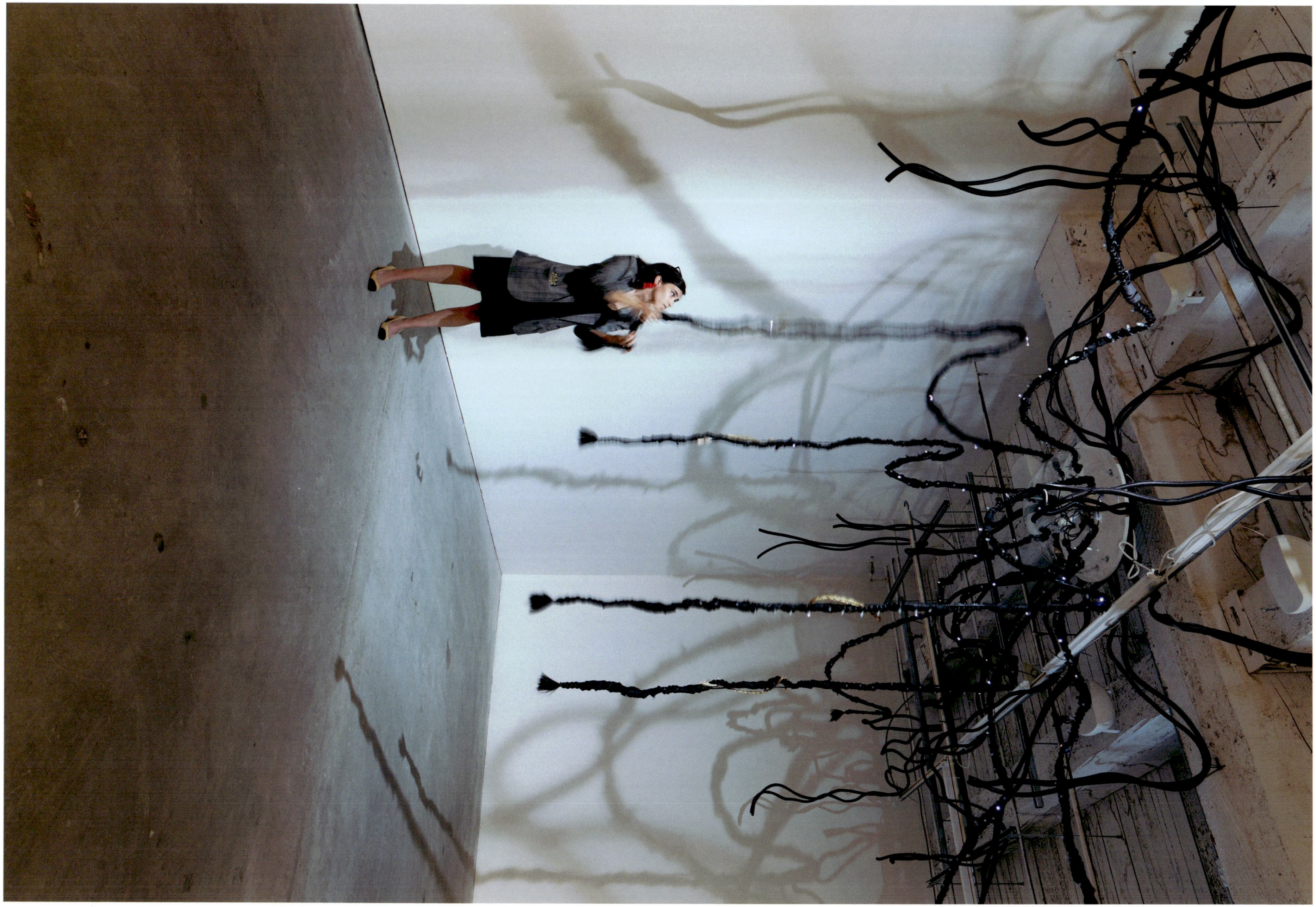

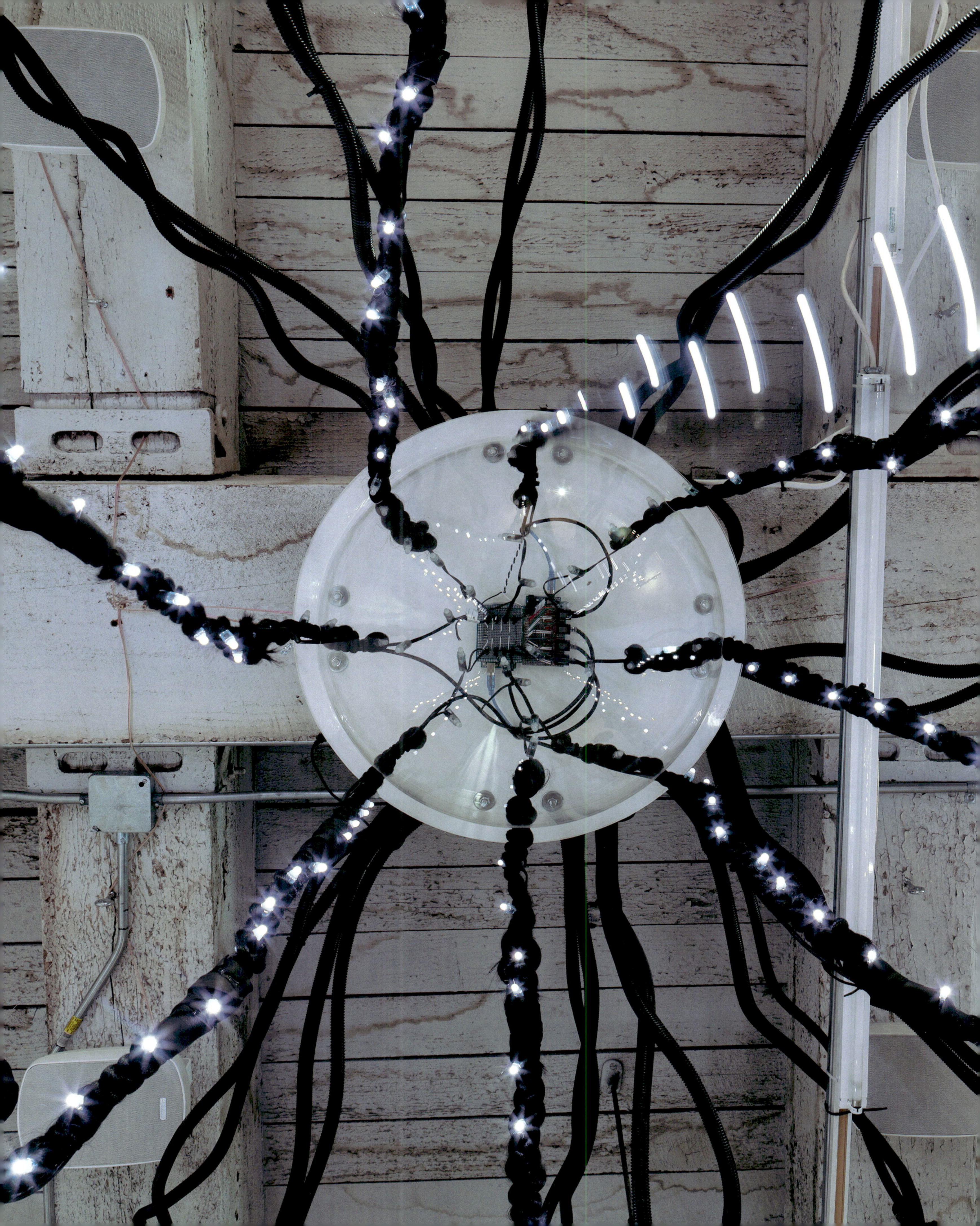

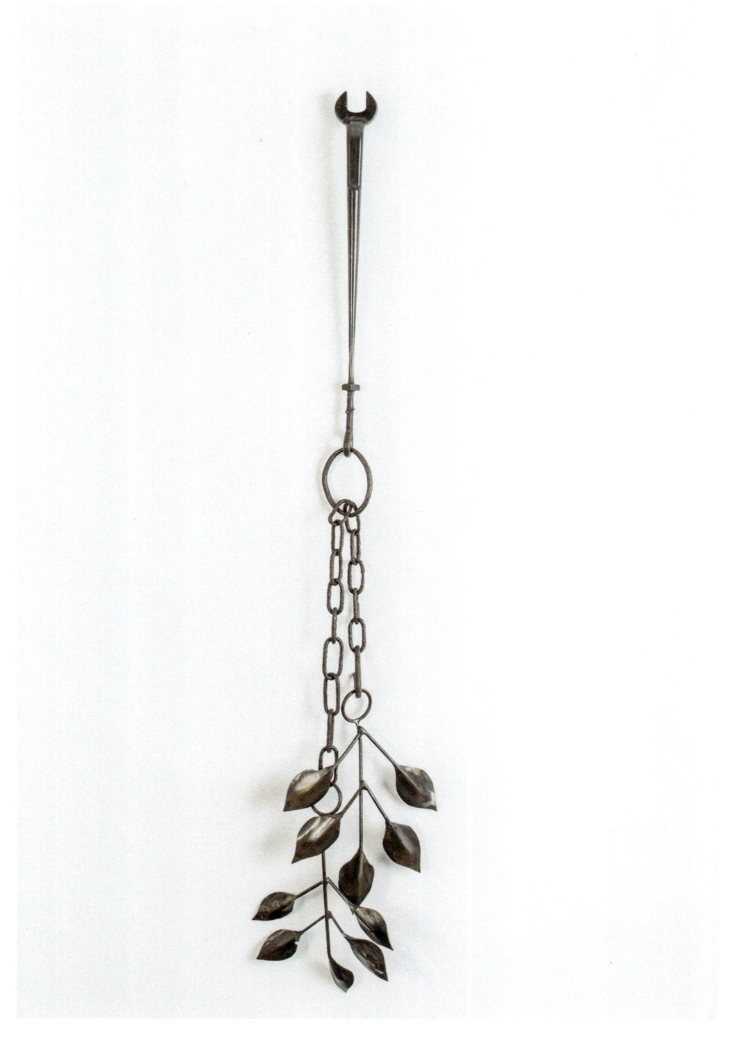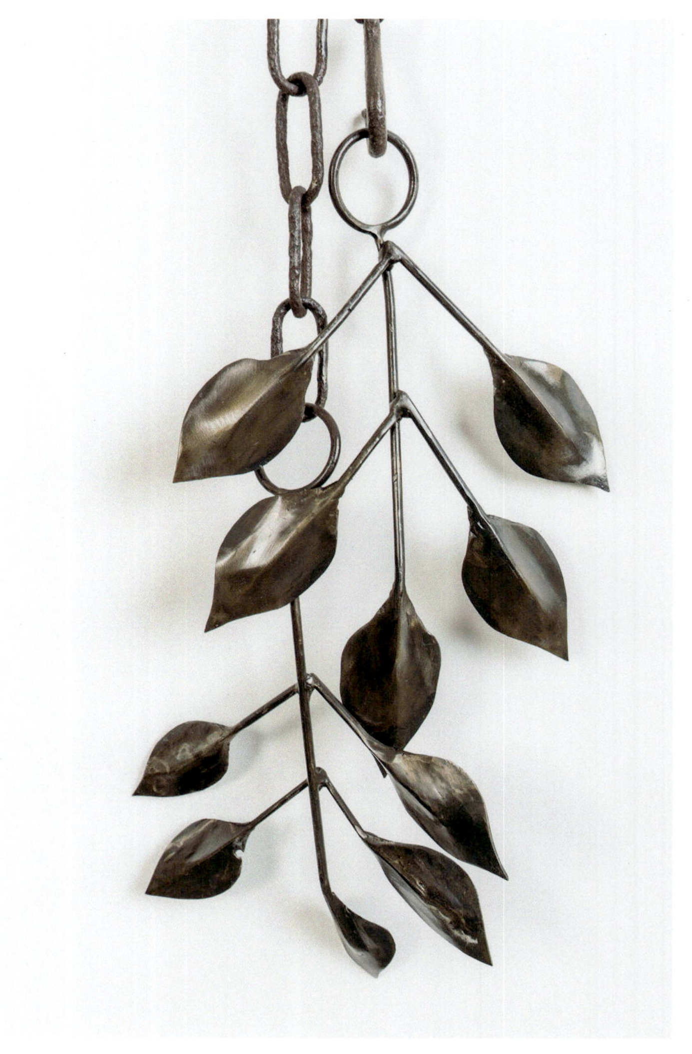

45. Margaret Jacobs (Akwesasne Mohawk), *Ash from Old Growth Series*, 2019. Steel, 48 × 12 × 4 in. Courtesy of the artist. Photography by GBH Photography

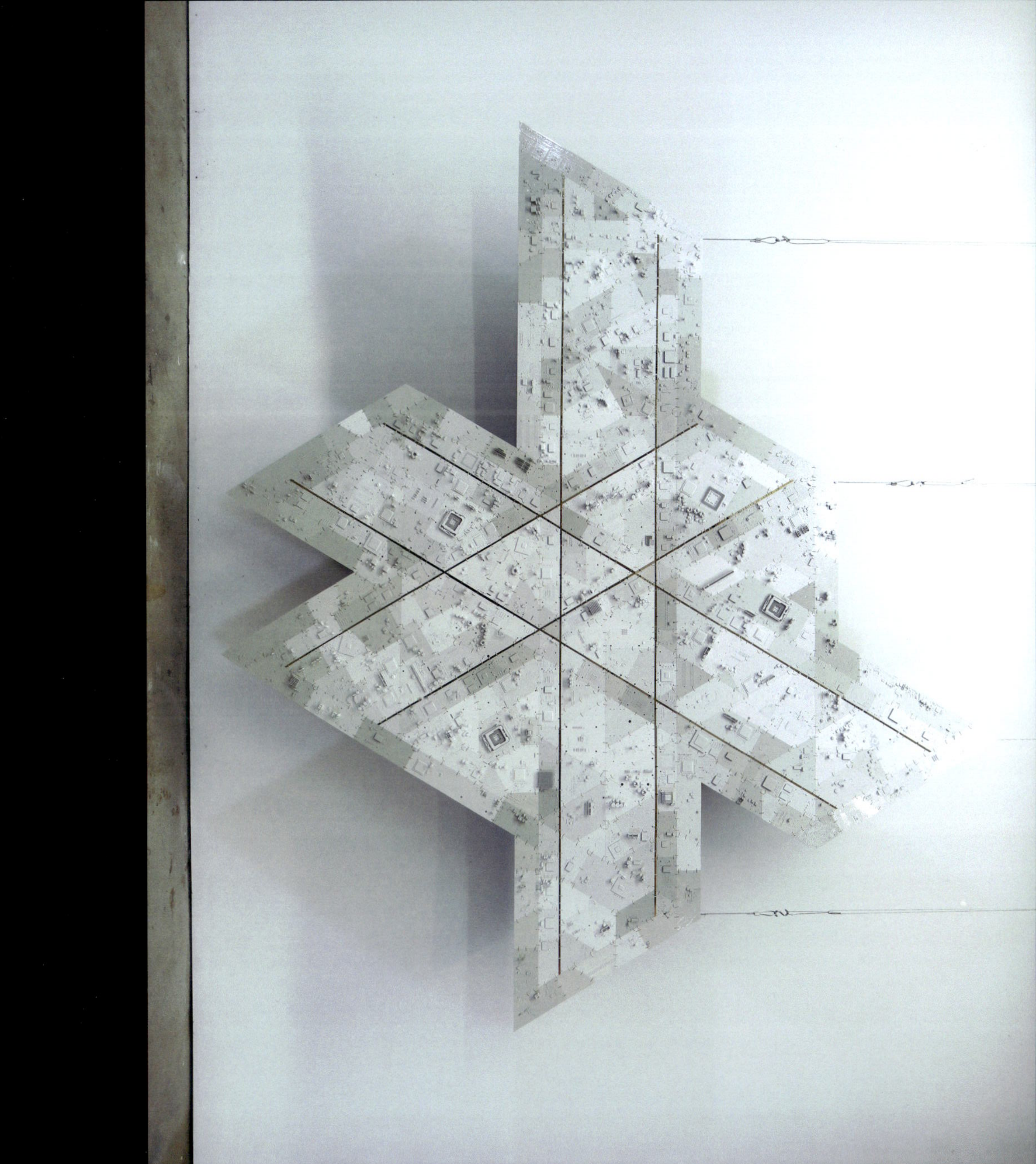

46. Wally Dion (Saulteaux), *Icosahedron*, 2016. Computer circuit boards, wire, enamel paint, 83 × 90 in. Courtesy of the artist and the University of Saskatchewan

Checklist of the Exhibition

Barry Ace (Odawa), *Efface*, 2017. Found shoes, vintage wooden shoe stand, vintage round circuit board, coated wire, capacitors, light-emitting diodes, resistors, vintage wooden shoe lasts, metal hardware, 28 × 15 × 15½ in. John O'Connell at Davis Rea Ltd.

KC Adams (Cree/Ojibway), *Cyborg Chicken Eggs*, 2005. Porcelain, lights, bleached flour, bleached sugar, feathers, audio, 10 × 10 ft. Collection of the artist

Neal Ambrose-Smith (Flathead Salish/Sho-Ban/Métis/Cree), *Get in the Relief Pod!*, 2013. Oil, acrylic, collage, 84 × 96 in. Collection of the artist

Sonny Assu (Ligwiłda'xw of the Kwakwaka'wakw Nations), *Tempest*, 2023. Wool and cotton Jacquard tapestry woven by Sophia Borowska, 41½ × 65½ in. Autry Museum of the American West

Nanibaa Beck (Diné), *Shí k'é, what has been your experience with coal?*, 2018. Sterling silver, coal, Acoma jet, mother-of-pearl, abalone, American Southwest turquoise, approx. 11½ × 9½ × 1 in. Collection of the artist

Catherine Blackburn (Dene/European), *Unsettle*, 2020. Beads, caribou hair, deer teeth, rabbit fur, sinew, bells, wool, dye-sublimated material, 12 × 8½ × 5½ in. (mask); single-channel video, 2:07 min. Eiteljorg Museum of American Indians and Western Art

Catherine Blackburn (Dene/European) and Rykelle "Ahlazua" Kemp (Mvskoke Creek Nation), *We Honor Bison* from the *Convergence* series, 2022. Bison horn, unsmoked caribou hide, antique beads, sterling silver, brass, gold foil, mother-of-pearl, vintage Swarovski pearls, rhinestone chain, 11¼ × 9⅜ × 2½ in. Denver Art Museum, Luncheon by Design Funds

Mona Cliff (Aaniiih/Nakota/Eastern European), *Stratification*, 2024. Preciosa seed beads, maple wood, beeswax, fabric, copal resin, pine rosin, thread, plywood, rhinestone banding, 90 × 21 × 1½ in. Collection of the artist

Mona Cliff (Aaniiih/Nakota/Eastern European), *Presence Stratified*, 2024. Gas mask, matte medium, acrylic paint, Oklahoma red dirt, brain-tanned leather, beeswax, pine resin, petroleum jelly, seed beads, shell, 3 × 10 × 5 in. Collection of the artist

Wally Dion (Saulteaux), *Gold Star Quilt*, 2024. Circuit boards, brass wire, copper pole, 76 × 96 in. Autry Museum of the American West

Mercedes Dorame (Tongva), *Asphaltum Seeps—Shaanat Chuuynok'e (I–VI)* from the *Everywhere is West* series, 2023. Inkjet prints, 30 × 30 in. Collection of the artist

Orlando Dugi (Diné), *Warrior Twins Coat*, 2022. Silk/wool blend fabric, silk charmeuse, gold flat metal wire, French bullion, silk dye paints, dimensions variable. Collection of the artist

Chase Kahwinhut Earles (Caddo), *Xi-nee'si I: Spiritual Leader Effigy Vessel*, 2022. Red River clay tempered with freshwater mussel shell, 4¼ × 10⁵⁄₁₆ × 7¼ in. Autry Museum of the American West

Andy Everson (K'ómoks/Kwakwaka'wakw), *Defender*, 2014. ABS plastic, rubber trim, cast resin, clear smokey acrylic, paint, approx. 11 × 11 × 11 in. Collection of the artist

Andy Everson (K'ómoks/Kwakwaka'wakw), *Northern Warrior*, 2014. ABS plastic, rubber trim, cast resin, turned maple (hat), clear smokey acrylic, paint, approx. 14 × 14 × 15 in. Collection of the artist

Andy Everson (K'ómoks/Kwakwaka'wakw), *Resilience*, 2014. Cast resin, acrylic, plastic, paint, approx. 10 × 10 × 10 in. Collection of the artist

Andy Everson (K'ómoks/Kwakwaka'wakw), *Resistance*, 2014. Digital print, dimensions variable. Collection of the artist

Jeffrey Gibson (Mississippi Band of Choctaw Indians/Cherokee descent), *Tribes File Suit to Protect Bears Ears*, 2018. Polyester satin, printed chiffon, canvas, neoprene, tin jingles, nylon fringe, glass and plastic beads, artificial sinew on tipi poles, 85 × 73½ × 8½ in. The Carl & Marilynn Thoma Foundation

Luzene Hill (Eastern Band of Cherokee Indians), *REVVV*, 2023. Mylar, silk organza, silver cord, tissue lamé, 26 in. shoulder width × 180 in. hem circumference × 52 in. length. Collection of the artist

Shawn Hunt (Heiltsuk) in collaboration with Microsoft Vancouver and the Garage, *Transformation Mask*, 2017. 3D-printed PLA and acrylic resin, LED lights, and Microsoft HoloLens, approx. 3¼ ft. Equinox Gallery, Vancouver

Margaret Jacobs (Akwesasne Mohawk), *Old Growth Series: Broadleaf Plantain, Cattail, Wild Blackberry, Chicory, Wild Strawberry*, 2024. Steel, dimensions variable. Autry Museum of the American West

Brian Jungen (Dane-zaa), *Variant #3*, 2016. Nike Air Jordans, leather, 50 × 71 × 14½ in. Collection of the artist and Casey Kaplan, New York

Brian Jungen (Dane-zaa), *Warrior I*, 2017. Nike Air Jordans, leather, 39 × 32 × 29 in. Dallas Museum of Art, TWO x TWO for AIDS and Art Fund

Jontay Kahm (Plains Cree), *Fossil 2.0 with Pebble Mask*, 2023. Organza twill, dimensions variable. Autry Museum of the American West

Kite (Oglala Lakota) and Devin Ronneberg (Hawaiian/Okinawan), *Ínyan yé (Telling Rock)*, 2019. Gold, silver, copper, aluminum, human hair, silicon, fiberglass with sound, processors, machine learning, handmade circuitry, dimensions variable. Collection of the artists

Cannupa Hanska Luger (Mandan/Hidatsa/Arikara/Lakota), *Watȟéča: Buzzard Regalia* from the *Future Ancestral Technologies* project, 2021. Mixed media, ceramic, repurposed materials; single-channel video, 6:04 min. Collection of the artist and Garth Greenan Gallery, New York

Meryl McMaster (nêhiyaw/Métis), *Of Universes We Have Just the One*, 2019. Chromogenic print mounted on aluminum composite panel, 45 × 30 in. Collection of the artist

Meryl McMaster (nêhiyaw/Métis), *Of Universes We Have Just the One*, 2019. Mixed media, 85¼ × 23 in. Collection of the artist

Caroline Monnet (Anishinaabe/French), *Aïcha's Regalia* from *Echoes from a Near Future*, 2022. Floor underlayment and reflective coating for laminate flooring, 37½ × 27 × 11 in. Collection of the artist

Caroline Monnet (Anishinaabe/French), *Echoes from a Near Future*, 2022. Inkjet print mounted on aluminum, 80 × 120 in. Collection of the artist

Jamie Okuma (Luiseño/Shoshone/Bannock), *Beaded High Heel Boots*, 2011. Hand-beaded Louboutin boots, 19 × 3½ × 8½ in. (each). Albuquerque Museum, Gift of the estate of Ruth and Sidney Schultz, PC2022.44.166.A-B

Virgil Ortiz (Cochiti Pueblo), *Sirens and Sikas* from the *ReVOlt 1680/2180* series, 2023. Multimedia installation, dimensions variable. Collection of the artist

Celeste Pedri-Spade (Anishinabekwe/Ojibwe), *Anti-Pipeline Society Kwe* from the *Material Kwe* series, 2019. Ribbon skirt, leather belt, brass tacks, metal jingle bells, fabric, acrylic hair, dimensions variable. Collection of the artist

Pat Pruitt (Pueblo ofLaguna), *Armorer of the Ice Infantry: Protectors of the Water*, 2024. Titanium, leather, 26 × 16 × 10 in. Autry Museum of the American West

Wendy Red Star (Apsáalooke), *Stirs Up the Dust* from the *Thunder Up Above* series, 2011. Pigment print on FineArt Pearl, 27 × 30 in. Autry Museum of the American West

Wendy Red Star (Apsáalooke), *Stirs Up the Dust* from the *Thunder Up Above* series, 2011. Faux feathers, polyester, beads, ribbon, dimensions variable. Autry Museum of the American West

Cara Romero (Chemehuevi), *Three Sisters*, 2022. Limited edition archival photograph, 40 × 55 in. The Carl & Marilynn Thoma Foundation, Santa Fe

Cara Romero (Chemehuevi), *The Zenith*, 2022. Limited edition archival photograph, 40 × 55 in. Trotta-Bono Collection, Santa Fe

Diego Romero (Cochiti Pueblo), *Cara*, 2018. Lithograph with gold leaf, 24 × 24 in. Gallery Hózhó, Albuquerque

Diego Romero (Cochiti Pueblo), *Prometheus,* 2021. Commercial clay, commercial gold luster, natural hand-gathered clay paint, 14 ½ in. ht. × 8 ½ in. dia. Collection of George and Martha Richards

Nep Sidhu (Punjabi Sikh) with Nicolas Galanin (Tlingit/Unangax̂), *SHE in Light Form* from *No Pigs in Paradise*, 2015-16. Melton wool, jute, silver zari, chenille, cotton, 72 × 20 in. Collection of the artists and Patel Brown, Toronto

Rose B. Simpson (Santa Clara Pueblo), *Ground (Witness)*, 2016. Ceramic, steel, leather, textile, 99 × 17 × 27 in. (standing figure), 153 × 59 × 37 in. (winged figure). Autry Museum of the American West

Ryan Singer (Diné), *Sand People Sand Painting*, 2019. Acrylic on canvas, 30 × 40 in. Gallery Hózhó, Albuquerque

Ryan Singer (Diné), *They Have Both Coffees*, 2023. Acrylic on canvas, 40 × 30 in. Autry Museum of the American West

Skawennati (Kanien'kehà:ka [Mohawk]), *Three Sisters: Regeneration*
from the machinima *Words Before All Else*, 2022. Machinimagraph,
dimensions variable. Collection of the artist

Skawennati (Kanien'kehà:ka [Mohawk]), *Words Before All Else*, 2022.
Machinima, 12:00 min. Artist's proof. Collection of the artist

Matagi Sorensen (Yavapai-Apache), *Gorget*, 2024. Bronze, 9 × 10 ×
2 in. Autry Museum of the American West

Adrian Stimson (Siksika) and Lucille Wright Payotapaihpiyakii
(Dancing the opposite direction woman) (Siksika), *Regalia
Naamoi'stotoohsin (Bumblebee Regalia)*, 2021. Cotton coveralls, fur
leggings, headgear, beaded gloves, beaded moccasins; dancing
stick with leather, bird talon, shell, horsehair, ribbon, feathers; painted
bison rawhide shield with ribbon, beads, feathers, dimensions
variable. Collection of the artist

Tammy Tallchief (Cayuga), *Space Farmer with Radishes*, 2010–22.
Assemblage, 12 in. dia. × 2½ in. depth. Collection of the artist

Jeffrey Veregge (Port Gamble S'Klallam), *Welcome*, 2014. Digital print,
dimensions variable. Collection of the artist

Jeffrey Veregge (Port Gamble S'Klallam), *She's Got It Where It
Counts*, 2016. Digital print, dimensions variable. Collection of the
artist

Marie Watt (Seneca), *Trek (Pleiades)*, 2014. Reclaimed wool blankets,
satin binding, embroidery floss, thread, 74 × 123½ in. Tia Collection,
Santa Fe

Will Wilson (Diné), *K'ómoks Imperial Stormtrooper (Andy Everson),
Citizen of the K'ómoks First Nation*, from the *Critical Indigenous
Photographic Exchange: dᶻidᶻəlalič* series, 2017, printed 2019.
Archival pigment print, 56¼ × 44¼ in. Collection of the artist

X (Koasati/CHamoru), *Glitch in Perpetual Time*, 2024. Extended
reality installation composed of original sound compositions,
dimensional renderings, and augmented digital artifacts, dimensions
variable. Autry Museum of the American West

Checklist current as of May 29, 2024

Contributors

WESHOYOT ALVITRE (Tongva/Scottish) is a comic book artist, writer, and illustrator. She was born in the Santa Monica Mountains on Satwiwa, a historic Indigenous territory and later the site of a cultural center founded by her father, Art Alvitre. She grew up close to the land, raised with traditional knowledge that inspires the work she does today, which focuses on an Indigenous lens and voice in projects ranging from children's books to adult-market graphic novels. Alvitre consciously works primarily with Native-owned publications and educational avenues to support and emphasize a self-directed narrative on past, present, and future Native issues.

SONNY ASSU (Ligwiłda'xw of the Kwakwaka'wakw Nations) explores multiple mediums to negotiate Western and Kwakwaka'wakw principles of artmaking. Often biographical, humorous, solemn, or political, his works deal with the realities of being Indigenous in the settler-colonial nation of Canada.

Assu received a BFA from Emily Carr University and an MFA from Concordia University. His awards and honors include the BC Creative Achievement Award in First Nations Art, a REVEAL Indigenous Art Award, and an Eiteljorg Contemporary Art Fellowship. His work is held in public and private collections across Canada, the United States, and the United Kingdom, including the National Gallery of Canada, Vancouver Art Gallery, the Sainsbury Centre for Visual Arts, the Art Gallery of Ontario, the Eiteljorg Museum of American Indians and Western Art, Thunder Bag Art Gallery, the Art Gallery of Guelph, the Art Gallery of Greater Victoria, the Museum of Anthropology at the University of British Columbia, the Seattle Art Museum, the Burke Museum, and the Audain Art Museum.

AMBER-DAWN BEAR ROBE (Siksika) is assistant faculty of Native American Art History in the Museum Studies department at the Institute of American Indian Arts (IAIA), Santa Fe, New Mexico, and Fashion Show Program Director for the Southwestern Association for Indian Arts (SWAIA), also in Santa Fe. Bear Robe's projects center on contemporary Indigenous fashion and how art practices intersect with fashion and design. In 2020 and 2021, Bear Robe received two Regional Emmys for producing two documentary short films on Indigenous fashion.

MERCEDES DORAME (Tongva) is a visual artist based in her Tovaangar (Los Angeles) homelands. She calls on her learned and ancestral connections to explore the problematics of (in)visibility and cultural construction in collaboration with the land and cosmos to empower the expansion of perception, experience, and imagination. Dorame completed a commission for the Getty Center in 2023 and has received grants from Creative Capital and the Eiteljorg Museum, among others. Her work has been exhibited internationally and is part of the permanent collections of several institutions, including the Hammer Museum, the Los Angeles County Museum of Art, and the San Francisco Museum of Modern Art. She is a faculty member at the California Institute of the Arts.

KRISTEN DORSEY (Chickasaw) is an independent curator and doctoral candidate in the Department of Gender Studies at the University of California, Los Angeles. She was also a jeweler and sculptor for over a decade. Her award-winning work has been exhibited nationally.

Dorsey's curatorial projects include the traveling exhibition and catalog *Visual Voices: Contemporary Chickasaw Art* (2018–2021) developed in collaboration with fellow Chickasaw artists. In 2018, she co-curated *Matriarchs* with Jaclyn Roessel (Diné) for the El Segundo Museum of Art. Dorsey has also facilitated public art installations by Indigenous artists through her service on the El Segundo Arts and Culture Committee (2018–2020), including a community mural by Nanibah Chacon (Diné/Chicana) in conversation with Mercedes Dorame (Tongva) for the El Segundo Public Library.

SUZANNE NEWMAN FRICKE, PhD, earned her doctorate in Native American art history from the University of New Mexico, specializing in contemporary Native American arts. She taught art history for over twenty-five years and curated multiple exhibits for museums in the United States and internationally. She frequently contributes to *First American Art Magazine* and has published in various journals and anthologies, including *As We See It: Conversations with Native American Photographers* (2023). In 2020, Fricke co-curated *Indigenous Futurisms: Transcending Past/Present/Future* for the IAIA Museum of Contemporary Native Arts and opened Gallery Hózhó, a fine art gallery dedicated to contemporary art from New Mexico.

JASON EDWARD LEWIS (Kanaka Maoli/Samoan) is University Research Chair in Computational Media and the Indigenous Future Imaginary at Concordia University. He co-directs the Abundant Intelligences research program exploring Indigenous approaches to artificial intelligence, as well as the Indigenous Futures Research Centre and the Skins Workshops on Aboriginal Storytelling in Digital Media. Lewis is lead author on the award-winning "Making Kin with the Machines" essay and editor of the Indigenous Protocol and AI Position Paper. His creative and production work has been recognized with the inaugural Robert Coover Award for Best Work of Electronic Literature, two Prix Ars Electronica Honorable Mentions, several imagineNATIVE Best New Media awards, and multiple solo exhibitions. Lewis is a Fellow of the Royal Society of Canada.

CANNUPA HANSKA LUGER (Mandan/Hidatsa/Arikara/Lakota) is a New Mexico-based multidisciplinary artist who creates monumental installations, sculpture, and performances to communicate urgent stories about twenty-first-century Indigeneity. Incorporating ceramics, steel, fiber, video, and repurposed materials, he activates speculative fiction, engages in land-based actions of repair, and practices empathetic response through social collaboration. Born on the Standing Rock Reservation in North Dakota, Luger is an enrolled member of the Three Affiliated Tribes of Fort Berthold. His work has been exhibited at numerous institutions, including the National Gallery of Art in DC, the Metropolitan Museum of Art in New York, the Gardiner Museum in Toronto, and the National Center for Civil and Human Rights in Georgia. Luger has been awarded fellowships from the Guggenheim, United States Artists, Creative Capital, the Smithsonian, and the Joan Mitchell Foundation.

NANCY MARIE MITHLO, PhD (Fort Sill Chiricahua Apache), is a scholar and writer whose work engages comparative global Indigeneity movements in the arts. Her training as a cultural anthropologist informs how she examines cultural, institutional, and political systems that often mask the normalization of bias in contested realms of power. She is the author of numerous publications including *Knowing Native Arts* (UNP, 2020). Mithlo is a professor of Gender and American Indian Studies at the University of California, Los Angeles.

VIRGIL ORTIZ (Cochiti Pueblo) fuses his Pueblo culture with apocalyptic sci-fi and fantasy genres to create futurist clay and multimedia works that challenge expectations and break taboos. Ortiz teaches Pueblo history to generations of viewers worldwide, telling the story of the 1680 Pueblo Revolt through his decades-spanning project, *ReVOlt 1680/2180*. This series of works, including ceramic vessels and figures, fashion, video, and live theater, depicts a dystopian future five hundred years after the Pueblo Revolt, in which a cast of time-traveling Indigenous superheroes return to the historical era of the revolt to gather songs, ceremonies, designs, artifacts, and culture to preserve and transport to the future. Ortiz's thought-provoking works are in museum collections worldwide, including the Design Museum Den Bosch, Fondation Cartier pour l'art contemporain, Triennale Milano, Smithsonian Institution, Minneapolis Museum of Art, and the Colby Museum of Art.

AMY SCOTT, PhD, is executive vice president of Research and Interpretation and the Marilyn B. and Calvin B. Gross Curator of Visual Arts at the Autry Museum of the American West. She has curated exhibitions on historical landscapes, Chicano photography, and contemporary Native art. Before joining the Autry, Scott was a curatorial assistant at the Nelson-Atkins Museum in Kansas City and a curator at the Gerald Peters Gallery in Santa Fe. She has published several books, including *LA RAZA* (2020), *Art of the West: Selected Works from the Autry Museum* (2018), and *Paul Pletka: Imagined Wests* (2017).

MATTHEW RYAN SMITH, PhD, is the curator and head of collections of Glenhyrst Art Gallery in Brantford, Ontario, and the literary editor of *First American Art Magazine*. He has published widely on Indigenous visual culture, curatorial studies, and autobiography in his academic work. Matthew has taught courses and seminars on art history, design theory, and film studies at the University of Toronto (Mississauga), Western University, OCAD University, and the Haliburton School of Art. He also served as editor for Eli Baxter's memoir, *Aki-wayn-zih: A Person as Worthy as the Earth*, which was awarded the 2022 Governor General's Award for English-language nonfiction.

GERALD VIZENOR (White Earth Nation) has published over thirty books, including historical fiction, speculative fiction, short stories, poetry, and critical literary studies. Vizenor is renowned for his works that examine Native American identity, culture, and politics, some of which include *Treaty Shirts: October 2034—a Familiar Treatise on the White Earth Reservation* (2016), *Favor of Crows* (2014), *Blue Ravens* (2014), *Hotline Healers* (1997), *Shadow Distance* (1994), *The Heirs of Columbus* (1991), *Landfill Meditation* (1991), and *Bearheart: The Heirship Chronicles* (1990). Vizenor has held academic appointments at the University of New Mexico, Lake Forest College, the University of California (Berkeley and Santa Cruz), the University of Oklahoma, and the University of Minnesota. He is professor emeritus at the University of California, Berkeley.

MANUELA WELL-OFF-MAN, PhD, is an art historian and chief curator at the IAIA Museum of Contemporary Native Arts in Santa Fe, New Mexico. She previously served as curator at Crystal Bridges Museum of American Art and the Montana Museum of Art and Culture. With more than twenty years of curatorial experience, she has organized national and international contemporary Native American art exhibitions and authored numerous catalogue essays and magazine articles on American art. Well-Off-Man received her PhD in art history from the Ruhr University Bochum and her MA in art history, archaeology, and pedagogy from the University of Cologne, Germany.

AMANDA K. WIXON (Chickasaw) is the associate curator of Native History and Culture at the Autry Museum of the American West. She is also a volunteer curator at Sherman Indian Museum in Riverside, California, and a doctoral candidate in Native American History at the University of California, Riverside. Her research interests are Native American boarding school histories, Native art, and American Indian identities. She is a co-editor of and contributor to the recent publications *Indigenous Activism: Profiles of Native Women in Contemporary America* (2021) and *Medicine, Education, and the Arts in Contemporary Native America: Strong Women, Resilient Nations* (2022).

Selected Bibliography

Ahlberg Yohe, Jill, and Teri Greeves. *Hearts of Our People: Native Women Artists*. Minneapolis Institute of Art and the University of Washington Press, 2019.

Barnard, Malcolm. *Fashion Theory: A Reader*. 2nd ed. Routledge, 2020.

Barthes, Roland. *The Language of Fashion*. Reprint ed. Bloomsbury Academic, 2013.

Baudemann, Kristina. *The Future Imaginary in Indigenous North American Arts and Literature*. Routledge, 2022.

Baudemann, Kristina. "Indigenous Futurisms in North American Indigenous Art: The Transforming Visions of Ryan Singer, Daniel McCoy, and Topaz Jones, Marla Allison, and Debra Yepa-Pappan." *Extrapolation* 57, nos. 1–2 (2016): 117–150.

Dillon, Grace, L. *Walking the Clouds: An Anthology of Indigenous Science Fiction*. University of Arizona Press, 2012.

Downing Peters, Laura. "A History of Fashion without Fashion." *Critical Studies in Fashion and Beauty* 10, no. 1 (2019).

Entwistle, Joanne. *The Fashioned Body: Fashion Dress and Modern Social Theory*. 3rd ed. Polity Press, 2023.

Finamore, Michelle. *Fashioning America: Grit to Glamour*. University of Arkansas Press, 2022.

Fricke, Suzanne, and Henrietta Lidchi. "The Force Will Be with You . . . Always: Science Fiction Imagery in Native American Art." *First American Art Magazine* 12 (2016): 34–39.

Fricke, Suzanne, and Henrietta Lidchi. "Introduction: Indigenous Futurisms in the Hyperpresent Now." *Future History: Indigenous Futurisms in North American Visual Arts*, special issue of *World Art* 9, no. 2 (2019): 107–121.

Gaertner, David. "Indigenous in Cyberspace: CyberPowWow, God's Lake Narrows, and the Contours of Online Indigenous Territory." *American Indian Culture and Research Journal* 39, no. 4 (2015): 55–78.

Gaertner, David. "Traditional Innovation: The Turn to a Decolonial New Media Studies." *Novel Alliances: Allied Perspectives on Literature, Art, and New Media*, November 25, 2014. https://novelalliances.com/2014/11/25/traditional-innovation-the-turn-to-a-decolonial-new-media-studies-2/.

Haas, Angela M. "Wampum as Hypertext: An American Indian Intellectual Tradition of Multimedia Theory and Practice." *Studies in American Indian Literatures* 19, no. 4 (2007): 77–100.

Heffel Gallery. "Encoding Culture: The Works of Barry Ace." Issuu.com/heffel, August 31, 2021. https://issuu.com/heffel/docs/2021_ace_brochure.

Herr, Chelsea M. "The Evolution of Revolution: Virgil Ortiz's *Pueblo Revolt 1680/2180* as an Assertion of Native Presence through Indigenous Futurisms." *Future History: Indigenous Futurisms in North American Visual Arts*, special issue of *World Art* 9, no. 2 (2019): 125–141.

Hickey, Amber. "Rupturing Settler Time: Visual Culture and Geographies of Indigenous Futurity." *Future History: Indigenous Futurisms in North American Visual Arts*, special issue of *World Art* 9, no. 2 (2019): 163–180.

Igloliorte, Heather, and Carla Taunton, eds. *The Routledge Companion to Indigenous Art Histories in the United States and Canada*. Routledge, 2022.

Jackinsky-Sethi, Nadia. "Gutskin Sewing in Alaska," *First American Art Magazine*, no. 39 (Summer 2023): 32-42.

Jameson, Fredric. "Progress versus Utopia: Or, Can We Access the Future?," *Science Fiction Studies* 9, no. 2 (July 1982): 147-158.

Kite, Suzanne, and Kristina Baudemann. "Fragmentary Transmissions: On the Poetics, Practice, and Futurism of Listener." *Future History: Indigenous Futurisms in North American Visual Arts*, special issue of *World Art* 9, no. 2 (2019): 183-203.

Lempert, William. "Navajos on Mars: Native Sci-fi Film Futures." *Space and Anthropology*, September 21, 2015. https://medium.com/space-anthropology/navajos-on-mars-4c336175d945.

Lempert, William. "Telling Their Own Stories: Indigenous Film as Critical Identity Discourse." *Applied Anthropologist* 32, no. 1 (2012): 23-32.

Lewis, Jason Edward, and Skawennati Tricia Fragnito. "Aboriginal Territories in Cyberspace." *Cultural Survival Quarterly* 29, no. 2 (2005): 29.

Lewis, Jason Edward. "A Brief (Media) History of the Indigenous Future." *Public* 27, no. 54 (2016): 36-50.

Lewis, Jason Edward, Noelani Arista, Archer Pechawis, and Suzanne Kite. "Making Kin with the Machines." *Journal of Design and Science* 3, no. 5 (2018): 1-18.

Lexileictous, Theo-Mass, and Sven Ehmann, eds. *Otherworldly: Avant-Garde Fashion and Style*. Gestalten, 2016.

Lippard, Lucy R., and Kathleen Howe, eds. *Rose Simpson: Ground*. Pomona College Museum of Art, 2016.

Meredith, America. "Spotlight: Powhatans Mantle," *First American Art Magazine*, issue no. 18 (Spring 2018): 93.

Mida, Ingrid E. *Reading Fashion in Art*. London: Bloomsbury Visual Arts, 2020.

Neidhardt, Nichole Roessel. *Stories Held in a Time Traveller's Hogan*. MFA thesis, OCAD University, 2021.

Paulicelli, Eugenia. "Fashion and Futurism: Performing Dress." *A Century of Futurism: 1909-2009*, special issue *Annali d'Italianistica* 27 (2009): 187-207.

Phillips, Patsy and Manuela Well-Off-Man, eds. *Indigenous Futurisms: Transcending Past/Present/Future*. IAIA Museum of Contemporary Native Arts, 2020.

Phillips, Ruth. *Trading Identities: The Souvenir in Native North American Art from the Northeast, 1700-1900*. University of Washington Press, 1998.

Rebick, Stephanie, ed. *Fashion Fictions*. Amsterdam: Information Office, 2023.

Rifkin, Mark. *Beyond Settler Time: Temporal Sovereignty and Indigenous Self-Determination*. Duke University Press, 2017.

Rocamora, Agnès, and Anneke Smelik. *Thinking through Fashion: A Guide to Key Theorists*. London: I.B. Tauris, 2016.

Smith, Matthew Ryan. *Skawennati: From Skyworld to Cyberspace*. London and Ontario, Canada: McIntosh Gallery, 2020.

Tuck, Eve, and K. Wayne Yang. "Decolonization Is Not a Metaphor." *Decolonization: Indigeneity, Education and Society* 1, no. 1 (2012): 1-40.

Vowell, Chelsea May. "Writing Toward a Definition of Indigenous Futurism." *Literary Hub*, June 10, 2022. https://lithub.com/writing-toward-a-definition-of-indigenous-futurism/.

Welters, Linda, and Abby Lillethun. *Fashion History: A Global View*. London: Bloomsbury Academic, 2018.

Whyte, Kyle. "Settler Colonialism,
Ecology, and Environmental Injustice."
Environment and Society 9, no. 1
(September 2018): 125-144.

Whyte, Kyle, and Julia D. Gibson.
"Science Fiction Futures and (Re)visions
of the Anthropocene," *The Oxford
Handbook of Philosophy of Technology*,
edited by Shannon Vallor. Oxford
University Press, 2021.

Wikler, Alexandra. "Indigenous Futurism:
Reimagining 'Reality' to Inspire an
Indigenous Future." *Exploring Indigenous
Knowledge Systems*, November 28, 2016.
https://blogs.ubc.ca/fnis401fwikler
/2016/11/28/indigenous-futurism
-reimagining-reality-to-inspire-an
-indigenous-future/.

This book is published in conjunction with the exhibition *Future Imaginaries: Indigenous Art, Fashion, Technology*, presented at the Autry Museum of the American West, September 7, 2024–June 21, 2026.

Future Imaginaries is among more than 60 exhibitions and programs presented as part of Pacific Standard Time. Returning in September 2024 with its latest edition, PST ART: *Art & Science Collide*, this landmark regional event explores the intersections of art and science, both past and present. PST ART is a Getty initiative. For more information about PST ART: *Art & Science Collide*, please visit: pst.art.

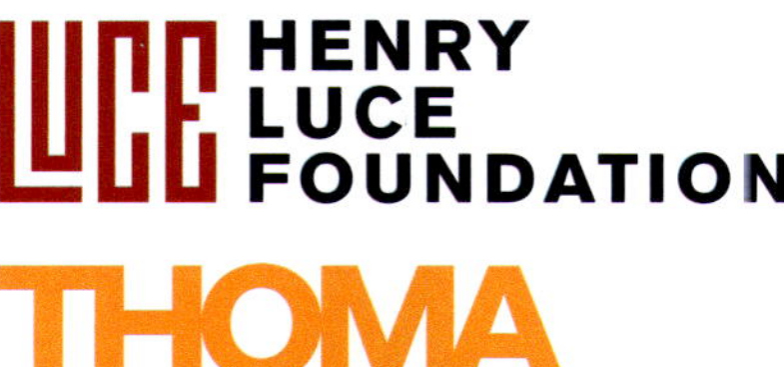

Presented by

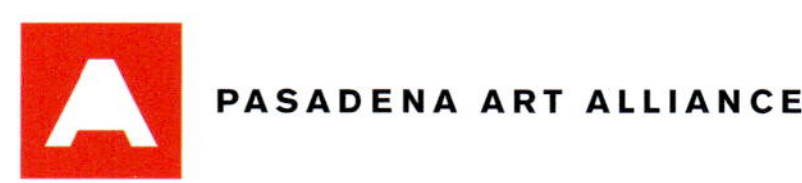

Additional support for *Future Imaginaries* is provided by the Carl & Marilynn Thoma Foundation, the Ethnic Arts Council, the Henry Luce Foundation, the Mildred E. and Harvey S. Mudd Foundation, Caryll and William Mingst, and the Pasadena Art Alliance.

Library of Congress Control Number: 2024936678
ISBN 978-0-295-75352-2

Autry Museum of the American West
4700 Western Heritage Way
Los Angeles, CA 90027
www.theautry.org

Published in association with University of Washington Press, Seattle
www.uwapress.uw.edu

Produced by Marquand Books, Seattle
www.marquandbooks.com

Edited by Jennifer A. Doyle
Designed by OTAMI—
Typeset in Maxeville
Proofread by Carrie Wicks
Index by Jane Friedman
Color management by I/O Color, Seattle
Printed and bound in China by Artron Art Group